ISBN 978-1-330-08666-7
PIBN 10022364

1 MONTH OF
FREE
READING

at

www.ForgottenBooks.com

By purchasing this book you are eligible for one month membership to ForgottenBooks.com, giving you unlimited access to our entire collection of over 1,000,000 titles via our web site and mobile apps.

To claim your free month visit:

www.forgottenbooks.com/free22364

English
Français
Deutsche
Italiano
Español
Português

www.forgottenbooks.com

Mythology Photography **Fiction** Fishing Christianity **Art** Cooking Essays Buddhism Freemasonry Medicine **Biology** Music **Ancient Egypt** Evolution Carpentry Physics Dance Geology **Mathematics** Fitness Shakespeare **Folklore** Yoga Marketing **Confidence** Immortality Biographies Poetry **Psychology** Witchcraft Electronics Chemistry History **Law** Accounting **Philosophy** Anthropology Alchemy Drama Quantum Mechanics Atheism Sexual Health **Ancient History** **Entrepreneurship** Languages Sport Paleontology Needlework Islam **Metaphysics** Investment Archaeology Parenting Statistics Criminology **Motivational**

MORE POT-POURRI

FROM A SURREY GARDEN

Earle, Maria Theresa,

BY

"MRS. C. W. EARLE"

New York

THE MACMILLAN COMPANY

LONDON: MACMILLAN & CO., LTD.

1899

Mount Pleasant Printery

J. Horace McFarland Company
Harrisburg, Pa.

TO THE READERS OF

'POT-POURRI FROM A SURREY GARDEN'

I DEDICATE THIS BOOK

'*Reading good Books of Morality is a little flat and dead. Observing our faults in others is sometimes improper for our case; but the best Receipt (best, I say, to work and best to take) is the Admonition of a Friend.*'

BACON.

CONTENTS

CONTENTS

CONTENTS

MAY

JUNE

JULY

AUGUST

MORE POT-POURRI

SEPTEMBER

September 1st, 1898.—It is now a year and a half since
I finished my first book, and the public have been almost
as appreciative and generous in their praise of it as my
nieces were.   Kind letters of all sorts have poured in,
and I have been overwhelmed with suggestions about the
future, and what I should or should not do.   Some have
said—and I admit that these, in all friendliness, are the
most earnest in their heartfelt appeals—that I should
rest on my laurels and write no more.   They urge that
a second book always falls flat.   If on the same subject
as the first, it is generally a failure.   If on a new subject, it is apt to be outside the writer's experience.   And
then they quote several incontestable examples which
jump to the recollection of everybody.   I really agree
with this view of the case up to the point of not acting
upon it.   Nothing can ever bear being done a second
time.   This is one of the sadnesses of life, and I do not
for a moment anticipate that No. 2 can please in the
same kind of way as did No. 1.   The method not
being new, my readers will know pretty well what to
expect; and this, probably, will immensely sharpen their

critical judgment. Then there were those who said and wrote—and need I state that they are the flatterers who come most home to the author's heart, as is but natural? —'We have read your book; we like it; we have found it useful and helpful, entertaining or suggestive. Cannot you give us more?' To these I answered: 'Give me time and I will try.' The result was that throughout the last year I have been making various notes about my life, things I saw and things I did, exactly as they occurred. These very likely will prove less interesting than former notes, which were more or less connected with the life that was behind me.

One newspaper had it that I must have a very good memory. As a matter of fact, I have no memory at all, but from my youth I have kept, more or less continuously, commonplace books — a jumble of all sorts of things as I came across them in my very desultory reading. These notes·were often so carelessly kept as not even to acknowledge where I stole the thought that gave me pleasure. This accounts for my having quotations at hand. Another reviewer kindly said that I had a 'marked grace of style.' My dear old mother used to say she never considered a compliment worth having that was not totally undeserved! I never had the slightest idea of possessing any style at all. But what is style? It is a weary topic when so much is said about 'getting style' (like 'getting religion'). Schopenhauer's remarks on the subject are worth noticing. He writes: 'There is no quality of style that can be got by reading writers who possess it. But if the qualities exist in us —exist, that is to say, potentially—we can call them forth and bring them into consciousness. We can learn the purposes to which they can be put. We can be strengthened in an inclination to use them, or get courage to do so. The only way in which reading can form style is by teaching us the use to which we can put our own natural gifts. We must have these gifts before we can learn the use of them. Without them reading teaches us nothing.'

One friend wrote : 'I should have liked the book still better if the moral and domestic reflections had been jumbled up with the rest, instead of being put, like an appendix, at the end.' With this I entirely agree, but my judgment in the matter was overruled by others. The most general criticism has been that the various subjects in the book are not kept enough apart. Some asked 'Won't you write a cookery book alone? or a gardening book alone?' I could only say that I am no specialist. Dozens of such books exist, and are much better than any I could write. I am and must remain an ignorant amateur. My mind only works, as I said before, on the lines of collecting knowledge, sweet and bitter, as I walk along life's way. What I have I can give, but I can neither create nor imagine. The accusations of the sudden jumps from gardening to surgery, or from cooking to art, which astonished my readers, are perfectly true. But are not these violent and sudden contrasts a marked characteristic of modern life? Do we not, many of us, any morning, go from our letters or newspapers—containing, perhaps, the most tragic human stories, affecting ourselves or those we love—to the ordering of the dinner for the friend who is to come in the evening, or seeing that the carriage or the fly is not forgotten for the guest who is leaving before noon? Such is life. So my months must remain quite as varied as before. It is sad to have to repeat the un-English name of 'Pot-Pourri,' which annoyed so many and was never very satisfactory to myself; but this book in no way aims at being more than a continuation of the first, a kind of second volume, a giving of more to those who ask for it. The word 'pot-pourri' is so generally accepted in England to mean a sweet and pleasant mixture, that we do not realize that the original word meant a mixed stew, as do its synonyms of 'hotch-potch' and *olla podrida,* a favourite Spanish dish consisting of a mixture of various kinds of meat chopped fine and stewed with vegetables.

Most of the letters I received were of kindly and affectionate appreciation. But some frankly criticised, while others marked shortcomings. As usual, however, in such cases, perfectly incompatible qualities were required. For instance, most of my gardening friends were disappointed at the information about gardening being so elementary, telling them little they did not know. They very likely overrated what I had to tell them, but they entirely missed the point of my omitting to make my information as detailed and special as I could have done — first, because I referred them to real gardening books, and secondly, because I wanted what I did tell to be particularly addressed to beginners with small gardens who wished to do their best, but had little time to spend in the study of other books. On the other hand, the ignorant amateurs, for whom it was specially written, mournfully complained that it still did not begin enough at the beginning. To these I always answered that Mr. Robinson must have realized this difficulty, as some years ago he reprinted the 'Amateur Gardener,' by Mrs. Loudon (Fredk. Warne & Co.), which is full of this elementary information, and to be had from any bookseller for the sum of ninepence.

A third difficulty was the slavish admirer, who, in all soils and even with different climates, said: 'I have strictly carried out your instructions, and utter failure has been the result.' I wish once more to reiterate that anything I say, both in the last volume and in this, with regard to plant life, is merely the result of my own personal experience. All that I state is by way of suggestion, not by any means as a law to be carried out at all times and in all places. Several letters of approval I received from working gardeners gave me great pleasure, and one said that he found the book 'very bright and holding.' This seems to me a most expressive word. Another complaint came from a Londoner, representing the opinion of the inhabitants of towns. He was in exact contrast to the gardener-friend in the suburbs and in the country. He complained bitterly of the long lists of plants, the many details about gardening, and asked pitifully if this part might not have been relegated to an appendix, suggesting that this would make the book much more readable.

One man, who professed to be no gardener at all, said his leading idea in gardening was to dismiss the under-gardener. This is a very common theory with the master of the house, who thinks gardens can be well kept very much underhanded. As a rule, the best gardens are those where the master of the house superintends the gardening himself.

A woman friend, who dislikes both garden books and gardening, wrote: 'Notices of gardening books might, for the sake of the village idiot, for whom everyone writes, have been put in a chapter quite at the end. "Fat," as the actors call it, should come at the beginning of a book to encourage the reader.' Perhaps she was not wrong, for I believe, so far as I can gather from the letters, that the non-gardening people like my book best — gardeners, after all, being, as they are the first to acknowledge, one-idea'd. And yet no, it cannot have been really so, as by far the most genuine and sympathetic letters I have received have been from real garden lovers — the sick, the old, the expatriated, all joining in one pæan of praise over the soul-satisfying occupation of gardening.

A few of the London booksellers were rather amusing on the subject, and I have considerable sympathy with their opinions. One said to a friend of mine, a few months after the book had come out, that it was going into the sixth edition and that he 'couldn't conceive why, as there was nothing in it.' Another shrewdly remarked that he called the book 'a social success, not a literary one.' There was a vein running through several letters which I thought perhaps accounted in some way for the success of the book, as it proved that many people wished to give it to someone else because they found in it a gentle rod wherewith to scourge their neighbour. One critic said that 'a spirit of benign and motherly materialism broods over the book'— an expression which I thought rather nice, as it was what I had aimed at. A second said the book was 'full of good spirits from beginning to end,' and a third discovered that 'a tone of sadness ran through it all.'

After critics came the friends, who amusingly said: 'The book is so extraordinarily like yourself, we can hear your voice speaking all through it.' Strangers, I am told, who know me only by reputation or not at all, kindly settled that it was not written by me, but by some mysterious unknown person they could not quite hit upon.

It is quite true, and I wish to state it again, as I did in my first preface, that I had very real and practical assistance from one of my nieces, who made a most efficient secretary. Our method of working was simple enough. I wrote what I wanted to say, and then dictated it to her. In reading aloud, the more flagrant mistakes and repetitions struck the ear quicker than the eye, as is but natural for one more accustomed to speak than to write. Two or three other people helped me by toning down my crude opinions and taking out whole sentences that might have been causes of offence. It has for a long time been a favourite theory of mine that, as people generally write books with a vague hope that they may be read, it is wise to consult a small number of people typical of the public, and to be guided, without too much self-esteem, by the opinions of these selected few. Of course, this opens up the further discussion whether, as I saw it well put the other day in the 'Spectator,' 'Success with the multitude is in itself desirable, or if it is not rather the hall-mark of a commonplace inferiority. Who pleases foolish readers must himself be a fool. If the general reader is, after all, quite such a fool as the superior *junta* think him, is another question altogether. But he has the marked advantage of holding the verdict in his hands.' The only *raison d'être* of ephemeral literature is that it should be read. The writer of genius comes under a different category. He stands on a mountain-top and breathes a rarer atmosphere, and often can only be understood from a distance. 'Bethia Hardacre' exactly expresses this in verse:

> I pray to fail, if to succeed
> Means faithlessness unto my creed.

Lady Eastlake says on this point: 'Genius, with its divine inspirations, may be left to find its way to the admiration of the few and in the end to the acknowledgment of all.' Many will remember when Mr. Quaritch brought out Fitzgerald's translation of 'Omar Khayyam,' disgusted at its complete failure, he threw the whole edition into a 'penny box.' Dante Rossetti found them, and we all know the rest.

Some people said that what really pleased them most in the book were the little bits of poetry. Considering that not one of these was mine, the remark by way of compliment was rather humorous. Another curious vein of flattery that ran through dozens of the letters was expressive of the writers' regret that they had not written '*Pot-Pourris*' of their own, proving the general truth of how easy everything is if we only take the trouble to do it.

The cooking receipts caused panic in some minds and indignation in others. One poor bachelor told his house-keeper to try the receipt in '*Pot-Pourri*' for making a soup. She happened to hit upon the French *chef's* extravagant directions for making *consommé* and, horrified by the numberless pounds of beef recommended, said : 'Really, sir, it would be far cheaper to have down a quantity of tinned soups from the Stores !' Another careful mistress of her own house complained very much of different meats, amounting to six pounds, being used for one pie. But in her case the household consisted of one thin brother and two thinner maids. My receipts, of course, were jumbled together for big and little establishments, to be used at the discretion of the housewife. A French lady writes that I make a mistake in thinking that it is usual in France to baste chickens with butter, and that they are much better done with the fat of bacon, or suet, or even common lard. I myself generally roast chickens with butter, and find that people like them very much. But, of course, only fresh butter must be used; never that horror called 'cooking butter.' It is true that basting them with the fat of good bacon does make them a better colour.

In a most humorous article from that delightful writer of the 'Pages from a Private Diary' in the 'Cornhill,' there were several funny allusions to my book. I quote the following as a specimen: 'While ''doing'' my Michaelmas accounts this morning, I found that the butter book (for we use Tom's dairy) was half as much again as last quarter, and the reason given by the responsible Eugenia is that Mrs. Earle protests against economy in butter. On referring to the passage, I find that she suggests instead an economy in meat, and I pointed this out to E.; but the butcher's book shows no proportionate diminution. This has led me to reflect how much more infectious extravagance is than economy.'

One of my most complimentary letters was from an old friend, Mrs. Roundell, asking me to allow her to quote some of my receipts in a new cookery book she was compiling. This has since appeared under the name of 'A Practical Cookery Book' (Bickers & Son), and is so excellent that it thoroughly convinces me of my wisdom in declining to write one myself. My praise of this book almost suggests a mutual admiration society, as Mrs. Roundell is very complimentary to me. She begins by thanking me for my receipts, and ends by a quotation from 'Pot-Pourri' on hospitality and housekeeping. It will be many a long year before her own book is superseded. The receipts are clear and economical, and its only fault seems to be that at present it costs seven-and-sixpence.

A literary friend writes that he has a point of dissent —'a bit of pedantic purism. You say "chickens." There is no such word: chicken is a plural. Hose, hosen; chick, chicken; and in old days many more — as house, housen; place, pleäsen. A farmer's wife, at least in the west, says correctly that she is going to feed her chicken—meaning not one, but many.' It is difficult to know when custom asserts itself sufficiently to change grammar, and my critic himself admits that many of the words he quotes are obsolete. I fear I shall hardly have the courage to say 'truss two fine chicken' if I come across such a phrase in a receipt.

I received very few letters on the nurse question. It

had been a good deal discussed in periodicals just before the book came out.

An old friend, a doctor, wrote: 'Your chapter on health I take some exception to. On the question that starvation is a cure for most of the minor ailments of life I agree with you, but I think you are wrong on the subject of nurses. You *may* get some affection and kindness on the part of a mother, or a sister, or a wife, but I have always held that in really bad cases all three make the worst possible nurses, because so few women can really control their feelings, and where there were great affection and grave anxiety they would be apt to fail in some small details which might be of the utmost importance, where a good trained nurse would not, because *she* looks on the patient only as a "case," which, if she is a conscientious woman, it is her one object to get well. My experience also does not tally with yours, that the nurse is the tool of the doctor and is bound to approve and agree with him. On the contrary, I think many of them, through "a little learning," think they know quite as much as, if not more than, the doctor, and often use their own *discretion* (?) as to whether they will carry out all the orders given them. If the doctor finds out this and remonstrates, he then makes an enemy of a person who at any time may have an opportunity of doing him much professional injury.' I am quite ready to acknowledge the correctness of these remarks, and if the nurse and doctor do not work well together, any opposition on the part of the nurse might make the situation very disagreeable for the doctor, and *vice versa*. If, on the other hand, they work extremely well together, the patient may be the sufferer, supposing the doctor were mistaken about the case, which does happen with men of the greatest talent. The too literal carrying out of the doctor's orders, especially with regard to medicines and sleeping-draughts, is often very injurious to the patient. I did not for a moment mean to imply that love and devotion could supply the qualities that are the result of training. But a kind of clear-sightedness and instinct that comes from love and devotion is by no means always to be found in the professional nurse.

I continue to quote typical letters on various subjects as they crop up. One kind old clergyman thought so flatteringly of my powers that he suggests that I should 'utilise the genius which has popularised your book in some of those fields into which your book affords glimpses — why not write on heredity?' The fact is, as I have already said, I am not able to write a treatise on cooking and gardening, much less could I pretend to give the world any information on great subjects connected with science ; and heredity more especially is peculiarly buried in darkness, even for experts. He concludes a long and interesting letter as follows: 'Some years ago Sir F. Galton sent me a paper of inquiries (which he was circulating among doctors) as to the physical and psychical history of three generations of ancestors.' This idea of Sir F. Galton's has been a favourite one with me for years. I have always thought that it would be of the greatest interest in families if a careful register were kept of people's health, diseases, and death, so that some idea might be formed of the general tendencies of family diseases, with their succeeding development and treatment during three or four generations.

It seems satisfactory that a great number of the newspaper critics gave me credit for common-sense. Some few passages in 'Sons and Daughters' raised opposition, but, I am bound to confess, much less than I expected. My great disappointment was that I got so little actual criticism—I may even say, so little correction. In this, I am told, I was ambitious, as most critics compose their articles by a few quotations, and have neither time nor inclination to really criticise. There was one excellent exception in an interesting and friendly article in the 'Spectator.' This critic seems to doubt, more even than I did, the courage of parents and nurses as regards giving independence to young children. But, in proof of the desirability of my recommendations, he quotes Stevenson's admirable saying with regard to a boy: 'It is better for him to break his neck than for you to break his spirit.' This article shows the *revers de la médaille* so well, as regards the atmosphere of a home, that I copy it. After approving my suggestions about giving allowances to both girls and boys, it goes on to say: 'The question of the frank criticism by children of their home is more doubtful. It is, of course, better that their dissatisfaction should, like the measles, "come out," but what about their home manners? Criticism is very apt to degenerate into grumbling, and the spectacle of children or young people grumbling about domestic arrangements is not edifying. Grumbling is always rude; and if manners make the man, it is an undoubted fact that perfect manners are incompatible with absolute brutal outspokenness. For instance, the wife and mother who is trying to attain the really lofty standard aimed at in this book cannot, of necessity, be absolutely outspoken. If her work is to be successful, she must not hint that any part of it is distasteful; that is, she must conceal some of her feelings. Surely children should not be brought up to feel that their father and mother are the only people they may be rude to. And if the money argument is to be applied to the wife, it must touch the children, too; they must not be allowed to take all the luxuries of the house they do not pay for, and then grumble because those luxuries are not arranged as they like best. And now that we apply this reasoning a second time, we see that in reality it is rather an ugly argument. It is a fact, but, like other facts, such as death and digestion, it need not be obtruded at every moment. The woman's work may be given from love of her home; and the children may forbear, also through love, to tell their mother that the dinner-hour is not quite the fashionable one, and "you might have remembered how I hate that pudding." The mother will look out for herself and see to the tastes of her family, and will, in talks with one and the other, ask for advice and hints on new ways of arranging the familiar details of life. And so good manners, which are really the Christian virtues of patience, charity, and self-control, will reign in that house, and it will be a far pleasanter place than if everyone in turn were loudly to volunteer their opinion of how it ought to be conducted.'

This has truth in it. All individuals must decide for themselves how to draw the line between good manners and what may end in whited sepulchres. This is doubly difficult with children, whose natural inclination is to speak as they feel, for not to do so appears to them rather as a deception than as a sparing of other people's feelings. Everyone's experience will tell them how early children say to others what they dare not say in their own home. The great difficulty is to keep the love of children. Goethe says: 'There is a politeness of the heart; this is closely allied to love. Those who possess this purest fountain of natural politeness find it easy to express the same in forms of outward propriety.'

Nothing was more amusing to me than this interesting variety in the letters about 'Sons and Daughters.' I will quote passages from several of them: 'I agree with your "Daughters" more than I thought I should. You do not lay such stress as I thought you would on the necessity of getting married and the "complete" point of view.' All the same, I maintain that an unmarried woman is not a complete human being.

'I think the chapter on "Sons" the better of the two. But I think independence in boys is far easier to manage than in girls. School-life brings boys to their proper level. Home-life with absolute freedom rather leads to a girl becoming too confident that her own opinion must be the right one. She rubs up against so few who can or will take her down. The independent girl generally rules those of her own age. Of course, you can not lay down a hard-and-fast rule for any child. Each one has its different character, to be formed and improved by those who live with it. This ought to be done by the mother, but it is more often left to an ignorant governess, who does not try to understand the child, who has her own narrow-minded ideas of right and wrong, and never makes allowance for high spirit and temper.'

'You must remember that the people I was brought up amongst take their duties as parents seriously, if narrowly — and many of these, as far as they still exist, will be a little startled at some of your theories, and the *un*moral (mind, I don't say *im*moral) tone. Parents and children are a subject of perennial interest. We have all been the one, and many of us the other — and the rest of us stand in *loco parentis* to some at least of the younger generation. But as long as the world lasts there will be difficulties in that relation. *Si jeunesse savait, si vieillesse pouvait*, is a saw which has many meanings. I totally disagree with your idea that the young must never be sacrificed to the old, or the healthy to the sick. Why, your own remarks on nursing testify to the good that may come of such a sacrifice.'

This last sentence proves to me that my remarks were

not clear, and the impression conveyed is certainly not what I intended. What I really think is that the old have no right to command the young to sacrifice their lives to them. But, on the other hand, the voluntary sacrifice by the young of their own lives, though it should be carefully watched by those about them, is certainly not without immense benefit to themselves, self-sacrifice being acknowledged by all moralists to be the greatest strengthener of human character. There is, however, the great risk and danger of self-suppression.

I continue my quotations:

'You put the question of unselfishness in parents or children as being a difficult one, but I have always felt that to help each person to be as they ought to be, in the best and highest way for their own characters, is the only right love and influence that each can have for the other, no matter in what relations of life. If you either spoil a child or a parent or husband or wife, so that you make them behave wrongly, you are sure to be distressed by their not doing right, and other people feel the same.' Everyone must agree that to make those we love behave well is the object to be attained. The difficulty is the best method of bringing it about. Is it by unselfish example or by exacting unselfishness on the part of others? Who can say?

Here is a severe condemnation from a father of several children: 'I don't agree one bit with your theoretical subordination of old to young. I think it innately ridiculous, essentially false, and at once morbid, superficial, and mischievous.'

Nobody actually wrote it to me, but I heard it from several people, that the advice about giving the latch-key to very young boys harassed and worried a great number of mothers. Why, I do not quite understand; as showing confidence in the boy seems to me the beginning of all true relations between a mother and a growing-up son. I still think that if boys are unfit to have a key at seventeen, or the recommended allowance at an earlier age, it shows that their education has been somewhat defective in fitting them, not for doing well at school, but for the general struggle of life as they get older, which is learnt so well by children in a lower class of life. There might, of course, be an exception in a family, but that merely means that he is more deficient in common-sense than his brothers, and should be gradually strengthened by some method fitted to his peculiar case. It is a delightful feeling of comfort to me to think that, whatever I suggest, nobody need follow it unless it seems to them good; but I wrote nothing without deliberate thought and practical experience.

As a rule, the book seemed to please the old and the young, rather than the middle-aged. Occasionally, however, some few parents wrote appreciating my hints about the modern danger of children growing up more and more apart from their parents. In our grandmothers' days this only happened among what have been called the 'upper ten thousand.' Now it pervades all classes, down to the labourer who has to send his children to the infant and Board school. Not that schools of any sort are necessarily bad in themselves, but it is a new position which has to be faced with courage and thoughtfulness by the parents.

A young mother wrote full of faith in her own excellent principles of how to bring up children, and how easy she had found it to gain an influence on their lives. This cocksureness, natural and even wholesome in the young, often brings about a good deal of disappointment. You may make a soil ever so good, and you may plant ever so good a seed, but even then there can be no security as to results. The very child who is most impressionable and easy to form in youth is also most affected by others as time goes on. The result of a powerful influence which we cannot even trace is what often makes children, as they grow up, almost unrecognisable to their parents. The forming of character, however, is totally different from moulding the impressionable clay, and, like casting bread upon the waters, it may return to us after many days.

Here are some pathetic groans from an intensely anxious mother of an only daughter: 'Needless to say that the chapter of your book which chiefly interested me is "Daughters," the education of my own being the burning question with me just now. You are certainly very comforting in what you say of "casual and superficial education," but I fear that would not satisfy the professed and professing educationalist. In our case, want of robustness on M.'s part has obliged us to put up with home education, and of course it is then a mere chance whether you happen to get a governess who can really *teach;* for the teacher is born, not made. When, however, I read the "Parents' Review," or the educational literature it recommends, I suffer agonies of remorse from the consciousness of not having made enough of these early years. My ambition is humble. I only wish my child to be average, but not to be at a disadvantage if, later on, she is prompted to take some part in the real work of the world. And yet how can I, with my own old-fashioned, defective education, train her in the right way! This fiend of education sits like a nightmare on me almost day and night—"Almost thou persuadest me it is impossible to be a parent." When I get up from the perusal of these books, I feel castigated to such an extent that my mind feels sore all over, and into those wounds *you* pour the oil and wine of consolation. My husband, highly educated as he is himself, is very much inclined to take your view, and has, if anything, kept me back rather than urged me on, always fearing that, instead of arousing an interest in a subject, one should simply cause a lasting distaste, if it is offered too early to the immature mind. We cannot, however, put off this "training of faculty" indefinitely, and I am becoming more and more awake to the fact that my child, in her cosy, comfortable home, does not know as much as I, immured in a boarding-school, knew at her age. The most tantalising part of the matter is that when I can shake off this incubus of *duty*, she and I are so happy together. I suppose there is some similarity in our minds and tastes that makes her very responsive to me. I cannot bring myself, owing, doubtless, to my own defective bringing-up, to stand at a distance, as it were, and criticise severely. As M. has no classes this afternoon, we are off to the British Museum — a sort of treat we both thoroughly enjoy. But, as you know, I am given to misgivings; the question arises sometimes whether the companionship of my mature mind is the best. "Childhood ought to be with childhood" is constantly being repeated to me.'

This letter seemed to me so touching that I sent it to a friend of mine much interested in the subject. She returned it with the following remarks, which express in strong terms very much what I feel myself: 'I quite agree — one of the most interesting letters you've had. But it is harrowing to me the way this poor mother won't let herself benefit by your advice, although she seems to approve of it. You ask for my comments. I should say she gives the receipt of what her line of conduct should be in the sentence "When I can shake off this incubus of *duty* she and I are so happy together. I suppose there is some similarity in our minds and tastes that makes her very responsive to me." Just fancy a mother having that opportunity and not using it! There's hardly a parent in fifty could boast as much. Personal contact and sympathy with an older person means hot-house growth to the mental capabilities of a child. The one fear is lest it should overforce them. What do the geography, history, arithmetic, and all the details of early education matter? The child's general intelligence and power of acquiring knowledge from her own observation, which is the only true educator, will develop much more fully and rapidly in the mother's company than with a governess, especially if the mother lays herself out to share all her knowledge, so far as possible, with her child. As she grows up, the child will be the first to discover where she is at a disadvantage compared to others. If she is indifferent about this, I should say no one else need mind for her, and she will be none the worse. But if she minds, and she probably will, she can then acquire the belated knowledge in half the time and with half the money spent on teachers that would be required if spread out over a childhood more or less reluctant to learn. Do try and stop the lady from taking in "educational literature," for I'm sure it's not only useless but harmful to fret one's conscience unless it leads to conviction, and, fortunately, this mother seems not convinced by the "professing educationalists." . . . If the child is already fifteen or sixteen, the only modification I should make to what I have said would be to recommend putting most forcibly before the girl herself that if she has to, or wishes to, "take some part in the real work of the world" she must utilise her best faculties to the full, and try to diminish her deficiencies.'

The burning question of what girls should or should not read called forth a good deal of comment and opposition. The following was one of the best of the letters on this subject: 'I think that, allowing for hereditary instincts and inherited character, or want of it, there can be no hard-and-fast rule as to allowing girl children to read without restriction. So much allowance must be made for the enormous difference in children, who are, quite unconsciously to themselves, swayed by temperament or feelings the real nature of which they are ignorant and innocent of. This question opens up a very wide field, and perhaps in your book you could only afford space for generalisation on such a subject. I also feel that children, like older people and plants and any living thing, are subject to the eternal and terrible order of change; have phases during which their whole nature may become either lethargic and indifferent, or, on the other hand, be dominated by sexual feeling, receptive or otherwise. One girl at the budding period feels and sees nothing harmful to her mind and morals ; while another, hitherto pure and simple-minded, may have her imagination stimulated and her morbid curiosity partially gratified by access to all and any kind of reading, and this may have the effect of soiling a mind in the first and most delicate stage of development. Children, too, are extraordinarily unexpected in their phases, and often turn out so much better or worse than one thought without any apparent reason.' As regards the reading, in spite of all that has been said, I cannot alter my view that, on the whole, it is better to leave a great deal of liberty from childhood upwards, allowing the child to form her own taste, it being better to manage the reading of the young by advice than by restrictions.

September 3rd.— A few days ago I returned home, after being abroad and away from my garden for over three months. I left towards the end of May, when all was fresh and green, bursting with bud and life, and full of the promise of the coming summer. In three months all seemed over ; the little place looked dried up and miserable, small, ugly, disappointing — in fact, hardly worth possessing at all.

I felt dreadfully depressed, but, of course, all this was in great measure due to the time of year, the end of August being the very worst month for this garden, and one that I have never attempted to struggle with, yielding rather to the difficulties and generally going away. Shall I also confess my own character had something to do with it ? Many people say, 'Absence makes the heart grow fonder.' This is not my case under any circumstances, and especially not with my little home and garden. The more I live here, the more I tend and cherish it ; the more pains I bestow upon it, the more I love it.

When I am urged to travel and change, I only feel that I agree with Mr. Watson in these lines:

> Nay, bid me not my cares to leave,
>   Who cannot from their shadow flee.
> I do but win a short reprieve,
>   'Scaping to pleasure and to thee.
>
> I may at best a moment's grace,
>   And grant of liberty, obtain;
> Respited for a little space,
>   To go back into bonds again.

After being away for only a short time I come back with the keenest excitement. But when I have been away for some long time, and got interested in other things, I come back in an ungardening mood, have forgotten all the horticultural names, and—if the time of year is unfavourable — I see, too clearly, nothing but the faults, and have a much too direct answer to Burns' prayer in the last verse of his queer little poem, 'To a Louse, on seeing One on a Lady's Bonnet at Church':

O wad some pow'r the giftie gi'e us
To see oursels as others see us!
It wad frae monie a blunder free us
    And foolish notion:
What airs in dress an' gait wad lea'e us,
    And ev'n Devotion!

I love what I am with, but with me, alas! *les absents
ont toujours tort*, and for weeks I had been used to
greater beauties and wider interests. Here the dome of
heaven is lower, and no cypresses point upwards. The
moral to me is quite clear: Gardeners should only go
away from home to learn, not to see how beautiful the
world is elsewhere without any gardens at all, the
science of life being to make the best of .what we have
to our hand, not to pine for what we have not.

September 5th.—The dryness continues, and we wait
in vain for rain. The weather makes us doubly appreciate the small square of cool water just in front of the
dining-room window, and the pleasure it seems to bring
to bird and insect. Great fat thrushes splash themselves in the shallow edges specially prepared for them
with big stones, as they seem much afraid of deep
water. Two of us were sitting at early breakfast, when
my companion said to me in a subdued voice, 'Look
there!' I saw, perched on a hanging branch of the
rose growing on the Pergola, the most beautiful Kingfisher. His blue wings flashed in the sunshine, and,
turning his red breast, it glowed like that of a tropical
bird. In a few seconds he flew away. I have never
before seen a Kingfisher in this dry garden, and I can
only account for it, as we are more than a mile from the
river, by something peculiar in the season and his being
attracted, in his search for food, by the gold-fish in my
little fountain. A friend told me that the same thing
happened in her garden, and that the Kingfisher, never
seen before, beat himself against the glass window.

One of the few things that looked really well in the garden when I came home was the Cape annual, *Nemesia strumosa*. The dryness apparently had suited the flowering capabilities of the annual, but, finding that it was forming no seed, I watered it daily, as it is one of the plants from which it is well worth while to save the seed, selecting it from the best-coloured flowers. The seed wants a good deal of care in the gathering, as it is so very ephemeral — unripe one day and gone the next. For a person of my age, it means groping on the ground each morning with one's spectacles on. I certainly must add it to the list of annuals worth growing in a small garden. We sow it in place the middle of May.

September 7th.—The old-fashioned *Zauschneria Californica*, when well grown, is a very pretty plant, with its soft gray leaves and scarlet flowers. I have had it for years, and it has stood any amount of moving about into different places. It never died, and yet never flowered. I grew it on rockwork, I grew it in shade, I grew it in the sun. It formed bushy little plants, but never had a single flower. My patience was nearly coming to an end, and I fell back on the gardener's usual solace—that the soil did not suit it. When I paid a visit to Mr. Thompson, of Ipswich, I found it flowering most satisfactorily, and learnt from him the eternal story that what it wanted was good feeding. It should have very good, rich soil, plenty of manure, and be put in a place that is free of damp in winter. This is the difficulty with so many of the foreign plants we try to grow. They want damp in their flowering-time, when we are dry; and dryness in the winter, when we are wet. I came home, broke up my *Zauschneria*, planted it on the edge of a raised vine-border, in full sunshine and with very well rotted manure. Helped, no doubt, also by the sunny season, it has flowered splendidly this year, and is even finer than the one I had seen at Ipswich. I think it is the better, like many other things, for watering when the buds are formed. I see in an un-modern gardening book that it only came to England in 1847. We find no difficulty in propagating it by division in spring. Cuttings strike easily in a little heat, and form blooming plants in the same season.

Phloxes have done very badly this year, whether removed from the reserve garden or left alone. In very dry seasons it is best to quickly cut them down; they flower again well when the rain comes. *Michauxia campanuloides* is flowering now for the second time. I have never grown it before, and its first bloom was in June, while I was away, so that I did not see it in its prime. The seed, unfortunately, does not ripen here, but it seems to me a plant worthy of all the trouble that biennials give; and experiments should be tried in growing it. I am now going to try it grown the second year in pots, under glass, in a cool house, in the same way as *Campanula pyramidalis* is grown. I expect it will be very fine. When grown out of doors it should be moved from the seed-bed into a dry, sunny place, and it wants as much water as you can give it when about to flower. It is figured in Vol. xvii of Curtis' 'Botanical Magazine,' but the flower there depicted gives little idea of the beauty of the whole plant, although the unusual shape and loveliness of the flower itself are well rendered. *Michauxia tchinatchewii* (see Thompson's list) is new to me and, I am told, good.

The Belladonna Lilies, treated as described in my first book, have flowered excellently, many having two flower-stems from apparently the same bulb. I immediately sent to Holland for two dozen more, as I believe there has been a disease among them in some places and that they are now rather scarce. As an example of how small a thing will affect the flowering of Cape bulbs, I noted this spring that the leaves in the more northern part of my little bed got injured by frost and east wind —not very severely, but slightly—and out of that dozen bulbs only one flowered.

A favourite little plant of mine, which I have had for years, has flowered unusually well this year. It is called *Tricyrtis hirta*, and is a small Japanese Lily—very quiet in colour, and spotted all over with lilac spots, but beautiful in its growth, and well worth cultivating. The dry rockwork seems to suit it, but I generally water it when coming into flower. Every year, as it comes round, it is a pleasurable excitement to see it develop its late flowers. In a book by Mrs. Brightwen ('Glimpses into Plant Life: an Easy Guide to the Study of Botany,' Fisher Unwin), it is alluded to as a typical pollenation plant. She says: 'We have seen that there are all kinds of devices by which the pollen of one flower may be made sure to reach the stigma of another; but if by any means this crossing fails, if the weather is such that insects are scarce or other conditions cause failure, then, in the case of many flowers, most curious contrivances are provided to secure seed by self-pollenation. Truly, this is one of the most beautiful of God's wonders in floral construction. One of the gems of my own flower-garden is a lovely little Japanese toad-lily (*Tricyrtis hirta*). In this flower there are three styles, which stand well above the stamens; the points of the styles are bent over, and the stigmatic surface grows mature before the anthers shed their pollen. If, however, no insect visits the flowers, pollenation is effected in the following way: The styles bend down and place their forked points in direct contact with the open anther-lobes, the style assuming almost the form of a semicircle. This is done very deliberately, for it is often a week before the act is complete.' I think that 'Glimpses into Plant Life' is a book that everyone interested in country life or a garden would very much enjoy. The illustrations are clear and good, and explain the text satisfactorily.

Nothing is more useful at this time of the year in a window or a greenhouse than *Vallota purpurea*. It is perfectly easy of cultivation, if the leaves are encouraged in their growth and thoroughly sunned and dried off. The bulb should be very rarely re-potted and well watered in its growing state. I am always hearing that people lose their plants; this is probably from the gardener's over-care and keeping them too warm and wet through the winter. I am going to try them out of doors next year, as Mr. Robinson recommends, now that I have plenty of offsets, but I confess I have never seen them doing well in England out of doors. They probably do not fear cold, as I saw many in full flower on cottage window-sills in Norway.

The west sides of rockeries are often very dull, especially in autumn. I find *Origanum hybridum* is a charming, interesting, curious little plant that flowers freely in a dry place in August and September. It is almost exactly the same as the old *O. dictamnus* figured in Vol. xix of Curtis' 'Botanical Magazine.' Curtis says: 'Turner, whose Herbal was printed in 1568, writes thus concerning it: "I have seen it growynge in England in Master Riches gardin naturally, but it groweth nowhere ellis that I know of saving only in Candy."' This is rather a nice way of telling us where the plant comes from. It seems easy of cultivation, and worth growing. *Caryopteris macranthe* is a little blue dwarf shrub that I have hardly ever seen anywhere, but which I grow and increase here quite easily, and find it very attractive. It wants a dry situation, and flowers better if cut back after flowering. It should be fed with a little mulching and watering when it comes into bud. I increase it easily from cuttings in spring.

As time goes on, I become fonder and fonder of the generally abused Polygonums. Mr. Robinson, in his latest edition of 'The English Flower Garden,' speaks of them also with much favour, and gives a splendid list of the varieties; but even he does not lay stress enough upon what entirely different plants they become if sufficiently thinned out and the suckers pulled off each spring. Otherwise they are ragged, intolerable weeds. If *P. sachalinense* is planted even under shade or in half shade, thinned out to three or four shoots, and watered or hosed in dry weather, the yearly growth is absolutely tropical. It turns a rich yellow colour in early autumn, and forms a splendid feature in places where many plants would not grow at all, such as under Fir-trees or in very poor soil. *P. molle* I do not think Mr. Robinson names, and yet it is a beautiful thing; though some years, if in an exposed place, it flowers so late that it gets injured by frost. It requires dividing every autumn, re-planting in better soil, and thinning every spring; it is well, if it can be watered, to grow it under some tree or shrub, which protects it in case of early frost. It is worth some trouble, as its flowering branches, almost like feathery white lilac, are very handsome, coming, as they do, so late in the year. *P. Leichtlini* is a very dwarf kind I brought from Germany, and will, I think, prove a useful little plant on the rockery for September flowering. The light blue Cape *Plumbago capensis* is doing very well this hot year, and is covered, out of doors, with its lovely cool china-blue flowers. No other colour in the garden is quite like it. It looks especially well planted against the posts of a verandah. We pot up the old plants in October,

cut them back, tie them up—when they take very little
room—and keep them rather dry all winter in a cold
shed just safe from the frost. We bring them on a
little in the spring, and plant them out the end of May
against a warm wall, though I am not at all sure that this
last is necessary. All they want is sunshine and copious
waterings. They are commonly treated in this way in
German gardens. Mr. Robinson says they can be increased by division of the roots, but we also find cuttings strike easily in spring; and three or four young
plants in a pot, as they flower at the top, are very pretty
in a greenhouse or window. *Solanum jasminoides* can
be treated in exactly the same way, though it will live
out through ordinary winters, especially if sheltered by
some other growth.

Last spring my jealousy was excited by seeing
Camellias flowering very well out of doors. The principle on which they were managed was to plant them in
a thick shrubbery with overhanging branches of Rhododendron or some other evergreen shrub. The ground
was prepared with a good deal of peat. In consequence
of the successful healthy look of these Camellias, I have
myself planted out two large old trees. The great
secret of success is that they should face due north, and
be well watered in dry weather. If *Dielytra spectabilis*
is planted in the same way, facing north and under the
protection of some shrub, it flowers well out of doors. It
always gets injured by spring winds and frosts in the
open borders here.

September 10th.—All the Funkias are worth growing,
but all might be left out of a small garden except *Funkia
Sieboldi*. That, anyhow, must be grown out of doors, as
it is a beautiful plant, gives no trouble, flowers every
year, and lasts very well in water. If kept in a pot it
flowers at the same time as out of doors, but under

glass the flowers are distinctly finer. It is not very often seen, but is quite the handsomest, I think, of the Funkias.

A friend asks me to recommend a really good book on the kitchen garden, including the proper treatment of fruit trees. I know no one book complete; the information on vegetables and fruit must be gleaned apart. For detailed directions on the culture of vegetables, none comes near the translation of Vilmorin's, mentioned before. But for ordinary purposes and as a cheap book, Sutton's 'The Culture of Vegetables and Flowers' (Simpkin, Marshall, Hamilton, Kent & Co.) is excellent. 'Profitable Fruit-growing,' by John Wright, F.R.H.S. (171 Fleet street, London), is clear, comprehensive, and concise, giving excellent information on pruning and general cultivation of all outdoor fruit trees, and currants, gooseberries, and raspberries. It makes no allusion to orchard-houses, nor to vines under glass or out of doors.

Samphire is a herb I have never yet tried to grow. I believe it is only to be had wild in its integrity from Norfolk, where they still make quite an industry of gathering and pickling it. The fresh Samphire is only to be found in August and September.

A critic in 'The Guardian' on 'Pot-Pourri' says it is a mistake to prune *Chymonanthus fragrans* after flowering in the winter, as I suggested; and adds, 'it should be done late in the summer by shortening back the year's growths to a quarter of their own length or less, to throw the vigour of the shrub into the short flowering spur rather than let it run into long, leafy and flowerless branches.' I think this quite true, but I call that cutting back. What I mean by 'pruning' is taking out real branches, and I think that is desirable here in this light soil with nearly all the flowering shrubs directly after flowering, as well as cutting back later in the year if they make too much growth.

I wonder the claret-coloured Vine is so seldom planted. The foliage is handsome and effective, and the little bunches of black grapes are interesting, and remind one of the ornaments in early Gothic churches. The stunted bunches are quite different in shape from those of ordinary grapes. They grow well up a pole, and make a good rough arch. Pancretiums are excellent greenhouse plants and well worth growing, especially *P. fragrans.* But in a small garden and greenhouse all these bulbs and plants want remembering and looking after, in order to get a good succession, and the head of the garden must help the gardener, as it is absolutely impossible, with the number of things requiring his constant attention, that he should remember them all himself.

September 11th.—What a week of excitement this has been, even for those without near relations in that faraway Nile Valley! Never in all my life do I remember what might be called the aggressive, grasping, ruling spirit of the typical John Bull to have been so united and so universal. War, and the pity of it, and the question why it has to be, which was so strong a feeling and which had such large numbers of supporters in the old Crimean day and even in the Indian Mutiny time, seems now simply non-existent. Is this gain or is it loss? Is it progress or is it retrogression? A most curious and, to me, poetic description, showing the conservativeness of the East, and how certain effects suggesting certain word-paintings were the same in the time of David as to-day, struck me very forcibly when I read it in yesterday's 'Spectator,' and I record it here. That a figure of speech which has long puzzled somewhat ignorant Bible commentators should be explained, as with a lime-light flash, by the unconscious wording of a war correspondent of to-day, seems indeed a drawing together of all historic times:

'The telegraphic despatch conveying the news of the battle of Omdurman contained an interesting illustration of a verse of the sixty-eighth Psalm which has caused some difficulty to commentators. The Prayer Book version reads (verse 14): "When the Almighty scattered kings for their sake: then were they as white as snow in Salmon" — *i. e.*, as generally explained, the flashing of the armour of the slain warriors resembled the snow shining on the dark boughs of the forest. Unconsciously, perhaps, the writer of the telegraphic despatch has used the same simile. His words are: "After the dense mass of the Dervishes had melted to companies and the companies to driblets, they broke and fled, leaving the field white with jibba-clad corpses, like a meadow dotted with snowdrifts."'

Is this really the last of these snow-flecked plains, or will another Mahdi and other Dervishes arise in future ages, to once more strew the ground with these white-clad corpses!

September 13th. — Last year, about this time, I drove to Mr. Barr's, at Long Ditton, and there I saw, planted out in an open bed, Tigridias, both white and red; and they looked splendid. I have never seen them grown out of doors in gardens, but Mrs. Loudon, in her 'Ladies' Flower Garden' (the volume on bulbous plants), speaks of them as easily cultivated if taken up in the autumn. Mrs. Loudon says: 'They have tunicated bulbs and very long, fibrous roots, which descend perpendicularly. They should be planted in a very deep, rich soil, which should either be of an open nature, or be kept so by a mixture of a sufficient quantity of sand, so as to allow a free passage for the descent of the roots, in the same way as is necessary for Hyacinths. If Tigridias are to be raised from seed, the seeds are sown in March or April in a hotbed and transplanted into the open border in May. Here they may remain till the leaves begin to wither in autumn, when the young bulbs should be taken up and kept for planting the ensuing spring. The splendid colours of this flower and the easiness of its culture render it a general favourite. Its only faults are that its flowers have no fragrance, and that they are of very short duration, never lasting more than a day. But they are produced in such abundance in succession as to compensate for this defect. It is a native of Mexico. In its native country its bulb is considered medicinal, and it was on this account that it was sent to Europe by Hernandez, physician to Philip II of Spain when he was employed by the Spanish Government to examine into 'the virtues' of the plants of the New World. It was not introduced into England till 1796. It is sufficiently hardy to be left in the ground all the winter, were it not on account of the danger to which it would be exposed from damp. It is better to take it up in September or October, tie it in bundles, and hang it up in a dry place till spring. Why it is always grown by gardeners in pots I do not know. In his last edition, Mr. Robinson speaks very favourably of growing it out of doors, and mentions particularly the ivory white one with carmine-red base, which I saw last year and thought very beautiful. What he says about cultivation is exactly what I have quoted above from Mrs. Loudon. In fact, treat them exactly as one would the *Gandavensis gladioli*. Gerarde, in his Herbal, speaks with delightful distrust of the very existence of the Tigridia as described by travellers. After trying to illustrate the plant from description, he goes on to say: 'The second feigned picture hath beene taken of the

Discouerer and others of later time, to be a kinde of Dragons not seene of any that haue written thereof; which hath moued them to thinke it a feigned picture likewise; notwithstanding you shall receiue the description thereof as it hath come to my hands. The root (saith my Author) is bulbous or Onion fashion, outwardly blacke; from the which springs vp long leaues, sharpe pointed, narrow, and of a fresh greene colour: in the middest of which leaues rise vp naked or bare stalkes, at the top whereof groweth a pleasant yellow floure, stained with many small red spots here and there confusedly cast abroad: and in the middest of the floure thrusteth forth a long red tongue or stile, which in time groweth to be the cod or seed-vessell, crooked or wreathed, wherein is the seed. The virtues and temperature are not to be spoken of, considering that we assuredly persuade our selues that there are no such plants, but meere fictions and deuices, as we terme them, to giue his friend a gudgeon.' 'Giving his friend a gudgeon' is apparently a Gerardian expression for what we should now call in familiar language 'pulling his leg.'

I alluded before (page 132 of '*Pot-Pourri*') to the cultivation of the large Japanese Stonecrop (*Sedum spectabile*). I have grown to like it more and more, because it is a very obliging plant, and will grow even in shade, though the specimens are far finer if grown in good soil and moved into a sunny place in July or August. I always take this little trouble, and in September I have my reward. Many people will not appreciate the great beauties of this plant because of the colour of the flowers, which are of rather an inartistic magenta-pink; but the insects do not find this so, and the reason I grow so much of it is that the bees simply love it. The little hard-working honey-bee, the

large, handsome bumble-bee, flies and beetles of all
kinds, and the beautiful common butterflies, all flop
about it with the keenest enjoyment, the colour of the
flower only making a groundwork to their bright hues
on a sunny September morning. I never fail either to
think, as I look at this scene, of a little poem by Victor
Hugo which was the delight of my youth, though perhaps for non-floral reasons:

La pauvre fleur disait au papillon céleste:
           'Ne fuis pas!
Vois comme nos destins sont différents. Je reste,
           Tu t'en vas!

'Pourtant nous nous aimons, nous vivons sans les hommes
           Et loin d'eux,
Et nous nous ressemblons, et l'on dit que nous sommes
           Fleurs tous deux!

'Mais, hélas! l'air t'emporte et la terre m'enchaîne;
           Sort cruel!
Je voudrais embaumer ton vol de mon haleine
           Dans le ciel!

'Mais non, tu vas trop loin! Parmi des fleurs sans nombre
           Vous fuyez,
Et moi je reste seul à voir tourner mon ombre
           A mes pieds!

'Tu fuis, puis tu reviens, puis tu t'en vas encore
           Luire ailleurs.
Aussi me trouves-tu toujours à chaque aurore
           Toute en pleurs!

'Oh! pour que notre amour coule des jours fidèles,
           O mon roi;
Prends comme moi racine, ou donne moi des ailes
           Comme à toi!'

Now and then quite strange insects appear just once,
and then never again. I have heard this is because
eggs of insects are sometimes deposited in baskets or

bales bringing goods from hot countries, which in dry
summers are hatched out in these northern climates.
One summer my Sedums were covered with a lovely
green beetle. I have never seen him again, but I am
too ignorant to know if he were a stranger or only an
insect common in our gardens and appearing in some
summers and not in others — a usual occurrence with all
insects. Sometimes there are a quantity of one kind,
they having triumphed over their natural enemies and
flourished abundantly. Then for a year or two they
disappear entirely. This is an especial characteristic
of butterflies. I thought there might be some way of
encouraging butterflies in my garden, where they seem
to have become rarer, and I asked a friend, who has
studied natural history all his life, whether he could help
me to do this. His answer was: 'The way to have
butterflies is to encourage the food-plants of the caterpillar.' He added: 'Fortunately, our three handsomest
English butterflies feed on the nettle — the Peacock, the
Small Tortoiseshell, and the Red Admiral. The Purple
Emperor is too rare for consideration.' I, being a
gardener before all things, did not think it was at all
fortunate that their natural food was nettles. I had
spent my whole life in eradicating nettles, so it is
perhaps not astonishing if butterflies have become less
in my garden.

We have had a great many figs this year, and they
have ripened well. No doubt they do better since we
have removed suckers and the small autumn figs that
never ripen here. It is curious how few people in England realize that, apparently, the fig never flowers, and
that what we call the fruit is the flower. Male and
female mixed are inside the fig, which when it enlarges
forms the receptacle and encloses numerous one-seeded
carpels imbedded in its pulp. This may be seen quite

plainly by cutting open a slightly unripe fig. I used to think the flower of the Fig was so small that it was invisible ! My little Mulberry tree, planted only fifteen years ago and now a good size, did wonderfully well this year. All over England Mulberries fruited in great quantities from the hot, dry season. They are trees that require much judicious pruning, and taking out of great branches now and then, or the fruit never ripens because of the size and thickness of the leaves. I have lately read that Leonardo da Vinci's great patron at Milan, Ludovico il Moro, was so named, not from the darkness of his complexion, as Gibbon supposes, but because he took a Mulberry tree (*moro*) for his device — from its being considered wiser than all other trees, as it buds later and does not flower until it has escaped the injuries of winter, when it immediately bears fruit. This the Prince considered was emblematic of his disposition. To us it means that Mulberry trees should be much more grown than they are, not only because they are beautiful and useful, but because of this late budding. The fruit is excellent cooked with apples, even if it is not quite ripe. Sweet Spanish Chestnuts are also very late trees in spring.

Sweet-scented Geraniums cut back in the spring do best for autumn and winter. For planting out the next year, they should be cut back hard, like show Pelargoniums, at the end of September .

My trees of *Magnolia grandiflora*, though still small, are covered this year with their beautiful flowers. These are, I am sure, best always cut off. It only strengthens the trees for forming flower-buds next year.

September 15th.—For those who care to have Sweet Peas early in the year, it is well to sow them now in the drills or holes, so as to earth them up a little after they come through the soil.

Cassia corymbosa is a yellow greenhouse plant now in flower and very useful. It is so nearly hardy that it will grow, like the blue Plumbago, against a south wall in the summer months. It comes from Buenos Ayres, and won't stand any frost.

September 25th.—I saw a Suffolk garden this September, where I learnt more in an hour than one would do in most places in a week. It was a beautiful, stately, flat garden and on a very large scale, with tall trees and broad expanses of lawn, which, in spite of my opinion stated before, and which angered so many of my readers (about overdoing grass in small places), I do immensely admire when sufficiently spacious and with spreading timber feathering to the ground. I saw in this garden the finest tubs of Hydrangeas I have ever seen anywhere. They were much raised above the ground, on a half-tub reversed or on bricks, so that the plants, which had been left alone for many years, fell all around, covering the tubs almost entirely. The tubs were painted white, and the gardener told me that instead of putting them into any house or shed in winter he put them under very thick shrubs. In his case he was fortunate to have an Ilex grove. Nothing was cut off the Hydrangeas but the faded flowers. By this means they get the damp and cold, which only strengthen them in their resting state. In the spring he cuts out the dead wood, mulches and copiously waters them when they begin to grow, and the result was certainly most satisfactory. Hydrangeas strike very easily in spring; and small young plants, especially if white or blue—which the pink ones will often turn to if planted in peat—make useful small decorative plants in a greenhouse or for late flowering. The tubs of Cape *Agapanthus* were less fine in foliage than mine are; but they had spike upon spike of bloom, which is really what one wants. He treated these in the same way as before described for Hydrangeas, leaving them out all the winter. Mine were kept in a cool greenhouse, and looked perfectly healthy, but had hardly any flowers at all this year. It's the old story. Everything from the Cape stands many kinds of treatment, but must have a long period of rest in order to flower well. Under a tall wall facing west in this Suffolk garden was a glorious border of many of the hardiest Bamboos, with a few strong-growing herbaceous plants in between and towards the front. The soil, in spite of the dryness of the year, was moist and very heavy, and the gardener told me he never dug up the border or touched it except to thin out and dig a big wedge out of the herbaceous plants with his spade in winter, filling up the hole with strong manure well stamped in. This, where size of clumps and filling up of large spaces are wanted, is quite an admirable plan. No re-planting is either necessary or desirable. In a small garden and light soil, where refinement and specimen plants are desired, re-planting and dividing, as well as thinning out, certainly seem to me to give finer blooms. On the top of a low wall, dividing this garden from another portion of it, were some flower-boxes well filled with trailing and half-hardy plants, brilliant in colour and easy to water and attend to ; and the effect was very good, and might be adopted on those dreary little walls that sometimes divide small villa gardens from their neighbours. The evaporation from painted wood is very much less than from flower-pots, and there is no fear of their being thrown over by a high wind.

Going about, I observe that — next to pruning and cutting back — there is nothing people are so ignorant about as watering, especially in dry weather. The ordinary non-gardening mind seems to think that if a thing looks blighted or faded or drooping, it is 'below par', and that water acts as the required tonic; whereas it is often that the dry weather has only hastened the period of rest, and when that is the case nothing is so hopeless as watering anything that is not in full growth. Consequently, in mixed borders, unless very carefully done, to a plant that is coming into bud, watering — and, above all, hosing — is best left alone; and much watering in the summer is very injurious to spring-flowering shrubs. At the same time, copious soaking once or twice a week is necessary very often to keep newly planted things alive. Half-hardy planted-out things, annuals, and plants lately moved from the reserve garden, can safely be watered. In this Suffolk garden all watering was done at four or five in the morning, the gardeners leaving off work at two in the afternoon. This plan, I think, would often work very well, both for the masters and men, during the long, hot days, but gardeners seldom like it.

RECEIPTS

I indiscreetly asked one of my rather intimate friends whether he had read 'Pot-Pourri.' He said, rather hastily: 'No; I gave it to my cook.' This impressed me with the idea that a good number of people valued the first 'Pot-Pourri' a great deal more for its cooking receipts than for anything else. Consequently, the book quickly leaves the library or the drawing-room for the kitchen, and I think it would be a distinct assistance to the cook if I keep these new receipts as much as possible together, though I allot them a place in each month, as the times and seasons have such a great influence on food and garden produce. In this book I reserve to myself the right to spell *recipe* 'receipt,' to which some of my friends objected before. I was taught that *recipe* meant a prescription, and it always seems to me a slight affectation when I see it in a cookery book. I believe 'receipt' to be quite as old and good a word used in this sense. In an old cookery book of mine, which was written by a lady and published in 1770, the word is spelt 'receipt.'

I take a great interest in cooks, and am always most anxious to help them, having agreed from my youth upwards with Owen, Meredith's delicious lines in 'Lucile':

> We may live without poetry, music, and art;
> We may live without conscience, and live without heart;
> We may live without friends; we may live without books;
> But civilised man cannot live without cooks.
> He may live without books—what is knowledge but grieving ?
> He may live without hope—what is hope but deceiving ?
> He may live without love—what is passion but pining ?
> But where is the man that can live without dining ?

There have been some complaints about the cooking receipts not being exact enough. I had tried them all myself, and with success, with several cooks, but I do not deny they were intended for those who understood cooking sufficiently to refer to more detailed books when they felt themselves to be ignorant. I shall continue to refer to 'Dainty Dishes' (by Lady Harriet St. Clair) as I did before, and without it my receipts are incomplete. Cooks differ very much in how they follow receipts. Some try to do it literally, but without judgment as regards increasing or decreasing quantities according to the number for whom they have to cook. Other cooks accept a receipt with the distinct conviction that their own way is far the best, and naturally then the new receipt does not turn out very satisfactorily. A good many cooks carry out a receipt very well the first time, and then think they know it by heart, and in a high-

handed way never look at it again. All this is where the
eye and the head of the mistress come in. Without
showing it, she must know the peculiarities of her own
particular cook, and by gentle flattery lead her back into
the right way. As my excuse for a certain vagueness in
some of the receipts, I give them as they were given to
me, for I did not by any means invent them all. Even
when they are mine, I instruct the cook, but do not
myself cook.

Some of my nieces scolded me for not putting the
receipt for my bread sauce in my last book, saying they
so seldom found it really good elsewhere. It is made in
every English kitchen, small and big; and yet how very
rarely is it excellent, as it ought to be, and with what
horror is it viewed by foreigners!

Bread Sauce.—It is very important that the bread
should be grated from a tin loaf, and allowed to dry in
a paper bag for some time before using it. It is absolutely impossible to make good bread sauce with new
bread. Cut up an onion in rather large pieces, boil it in
milk, pass it through a sieve, or remove the onion. Pour
the milk boiling over the crumbs, and add a few pepper-
corns. Boil the whole in a china saucepan for about
twenty minutes. As the milk is absorbed, add a little
more until it is an even mass, neither too moist nor too
dry. Remove the pepper-corns before serving, and stir
in a large piece of fresh butter. Many people add
cream, which spoils it. Cream makes the sauce tasteless
and *fade*.

The following is a much simpler receipt and suggests
a poultice rather more than I quite like; but it is excellent
to eat, and useful to know, as it can be carried out in a
sick-room or a lodging-house kitchen. Take a breakfastcupful of fresh breadcrumbs, rubbed, not grated; a
breakfastcupful of milk. Cut up into it an onion, and

add two or three pepper-corns. Boil the milk up and pour it on the crumbs, which have been put into a small basin. Cover over, and let it stand for two hours. Remove any pieces of onion that show. Warm up before it is wanted, with a small piece of fresh butter the size of a walnut.

It is also, under the same circumstances, useful to know that chickens or game of any kind can be perfectly well roasted in a baking-tin on a little kettle-stand in front of any ordinary fire in the following way: Put a little bacon fat in the pan, lay the bird in it on its side, with the back towards the fire. Baste well. When sufficiently done, turn it onto the other leg, with the back still towards the fire. For ten minutes at the end, with a large fowl or pheasant, turn the breast to the fire, basting it well. The time a bird will take to roast must depend on its size. Woodcocks, snipe, and larks will take a very short time.

Vegetable Marrow.— Peel a young vegetable marrow, cut it across in slices the thickness of a finger, and put them in a tin in a moderate oven, with a little piece of butter on each. Bake for nearly an hour. Prepare some pieces of toast slightly buttered and hot. Lay a slice of the vegetable marrow on each piece. Warm in butter a little of the sweet-chutney (see '*Pot-Pourri*,' page 126), put half a teaspoonful of it onto each slice, and serve.

If vegetable marrows get past being young, let them ripen well, then dry and store them on a shelf in the fruit-house or elsewhere. In winter break one up by hammering a knife through it, clean out the seeds, cut the pieces into small dice half an inch square, boil them with very little salt in cold water till soft, strain them, and make a nice thick white sauce (*Béchamel*). Put the marrow in the sauce, add a small piece of sugar, and serve hot. Pumpkins can be treated in the same way.

If you have grown the little ridge cucumbers — those recommended in Sutton's book do very well either in a cool house or outside — and have had any left over in this month, which I never have, this German receipt for preserving them — in Germany they always grow them in large quantities — is very useful and good.

Cucumbers preserved in salt (in a barrel or stone jar).—Pick the outdoor cucumbers when about three inches long and one inch thick. Brush them in a large tub of cold water till quite clean. Spread them on a table to dry. Meanwhile, boil up a large quantity of water. Measure it carefully, and for each quart of water add a *small* teacupful of salt and a small teacupful of vinegar. Boil all well together, and let it get cold˙ Then put some vine-leaves, fennel, tarragon, pimpernel, and a few bay-leaves and pepper-corns at the bottom of a small barrel or stone jar. Place four layers of cucumber, one of herbs and leaves, and so on till full. Cover the top thickly with leaves, and pour on the salt water till the jar is quite full. Put a clean slate over the top of the jar, and weight it with a stone. They should stand for at least six weeks.

A Purée of Vegetables.—A pretty dish can be made with a *purée* of any kind of green vegetables surrounded by macaroni cut into small pieces, boiled plain with a little onion in the water, drained, and warmed up in a little strong stock (or water), butter, and a little sugar. The New Zealand Spinach or the Spinach Beet is sure to be still quite good in the garden.

A friend of mine who has been much in the East makes the following comments on my curry receipt and my cooking of rice: 'You say meat in curry is to be cut in *dice*. An old Indian uncle of mine always taught his cooks to make curries, and there were never better curries; and he always said, *No* dice, but thinnish slices about the size of two small mouthfuls. I think he was right.' The Indian uncle also said that rice can never be really properly cooked except in earthenware vessels. I think I agree with both these criticisms.

Here is a good receipt for those troubled with a superabundance of grouse :

Grouse Salad.—Select fresh salad material. Place this in a shallow dish on which has been constructed a border of hard-boiled eggs, set off with pieces of anchovies and sliced beetroot.

Sauce.—Two tablespoonfuls of eschalots minced small, seven teaspoonfuls of chopped tarragon and chervil, five dessertspoonfuls of pounded sugar, the yolks of two eggs, five saltspoonfuls of pepper and salt mixed, and a very small pinch of cayenne. Mix slowly with twelve or thirteen tablespoonfuls of salad oil and six dessertspoonfuls of chili vinegar. Add half a pint of whipped cream.

The grouse may be roasted or fried. Build up the grouse tastefully in pyramidal form on the greenstuff, then pour the sauce over the whole, and serve.

This receipt for pickled damsons was sent me by one of my very kind readers, with a bottle of the same, which certainly was quite excellent.

Pickled Damsons.—Six pounds of damsons, six pounds of sugar, two quarts of vinegar, quarter of an ounce of cinnamon (stick), quarter of an ounce of cloves, one onion (about as large as a nutmeg), half tablespoonful of cayenne tied in muslin, and a little salt.

Put all except the damsons into a pan, and boil; then pour the liquid over the fruit, and allow the whole to remain until the next day, when strain it, putting the fruit back into a basin; boil up the liquid, and pour it over the fruit again. Let the whole stand for another twenty-four hours, and on the third day boil for four or five minutes. Strain and press through a sieve, to remove the stones and skins. The pickle will then be ready to bottle for use.

Both the following receipts are Belgian. The eight stumps of endive make my economical hair stand on end, as the curly endive, which is the one intended, is a very shy grower in this hot soil, and we blanch it rather preciously under boards for November salads. But the broad-leaved Batavian endive is very nearly as good, only it requires longer cooking. Take eight stumps of endive, a good bit of butter (say, the size of two walnuts), a good teaspoonful of flour, half a teacupful of milk, and a little salt. Throw away the bad leaves, cut the others in small pieces till near the stump. Wash several times, so that the sand may sink. Let the endive boil in plenty of water with a little salt for about an hour; then put it on a sieve to drip out well. Make a sauce of the milk, flour, and butter, and let it stew for a few minutes.

Purslane.—The purslane, after being picked and washed, is put on a gentle fire to melt, without adding any water. When quite soft, add some salt (a very little) to taste. If too watery, pour it off; then add butter (a rather larger piece than the size of a walnut), and carefully mix a well-beaten egg; or, if this does not suit the taste, bind it with a little flour.

Here is an excellent aromatic herb-seasoning which does equally well for use with vegetables or meat. I found it in an old-fashioned book called 'The Gentle-woman,' published in 1864, which I shall notice again further on. The author took this receipt from Fran-catelli, the famous cook of the day. Take of nutmegs

one ounce; mace, one ounce; cloves, two ounces; dried
bay-leaves, one ounce; basil, three ounces; marjoram,
three ounces; winter savoury, two ounces; thyme, three
ounces; cayenne pepper, half an ounce; grated lemon-
peel, half an ounce; two cloves of garlic. All to be
well pulverised in a mortar and sifted through a fine
wire sieve, and put away in dry corked bottles. We
made this last year, and used it frequently through
the winter for flavouring a great many things, such
as *purées* of cabbage, preserved French beans, soups,
sauces, etc. I reduced the cayenne pepper to half the
prescribed quantity.

Blackberry Jelly.—Boil the blackberries. Strain
them and stiffen with isinglass. This keeps splendidly,
and is not too sweet.

Gardening—Echeverias—Ignorance about bulbs—Gossamer time and insects—The East Coast—A new rockery—*Oxalis flori-bunda* as a vegetable — Previous ' *Pot-Pourris* ' — Cooking receipts, various—Journey to Frankfort in 1897—Cronberg—Boecklin's *Todten-Insel*—Jewish Cemetery—Goethe's house—Staedal Art Institute—German treatment of tuberculosis.

October 5th.—The other day I was going round the garden, giving away plants, when I came to a bed where there were several fine Echeverias. They had been planted out to grow naturally into better plants. I offered my friend some, but she said, with a shudder: 'What! those artichoke-looking things? No; thank you.' I think the dislike of these plants arises very likely from their having been used so much in those old-fashioned beds arranged in fancy designs as ugly and incongruous as the patterns on a Turkish smoking-cap.

These plants are not only kind friends that give little trouble, and can be grown in pots and allowed to assume their natural growth, but they are also exceedingly beautiful. I have an *Echeveria metallica crispa* grown to a large plant in a pot. It has been perhaps retarded in its growth by dryness this summer, and is now throwing up a fine pink flower-spike. The whole tone of the plant is lovely to a degree, shot with pale purples, grays, and pinks, and as full of drawing as the cone of an Italian pine. The thick stem is beautifully marked by the leaves as they have dried up and fallen away. The plant is altogether very picturesque in its quaint growth, and admirably adapted for a room or window-sill in late autumn, and reminds one of the corner of a Dutch picture. The Echeverias and Cotyledons are closely allied (natural order *Crassulaceæ*), and there are many varieties of these plants, all requiring much the same treatment — protection and very little watering in winter, but otherwise next to no care. They can be increased easily by cuttings at any time, starved and re-potted at will, which alters their flowering-time. They will grow in china pots, with only a few stones for drainage; or will hang out of Japanese vases, suspended by wires, containing hardly any earth. A large earthenware pan of the ordinary *Echeveria glauca* is a very pretty sight in summer, and does well in a north window. It can be planted with a little peat, charcoal, and a few stones.

I never knew till this year that Marvels of Peru can be kept, like Dahlias, free from frost and started the following spring, when they make much handsomer plants than if grown each year from seed. In gardens where you are pressed for room — and where is it that you are not? — it is an excellent plan to make a hole in the ground, put some straw at the bottom, and lay in Geraniums, Dahlias, Marvels of Peru, and many other half-hardy things, cover them with straw, and earth up just as you would potatoes or mangolds in a field.

October 10th.—It is extraordinary how vague are people's ideas about plants, bulbs, etc.; and it is not till one is asked questions that one realises how much most people have to learn. I was asked the other day by a friend, who had had a lot of Narcissus bulbs given her, if she might plant them in a Tea-rose bed! That is the last place where they ought to be put, as, if planted in too rich a soil, they all go to leaf and flower badly; and

Roses are the better for being heavily mulched in the winter and spring.

Mr. Robert Sydenham, of Tenby street, Birmingham, publishes a catalogue of bulbs, in which are the clearest possible instructions of how to cultivate them, both in pots and in the open, with an interesting account of his own first experiences. If these instructions are carefully followed, I do not believe the disappointing failures, so often seen when amateurs try to force bulbs, will occur. He also makes it quite plain which are the bulbs that should be planted in poor places and left alone, and those which have to be taken up, dried, and re-planted. Tulips, at least in this soil, require much better feeding than any of the Narcissus tribe, and are certainly the better for taking up and drying after their leaves have thoroughly died down. I planted my Roman Hyacinths, according to Mr. Sydenham's directions, early in October, and the result was more satisfactory than I have ever had before, and they were in full flower by Christmas. It is a very pretty conceit to plant Hyacinths in shallow earthenware or china pans with jadoo, cocoanut fibre or moss, and place small stones and charcoal at the bottom for the roots to cling to as they grow up. They must be kept very wet. Planted in this way they look much more decorative in the room than when grown in pots or glasses. Any fancy or ornamental vase can be used for the purpose, whether it is flat or not. Many kind hints have been given me by various correspondents about the growing of Hepaticas. One lady said that small beds with pieces of sandstone were a great help. Another writes as follows: 'I thought you might be glad of certain facts about Hepaticas that have come under my own observation. When a child I lived in Somersetshire, where the soil was heavy clay. The most beautiful show of Hepaticas I ever saw anywhere was a row in an old lady's garden, close under a thick hedge of Laurestinus, with a due north aspect. They were single-blue and double-pink. In the same village there was for many years a large clump of double-pink close under a cottage wall with a south-east aspect. That also flowered abundantly, so for double-pink, at any rate, shade is not essential, though I remember that the late James Backhouse told me many years ago that the Hepaticas did best and flowered earliest with a north aspect, as then they went to sleep sooner in the autumn. The wild ones in Swiss and French woods are always where they would be shaded in summer, and grow with the Primroses. I was also unsuccessful with Hepaticas for many years, as long as I grew them on the flat, but when I at last tried them on the shady side of the rockery, between the stones, the blue ones have done well, the plants increasing in size year by year and flowering abundantly.' I found by my letters that a good many people thought when I did not mention some plants that I either had not got them, or did not care for them, or did not know them. The last was sometimes the case, but I have, of course, a great many things in the garden, grown in the usual way and doing well, which I did not mention.

October 15th.—I suppose there are still some few people who plant trees for their children or grandchildren, although it is rather the fashion to expect gardens and woods to be made in a day, and always to be planting quick-growing things, Scotch Firs being discarded and the ugly-growing *Pinus austriaca* planted in its stead, etc. One of the loveliest things I know in this neighbourhood is a road running through a Beech-tree copse, planted thickly but varying in depth on each side of the road. The trees when they were young were evidently cut down, as many of them have two or three stems. At all times of the year the drive up this chalk slope is perfectly enchanting — whether in the autumn, when the stems are gray and green against the leaf-strewn ground, rich and golden in the slanting sunlight; or in spring, when the tiny leaves make flickering light and shade; or in the cool thickness on a summer's day. The fact that nothing grows under beech-wood gives a very distinguished and unusual effect, accustomed as we are to the dull walls of evergreens. For the young who wish to plant a most unusual approach, I can suggest nothing better.

The planting along the roads and hedgerows of England of Apples, Cherries and Damsons, would cost no more than any other trees, and would be both ornamental and useful. These three fruit trees, once well planted, require no other care. The impression is that the fruit would be stolen, but I believe that to be a matter of custom, and when once people understand that taking fruit is stealing they cease to do it. Growing fruit trees in open fields is universal on the Continent, and I am told that they are never touched.

My love of autumn, with its recurring beauty, does not dull with age or loneliness, and I am often astonished at the interest that is still so keen about all that surrounds me. Perhaps it ought not to be so, for I find quoted in my notebook the following complaint:

> How much is lost when neither heart nor eye
>   Rose-winged desire or fabling hope deceives;
> When boyhood with quick throb has ceased to spy
>   The dubious apple in the yellow leaves;
> When, rising from the turf where youth reposed,
>   We find but deserts in the far-sought shore;
> When the huge book of fairy-land lies closed,
>   And those strong brazen clasps will yield no more!

October 16th.— The beautiful gossamer time has come again. Most mothers now cultivate in their children a love of flowers, but it is astonishing how rarely a love of insects is taught. I do not mean a mawkish fear of killing them, for very often they have to be killed. I remember a boy who was fond, on wet summer days, of killing flies on his nursery window. I remonstrated and said it was cruel, upon which he answered : ' Why ? Father goes out fishing, and brothers go out shooting ; why may I not kill flies ? ' The only answer that came to my mind was that I could stop the one and I could not the other; this remained for ever with him as an injustice. But I do think that probably the more children understand and admire, the less they would wish wantonly to kill, and at any rate it might do away with so much of that groundless dread and uncontrollable nervous fear of insects which stick to some people through life. I know some girls who have to leave the room if moths — innocent, soft, downy moths ! — come in, attracted to their doom by the cruel lamp. I know others who dare not pick certain flowers for fear of an earwig, which from its silly name they believe to be really a dangerous enemy. Others, again, will injure their health and remain, all through the hot summer nights, perhaps in quite a small room, with window and door closed, for fear of the inroad of some winged wanderer of the darkness. All this seems to me so silly, so ignorant, so unnecessary ! And if children were early introduced to the wonders of insect life — ants, bees, butterflies, moths, etc.— I think they would fear them as little as the ordinary house-fly, which is really more objectionable than many of them. I never cared much for spiders till I heard a most interesting lecture about them, when I longed to know more. The process by which they weave their beautiful webs has only been understood in comparatively recent years. Everyone knows now that the gossamer which covers our commons is spun by spiders. In old days all sorts of fairy traditions hung about it, as it was quite unlike the web of other spiders. The lecturer said that spiders place themselves with their face to the gentle breeze. This carries the thin thread they have power to eject, with its glutinous end, into the air till it reaches some branch or stone or corner of leaf, to which it adheres instantly. When this happens, the spider turns quickly round and pulls, like any British tar, with his two front claws till the fairy rope is tight. Then he fixes it and can travel along it, and that is the first stage in the 'weaving,' as the old language puts it, of his beautiful web. Spiders belong to a kingdom ruled by women, and the female eats up the male if she finds him troublesome and unsatisfactory. There is a very good book about British spiders by E. F. Staveley (L. Reeve & Co.), which would tell all that anyone might want to know about these insects. The first page illustrates spiders' heads, with the varying numbers of eyes the different kinds possess.

'Gleanings in Natural History,' by Edward Jesse, is a book I can indeed recommend to all lovers of natural history. The first edition is dated 'Hampton Court, 1842.' For all of us who live near Hampton Court the book has a double interest, as he was Surveyor of Her Majesty's Parks and Palaces, and lived there, and many of his anecdotes are connected with the neighbourhood. His opening words are: 'One of the chief objects I had in writing the following pages was to portray the character of animals, and to endeavour to excite more kindly feelings towards them.' It is a kind of half-way book between Gilbert White and the scientific writings of the present day; and all natural instincts and facts are accounted for in what the most ignorant, since the days of Darwin, would describe as the unscientific language belonging to that date. To my mind, that in no way detracts from the interest of its shrewd observations on the facts of nature.

To name another book in this place, 'Country Pleasures : Chronicle of a Year chiefly in a Garden,' by George Milner, has been lately republished and thoroughly deserves it, as it is one of the best of its kind, and must be an especial favourite with all nature lovers. Its charm is of rather a different kind from either of the other two. The writing is beautiful, and the quotations are pointed, and chosen with literary taste and knowledge. Here are two sentences which I give in order that the charm may be felt. One is dated 'May 22d,' for the book is arranged in months, which seems to me the only natural system when speaking of the year's produce and colour-effects in field, wood, or garden :

'In the present general outburst of vernal foliage, we naturally forget that the evergreens, as well as the deciduous trees, are putting forth their new leaves. This is one of those lesser beauties of the spring, easily overlooked, but full of interest when once observed. The yew-tree now shows itself as a mass of leafage, so dark as to be almost black, but wearing a fringe of yellowish green ; the box has six or seven bright new leaves at the end of each spray, in sharp contrast with the sombre but polished growth of last year ; the ivy buds are silver-gray, like the willow ; those of the holly are edged with red, and the rhododendron is a light green. In that delightfully child-like carol of Kit Marlowe, which gave such pleasure to the gentle soul of dear old Izaak Walton, the Passionate Shepherd promises to his Love

'A belt of straw and ivy buds,
With coral clasps and amber studs.'

Once every year, in the autumn, and sometimes twice, I go to the east coast, and the house is so absolutely on the seashore that this description in 'Country Pleasures' exactly suits what I feel when I am there. It is, I think, so good that it may be an inducement for my readers to get the book for themselves: 'It is often said that the sea is both monotonous and melancholy, but the longer we remain in its close neighbourhood the less are we disposed to allow that it is monotonous. Melancholy it may be, as it is fierce or wild or lovely by turns, but it is not monotonous. Rather it is, next to the sky, the most changeful thing we know: and by this I do not mean only the obvious motion and restlessness of the waves, but the more subtle and ever-varying alternation of the whole aspect of the sea. It is usual to suppose that these moods are mainly in the mind of the observer; but that is not so. The sea, like nature generally, has its own absolute conditions—conditions which prompt and suggest, rather than follow, emotions in the mind of man. To feel all this, however, one must live continuously near the sea.' I do not agree that this is really necessary in order to appreciate the sea. I think one does feel all Mr. Milner describes, even if one goes only for a short time, so long as one lives close to the shore, no going out of the house being necessary in order to see the sea, still less a long walk, which means remaining only a few minutes by the waves. Mr. Milner continues: 'We are so contiguous to the sea here that, looking through the window as I write, I can see nothing but the wide stretch of waters, just as I should if I were sitting in the cabin of a vessel; and if I stand at the door I can fling a stone into the fringe of the tide. Crossing the road, one step brings me to the shore; and here you may sit all the day long, with the sea breeze blowing round you and the sound of the water ever in your ears. This sound is usually resolvable into three elements. There is, first, the great boom of the waves, the chorus of many waters, far and near, heard in one deep unison; then there is a noise as of liquid being poured continuously out of one vessel into another — that, I think, is caused by the falling crest of the waves; and lastly, there is a low and lisping talk ever going on between the water and the pebbles.' I call that an excellent word-rendering of sea-sounds. Then: 'In the pools and tiny basins there are a thousand fairy creatures, whose motions you may watch even as you lie reposing — green and thread-like tentacula issuing and retreating, purple atoms spinning round and round in some strange dance which is the beginning and end of their existence, gorgeous anemones, and many a tiny shell, delicately built and cunningly colored:

'Slight, to be crush'd with a tap
Of my finger-nail on the sand,
  Small, but a work divine;
Frail, but of force to withstand,
Year upon year, the shock
Of cataract seas that snap
  The three-decker's oaken spine
Athwart the ledges of rock.'

In mentioning these books, I mean no slight on any that I am not fortunate enough to know. I have kept to the same rule which I found necessary with the old garden-books — of only naming those that I not only know, but possess.

October 20th.—I have been very busy here hollowing out new rockeries and digging deep holes, eight to twelve feet deep, and throwing up the sandy earth on either side, so making slopes and mounds of earth. Small, narrow paths lead into these hollows, and instead of catching the water at the bottom, as I did before, I keep the bottom dry, and sink petroleum barrels level with the ground to catch the water as it runs down the paths when rain falls, or after watering with a hose. In the tall walls of sandy earth every sort of aspect is to be found, little hollows are made, and all kinds of treasures can be planted on the flat or the slope. By making holes in the sandy walls, and helping to fix the plants with a mixture of cow-dung and clay, they adhere quite well on the steep slope. On one side of these sunk rockeries, so as still more to keep off the north-east wind, there is a wall about four feet in width and four feet high, built up gradually with pieces of stone and earth between them—no mortar. This makes an excellent cool depth of soil for many precious plants. A small boggy bed can be made, by guiding the rain as it runs away into a hole, anywhere by the sides of paths and where the earth slopes. This immensely increases the effect of rainfall for individual plants, and it is a great help to gardening on sandy soils. The fault of my rockery, unavoidable from the situation, is that it has very little eastern aspect, being shaded in that direction by trees; and morning sun is what early Alpines require. As the holes approach the large trees, the banks are planted with Ferns, various Ivies, Periwinkles (*Vinca*), and shade-loving plants. Pernettyas, which are lovely little shrubs, will not do in sun at all; but in shade they seem to do excellently, and are quite healthy in sandy soil. All those I planted in full sun have simply died this dry year, having been very much parched up. *Cotoneaster microphylla*, on the contrary, never berries so well or is so satisfactory as in a very dry place fully exposed to the southern sun.

The other day, as I was working in this new Alpine garden, a caterpillar fell off a tree just in front of me. His head was round; he had a hairy body, plump and thickest in the middle, covered with moderately abundant hairs; and four square-topped bunches of hair of a pale yellow colour grew on his back. His head and body were green; his long, pointed tail bright pink. The spaces between the tufts of hair were deep black. His legs and pro-legs were green. I thought I had got hold of some wonderful rare beast, as I had never before found a caterpillar with a pink tail like a horn. A friend to whom I refer all my natural history questions informed me that this was the caterpillar of a moth called the 'Pale Tussock' because of the tussocks upon his body. The moth is pale gray coloured, with various markings, and is fairly common. He feeds upon most trees, often on Oak, but also on Hazel, Birch, and—oddly enough —Hops. He will eat Plum and Pear.

October 23rd.—I have found that *Crocus speciosus* does admirably in this very light soil, and comes up year after year, but is very much better not disturbed, when it decidedly increases. Young plants of variegated Maple look very pretty planted in clumps in front of a shrubbery, especially if backed by small plants of *Prunus pissardi*. The planting of Rosemary under shrubs, no matter what aspect, has answered perfectly, and in this way I have a lot of the delicious stuff, not only to burn in my own house, but to give away.

October 25th.— We have improved on the cultivation of watercress in a dry garden by sowing it in a wide trench with the sides supported by two old boards, and close to a tap, so that it can be easily watered. In October some of the plants are dug up, put into a box and then placed in a cold frame, so I get fresh watercress for tea through the cold weather. In London it is easy to get everything more or less good, but this is not at all the case in the country. What you do not grow you generally have to do without, and even if watercress can be bought, there is the additional advantage of safety in growing it on clean ground instead of buying it out of a dirty ditch, when it often tastes of mud.

I find that in Germany the roots of the pink *Oxalis floribunda* are eaten as a vegetable, and a most excellent vegetable it is. It is not quite hardy. The way to treat it is to take it up about this time of year, eat the big roots, preserve the small ones in sand, and re-plant them in the spring. Celeriac and salsifies are also much better taken up now and stored in dry sand under cover, like carrots. They grow old and spotty if left in the ground in the usual English way.

Before cutting down our asparagus we collect the pretty red seeds, sow them at once very thickly in ordinary or fancy china pots, and keep some for later sowing. The seedlings come in well as an ornament in the greenhouse at Christmas, look green and fresh and refined, and most people do not know what they are. They have the great merit of costing nothing and of being very easy to grow for anyone who has a warm greenhouse.

October 28th. — We are benefiting now by the extraordinarily dry autumn and no early frost. The number of flowers in the garden is quite surprising. I picked this morning a large bunch of Nemesia. The Lavenders are flowering a second time, and there are plenty of Tea Roses.

The following instructions for growing the *Tropæolum speciosum*, which has failed here so often, were sent me by a lady: 'The two great needs seem to be moisture — but not great moisture — at the roots and dampness of atmosphere round the foliage when in summer growth. These objects are best obtained by — first, in England, or at least in the southern counties, a north wall; second, by being planted about two feet deep in a trench properly prepared for it; third, by frequently syringing in the summer. I have found a trench a foot wide and a foot and a half deep suit it best. But if the subsoil is clay or a tenacious soil, the trench should be made two feet deep, the bottom six inches being filled with drainage — pieces of broken stones or brick. The soil with which it is next filled should be peat and ordinary loam in equal proportions, with a little sand and leaf-mould thrown in and thoroughly mixed with the whole. Sphagnum cut and chopped into small bits — this retains the moisture, which is as essential as that it should not be stagnant. The young plants should be put in in the autumn preferably to the spring. It is important that the soil in which the roots are growing should vary as little as possible in moistness, never getting dryer at one time than at another.'

The two Japanese grasses, *Eulalia Japonica variegata* and *zebrina*, do not throw up their flower panicles here quite early enough to come to perfection, but I learnt last summer that if the cane containing the flower (this is easily distinguished by feeling a certain fulness near the top) is picked and brought into the house, the grass will dry; it should then be peeled off, and the feathery panicles will display themselves (see illustration in 'English Flower Garden'). They make a pretty and refined winter decoration, and they are just the right size to mix with the red-berried pods of *Iris fœtidissima*. The seed-branches of Montbretias are also a pretty addition to a dry winter bouquet.

Plumbago rosea is a very pretty autumn-flowering greenhouse plant. It wants to be grown in a fairly warm house; but, once in flower, a cool greenhouse seems to suit it well. Its growth is very different from the other Plumbagos, and the pink of its flower is of an unusually beautiful hue. It is not difficult to strike.

RECEIPTS

I have two amusing little books by the same author—
kind of '*Pot Pourri*' of the early 'sixties—one called
'Dinners and Dinner Parties' and the other 'The Gentlewoman.' They are full of good advice and receipts,
some of which I think are worth copying, but the chief
amusement is to see how the advice they give has grown
and spread, and is so much less really wanted than it
was thirty-five years ago. The anonymous writer is
extremely sarcastic about the neglect of household duties
by women of all classes. Now, perhaps, the absorption
in domestic arrangements and refined luxuries is almost
carried to the extreme. Most newspapers have *menus*,
and the cookery books are innumerable. One paragraph
in 'The Gentlewoman' is headed, 'The Great Evil in
England,' and runs as follows : 'The great social evil is
not that which is talked of by gentlemen in black at
midnight meetings; but it is the great evil that besets
the English from the highest to the lowest. Every man,
woman, and child suffers from it, and thousands die or
only experience a lingering existence from its neglect.
The great social evil is the want of persons of education
and practical knowledge worthy to be entrusted in the
preparation of food with that care and nicety that is
practised in every nation in Europe except England,
whereby health would be no longer jeopardised, and
twenty millions of money would annually be saved.
There would be ample employment for every poor lady
who, for the want of domestic knowledge, is doomed to
life-long misery.' The writer further complains that
ladies do not go to market, that young gentlewomen do
not look after their own wardrobes, and is full of com-
passion for the poor father who has the task of providing a sufficient dowry for each girl. His language must

always have been exaggerated, and it is certainly untrue in our day. The 'Stores' have replaced the old markets, and without doubt ladies, and even gentlemen, do go to them — tiresome places though they are — and the girls of the present day are very few who do not look after and think about their clothes. Fathers still find the same difficulty in providing dowries for their daughters; but the girls themselves — among them those who have every right, from the way they have been brought up, to look for dowries — are now always striving to do some work of their own. The over-strained gentility that my author speaks of does still and must always exist. He touches on too many subjects for me to go on quoting him. But the employments he recommends for women, laying especial stress on nursing, do make one realize the changes and the improvements of the last thirty years. All his advice about stores and cooking utensils and general management of the kitchen is excellent. It is carried out far more in the beautiful kitchens of modern Germany than anywhere here. He is as strong as even I could wish about the use of earthenware *casseroles* and fireproof dishes. But both servants and mistresses hate them because of the breakage, which, of course, is very troublesome; and the excessive heat of our fireplaces makes them more difficult to manage. English servants, too, are so conservative that it is extremely difficult to interfere in any way with their method of work. They only like to do things as they have always been done.

On looking over these two books, I find the receipts so good and so unlike those in the ordinary cookery book that I shall copy several of them to disperse through the months as they seem to me seasonable. It is often difficult to remember how each generation requires to be told the same things over again. Among other good and useful hints, one is to keep a supply of corks for putting into any bottle that has been opened, so that it can be turned over on its head in the store closet and thus prevent the air from getting to the contents. This ensures your not having to buy a fresh bottle of oil for every third salad, or a fresh bottle of anchovy when you require only a teaspoonful. I am afraid the modern cooks are rare who will take the trouble to attend to such details.

This dressing of two chickens in different ways for one dinner party is rather original, so I copy it out of 'The Gentlewoman' just as it is:

'**Two Chickens for Eight Persons.**— Abandon the boiled fowl fashion; order a pair of fowls to be sent without being trussed, and let the heads and necks be sent with them. Cut up one of the fowls into pieces — the leg and thigh into two pieces, the back into three pieces, and the breast into two pieces, which, with the merry-thought, will be fourteen pieces.

'Take a Spanish onion, cut it up small, put it into a stewpan with two ounces of butter and a little pepper and salt ; let it stew gently for about an hour, until it is in a complete pulp. Half an hour before you want it, put in the fourteen pieces of chicken, let them stew half an hour, and when done put into your silver dish a tea-spoonful of Spanish or French garlic vinegar, or, if that is not liked, the squeeze of half a lemon, and you will never again want to taste insipid boiled fowl. Mind, it requires no water ; the fowl will be done in its own gravy.

'Cut the other fowl in the same way; viz., fourteen pieces. Let the heads and necks be picked and scalded; stew them in half a pint of water, and when all the goodness is extracted strain off the liquor, put it into a stewpan with a pint of button mushrooms, a little pepper and salt, and put in the fourteen pieces of fowl, stew them until done (about half an hour), thicken with a little arrowroot. When you dish them up, put into your silver dish a tablespoonful of mushroom catchup. These two fowls will be a variety, will require only the effort of serving, will be enough for eight or ten persons, and each *convive* will want to taste each dish.

'Pigeons, when in season, cooked in the same manner are equally good, and make a change — such a change that those who taste it never forget. Grouse and partridges treated the same way are better than roasted.

'A young turkey poult dressed in the same way is a very inviting dish.'

Towards the middle of October I buy two or three young turkeys in Suffolk, and feed them here till a fortnight before Christmas. They must be starved twenty-four hours before killing, and require to hang about a fortnight. They should not be plucked or cleaned out till they are going to be cooked.

Chervil Soup.— Pick, wash, and chop fine a very large handful of chervil. Melt a piece of butter the size of an egg, with two tablespoonfuls of good flour. Stir smooth. Do not let it colour at all; then add the chervil, and let it simmer ten minutes, stirring well. Pour on it sufficient stock or water (water is quite as good as stock, in my opinion) to make the soup (rather less than more, as one can easily add a drop if too thick). Let it boil half an hour. Just before serving the soup, put the yolks of two fresh eggs, one teacupful of milk or cream and a bit of sweet butter, well mixed together and beaten up, into the soup tureen; pour the boiling soup into this thickening, stirring it well till mixed. The same receipt exactly applies to sorrel soup.

To Dress Fresh-water Fish.—Bone the fish and lay it flat in a fireproof dish, with small pieces of butter underneath the fish. Chop half an onion and three or four washed anchovies, brown them in a little butter in a small copper saucepan; pour this mixture all along over the fish. Strew lightly with very dry breadcrumbs grated from a brown roll or the crust of a loaf. Add in the dish a few spoonfuls of good brown sauce, and baste the fish in the oven till cooked. Serve in the fireproof dish in which it was cooked.

In Germany they still use fresh-water fish almost as much as they do in France, and obviously for the same reasons. A full account of these reasons is most excellently given in Mrs. Roundell's 'Practical Cookery Book,' under the head of 'Pond Fish.' Sea fish in England is so plentiful that I do not believe, in these days of quick carriage, that fresh-water fish will ever be again a matter of trade, though even this we cannot say for certain. The fishmongers and fishermen are so absolutely determined to ruin our fish supply by covering it with that injurious chemical, boracic acid, very often before it leaves the coast, that I, for one, would greatly prefer a freshly netted pond fish. Boracic acid can be easily recognised, when the fish is cooked, by the purple line that lies along the spine in soles, whiting, haddock, plaice, etc. It is introduced under the gill, and I fancy with experience one would soon recognise it even before the fish is cooked. But the use of it is now so universal, alas! that a young cook can hardly be expected to know what fish looked like without it. I cannot understand why people who possess large places with rivers, lakes, ponds, game-keepers, and, in fact, every facility for having fresh-water fish, are yet content to do without so good a variety of food.

One reason is that the cooks do not know how to cook it properly, and the mistresses of the house do not take the trouble to teach them. The Izaak Walton receipts are very inadequate, and depend almost entirely for success on cooking the fish the very moment it is taken out of the water. In France, fish that cannot be cooked immediately is always marinaded. (See 'Dainty Dishes.') Mrs. Roundell entirely does away with the terrible superstition that has always haunted my imagination as a fact, that eels have to be skinned alive as lobsters are boiled alive. She is silent on the subject of lobsters, but with regard to eels she distinctly says : 'Kill them first, and skin them afterwards.'

Endive (French receipt).— Boil the leaves in lots of salt and water, just as if you were doing spinach or cabbage. When tender, pour the whole thing on to a large sieve, and as soon as the hot water has drained away put the sieve under a tap and let cold water run on it for some minutes. This applies to the boiling of all green vegetables — cabbages, sorrel, cauliflowers, cos-lettuce, cabbage-lettuce, etc. After the cold water, put the endive on a chopping-board, or, if required to be quite smooth as a *purée*, rub it through a fine hair sieve. In both these cases return it to the fire, after having first put, in a china saucepan, a pat of butter to dissolve with one spoonful of fine flour. Do not put the vegetable in before the butter and flour are well amalgamated. When this is achieved, stir the vegetable well up with the butter and flour, and let it simmer for another fifteen minutes. Add a little cream or milk quite at the last moment, just to make it soft and pretty. It must not be thicker than a thin *purée*.

Endive (in the German way).— Cut up the endive quite coarsely, wash it in lots of cold water, and throw it, very wet, into an earthenware pot in which a large piece of butter has been dissolved; no salt nor anything else. Put the lid on, and simmer gently for three or four hours. Add salt the last minute, and no flour at all.

Canard à la Rouennaise.—Take the fillets of two ducks. Put them into a buttered sauté-pan, and poach for five minutes in a good oven. When done, cut them out with a cutlet-cutter, and spread on one side of each fillet some liver force-meat, then *chaud-froid* over with some tomato sauce. When set, dish them flat on the entrée dish with some aspic, some skinned grapes in the centre, and a grape here and there. Serve with grape salad.

Purée of Carrots.—Get some nice red carrots; slice them thin. Add an onion, also sliced, a little celery, and a turnip. Braise all together in some weak stock, or water, until quite tender. Pass the whole through a tammy or hair sieve. About an hour before serving, place it in a stewpan over the fire and let it gently simmer to clarify. Season with sugar and salt, and work in a little cream just before serving.

Poulet à la Marengo.—Have some nice young chickens, cut them up neatly, and put them into a sauté-pan with a little salad oil, one onion, a small piece of parsley, and thyme; season with pepper and salt, cover the sauté-pan with the lid, and boil till sufficiently browned. Then add some good brown stock, and stew for some time, finish with a good glass of madeira (optional). Dish up with fried eggs round. Fry the eggs in salad oil.

Chestnuts au Jus.—Remove the outer skin and throw the chestnuts into boiling water, to enable you to remove the inner skin as well; then lay them in cold water while the following mixture is prepared: Stir two tablespoonfuls of sugar into an ounce of butter, in a sauce-pan, till the sugar is browned, let it boil up, add a little *cold* water. Put in the chestnuts, simmer till tender, but do not shake them (to avoid crumbling). Just before serving, add a few spoonfuls of very good strong glaze. Onions, small turnips, and oxalises can be done in the same way. We find all these equally good without the meat glaze.

Celeriac Salad.— A most excellent autumn salad is celeriac well boiled, cut in slices like beetroot, mixed with a light mayonnaise sauce, half oil and half cream, surrounded by a wreath of what they call in Germany 'garden-cress,' which is merely the cress we grow in spring in a box, allowed to grow out of doors in summer till about the size of parsley. It grows all the summer through in the garden, and can be cut over and over again. When grown in boxes in the winter, it should be allowed to grow on, instead of cutting it quite young.

I have always considered salads a strong point with me, and was much amused the other day, when reading Sydney Smith's 'Memoirs' by his daughter, at the following description of his experiences with salads. I think his receipt so clever that I have extracted it, with the feeling that it was better to have it in two books than in only one, so that it may give pleasure to more people. He says: 'Our *forte* in the culinary line is our salad. I pique myself on our salads. Saba always dresses them after my recipe. I have put it into verse. Taste it, and if you like it I will give it to you. I was not aware how much it had contributed to my reputation till I met Lady——, at Bowood, who begged to be introduced to me, saying she had so long wished to know me. I was, of course, highly flattered, till she added : "For, Mr. Smith, I have heard so much of your recipe for salads that I was most anxious to obtain it from you." Such and so various are the sources of fame !

> 'To make this condiment your poet begs
> The pounded yellow of two hard-boil'd eggs;
> Two boil'd potatoes, passed through kitchen sieve,
> Smoothness and softness to the salad give.

Let onion atoms lurk within the bowl
And, half-suspected, animate the whole.
Of mordant mustard add a single spoon,
Distrust the condiment that bites so soon;
But deem it not, thou man of herbs, a fault
To add a double quantity of salt.
Four times the spoon with oil from Lucca brown,
And twice with vinegar procured from town;
And, lastly, o'er the flavoured compound toss
A magic *soupçon* of anchovy sauce.
Oh, green and glorious! Oh, herbaceous treat!
'Twould tempt the dying anchorite to eat;
Back to the world he'd turn his fleeting soul,
And plunge his fingers in the salad bowl!
Serenely full, the epicure would say,
"Fate cannot harm me—I have dined to-day."'

Fried (German) Pudding.—To make the batter put two pints of milk to boil, with a tiny pinch of salt and two ounces of butter. When boiling, stir in very smoothly eight ounces of finest Hungarian flour. (Use no other flour than Hungarian or Austrian for all sweets and sauces.) Stir till the batter recedes from the sides of the stewpan, then pour it into a dish to get cold. Add six eggs and two spoonfuls of rum; mix gently. Put a deep iron pan full of frying-fat on the fire, but let it get only moderately hot. Fry the batter in round balls in the following way: To make this very German pudding properly, one should have a large tin syringe, made specially for the purpose, but in its absence the batter must be taken up by small teaspoonfuls and dropped into the frying-fat. It will form round balls, which should be constantly moved about with a spoon to get them golden-coloured all over. When they show little cracks they are sufficiently done. For this method the batter should be made a little stiffer than for the syringe by adding a little more flour. Serve with dissolved fruit syrup or custard.

Gâteau Savarin.—Ingredients : A little less than one pint of milk, six ounces of butter, ten eggs, two ounces of pounded sugar, one pound of good Hungarian flour, sifted, grated peel of two lemons, two ounces of good German yeast, a pinch of salt. Put one-fifth part of the flour, the yeast, and the milk together in a deep basin, and work them to a stiff paste; cover with a cloth, and stand in a tepid place till it swells to double its size. Put all the other ingredients into a much larger basin, mix them very vigorously and thoroughly with the hands for ten minutes, then work into this the first paste with the yeast in it. When all is well incorporated, work it for another fifteen minutes. Fill the tin or earthenware Savarin shapes with paste to one-third of their height, having first greased them well inside with melted butter. Stand them in a warm place till the paste has risen to the very top. Put them in a rather slow oven for twenty-five to thirty minutes. When well coloured, but not brown, turn them out and pour rum punch over them, taking care not to sodden them.

I had occasion, at the end of this month last year (1897), to go to Germany, to the neighbourhood of Frankfort. The journey, about twenty-five hours from London, is wonderfully easy. My friends said : 'What ! go all that way for ten days ?' But, in fact, it means far less time and money than did a journey to Devonshire, or even the Isle of Wight, to our grandmothers. I had never seen the Rhine before in late autumn. The late vintage was just over, and the vines and the earth seemed one even brown, diversified at times with yellow leaves hanging thinly on the poplars and the low oak brushwood bronze and gold against the sky. It seems bathos to say so, but the Rhine runs so due north and south that it reminded me of my winter walks in Sloane street. The sun was always in one's eyes in the middle of the day, and behind the hills morning and evening; and the fogs hung about the river as they do between the houses in the street. How entirely the Rhine of Turner and Byron has ceased to be! All the beautiful, picturesque boats, barges, rafts, etc., with white or tan sails, that trailed their long reflections in the broad river, representing the commercial industries of the people, which had been growing from the commencement of history — all this has completely disappeared. On the main, I saw one or two of the old-fashioned large rafts, not towed by steamers, but punted by the graceful little black figures, ceaselessly labouring up and down a small portion of the raft and pushing it with long poles. On the Rhine, everything was towed by steamers of various sizes and kinds. As I sped along in the luxurious railway carriage, and noticed the road beside the river turning and twisting along the bank, I could not but think of the changes since the days when all travelling was done by carriages and lumbering diligences. In Moore's 'Life of Byron,' which I used to think such a delightful book, but which now is somewhat sneered at as unfair book-making by Byron biographers, there is a detailed account of the way the rich and great journeyed at the beginning of the century: 'Lord Byron travelled in a huge coach copied from the celebrated one of Napoleon, taken at Genappe, with additions. Besides a *lit de repos*, it contained a library, a plate chest, and every apparatus for dining in it. It was not, however, found sufficiently capacious for his baggage and suite, and he purchased a *calèche* at Brussels for his servants.' So travelled the man whom Lady Caroline Lamb attempts to describe, in her famous though dull novel of 'Glenavon,' with the motto:

He left a name to all succeeding times
Link'd with one virtue and a thousand crimes.

The train sped along, and the weather was beautiful. We were not parboiled in the carriages, as they do not warm them before the 1st of November. My friend lived out of Frankfort, on the slopes of the Taunus Mountains, under the towers of the mediæval Castle of Cronberg. Land is not, I fancy, to be bought in Germany except close to the towns; all the forests belong to the State, and are not sold. I was surprised to find in this delightful home of my Cronberg friends, in the very kingdom of stoves, as we consider Germany, that one of the rooms was warmed by an Irish stove, made by Messrs. Musgrave, of Bond street, exactly like the one I find so invaluable for keeping my own little house at an even temperature. I cannot imagine why any English house not warmed with hot pipes is ever without one of these stoves. They burn only coke, they require very little stoking, they keep in a very long time, and they never unpleasantly dry the air or cause the least smell. I afterwards found that the shops in Frankfort were full of English goods. This is some consolation for us when things we buy are so constantly marked 'made in Germany'.

My bedroom at Cronberg looked north, and faced a long line of sunlit Taunus Mountains, clothed with oak woods in all their autumn glory. They were intersected with pine woods, which in previous months must have looked dull and dark against the summer green, but in late October they were shining bright against the red gold of the dying woods. They reminded me of one of 'Bethia Hardacre's' truest touches of colour:

> Silver and pearl-white sky,
> Hills of dim amethyst,
> Bracken to gold changed by
> Autumn, the Alchemist.

Spikes of bright yellow poplars here and there marked the road as it wound up the hill, to lose itself in the silent forest. The walls of my bedroom were hung round with photographs and prints, remembrances brought back by my cosmopolitan hostess from various countries. They were most of them known to me, but one print was quite a stranger and very striking. It was of a picture, I was told, by a Swiss artist called Arnold Boecklin, a celebrated man, though unknown to me. On the white margin of the print were written the simple words: *Todten-Insel*. The print represents an imaginary burial-place: A high, rocky island, with a suggestion of big caves in the rock and windows made by man. In the middle a little open space, with tall, upright groups of splendid Italian cypresses, which seem to be mournfully swaying in the wind. Down the rocks on each side tumble somewhat conventional waterfalls into a fathomless ocean, perhaps meant to be typical of life and death. Two white stone posts on each side of a step mark the entrance to this sombre garden of peace and rest. On the foreground of calm water floats a black boat, which approaches this entrance rowed by a solitary dark figure — a realistic Charon. Across the front of the boat lies the dead; and a radiant, draped, mysterious mourner, with head bowed over the inevitable sorrow of mankind, stands erect in the middle of the boat. The combination of the horizontal dead figure and the upright mourner, in their white draperies, seems to form a shining cross against the deep shade of the cypresses. This print fascinated me, with its eternal facts transcribed into an allegory by a man of genius. The picture from which it is taken is a replica, with many alterations, of one painted some years ago which I have seen. But, judging from the print, I believe that the last-painted one is the finest. Certainly the allegorical details in this later one are brought out with greater distinctness. Several of Herr Boecklin's pictures have been bought by his native town of Bâle, and, later on, I will describe how I spent a night there on purpose to see them. After my return home I came across an interesting description of Herr Boecklin and his work, in a lately published book called 'The History of Modern Painting,' by Richard Muther, from which the following extract will perhaps make others wish as much as I do to see his pictures. Mr. Muther says of him that: 'He belonged to the very time when Richard Wagner lured the colours of sound from music with a glow and light such as no master had kindled before Boecklin's symphonies of colour streamed forth like a crashing orchestra. The whole scale, from the most sombre depth to the most chromatic light, was at his command. In his pictures of spring the colour laughs, rejoices, and exults. In the "Isle of the Dead," it seems as though a veil of crêpe were spread over the sea, the sky, and the trees. . . . Many of his pictures have such an ensnaring brilliancy that the eye is never weary of feasting upon their floating splendour. Indeed, later generations will probably do him honour as the greatest colour-poet of the century, and, at the same time, they will learn from his works that at the close of this same unstable century there were complete and healthy human beings. . . . The more modern sentiment became emancipated, the more did artists venture to feel with their own nerves and not with those of earlier generations, and the more it became evident that modern sentiment is almost always disordered, recklessly despairing, unbelieving, and weary of life. Boecklin, the most modern of modern painters, possesses that quality of iron health of which modernity knows so little.'

To return to my time in Germany. The weather grew cold and foggy, and my expeditions from Cronberg into Frankfort were fewer than I could have wished, and many sights I did not see at all.

Among the towns of which I have an early, though faint, recollection, not even Paris itself is more utterly and entirely changed than Frankfort. Only here and there does anything remain that recalls Goethe's description, so familiar to the readers of his ever-enchanting autobiography, that perfect mixture, 'Truth and Poetry.' The Jewish cemetery, full of interest with its unbroken record from the twelfth century, I did not see, though to my mind it must be one of the most interesting spots in Europe. This feeling would only be understood by the English, the awful hatred of the Jews — universal on the Continent — being happily unknown to us. The world changes so much, and yet so much remains the same. Who would have imagined that at the end of the nineteenth century Jewish persecution would be the same as in the Middle Ages? If it were possible, would not the gates of the Ghetto be shut in the same cruel and unjust way as years ago? Hatred of the Jews seems to me the one real bond that unites France, Germany, and Russia. It is generally attributed to Disraeli, but I believe it was Heine who first said: 'Every nation has the kind of Jew it deserves.'

I am told that in this Jewish cemetery at Frankfort the surnames on the tombstones date back in many cases three hundred years. The old graves have generally only a first name (one cannot say Christian name), with a locality, mentioned; as, for instance, 'Hannah of Hamburg.' The Jews seem to regard this cemetery as an even truer record of their families than we consider our peerage. The *Judengasse* has virtually disappeared. I never saw it but once in my childhood, when I felt the same kind of mixed awe and curiosity with which Goethe speaks of it. There is a sketch of it in that never-to-be-forgotten volume of our young days, 'The Foreign Tour of Messrs. Brown, Jones, and Robinson,' by Dickie Doyle. His drawing gives a somewhat spiteful version of it, but it is a funny remembrance of this swept-away quarter. Lewes says Goethe learnt much from the society of the Jews in the strange, old, filthy, but deeply interesting *Judengasse*. Like him, we have all pondered over 'the sun standing still on Gideon and the moon in the valley of Ajalon.'

It was with a genuine thrill that I entered Goethe's house, where he was born, where he lived, where he played and ate and slept and loved Gretchen, and which — angry and disappointed at being described as the boy he really was — he left, with the indifference usual at that age, to seek his fortunes in the world. As he says himself: 'At certain epochs children part from parents, servants from masters, *protégés* from their patrons; and whether it succeed or not, such an attempt to stand on one's own feet, to make one's self independent, to live for one's self, is always in accordance with the will of nature.'

I am so fond of Goethe's sayings that they stick somehow in my mind, in spite of my bad memory. He says somewhere so truly, and it refers to this entrance into life that all have to face: 'Every man has his decoy, and every man is led or misled in a way peculiar to himself.' How frequently Goethe's sayings remind one of Lord John Russell's apt definition of a proverb, 'One man's wit and all men's wisdom!' Goethe's house in the *Hirschgraben* is now a museum, bought by the Goethe Society, whose headquarters are at Weimar, and restored by them with reverent care. Every effort is made to preserve it and what it contains from decay.

Such guardians are necessary; they hold the hand of the destroyer and arrest decay, keeping for posterity what we ourselves highly value. The old house where Luther rested for the night on his way to the Diet of Worms was being levelled to the ground this summer before my eyes, to make room for a handsome entrance into the courtyard of a large white stucco house. So incongruous was this building to the old sixteenth-century street that had I seen it suddenly I should have said it was a residence, not in Frankfort, but in the *Quartier St. Germain* in Paris. I honour all societies that save us from this wholesale destruction of the past. In the Goethe house-museum there were some of Goethe's drawings, which made me sympathise more than I had ever done before with Lewes' somewhat bitter reproaches about the time Goethe wasted on drawing. Lewes says: 'All his study and all his practice were vain; he never attained even the excellence of an amateur. To think of a Goethe thus obstinately cultivating a branch of art for which he had no talent makes us look with kinder appreciation on the spectacle, so frequently presented, of really able men obstinately devoting themselves to produce poetry no cultivated man can read; men whose culture and insight are insufficient to make them perceive in themselves the difference between aspiration and inspiration.'

I also went alone to the suburb of Sachsenhausen to see the Staedel Art Institute. Frederick Staedel, in 1816, bequeathed his pictures and engravings and 100,000*l.* to his native town. This formed the nucleus of the present gallery. Many pictures have been added since his death, and in many ways the collection is an interesting one. I stood long before a picture which the inscription on the frame told me had been presented by a Baroness Rothschild. Having no catalogue, and feeling shy about asking in German, I neither knew nor guessed what it was or why it was there. It powerfully arrested my attention — a life-sized picture of a man of about forty, sitting in a gray, flowing overcoat, on gray stones in the gray Campagna of Rome. Afterwards I was told that it was the famous picture of Goethe by Johann Friedrich Tischbein. This painter lived from 1750 to 1812 — that is to say, only a part of the life of Goethe, who was born a year before Tischbein and died in 1832. He, therefore, was thirty-seven when he wrote in the letters from Italy, December, 1786, as follows : 'Latterly I have often observed Tischbein attentively regarding me ; and now it appears he has long cherished the idea of painting my portrait. His design is already settled and the canvas stretched. I am to be drawn the size of life, enveloped in a white mantle, and sitting on a fallen obelisk, viewing the ruins of the *Campagna di Roma*, which are to fill up the background of the picture. It will form a beautiful piece, only it will be rather too large for our northern habitations. I indeed may crawl into them, but the portrait will never be able to enter their door.'

This is the exact description of the picture as it now is. Later on, in the letters in February of the following year, Goethe again alludes to the picture: 'The great portrait of myself which Tischbein had taken in hand begins already to stand out from the canvas. The painter has employed a clever statuary to make him a little model in clay, which is elegantly draped with the mantle. With this he is working away diligently.' The last fact is curious, as it is exactly the way Meissonier worked a hundred years after. I went to his studio shortly after his death, and saw all his little clay models of cannons, figures, horses, roads, from which all his highly finished pictures were painted. The Goethe portrait has a distinct dash of affectation in it, and the whole pose, excusable enough in Goethe, is of a man in the prime of his life who felt himself to be famous and knew himself to be handsome. To our ideas, the picture is singularly devoid of colour, almost monochrome; but it strikes one as very modern in treatment, considering its date, and for every reason it must always remain one of the interesting portraits of the world. In the early part of this century and during the Napoleonic days, when the Rothschilds of Frankfort began to spread themselves through Europe and establish their banking-houses in so many capitals, the son who went to Naples bought this great canvas of Tischbein's. In this way it has ultimately found a most fitting home — not in the small house which, Goethe truly said, would not admit it, but on the walls of this museum in his native town.

The Staedel Institute has many artistically interesting pictures, most instructive to the student of the old masters, both German and Italian. For those who wish to understand modern criticism and the altering of long-accepted catalogues attributing pictures to wrong artists, I can most strongly recommend ' Italian Painters,' by Giovanni Morelli (John Murray), translated into English by Constance Jocelyn Ffoulkes. Giovanni Morelli lived at Bergamo in Lombardy. He left as a legacy to his native town a small, but very remarkable, collection of pictures, the chief treasures of which are Dutch master-pieces. I imagine the ' Italian Painters ' is almost the root of the kind of modern criticism which has torn from us of the older generation many of the faiths of our youth. For instance, the famous Guido's ' Cenci ' of the Barberini Palace for more than a century drew tears of pity from the eyes of poets and their followers as being a most tender representation of a famous criminal painted in prison, who, but for this supposed portrait of her, would never have been known to posterity. As a fact, she was executed six or seven years before Guido arrived in Rome. Neither is the picture a Guido at all, but a study by some inferior painter of an unknown model. At least, this, I believe, is the last word on the subject. The favourite portrait of Raphael by himself in the Louvre, leaning on his hand, is not a portrait of him, nor is the picture painted by him. The great Holbein at Dresden is said now not to be the original, which is at Darmstadt; and so on. In this Frankfort gallery there is an extraordinarily fine and interesting female portrait, hitherto attributed to Sebastiano del Piombo, but now supposed to be by Sodoma. It is one of the gems of the collection.

Before leaving England last year (1897), I had been immensely interested at hearing of the open-air treatment for phthisis as practised in Germany, the parent establishment of which is at Falkenstein, in the Taunus Mountains, close to Cronberg, where I was staying. I wished very much to visit this sanatorium myself, but circumstances rendered it impossible.

A good account of it was published just after I came home, in the 'Practitioner' for November, by Dr. Karl Hess, senior physician to the establishment.

It cannot fail to strike us as we walk or drive past the Brompton hospital, with its airless situation and its closed windows, how hopelessly different its conditions and treatment must be from those recommended — and apparently so successfully carried out — at Falkenstein. In Germany twenty sister establishments have been started, and the medical management is supposed to be now so complete against infection that German parents have no fear of sending delicate children to these cures, at the age of sixteen or seventeen, to be benefited by the outdoor treatment as a strengthener against the possibility of their catching tuberculosis. At Falkenstein, the parent institution, much meat is insisted on; but I am told that at Nordrach Dr. Walther now gives very little meat, and sends away patients if they take any stimulant at all. He does cram them, but it is with enormous quantities of milk, cheese, butter, brown bread, and other farinaceous foods.

When I came home from Germany last year I noted three things which I hold to be of the utmost importance, and in which we seemed in England to be decidedly behind other nations. First, I wished to see established public slaughterhouses, duly inspected, not only in large towns, but in every village where beasts are slaughtered. It seems to me absurd to expect that the man who buys a beast, kills it himself, and counts on selling the meat at a profit, should forego his gains solely for the public good. Meat is constantly eaten which is rejected by the Jewish priests, and I believe it is a statistically established fact that Jews have a great immunity from both consumption and cancer. It used to be supposed that this was because they were of a different race from ourselves. I believe it is because they are much cleaner feeders than we are.

Secondly, I would gladly have seen greater intelligence and knowledge on the part of the public as regards the danger to children and invalids who live almost exclusively on milk of drinking it unsterilised or unboiled, since one tuberculous cow infects the whole supply, and this is not possible to detect by any analysis of the milk.

Thirdly, I wished that the German rational outdoor treatment of consumptive patients, when once they have caught tuberculosis, or are so constituted that they are likely to catch it, should be understood and practised in England.

F

The strides that have been made towards the accomplishment of these three wishes of mine during the last year is simply astonishing. The newly formed National Association for the Prevention of Tuberculosis, whose office is in Hanover Square, has for its great object to instruct people on the infectiousness of tuberculosis and the best methods of arresting it. Everyone who read the account of the first meeting of this society at Marlborough House must have been struck with the fact that when the Queen's herd of cows were tested, thirty-six of them were condemned to be slaughtered.

A century ago, when first invalids were sent to the Riviera and Madeira, all the doctors distinctly taught that the disease was hereditary, and not infectious. The natives of these health resorts soon discovered, to their cost, that the disease was infectious; for it spread amongst the population in the same way as it now has at Davos, where tuberculosis was formerly unknown. The superstition, as the doctors of the 'forties thought it, of the peasants round Nice — who held that consumption was really catching — made such an impression on my mother, whose whole soul was bent on saving her children from the disease of which their father died, that she brought us up on the lines of that belief, and kept us from every one whom she in any way suspected of being consumptive, even when their complaint may have been but a constitutional cough.

Perhaps this training is what has made me somewhat sceptical about the medical science of any day being absolutely conclusive. I sometimes think that the implicit faith that people are apt to place in doctors may be injurious to the community, and that experience and quackery sometimes turn out to be scientifically truer than the medical theory of the hour. Shocking as many will think the suggestion, I believe this may eventually prove to be the case even with regard to vaccination as a necessary preventive against small-pox epidemics, the great decrease of which may have been effected by many other circumstances. The itch, scurvy, and leprosy have practically also disappeared in England with improved food and cleanliness. Nowadays, why should not a case of small-pox be stamped out as the plague was this year in Vienna? Before Jenner's great discovery, even the most primitive methods of preventing infection were unknown. It is only within the last twenty years that these have been brought to anything like perfection, and only in the last ten years with regard to crowded localities.

To return to tuberculosis. In spite of Tyndall's wonderfully clear, instructive, and interesting letters to the 'Times,' published more than twenty years ago, and which explained most thoroughly the infectiousness of consumption, the public have remained curiously ignorant on the subject. As an illustration of this, a sad case occurred this year not far from here. A signalman who was mortally ill of consumption remained at his work, in his signal-box on the line, as long as it was possible for him to get there. When the day came that he had to give in and remain at home to die, a young and healthy man replaced him in the signal-box, which had in no way been disinfected or whitewashed, and which, from its construction, was a sun-trap and the best dust-and-germ-producer that could be. A cattle-truck would have been differently treated! The young man caught the disease, and died in a few months.

I find, in talking even to educated people, a considerable tone of resentment on this subject. 'What!' they say, 'are our consumptives to be treated like lepers?' The poetry that hung about consumption in the early days of this sentimental century, its association with the South, with Madeira's orange groves and the sunshine of the Mediterranean, is now not easy to eradicate. The modern cure is stern, rough, and unattractive, and it is difficult at first to believe it to be the best for the hard, hacking cough and hectic flush of the patients.

The homeward journey from Germany was much less pleasant than my journey out had been, in consequence of the fatal date having come which decides that German railway carriages shall be heated — or, as we English think, over-heated. This causes considerable suffering to those who stupidly, like myself, forget that an almost summer dress is required, with plenty of wraps to prevent any chill on leaving the carriage. We passed Coblentz at early winter sunset-time, and I never saw anything more beautiful than all the tones of blues and pearly grays under a sky spread with wave upon wave of bright pink clouds. Not Turner himself could have come near to the delicate yet brilliant effect. Skies are fleeting enough, and the waves of rosy clouds quickly disappear, but the despairing swiftness of an express train is the quickest of all; and in a moment Coblentz, with its towers, its fortress, and its beautiful sunlit sky, was out of sight.

I do think that if we would enjoy the Rhine in its beauty we must visit it in winter, when we see it as Turner saw it. What a pleasure it is now to go to those rooms on the ground floor of the National Gallery where Turner's sketches are ! I went there again the other day to see the Rhine of one's youth. What a king and creator of Impressionist sketching was Turner in his later manner ! He lifted the hilltops till they grew pink in the setting sun, and he trailed the long reflections to fathomless depths in the broad river. And was not the fortress defiantly impregnable in those days, and so rendered by him in those two wonderful pink and yellow and blue Ehrenbreitstein sketches ? How quickly and easily all his effects and gradations are produced! If they were not consummate, we should now call them cheap. I had not seen these rooms in the National Gallery for some years. They are beautifully arranged — so warm, so light, and, alas! so empty. At least, when I was there I wandered alone. How true it is that what we can have always we care for so little, and how we toil as tourists in foreign towns!

It seems rather ridiculous to have brought back from Germany a French poem. But I heard there, for the first time, one of Tosti's earlier songs, the words of which seemed to me sympathetic and full of charm. They are written by a Comtesse de Castellane, and, as they are very little known apart from the music, I quote them here for the benefit of the non-singing world — which, after all, is rather a large one:

VOUS ET MOI

Vos yeux sereins et purs ont voulu me sourire,
    Votre main comme une aile a caressé ma main,
Mais je ne sais trouver, hélas! rien à vous dire,
    Car nous ne marchons pas dans le même chemin.

Vous êtes le soleil d'un beau jour qui commence,
    Et moi la nuit profonde et l'horizon couvert;
Vous êtes fleur, étoile, et joyeuse cadence,
    Vous êtes le printemps, et moi je suis l'hiver!

Vous buvez les rayons et respirez les roses,
    Car vous êtes l'aurore, et moi la fin du jour;
Il faut nous dire adieu sans en chercher les causes,
    Car je suis le regret, et vous êtes l'amour.

There are few acts, in my opinion, so blamable and so selfish as an old man marrying a young girl. He understands life and she does not, and the responsibility rests with him. Of course this does not apply to a woman past thirty who wants a home.

Present of 'The Botanist'—Echeveria and *Euphorbia splendens*—
   Cowper on greenhouses — Cultivation of greenhouse plants —
   Bookseller at Frankfort — Dr. Wallace on Lilies — Receipts —
   Winter in the country — The sorting of old letters.

November 1st.—One of those most pleasant echoes of
my first book came to me to-day. I received a letter,
addressed to the care of my publisher, from a lady who
was so pleased with my commendation of her father's
work ('The Botanic Garden,' by B. Maund) that she
kindly asked to be allowed to send me, what I had long
wished to have, the five volumes of his second book,
'The Botanist'—a gardening periodical which was
published only for five years, as the coloured illustrations were too costly to be continued. The first number
was issued in January, 1825. It contains full-page
illustrations of stove, greenhouse, and new hardy plants
— new, that is, in 1825. I have had it bound, and it is
a great addition to my collection of flower-books. The
original drawings were chiefly made by Mrs. Withers,
who was the first flower-painter of that day. The title-
page bears the following inscription:
   The Botanist: containing Accurately Coloured
Figures of Tender and Hardy Ornamental Plants,
with Descriptions Scientific and Popular, intended to
convey both Moral and Intellectual Gratification.' A
quotation is added from Sir J. E. Smith: 'The world
seems to have discovered that nothing about which
Infinite Wisdom has deigned to employ itself can, properly speaking, be unworthy of any of its creatures, how

(86) .

lofty soever their pursuits and pretensions may be.'
The flowers are beautifully drawn and delicately coloured, one on a page — not on the same principle as
'The Botanic Garden.' But it is as full as that is of
interesting information, not the least, perhaps, being
the derivation of the names of plants, some of which we
use every day. For instance, 'Echeveria' is derived
from M. Echever, a botanical painter.

Euphorbia splendens is an interesting and effective
stove-plant. It is a native of Madagascar, and the
name it bears in its own country is 'Soongo-Soongo.'
It is among the plants one need not fear to buy, as
cuttings strike easily under a hand-glass. I mention
it, as I bought it last year at a sale not knowing what
it was. *Oxalis Bowiei* I also have, and try to grow it
out of doors in a very sheltered place. Like most of the
finer Oxalises, it is a native of the Cape. I was not
here, as I have said, in the summer this year; but when
I returned, it looked very dried up and unsatisfactory.
This is what William Herbert, the author of 'Amaryl-
lidaceae,' before mentioned, says of its cultivation: 'This
most beautiful and florid plant is hardy' (where mine
came from it had been out of doors for years) 'and in
the open ground will flower in the autumn.' (I expect
a bell-glass would greatly help this.) 'But it blossoms
most profusely when kept in a pot under glass, especially if, after a short period of rest at midsummer, it is
placed in a stove or warm greenhouse for a very short
time to make it start freely. Its flowers expand in very
moderate temperature. Like all the Oxalises, the
flowers are very sensible to light, and only expand
thoroughly when the strong, clear sunshine falls upon
them.' These early-going-to-sleep plants are rather
trying, as they never look their best when one wants to
show them off in the afternoon.

The stalks or canes of Michaelmas Daisies should be cut down carefully, trimmed, and dried, as they make excellent sticks for plants in pots or even out of doors, and are well worth saving.

November 3rd.—A lady writes strongly recommending a Tea Rose called 'Ma Capucine.' 'Such lovely red-scarlet buds from June to December,' she says. This I have now ordered. I have moved my white 'Lamarque Rose,' but I cannot get it to do well here. The Dean of Rochester wrote me a most kind letter reproaching me for saying I could not grow Roses, and implying that the fault is mine. This I know to be true, but the fact is I am so fond of variety in flowers, as in all else, that I grudge too much room in the garden being given to Roses ; and the attention and hand-picking they require in the spring, when I am very busy with other things, cause them to be neglected.

Another correspondent from the north of London wrote that I exaggerated the difficulty of growing Roses near London. He says he has had good success with his. But then he lives on heavy soil, and that makes an extraordinary difference in their power of resisting their enemies—smoke, blight, etc.

This year a Crimson Rambler that failed near a wall (I believe they never do well on walls) has made prodigious growth out in the open. I have cut out the old wood, spread out the long shoots, and tied them down to canes on either side, so as to increase the flowering all along the branches. Underneath is a large bed of 'Mrs. Simpkin' Pinks, and I think the two together will be pretty.

November 7th.—I am always being asked about greenhouse plants, and how to get variety both for picking and for ornamenting a small greenhouse next a room. It has been rather the fashion of late to say : 'Oh ! I don't care for greenhouse plants; I only like hardy things.' This surely is a mistake. Cowper, that now-neglected poet, says:

> Who loves a garden, loves a greenhouse too.
> Unconscious of a less propitious clime,
> There blooms exotic beauty, warm and snug,
> While the winds whistle and the snows descend.
> The spiry Myrtle, with unwithering leaf,
> Shines there and flourishes. The Golden Boast
> Of Portugal and Western India there,
> The ruddier Orange and the paler Lime,
> Peep through their polish'd foliage at the storm,
> And seem to smile at what they need not fear.
> The Amomum there, with intermingling flowers
> And Cherries, hangs her twigs. Geranium boasts
> Her crimson honours, and the spangled Bean,
> Ficoides, glitters bright the winter long.
> All plants, of every leaf that can endure
> The winter's frown if screen'd from its shrewd bite,
> Live there and prosper. Those Ausonia claims,
> Levantine regions these; the Azores send
> Their Jessamine, her Jessamine remote
> Caffraria. Foreigners from many lands,
> They form one social shade, as if convened
> By magic summons of the Orphean lyre.
> Yet just arrangement, rarely brought to pass
> But by a master's hand, disposing well
> The gay diversities of leaf and flower,
> Must lend its aid to illustrate all their charms,
> And dress the regular yet various scene.
> Plant behind plant aspiring: in the van
> The dwarfish; in the rear retired, but still
> Sublime above the rest, the statelier stand.

In spite of what I consider the excellent gardening spirit in these lines, how curiously non-poetical they are according to the ideas of our day! In my edition of Cowper there is a footnote to the word 'Ficoides,' explaining it as 'Ice-plant,' which is an annual Mesembrianthemum; whereas he probably meant some of the perennial flowering Mesembrianthemums, which, I think, are beautiful things in a winter greenhouse, in a pot, and hanging from a shelf. All the same, I imagine it would be possible to sow the Ice-plant so late that it might go on growing through the winter in a pot, though its beauty can never be so great as on a broiling hot summer's day.

I agree with every word that Cowper says, and his lines suggest what I want specially to urge on those who pass the winter in the country. Greenhouses were new in Cowper's time, and the pleasure of them has probably been wiped out—or, at any rate, greatly diminished—by the way people who can afford such luxuries are now always rushing away in search of sunshine in other climes, and are content to come back in June and find their flourishing herbaceous borders, that have been asleep under manure all the winter, surpassing in luxuriance of colour and form the gardens of the South. One of the least helpful volumes of the large edition of Mrs. Loudon's 'Lady's Flower Garden' is the one called 'Ornamental Greenhouse Plants'—so many things she recommends to grow are now proved to be hardy, and so many others that we now know to be well worth the trouble of cultivation for flowering in the winter are omitted altogether. I know no modern book that quite tells one enough how to keep a small conservatory furnished all the year round.

Greenhouse flowers can be most interesting and various, and I propose each month through the winter to name fresh things as they come on and are brought into the small conservatory next my sitting-room. I am too ignorant to speak of any plants except those I grow. The conservatory faces east and south, so it gets what sun there is to be had in winter. I removed the stages that were there, except two shelves close to the glass on the east side. I took up the tiles and dug a bed close to the north wall, which is against the drawing-room chimney, and another bed on the west side of the small square. These beds make the difference between a greenhouse and a conservatory. When I speak of a bed I mean that, though the floor of the greenhouse is tiled, the plants are planted in the ground. This is very essential in any conservatory, whether large or small. On the north side, facing south, is planted out what has now grown into a huge plant of Henry Jacobi. It has been there some years, and is cut down very severely about this time every year. Next to it is a quaint plant, one of the Platyceriums, growing on a piece of board hung on the wall, which requires nothing but occasional watering. Below that are two French flower-pots that hang flat against the wall and are filled with Maidenhair. A plant of the sweet yellow Jasmine and a plant of pale Heliotrope, both in the ground, are all the wall will hold on this side. In the middle of the other bed next the west wall, and also planted out, are a large sweet-scented double-white Datura; a white *Niphetos* Rose, which runs up a pole to the glass roof; a common Passion Flower, to make shade in summer; and a blue *Plumbago capense*. By the side of the door, growing up a wire, is a dark green Smilax, that has been there for many years and gives no trouble. The other things are in pots, and are constantly changed and moved. I grow both Pancretiums and Crinums; they are indeed worthy of every attention, and ought to be in all carefully selected collections. They are so sweet, so delicate, and so lovely! —all that we prize most in single flowers. There are a great many kinds of both Pancretiums and Crinums. (See Johnson's 'Gardener's Dictionary.') Even the hardier Crinums in pots require heat at the growing time, and they often have to be grown for several years after they are bought before they flower at all; but, once started, they seem to flower each year. I have a *Crinum Moorei* out of doors which makes its leaves every year, but has not yet flowered.

I try to arrange the plants in groups in this conservatory. Whether there are ten plants of one kind, or only two, they are placed together; and if there are different plants more or less of one colour, they, too, are massed together. I think this makes the most immense difference in the pleasure to be got out of a greenhouse, and increases the colour-value of everything grown in it, as the power of one plant to kill or injure the colour of another is far more felt in a greenhouse than even in the open border. I have, now flowering, my usual number of the protected Chrysanthemums. They are less good than last year, the wet June and dry August not having suited them. Last year the hardy early outdoor Chrysanthemums were very good indeed; this year the season has been even harder on them than on the pot-plants. All the same, they should be very much grown in all gardens. They transplant quite easily from the reserve garden at any time from August onwards. I have yellow, orange, pink, white, dark red, and a very dark yellow, which seems to last the longest and be the hardiest. Some few cottage gardens have better varieties than I can boast. The great secret for the late-flowering hardy Chrysanthemums is to get them against walls, and, still better, under the protection of shrubs. Many of the greenhouse Chrysanthemums will also flower perfectly out of doors, if only planted late in the summer under shrubs, as I have just said. In this way they get a natural protection on cold nights. The last two years I have grown for the greenhouse, in pots, a Michaelmas Daisy that is new to me, called *Aster grandiflora*. It has a stiff, pretty growth, and is quite hardy;

but it flowers so late that it does not come to perfection
out of doors. It looks very well under glass in front of
a group of white Chrysanthemums. The flowers are as
large as *Aster amellus*, and of the same colour, which is
so different in tone from that of any of the Chrysanthemums. It reminds me a little of *Stokesia cyanea*, which
I used to grow in the same way; only that did not stand
the moving and potting up nearly so well as this Aster
does. I dare say I did not manage it rightly.

November 8th.— There is a famous seller of old books
in Frankfort named Baer. He lives in the Rossmarkt,
and some of my best old flower-books I have had from
him. I brought home this time one of those books that
delight a collector's heart, a really very fine one. I
have been told by an artist who saw it here that it must
have cost more than 2,000*l.* to bring it out. The book
consists of two elephant folios bound in old stamped
white vellum, and bringing them back as a parcel was
not exactly easy. There is no letterpress at all in the
first volume. It has two handsome frontispieces in the
Dutch manner, with Flora and another goddess holding
a large straw bee-hive. In the middle is the title, written in Latin and printed on what is supposed to
represent a sheet of parchment, hung from a classical
building with columns on each side. At the bottom is a
representation of the Garden of Eden, with trees and
various animals, all well drawn. Adam is walking with
the Almighty, who is represented by the figure of an old
man surrounded by what in early Italian art is called a
mandorla, or almond-shaped glory. Miss Hope Rea, in
'Tuscan Artists,' says of this almond-shaped glory:
'In Christian symbolism and art it is reserved 'for
Christ, and has a profound signification. Though called
a *mandorla,* or almond, it is really intended to represent
the form of a fish; and this, from the days of the

Church of the Catacombs, was the accepted symbol of
Christ, because the letters of the Greek *ichthus* = fish,
give the initials for the Greek words, 'Jesus Christ, Son
of God, the Saviour.' Mrs. Jameson, in 'Sacred and
Legendary Art,' gives the Latin name, *vesica piscis*, for
the oblong glory surrounding the whole person. She
says that it is 'confined to figures of Christ and the
Virgin, or Saints who are in the act of ascending into
heaven.' It is, therefore, in ignorance that this German
of the early days of the seventeenth century surrounds
the Almighty with this almond-shaped glory instead of
a glory round the head. The book is called 'Hortus
Eystettensis,' and was brought out in 1613 by Basil
Besler, an apothecary. On each side of the columns are
two draped male figures, representing Solomon and
Cyrus. The whole page is coloured (highly rather than
beautifully) by hand; and the large first volume must
contain over three hundred pages, with designs of all
kinds of flowers and fruit beautifully drawn and
coloured. I believe the book with only outline represen-
tations of the flowers is not very uncommon, but coloured
copies are exceedingly rare. In fact, Herr Baer told
me he had never seen another. Whether the colouring
dates from the time of printing or not it is difficult to
say. The paper is beautiful, the whole in excellent
condition, and it is a treasure, from a collector's point of
view. Binders were careless in those days, as one sheet
is bound upside down. The second volume is not quite
so thick, but the plates are of even greater beauty. It
contains a curious copyright, given by Louis XIII.,
King of France and Navarre. The date of the book
being 1613, the young king was only twelve years old
when he granted this protection to his good servant,
Basil Besler, who had been put to such great expense
in producing his book.

November 10th.—I find several of the Japanese Maples so well worth growing and quite hardy here. They make very little growth, and want dry, sunny, protected places, where they suffer sometimes from drought, but recover by the following year, and are delightful plants. Golden Privet is a very pretty-growing plant when young, out of doors or in pots. It has been much used of late in London in window-boxes. I have never tried to see if it would keep its leaves in a room.

November 13th.—I gathered to-day a small but bright, well-grown Oriental Poppy; and several of the Delphiniums, cut down in summer, have flowered beautifully a second time. One cannot provide for or be sure of these out-of-season garden surprises; but when they come by chance—some one year, some another—they are very delightful, interesting, and precious. They are like an unexpected piece of good fortune, or the return of a long-absent friend, who, one thought, had quite forgotten one, and who returns as on the day he left—as friendly, as kind, and as confidential. Such surprises push back for a moment the dial of the clock —a thing not to be despised even as a passing illusion, whether in the late autumn of a garden or of life.

November 18th.—Two days later than I have ever before remained down here! It is such beautiful weather. In these mild days the singing of birds comes slightly as a surprise, so different from the silence of August and September. How little one realizes during this silence that the birds, thrushes especially, begin to sing now, in November, and keep on all through the winter, in mild weather, till the end of June. The robin did not like the dry season; he began to sing so late this season.

November 20th.—Most people who have gardens wish

to grow Lilies, and yet very few are really successful
with them. By far the finest I have seen in this part of
the world were grown in an Azalea bed, in more than
half shade, and copiously hosed all through the hot, dry
weather. They were really beautiful. A book called
'Notes on Lilies and their Culture,' by Dr. Wallace, of
Colchester, has only lately come to my knowledge, and I
am quite sure anyone who wishes to grow Lilies will not
get on well without it. It is an admirable book; in
fact, its only fault is that it is so comprehensive one
feels, as with most of the specialist gardening books,
that the rest of one's life must be spent in trying to
understand that one plant. I think there is a good deal
to be said for this kind of gardening. As the amateur
advances in knowledge, he naturally wishes to grow with
extra perfection some plants with which everybody
cannot succeed. And I think, in the case of small
gardens near towns, that it would be a real interest for
a man to grow, let us say, Lilies from Dr. Wallace's
book, or Irises by the advice of Professor Foster, or
Cactuses according to Mr. Watson. This has been done
over and over again in the case of Roses; but rarely, in
my experience, with other plants.

November 27th.—My principal flower-table in summer is in a cool hall away from the sun. In winter,
now that I live here all the year round, I have it in the
sitting-room, close to a large south window. The sun
in summer quickly kills flowers that are cut and in
water, but in winter this is not so. On the contrary, it
seems to cheer them up and make them open out and
look happy. I will describe this flower-table as it stands
before me. At the back, in a pot, is a baby Araucaria
(Puzzle-monkey). These trees, so ugly when growing
on a lawn, are charming in the baby stage. They can
be grown from seed, and they do very well in a room.

little **tree is rais**ed on a Japanese stand. Beside it
pot **containing** a small orchid, *Odontoglossum pic-*
um, **one mass** of flowers like yellow Violets.
ous **Cypripediums** are in front in a glass, and
tophyllums **that** have stood out all the summer
thrown **up a few** late autumn flowers; they are
ys most effective picked. There are also pieces cut
m a bright yellow Coronilla flowering out of doors
a greenhouse wall, a bunch of white Paris
ies that were left out to be killed by the frost and
still flourishing, and a bunch of the black berries of
common Privet, which contrast well with a few bright
ge Gazanias, also left out to perish early in the year
m cold and dryness, but of which we always take
tings, as it has this great merit of late flowering out
doors. Finally, there is a precious bunch of Neapoli-
Violets. For the first hour or two after they are
cked I always put a small bell-glass over them, as the
moisture from condensation under the glass very
uch increases their sweetness.

I do not find it recommended in any of the modern
gardening books that I have, but I am sure, if you want
your Lilacs to flower well and never assume that weedy,
choked appearance that they generally have in gardens,
it is most important to remove, every winter, the
numerous suckers that surround Lilac bushes. When
this is done, it is as well to introduce a little manure
round the roots.

RECEIPTS

An excellent winter salad is made by mashing potatoes as if for a *purée*, and beating them up with a little
lukewarm weak stock or warm water instead of milk,
and no butter. Then dress them with a little chopped
chive, oil and vinegar, pepper and salt. This is good

with braised meats or boiled salt beef, and can be endlessly improved and varied by covering it up, after it
is dressed, with chopped hard-boiled eggs, beetroot,
cucumbers bottled in vinegar, anchovies, etc., etc. In
fact, with these kinds of salads one can give hardly any
rule, as imagination and experiments are everything.
The ordinary red cabbage makes a very good salad. It
must be cut into very fine shreds, then scalded by pouring a large kettle of boiling water over it. When cool,
but not cold, it should be dressed with oil and vinegar,
like ordinary salad, covered up, and allowed to stand for
two or three hours.

Pheasant stuffed with Woodcocks.— The French
say : ' To the uninitiated this bird is as a sealed book ;
eaten after it has been killed but three days, it is insipid
and bad — neither so delicate as a pullet, nor so odor-
iferous as quail. Cooked at the right moment, the flesh
is tender and the flavour sublime, partaking equally of
the qualities of poultry and game. The moment so
necessary to be known and seized on is when decomposition is about to take place. A trifling odour and a
change in the colour of the breast are manifested, and
great care must be taken not to pluck the bird till it is
to be larded and cooked, as the contact of the air will
completely neutralise the aroma, consisting of a subtle
oil, to which hydrogen is fatal. The bird being larded,
the first thing to do is to stuff it, which is effected in the
following manner : Provide two woodcocks, bone and
divide them into two portions, the one being the flesh,
and the other trail, brains, and livers. You then take
the flesh and make a forcemeat by chopping it up with
some beef-marrow cooked by steam, a little rasped
bacon, pepper, salt, fine herbs, and so much of the best
truffles as will, with the above, quite fill the interior of
the pheasant. You must take care to secure this force-

meat in such a manner that it shall not escape, which is sometimes sufficiently difficult if the bird is in an. advanced state; however, it is possible to do so in diverse ways, one of which is by fitting a crust of bread and attaching it with a bit of ribbon. Take a slice of bread one-third of an inch thick and two inches wider on each side than the bird when laid on it. Then take the livers, brains, and the trail of the woodcocks; pound them up with two large truffles, an anchovy, a little rasped bacon, and as much of the finest fresh butter as may seem necessary. Spread, then, this paste on the toast equally, and let the pheasant, prepared as above, be roasted over it in such a manner as that the toast may be saturated with the juices that drop during the operation of roasting. When that is done, serve the pheasant gracefully laid on its bed (the toast). Garnish with Seville orange, and be tranquil as to the result.' This extract from 'Les Classiques de la Table' (p. 129) I have taken from 'The Gentlewoman.' The *gourmets* must make haste and try this dish, for fear the woodcocks, which are getting very scarce, should disappear altogether. It is rather a mystery why they are becoming so rare in England, for they are birds that migrate. It has been suggested as as explanation that sport is now so cosmopolitan, and breech-loading weapons have so favourably handicapped the modern gunner, that the woodcock is being gradually eliminated. Poor little, clever, swift-flying thing, he is safe nowhere !

Mince-meat for Christmas should be made about the 20th of this month. I think this old Suffolk receipt is better than the one in 'Dainty Dishes' or in Mrs. Roundell's 'Practical Cookery.' The following directions are for a large quantity, but, of course, the proportions can be greatly reduced: Two pounds of beef suet finely chopped, two pounds of raisins stoned and chopped, two pounds of currants washed and picked, two pounds of apples chopped fine, one pound and a half of raw beef scraped and chopped fine (every little bit of gristle having first been removed), one pound of finely preserved ginger, six lemons (juice and peel), twelve oranges (only the juice), a little salt, one pound and a half of sugar, a little spice. Mix well with brandy and sherry to taste. Keep in stone jars in a cool place.

German Way of Warming Up Potatoes.—Boil them, let them get cold, cut them in thin slices into a fireproof dish, add a little butter and milk, grate some Parmesan cheese on the top, and bake in the oven.

Boiled Beef.—Take six to eight pounds of good fat top-side or silver-side, beat it very hard on all sides with a heavy wooden oak-log, to break the fibre. Put it into a deep earthenware pot or copper stewpan, with about five to five and a half quarts of cold water, adding all its bones and all the parings and bones you may have over from the joints, chickens, etc., of previous days. Let it come gently to the boil, remove all the rising scum, then add two leeks, two carrots, half a celeriac, one turnip, and several sprigs of parsley and chervil. Put the lid on so that a small slit remains open. Place it by the side of the fire, so that it should not get off the boil, and yet only boil quite gently. Leave to boil for three and a half to four hours from its first boil. Serve with a garnish of the vegetables cooked in the broth and little *hors-d'-œuvre* of salted cucumbers, horse-radish grated finely and dressed with oil and vinegar, beetroot salad, cress salad, celeriac salad—in fact, endless variations. It is very good with a plain tomato sauce (French system).

Minced Collops.—Pass as much raw lean gravy beef

as you require two or three times through a mincing machine. Fry it in about two ounces of butter for a few minutes. Add pepper, salt, a little flour, and gravy or water. Let this simmer for about twenty minutes, keeping it well stirred to prevent it getting lumpy. A little minced onion may be fried with the butter, and is a great improvement. This receipt is very useful in wild countries where the meat is hard and bad, and where other food is deficient.

How to Dress Cod.—Take some slices of a small cod and bake them in the oven in a little butter, with a squeeze of lemon-juice, exactly as you would do salmon. Serve with Tartare Sauce, as in 'Dainty Dishes'; only, instead of putting it in a boat, which means a wastefully large quantity, serve it in a little flat dish with a small spoon. Brown bread and butter should also be handed with it.

November 21st.—This is the first time in my life that the short days have drawn in shorter and shorter and that I have found myself alone, having to make up my mind that being alone is my future, that my time is at my own disposal, and that I am to live so always, except for occasional visitors, who will grow fewer as time goes on.

> It is not sad to turn the face towards home,
>   Even though it shows the journey nearly done;
>   It is not sad to mark the westering sun,
> Even though we know the night doth come.

I do not dread loneliness in itself; but those who live with one, if they are kind and just, do take their share of the burden of life, and it is hard to have no one to whom one can go with those numberless little things which are often big things in life's routine, and that one hides away from those who come in from the outside world as guests, be they ever so near and dear. It is best to keep oneself continually occupied, and one realises that though the end cannot be so very far off, yet the natural love of life is very strong indeed, and an immense help. In a little volume of poems called 'Ionica,' very well known to a few, but which I believe has not spread to a large public, there are two poems which I think strike singularly sympathetic notes. The four lines of 'Remember,' do they not come home to one with all the tenderness of a message?

> You come not, as aforetime, to the headstone every day,
> And I, who died, I do not chide because, my friend, you play;
> Only, in playing, think of him who once was kind and dear,
> And, if you see a beauteous thing, just say, 'He is not here.'

I reverse the position of these poems in the volume, this short one being at the very end, and the following almost in the beginning. I wonder if those who don't know them will like them as much as I do.

> You promise heavens free from strife,
>   Pure truth, and perfect change of will;
> But sweet, sweet is this human life—
>   So sweet I fain would breathe it still;
>   Your chilly stars I can forego;
>   This warm, kind world is all I know.
>
> You say there is no substance here,
>   One great reality above;
> Back from that void I shrink in fear,
>   And, child-like, hide myself in love;
>   Show me what angels feel. Till then
>   I cling, a mere weak man, to men.
>
> You bid me lift my mean desires
>   From faltering lips and fitful veins,
> To sexless souls, ideal quires,
>   Unwearied voices, wordless strains;
>   My mind with fonder welcome owns
>   One dear dead friend's remembered tones.

Forsooth, the present we must give
To that which cannot pass away;
All beauteous things for which we live
By laws of time and space decay.
But oh, the very reason why
I clasp them is because they die.

Great grief, like great joy, has a right to be selfish — for a time, at any rate. Everyone recognizes this, and, in fact, wishes to minister to it so long as the selfishness does not extend, as it were, to the grief itself or to a feeling of rebellion against the inevitable, which tends to hardness and paralyses the sympathy of friends and relations. 'To the old sorrow is sorrow, to the young it is despair.' We must not forget this. The highest ideal of how to receive grief with dignity is admirably expressed in this sonnet by Mr. Aubrey de Vere, though the moral reaches almost unattainable heights:

Count each affliction, whether light or grave,
    God's messenger sent down to thee; do thou
    With courtesy receive him; rise and bow
And, ere his footsteps cross thy threshold, crave
Permission first his heavenly feet to lave.
    Then lay before him all thou hast, allow
    No cloud of passion to usurp thy brow
Or mar thy hospitality; no wave
Of mortal tumult to obliterate
The soul's marmoreal calmness. Grief should be,
    Like joy, majestic, equable, sedate,
Conforming, cleansing, raising, making free,
    Strong to control small troubles, to command
    Great thoughts, grave thoughts, thoughts lasting to the end.

November 30th.—A long, gloomy, lonely day. I thought this evening I would look through a large box I have upstairs full of old letters and papers left to me, and which I have always intended to sort at my leisure. They have been there for years, but I have never had

time, in the hurry and business of life, even to glance
through them. It is an employment that requires rather
a peculiar state of mind, a quiet eddy away from the too
rapid swirl of ordinary life. Such an occupation must
recall to the memory of anyone who has ever read it
Professor Max Müller's preface to his charming little
story called 'German Love,' which was published as long
ago as 1877. The little book treats of love—the eternal
familiar subject—with that touch of genius that makes
originality, and the preface fits so curiously with my
thoughts to-night that I think I must quote it:

'Who has not, once in his life, sat down at a desk
where shortly before another sat who now rests in the
grave? Who has not had to open the locks which for
long years hid the most sacred secrets of a heart that
now lies hidden in the holy calm of the churchyard?
Here are the letters which were so loved by him whom
we all loved so well; here are pictures and ribbons, and
books with marks on every page. Who can now read
and decipher them? Who can gather together the faded
and broken leaves of this rose, and endow them once
more with living fragrance? The flames which among
the Greeks received the body of the departed for fiery
destruction—the flames into which the ancients cast
everything that had been most dear to the living—are
still the safest resting-places for such relics. With
trembling hesitation, the bereaved friend reads the pages
which no eye had ever seen, save the one now closed for
ever; and when he has satisfied himself by a rapid
glance that these pages and letters contain nothing
which the world calls important, he throws them hastily
on the glowing coals; they flame up, and are gone.

'From such flames the following pages were saved.
They were intended at first for the friends only of the
lost one; but as they have found friends amongst

strangers they may, since so it is to be, wander forth again into the wide world.'

I began my task, turned over the old, mouldy papers of long, long ago, and came across a bundle of the early love-letters of my father and mother. So long as I live I cannot allow them to be consigned to the flames, as Professor Max Müller recommends. They are so simple, so touching and interesting in their old-world language, that my first impulse was to string them together anonymously, adding the little tale of the love affair as perhaps no one but I could do. But even without names this might possibly have shocked the taste of people who are sensitive on the subject of letters. I am not one of those who object to the publishing of love-letters, given sufficient time for personal knowledge and recollection of the writers to have crumbled away. Voltaire said: 'On doit des regards aux vivants: on ne doit aux morts que la vérité.' Had I myself written beautiful love-letters in my youth, it would be a pride and joy to me to think that generations unborn should appreciate and enjoy the depths of my devotion, and forgive my weaknesses for the one great reason which will endure for ever, 'because she loved much.' A little boy asked: 'Why is everyone called ''poor'' and ''good'' when they are put into a box in the ground?' I say: What is it all the world forgives in the future, though at the time society must defend itself by hard judgments and stern morality? What we all think vile and odious, and what shocks our best sensibility, though it is inevitable, is the publication of the most commonplace love-letters in the police or divorce courts. But does not love, above everything that we share with our common humanity, belong to all? Is it not the most brilliant, glorious possession we have? Are we not really proud of it even when it is misdirected? Is not the perusal of unselfish, passionate, devoted letters—such as, for instance, Mary Wollstonecraft's letters to Imlay (a perfectly unworthy object)—a better lesson to women than all the articles, all the lectures, and all the sermons ever preached? And why should we not, each of us, gain strength through the publication of letters which show the weakness of love in gifted beings like Keats and Shelley? I cannot see any objection, and with pride and joy would I have given, to those who cared to read it, this interesting little bundle of papers, yellowed by time, and written by my parents in the sunshine of their youth, portraying that nothing really came between the two but that old struggle—difference of opinion on religious subjects — and also showing the confident hope on both sides that love ought to conquer.

Time crystallises, to my mind, such material into biography ; and the more absolutely true biography is, the more interesting it becomes to the public. I have noted down from some book—perhaps Symonds' Life—that 'the first cannon in the art of unsophisticated letter-writing is that, just as a speech is intended for hearers rather than for readers, so is a letter meant for the eye of a friend and not for the world. The very essence of good letter-writing is, in truth, the deliberate exclusion of outsiders, and the full surrender of the writer to the spirit of egotism — amicable, free, light-handed, unpretending, harmless, but still egotism. The best letters are always improvisations, directly or indirectly, about yourself and your correspondent.' Letters of this kind are, in my opinion, the very ones most worth giving to the public. The man of the world says : 'Burn all letters, and only write insignificant notes with little meaning in them, so that there may be nothing for others to keep.' Goethe says : 'Letters are among the most significant memorials a man can leave behind him.' This seems to me true of private individuals, as well as of those who have played a notable or distinguished part on life's stage. But this is not the general opinion — to which I, being only a prudent old woman, am content to bow — and once more return to the box this touching, interesting, and characteristic love-story of my father and mother. I find, however, one letter written by my father, and dated 1834, which is so impersonal and so different from the ordinary love-letter to a young girl that I think it can appear an indiscretion to no one that I should publish it.

They met for the first time, by chance, on a summer's afternoon for a little over an hour, and so completely was it love at first sight on his side that he told my mother afterwards he would gladly have married her there and then had it been possible. She belonged to a Tory family, so bigoted and narrow in their ideas that they could hardly find a parallel in our day ; and on to this training, with her hatred for worldliness and with all the enthusiasm of her youthful aspirations, she had grafted an almost Methodistical view of the duties of a Christian. His views, on the other hand, were on all points those of an advanced Liberal of the early days of John Stuart Mill. Circumstances kept them apart for four years, and at the end of three, after an accidental meeting, he wrote her the following letter. With all its humility, one can easily see that his object was the enlightenment of a mind which had been narrowed by its training :

'Sunday night, July, 1834.

'Pray do not think I mean to force another letter upon you. Your word is law to me, and I feel too deeply obliged to you for all you have so kindly and generously risked, in order to afford me the gratification of hearing from you, to think of going myself or endeavouring to force you one step beyond what you think right and proper in this respect. I only wish to say one word upon the two or three books I am venturing to send you. I was delighted with your intention of continuing German, because I am convinced that you will derive great pleasure and benefit from your study of it. It is a language which, from its power of expressing abstract ideas, to say nothing of its structure and the facility which exists in it of forming endless combinations of words, is of a much higher order than any other European language. It approaches nearest to the Greek, and is no bad substitute to those who have never had an opportunity of studying that language. No foreigner can learn it without acquiring many new ideas and rendering clearer some which he possessed before. There is much, too, in the mind of the Germans as reflected in their literature, the high tone of sentiment in their moral writings, and the constant reference to the ideal in their philosophy, which could not fail to be interesting and attractive to you. Unfortunately, I do not know how far you are advanced in your study of the language, but I think I remember your telling me that you had but just begun it. I have therefore sent you "Klauer's Manual," the best book for self-tuition which has been published, and I have marked in the Index a few of the selections which are perhaps the easiest to begin with. There is this advantage in the book, that should you be so far advanced as not to need the interlinear translation, the selections which are given without it contain some admirable passages from the best authors. Should you be but just beginning, I should advise you to learn by heart only the articles, yͤ five personal pronouns, and yͤ three auxiliary verbs: and then, looking over the conjugation of the regular verb, proceed at once to read the pieces in the

1st vol. in the order in which they are marked, using the 2nd vol. (in which they are translated) as the key. You will find the numbers of the pieces in the 2nd vol. corresponding with those in the 1st. I have also sent you a little volume of Schiller's poems, with a few which I like marked. I should advise you, if any took your fancy, to learn them by heart; it is an agreeable way of getting into one's mind a great fund of words to be serviceable on all occasions. I had some difficulty in getting you the "Morgen und Abendopfer," but I was anxious that you should have these little poems. They are written by a German clergyman. The poetry is very pretty and simple, and I like them for the cheerful view which they take of religion. I have also ventured to send you a little book of selections from different authors, principally for the sake of those which have been made from the works of four men whose writings I have often perused with almost unmixed satisfaction. I mean Jeremy Taylor, South, Bacon, and Milton. I send them to you, not only as samples which will, I think, please you, but in the hope that they will induce you to look further into the works from which they are taken. I had inserted some loose pages containing parallel passages and observations upon the text, but think, upon the whole, it would be to expose you to observation were I to send the book with them in and anybody but yourself happened to look into it. I only send you with it some verses of Southey's which struck me as very pretty, and which I have but lately met with. You can take them out. Taylor is a writer of the greatest eloquence and the most exuberant imagination I am acquainted with in any language. He had at the same time an humble mind, and was thoroughly imbued with a true spirit of Christian charity. South is distinguished for ye vigour and nervous energy of his style and thoughts. He had a thoroughly strong mind — too confident, however, and uncompromising to admit of his being really tolerant of the opinions of others. His conception of the state of man before the Fall, though it savours of course of ye ideal, is a very remarkable performance. Bacon had a practical mind, and no man perhaps ever so thoroughly mastered the subject of human nature as he did. If you can get his Essays, which are sold almost everywhere, pray read them — or rather, I should say, study them, for they are models of conciseness. Every sentence admits of development. They force one to think for oneself, which is the best service an author can render one. Justice has not been done to Milton's prose works in this little book, but, as they are mostly confined to political subjects, they might not perhaps interest you so much. Milton's mind was not wholly free from bigotry. But I love him for his hatred of tyranny and persecution under every shape, for his unquenchable ardour for liberty, and his hearty and fearless advocacy of the enlightenment of mankind. Among his poetical works do you know the "Comus" well? There are parts of it which, I think, he never surpassed. I am sure you must like it. His "Paradise Lost" is indeed a study — a noble and improving one for all who can comprehend his sublime conceptions and the beautiful and powerful language in which he has clothed them. But I must think he was unfortunate in his subject. A lover of pure religion can hardly fail to think that the effect of parts is to degrade and humanise the Divinity. I can hardly conceive that the 3rd Book, in which he propounds the mystery of the Redemption and details its origin, should not be in some degree shocking to a true Christian. The poetry of it is certainly most sublime, but there is, on the whole, a familiarity in the scene described which makes me think it would have found a fitter place in the writings of a heathen. I had also got you one or two more books, but I am afraid to send them, lest you should think I presume too much upon ye permission you gave me. One of them was an Essay upon the nature and true value of military glory, and another upon the education of the poor as the best kind of charity we can do them. Depend upon it, it is so ; and all indiscriminate relief, given as it generally is for the selfish purpose of gratifying our own benevolence, partakes not of the real nature of charity, which regards the good of the object ; and, while it tends to diminish their own exertions in the present, prevents them from acquiring those habits of providence and self-dependence which, in the long run, constitute their only chance of respectability and happiness. There is no fear the stream of charity will want channels in which to flow, and I also do not believe that its sources are the least likely to be dried up. There are more funds required for education and ye support of some kinds of hospitals than will, I fear, ever be supplied. You would find Mrs. Marcet's "Conversations on Political Economy" very useful, and there are some good reasons given in the beginning why ladies should be acquainted with the principles of the science. Let me recommend to you, as connected with your German reading, Madame de Staël's work on Germany. I have derived great pleasure from reading it. And though she occasionally goes out of her depth, and her facts are not always correct, there is a good deal still of profound reflection and much valuable information in the work. I will mention to you a few others of the books which I have most admired. I am not, however, a miscellaneous reader ; I wish I could be ; but I have not a retentive memory, and as reading is to me valuable only in proportion as I retain what I read, I confine my studies as much as possible to those works which I can bear to read over and over again. Of such character is Wordsworth's poetry, and I should be glad if no day elapsed without my reading some portion of it. If you have his works with you, pray read the "Ruth," the "Laodamia," the "Ode to Duty," the "Lines Written Near Tintern Abbey" (I know nothing more beautiful than this), the "Cumberland Beggar," and a little poem—I think he calls it the "Yew Tree" or the "Yew Tree Seat" (for I have not the book with me)—in which there are some lines beginning, "The man whose eye is ever on himself doth look on one the least of Nature's works," etc. I like Coleridge's poetry, but less well. Of all his long pieces I like his translation of Schiller's Wallenstein the best. It is admirable as a poem, while it is perfect as a translation. His "Ancient Mariner" and his "Love" or "Geneviève" are very beautiful. I hope you will be able to read my friend's play, which my sister told you of.[1] I longed to send it to you. It is a work of genius, and at the same time of great labour. He is a man of humble birth, but of an exalted mind; and that, I am sure, you will think better than being "some tenth transmitter of a foolish face"! In religious works, I have best liked Butler's "Analogy" and "Sermons," Taylor's and South's sermons, Paley's "Evidences," all Whateley's works—especially his "Romish Errors" and the "Peculiarities of Christianity"—and Davison on prophecy. This is a work which will survive the present day. Its author is just dead, prematurely. He was a man of great powers of mind, but his health prevented him from sustaining any great intellectual labour. Sumner's "Records of the Creation" is a very instructive work, as well as a most interesting one. I should like to recommend to you

---

[1] *Philip van Artevelde.*

also Southey's "Life of Wesley." It is not very easy to get it, but I am sure it would well repay you for reading. Among lighter books, I will mention Scott's "Lives of the Novelists." It is not only a very interesting book, but there is a great deal of sound criticism in it — particularly, for instance, in his lives of Richardson and Fielding — and it would be well if the generality of novel-readers had some fixed and firm certain principles of taste by which to judge of the merits of what they read. I was much struck, I assure you, with your remarks upon the "Admiral's Daughter" to my sister. The criticism seemed to me as just as it was well expressed. What I had objected to in the work was the intention of placing the man of intellect and of cultivation in unfavourable contrast with the man of impulse and feeling. You will say that religion made the difference; but I am not aware that anything which is good in the good man is supposed to arise from the presence of religion. But I will not write you a letter, though I feel as if I could go on for ever. No. I fear, for so long as you desire it, all direct communication must cease between us. I doubt not you are right. Heaven grant that it may be renewed at no distant time and under happy circumstances! May God for ever bless and protect you!'

In 1835 they were married, and had eight short years of great happiness. This was constantly described to me in a way to make a deep impression on a child's mind, and to account for a sentimental vein in me that was perhaps beyond what was usual even in the days when a very different tone was prevalent among girls than at present. Though my recollection of my father was of the faintest, my hero-worship for him amounted almost to idolatry all through my childhood. I so ven-

H

erated the few of his written sayings that my mother brought to my notice that I think they powerfully affected my character. I confess it gave me great pleasure when, a few years ago, I saw two references to him in a volume of Lady Carlisle's letters written from Paris in 1832. The allusion was in a letter dated 'Paris, September 1st, 1832,' and was as follows: 'Edward Villiers is here, only for one day. He is the image of George' (his eldest brother), 'only handsomer and graver. I think him uncommonly pleasing.' The other notice was on November 5th, when the old lady says: 'Edward Villiers is my love. He is delightful, excellent, and interesting. A Villiers without any of the shades.' He died of consumption at Nice in October, 1843. In Charles Greville's 'Memoirs' is the obituary notice which he wrote for the 'Times' of November 7th. It has a certain literary interest, as being so much more personal in tone and more deliberately the act of a friend than is usual in notices of the same kind to-day:

'Last night came intelligence from Nice that Edward Villiers was dead. He went there in a hopeless state, was worse after his arrival; then an abscess broke in his lungs, which gave a momentary gleam of hope, but he expired very soon after. I had a very great regard for him, and he deserved it. He was a man little known to the world in general—shy, reserved to strangers, cold and rather austere in his manners, and, being very short-sighted, made people think he meant to slight them when he had no such intention. He was not fitted to bustle into public notice, and such ambition as he had was not of the noisy and ostentatious kind. But no man was more beloved by his family and friends, and none could be more agreeable in any society when he was completely at his ease. He was most warm-hearted and affectionate, sincere, obliging,

disinterested, unselfish, and of unscrupulous integrity;
by which I mean integrity in the largest sense, not
merely that which shrinks from doing a dishonourable
or questionable action, but which habitually refers to
conscientious principles in every transaction of life. He
viewed things with the eye of a philosopher, and aimed
at establishing a perfect consistency between his theory
and his practice. He had a remarkably acute and
searching intellect, with habits of patient investigation
and mature deliberation; his soul was animated · by
ardent aspirations after the improvement and the happiness of mankind, and he abhorred injustice and
oppression, in all their shapes and disguises, with an
honest intensity which produced something of a morbid
sentiment in his mind and sometimes betrayed him into
mistaken impressions and erroneous conclusions.

' The expansive benevolence of his moral sentiments
powerfully influenced his political opinions, and his deep
sympathy with the poor not only rendered him inexor-
ably severe to the vices of the rich, but made him regard
with aversion and distrust the aristocratic elements of
our institutions, and rendered him an ardent promoter
of the most extensive schemes of progressive reform.
But, while he clung with inflexible constancy to his own
opinions, no man was more tolerant of the opinions of
others. In conversation he was animated, brilliant,
amusing, and profound, bringing sincerity, single-mind-
edness, and knowledge to bear upon every discussion.
His life, though short, uneventful, and retired, was
passed in the contemplation of subjects of interest and
worthiest to occupy the thoughts of a good and wise
man; and the few intimacies he cultivated were with
congenial minds, estimable for their moral excellence or
distinguished by their intellectual qualities and attain-
ments. The world at large will never know what vir-

tues and talents have been prematurely snatched away from it, for those only who have seen Edward Villiers in the unrestraint and unreserve of domestic familiarity can appreciate the charm of his disposition and the vigour of his understanding. No stranger would have divined that under that cold and grave exterior there lay concealed an exquisite sensibility, the most ardent affections, and a mind fertile in every good and noble quality. To the relations and friends, who were devotedly attached to him, the loss is irreparable, and will long be deplored, and the only consolation which offers itself is to be found in the circumstances of his end. He was surrounded by kind and affectionate friends, and expired in the arms of his wife, whose conduct he himself described to have been that of a heroine as well as an angel. He was in possession of all his faculties, and was free from bodily pain. He died with the cheerfulness of a philosopher and the resignation of a Christian —happy, devout and hopeful, and joyfully contemplating death in an assured faith of a resurrection from the dead.'

Only those who have been brought up by a widowed mother whose whole life had been snapped asunder by such a loss, can quite realise how very peculiar and unlike other homes it is.

How rare it is to be perfectly natural under a great grief ! There is so often an element of self-consciousness, an honest wondering how our attitude will strike others. If we use self-control and try to let life flow in its usual currents, we fear to be thought indifferent, cold, and hard. If once the smallest display of grief becomes in any way a habit, it is difficult to resume again that perfect sincerity of manner which, after all, is the only outward expression of true feeling. A short time ago in 'The Weekly Sun,' in one of Mr. T. P.

O'Connor's wonderful reviews of a Life of Tolstoi, he quotes a passage which is a very vivid picture of self-consciousness in grief. 'Tolstoi describes his visit to his mother's death-chamber: "I could not believe it was her face." How this comes home to us all! The change made by death, the effort of the brain to recognise that what we see before us *is* the loved object, whom, living, we should instantly have recognised among a million. Tolstoi continues: "I looked fixedly at it, and by degrees began to recognise in it the dear familiar features. I shuddered when I did so, and knew that this something was my mother. But why had her closed eyes sunk thus into her head? Why was she so dreadfully pale? and why was a dark spot visible through her transparent skin on one of her cheeks? Why was the expression of her face so stern and so cold? Why were her lips so bloodless and their lines so fair, so grand? Why did they express such unearthly calmness that a cold shiver passed through me as I looked at them? . . . Both before the funeral and after I did not cease to weep and feel melancholy. But I do not like to remember it, because a feeling of self-love mingled with all its manifestations; either a desire to show that I was more afflicted than the rest, or thoughts about the impression I produced upon others; or idle curiosity which made me examine Mimi's cap or the faces of those around me."' The reviewer adds: 'Now I call this passage morbid.' It may be, but the description is extraordinarily true to many under the influence of grief, though they fail to analyse or understand their own mental state.

We all say, we all think, we all know, that 'in the midst of life we are in death'; and yet when the blow falls with appalling startlingness on someone who is near to us, how we all must feel—with a piercing, heartrending reality—'If I had known'!

If I had known, O loyal heart,
  When, hand to hand, we said 'Farewell,'
How for all times our paths would part,
  What shadow o'er our friendship fell,
I should have clasped your hand so close
  In the warm pressure of my own
That memory still might keep its grasp—
  If I had known.

. If I had known when far and wide
  We loitered through the summer land,
What presence wandered by our side,
  And o'er you stretched its awful hand,
I should have hushed my careless speech
  To listen well to every tone
That from your lips fell low and sweet—
  If I had known.

If I had known when your kind eyes
  Met mine in parting, true and sad—
Eyes gravely tender, gently wise,
  And earnest rather more than glad—
How soon the lids would lie above,
  As cold and white as sculptured stone,
I should have treasured every glance—
  If I had known.

If I had known that, until Death
  Shall with his fingers touch my brow,
And still the quickening of the breath
  That stirs with life's full meaning now,
So long my feet must tread the way
  Of our accustomed paths alone,
I should have prized your presence more—
  If I had known.

CHRISTIAN REED ('Weekly Sun,' 1897).

Oh! the anguish of that thought—that we can never atone to our dead for the stinted affection we gave them, for the light answers we returned to their plaints or their pleadings, for the little reverence we showed to that sacred human soul that lived so close to us and was the divinest thing God had given us to know.

DECEMBER

December 1st.—I have been turning out more old letters, and among other papers, with other memories and connected with other times, I found this fragment of what was evidently intended to be an autobiography of a long life. As a sketch of a little boy's life nearly seventy years ago, with its allusions to foreign lands and customs now nearly extinct, I think it is not entirely devoid of interest. I omit an account given of the writer's family, the story of his father and mother, and his own birth in Switzerland:

' My early youth was passed in many different places, but I have not much recollection of them. One season we had a house in Hereford Street, Park Lane—a site now occupied by Hereford Gardens. I remember cows being milked for purchasers in Hyde Park, and Blacks playing the cymbals in the bands of the Guards.

' When very young we went to Scotland, where my father, who was very devoted to every sort of sport, enjoyed his life immensely. Those days were before the railway period, and an Englishman in Scotland was a comparatively rare person.

' Whilst I was in Edinburgh I went with my brother

Augustus to a large day-school called the Circus Place
School. It was attended by boys and girls of every
class that could afford to pay the fees, and the little
Scotch roughs used rather to bully us two English lads.
My dear mother, in her anxiety that we should not catch
cold by walking to school in the snow and sitting with
wet feet, used to send us there on bad days—of which
there were a good many in that abominable climate—in
a Sedan chair, the customary conveyance at that time in
Edinburgh. I shall never forget the jeers with which we
were greeted when, on arriving at the school, the chair
was opened by lifting up the top to release the door, and
we were shot out, spick and span, among the crowd of
little hardy brats who had trudged with their satchels on
their backs through the snow-slush which our mother so
dreaded for us !

'At this time I remember " Pickwick " coming out in
monthly numbers, and my father's anxiety for their
appearance as the month's end approached.

'Another subject of recollection is the efforts that
were made to get franks for letters from Members of
Parliament. The penny postage had not then been invented, and my impression is that a letter to London
from Scotland was charged a shilling. I do not know
how many franks a day a Member had, but I think there
was a limit. If he did not require his full allowance for
his own correspondence, he used to oblige his friends by
signing his name on an envelope, as a Secretary of State
does now, and handing it to his applicant. It did not
seem to occur to anyone that the privilege was given to
facilitate a Member's official correspondence, and that
handing it on to others was an abuse of it.

'Whilst in Paris, Augustus and I attended a little
day-school of French boys. It was in a small street
somewhere near the Rue St. Honoré. The great pump-

kins then so much used in the poorer parts of Paris, exhibited outside the little shops partly cut and showing their yellow flesh, are among the recollections of those daily walks to and from school.

'We used to have our midday meal at the school, and I have grim memories of the Friday *maigre* dinner, with a sour *bonne femme* soup which did not please our British beef- and mutton-trained appetites. But what do I not owe to the admirable woman who assisted her husband in his educational duties, and who stood over Augustus and myself while with rigorous efforts she endeavoured to convert our pronunciation of the French word for bread from "pang" to "pain"! How persistent she was, that dear, conscientious Frenchwoman! How often, with repeated and exaggerated aspiration of the final "n," did she drive into our unaccustomed ears the proper sound of that much (by Britons) murdered monosyllable! And she succeeded at last, and broke the neck of our initial difficulties in French pronunciation. I think I was nine years old at this time; but the gloomy little garden, with a horizontal gymnastic pole, and the parallel bars under the one Lime tree, the whole screened off from the next-door estate by an ivy-covered trellis, are present to my sight.

'I have no recollection whatever of the journey from Paris to Tours. We children, with the tutor and servants, must have made it by *diligence*, and perhaps my remembrance of it has been obscured by the more vivid impressions of the joys or the sufferings—the difference depending upon which direction I was going in—of the same journey several times performed on my way to and from a school at Paris, which I will refer to later on.

'The house my father had taken at Tours was called the "Grands Capucins"—I believe, from being a house of retreat or "pleasaunce" house belonging to a Capucin monastery. And surely no monks, skilful as they were in the selection of localities, ever chose a more charming spot for a small villa-like residence where they could retire from the austerities and the duties of the convent.

'Situated on the heights which rise on the right bank of the Loire at this point in its course, and immediately over the little faubourg of Tours, St. Symphorien, it commanded an extensive and beautiful view of the river, the town of Tours, and the rich plains to the south watered by the rivers Cher and Indre. The grounds, I fancy, were in extent about five acres, but there were vineyards and other appurtenances belonging to the estate, though not comprised in the lease, which made an almost boundless playground for children, and were so varied by terraces, caves in the side of the hill, and other strange incidents of site, that a great excitement was lent to the games of mimic wars and surprises at which we were constantly playing. There was a large tank under one side of the old house — you descended to it by steps from the garden — and armed with candles, for it was pitch-dark, and provided with planks, we used to embark on its water and navigate the mysterious cavern — an amusement that led to wet feet and friction with Mrs. Hunt, the old nurse, in consequence.

'The front part of the house was modern; it stood on a platform raised above the large formal garden before it. The boundary of the garden was a terrace-walk looking down on the river and the town. There were no steamers, or very few, in those days, and, of course, no railway; and the long strings of flat-bottomed barges, with their great white square sails, that carried the merchandise from Nantes up the river when the wind served, made a striking feature in the scene.

'There was a wine-press attached to the rambling

old house, and the proprietor made his wine from the vineyards every autumn. There was also an old bil-liard-table, and we used to do a little wine-pressing of our own by putting the bunches of fat black grapes into the net pockets and squeezing the juice into a jug. The fruit of all sorts was magnificent; the greengages, the muscat grapes on the face of the cliff, the gooseberries, strawberries, currants, and in autumn the walnuts, were splendid objects for youthful greediness, and are matters of life-long remembrance to me.

'The grounds and gardens were under the care of a family who resided in a cottage and bore the name of Diète. There were the Père and Mère Diète, good old sabot-wearing peasants who worked in and overlooked the vineyards, while their son Martin attended to the garden. We had a coachman called Joseph, an old cavalry soldier who interested us children with his tales of the siege of Antwerp by the French in 1832, and particularly by his account of a cavalry charge in which he took part. The noise of its galloping, he used to say, was like the *tonnerre de Dieu*. His contempt of the infantry soldier, whom he spoke of as *le piou-piou*, was characteristic of the attitude of the dragoon towards the foot-soldier in all armies.

'Augustus and I learnt to swim in the Loire. We used to go out in a punt with a *maître de natation*, who hooked us on to a pole by a belt round our waists, and so supported us in the water till we could keep our-selves afloat. We also amused ourselves by sailing a toy boat in the lagunes and back-waters of the river. One day, while so occupied, a French lad of about fif-teen or sixteen began throwing stones at our cutter. Augustus, who was taller than I and much more daring, rushed at the Frenchman, and, after a struggle with him, was thrown on the sand. The French lad, who had the best of the wrestle, improved his advantage by taking up handfuls of sand and rubbing it into Augustus' eyes while he was lying helpless underneath. A stout stick the French boy had brought with him had fallen in the struggle under Augustus. I, seeing the position, dragged the stick out from under the combatants, and began belabouring the Frenchman with all my might. This soon converted our defeat into a victory, and the enemy, extricating himself from his antagonist, fled from the field. The lad's father then appeared on the scene and relieved himself by a torrent of abuse. In those days the memories of the old struggles between England and France were still alive among the populace, and we were constantly followed by gamins shouting after us "Goddam Anglish" and other contemptuous expressions.

'During our residence in Touraine, Augustus and I went with Mr. Nicholl, the tutor, to visit the old castles of the neighbourhood, and I remember going to Loches, Chinon, Chenonceaux, and Chambord, travelling in the little country *diligences.*

'In the winter evenings, at the "Capucins," my father used to read Walter Scott's novels to us, and I recall how we looked forward with excitement to the time of resumption of the stories. "Quentin Durward" was especially interesting to us, as the scene of a great part of his adventures was within sight of our own house, Plessis les Tours being just across the river.

'On the whole, my life at Tours was the part of my youth to which I look back with the greatest pleasure. It has tinged my whole existence with a great love of France, and, until the experience of late years showed me the childish petulance in political affairs of her people, I had a sincere admiration and affection for them.

'The time came at last when I had to go to school.

I was eleven years old when my father took me to Paris, to a school for English boys kept by a M. Rosin, a Swiss. It was established in a fair-sized house with grounds round it, something like a superior villa at Putney, near the Arc de Triomphe and to the north of the Champs Elysées. It was distinguished as No. 15 Avenue Châteaubriand, Quartier Beaujon, and has long since disappeared. The whole region has become the site of the fine *hôtels* of the magnates of finance who have since the 'forties peopled the neighbourhood of the Champs Elysées. When I was at school, the Bois de Boulogne was a scrubby waste. The only road of importance through it from the Arc de Triomphe was that to Neuilly.

'A few sorry hacks and donkeys stood saddled for hire at the fringe of the Bois. There were no houses of any size farther up the Champs Elysées than the Rond Point, and near the Arc was a waste occupied by the earth thrown out of the road in the leveling operations of its construction. I remember it well, for it was on the heaps resulting from the excavations that we stood one bitterly cold day in the winter of 1840, from 8 A. M. to 1.30, to see the funeral of the great Napoleon pass through the arch on its way down the Champs Elysées to his burial-place, in the crypt of the Invalides.

'Augustus followed me to the same school. I do not think I could have been there more than eighteen months, but it was long enough to have the recollection of the journeyings in the *diligence* to and from Tours at Christmas and at midsummer. Very happy migrations they were on the way home, and very much the reverse on the return to school.

'In the winter my father and mother used to come to Paris, and take an apartment for a time in the Hôtel Mirabeau in the Rue de la Paix. And every Saturday while they were there we passed the afternoon and the following day with them, sleeping in the hotel. There was not much of the present luxury of washing at schools in those days. At Rosin's, once in three weeks, we were marched off to some *bains* where we could enjoy a good wash in a warm bath and a surreptitious cake of chocolate, provided by the *garçon de bains* for a consideration. So there were great washings on the Saturday nights at the hotel, superintended by our dear mother, after our return from the "Français," where we were always taken on the Saturday evenings for a lesson in French. Rachel was just coming into celebrity, and we sat through the long and, to us, unexciting Racine plays in which she appeared, rather sleepy after dinner at a restaurant and an afternoon of exceptional interest, driving about the streets. Those strictly classical plays, in which the three unities are rigidly observed, were very tedious to us boys, and the prospect of an ice at Tortoni's on the way home was more engrossing, I am ashamed to own, than the passionate scenes rendered by the great actress.

'I remember, while at Rosin's, going sometimes to spend the afternoon and dine at Lord Elgin's, the hero of the Elgin Marbles acquisition. He seemed to me then a very old man, and always sitting at a writing-table in a corner of a large room in their house in the Faubourg St. Germain, while his daughters performed the up-hill duty of trying to amuse me, a stupid, shy boy of eleven. I was also taken out by other friends of my father's, and can recall the intense sleepiness following an unwonted dinner at seven o'clock, before the time came for being packed off in a *fiacre* to the Avenue Châteaubriand.

'But the time came when Augustus and I, both destined for the army, had to prepare, he for Woolwich and

I for Sandhurst. It was decided that we should go to a great preparatory school of those days for the military colleges of the Queen's and East India Company's services, kept by Messrs. Stoton and Mayor at Wimbledon. The school was a large one, and would be thought a rough one now. The only washing place was a room on the ground floor, with sinks and leaden basins in them, to which we came down in the morning to wash our hands and faces. There was very little taught but mathematics for the army boys, and classics for those destined for Haileybury, the East India Company's college for the Indian Civil Service. Copley Fielding taught some boys drawing and water-colour painting. There was also a French class, presided over by a poor little old Frenchman, M. Dell. I never in my life met a being to whom the term "master" was less applicable. The French master at the schools of sixty years ago was not a happy person. He was despised of all men and boys, and his position was one of such inferiority that no man of any power or spirit was likely to fill it. Stoton allowed no prize for the French class, and it has been one of the most touching incidents of my life that the poor old Frenchman gave me a little prize which he paid for himself. It was a small edition of Florian's fables. I had it with me for years, but where it has gone to now I know not. It is perhaps buried somewhere among the increased belongings that inheritances and a settled life have accumulated about me ; I wish I could find it again. Augustus and I were probably the only boys that had been in France, and certainly the only ones with any pretension of speaking French, and I think the good little man had a predilection for us among the crowd of sneering John Bulls — hating him, his language, and his country — that it was his hard fate to teach. It would be a great delight if I could perform an anachronistic miracle and find him as he then was, to give him a hundred times the value of his poor little book.

'From Stoton's, at the age of fourteen, I went to the Royal Military College at Sandhurst, and Augustus must have gone to the Military Academy at Woolwich about a year later. My father took me to the college, and we slept the night before the entrance examination at the "Tumble-down Dick" inn at Farnborough, which was then the nearest station. The examination was a farce, of course. I suppose they ascertained that one could read and write, and the doctor satisfied himself you were not deformed, but I don't believe it went much farther.' (Here the fragment ends.)

December 5th.—The weather is wonderfully mild. I have a bunch of Tea Roses flowering in the room that were picked out of doors yesterday. Have seasons changed, or have the Roses? I used to think Owen Meredith's allusion to the Rose of October so true:

> If Sorrow have taught me anything,
> She hath taught me to weep for you;
> And if Falsehood have left me a tear to shed
> For Truth, these tears are true.
>
> If the one star left by the morning
> Be dear to the dying night,
> If the late lone rose of October
> Be sweetest to scent and sight,
>
> If the last of the leaves in December
> Be dear to the desolate tree,
> Remember, belov'd — O remember,
> How dear is your beauty to me!

December 10th.—I have again been away. At last it is quite winter, and everything is at rest outside. But if all the outdoor Chrysanthemums, or even the hardiest indoor ones, had been moved in October or November into sheltered places under shrubs and trees, or against walls, there has been, up to now, no frost to hurt them in such situations. Some that I moved twice this autumn are not feeling it at all.

If Camellias are grown in pots, they make far more buds than they can possibly carry, and severe disbudding is most useful.

Outdoor Heaths seem to do better for cutting back after flowering.

Just lately I have received from the south of France a box of dried figs, not pressed at all, but just dried in the sun, as the peasants eat them. They are delicious, I think; far better than the usual dried figs we get in England, the inside seeds of which, as a rule, are much too hard.

December 11th.—The Hornbeam—one of the old indigenous trees of England, and among the very best for firewood—is, judging from what I notice, very little planted now and rarely named in catalogues. And yet for many purposes it is useful and beautiful. It stands the knife to any extent, and makes most satisfactory hedges.

In my last book I spoke of pergolas—those covered walks made with poles, or columns of bricks or stone, and overgrown with creepers of all kinds. Now I would speak of the 'charmilles'—walks either of turf or gravel, covered over with arches of growing trees, with no supports or wires or wood, merely the interlacing of the boughs till they grow thick overhead with continual pruning. There is a little short walk of this kind at Hampton Court—I forget how it is made (I mean, with what trees it is planted)—and in the Boboli Gardens at Florence there are endless varieties, as everyone knows, of these covered walks. They would be very beautiful on the north or east side of many a sunny lawn; and if a garden were too small for such a walk, there might still be room for an occasional self-forming arch, which adds mystery and charm to any garden. It could be made either with Hornbeam, Beech, or (perhaps best of all in light soil) Mountain Ash, which flowers—and berries too—all the better for judicious pruning, and which could make a support as well for Honeysuckle or a climbing Rose. This kind of planting to gain deep shade can be done over a seat, and would not take very long to grow into a natural arbour. A Weeping Hornbeam—which, I suppose, must be a modern gardening invention, as it is not mentioned in Loudon's very comprehensive 'Arboretum et Fruticetum'—is also a splendid tree for a sunny lawn; and in the female plant the long, loose, pendulous catkins are very attractive. The seeds ripen in October, and the bunches or cones which contain them should be gathered by hand when the nuts are ready to drop out. The nuts separate easily from the envelope, and if sown at once will come up the following spring. All this sounds rather slow, for in these days people buy all they want and never wait. Messrs. Veitch sell both kinds of Hornbeams, and even tall, well-grown plants of the weeping kind are not expensive.

'Bosquets, or groves, are so called from *bouquet*, a nosegay; and I believe gardeners never meant anything else by giving this term to this compartment, which is a sort of green knot, formed by branches and leaves of trees that compose it placed in rows opposite each other.' The author of 'The Retired Gardener' then adds: 'I have named a great many compartments in which Hornbeam is made use of; yet methinks none of them look so beautiful and magnificent as a gallery with arches.'

December 13th.—We have just been digging up and preparing a good-sized oblong piece of ground in the best and sunniest part of the kitchen garden, and moving into it gooseberries and currants — red, white, and black. Round this I am going to place, after considerable deliberation and doubt, a high fine-wire fencing, with an opening on one side instead of a gate — which reduces the expense — and the opening can be covered when necessary with a net. The reason for not wiring over the top, besides the expense, is that it causes a rather injurious drip in rainy weather and breaks down under the snow. I am also assured by good gardeners that it is unnecessary, and that the wire netting round the sides is a most effectual protection to the bushes, as small birds do not fly downwards into a wire-netted enclosure. My gardener is very skeptical on this point, and says he thinks our birds are too clever to be kept out by such half-measures. I think we have an undue share of birds, as on one side of the kitchen garden there is a small copse, belonging to a neighbour, which has been entirely neglected for years, and presents the appearance of what one would imagine a virgin forest might be. This affords the most extraordinary protection for birds, and bullfinches and greenfinches abound. They not only do harm to the fruit when it is ripe, but they strip the trees of their buds in dry weather in early spring. If this new wire netting answers, I am told we ought to have three times the fruit for a less quantity of bushes. I shall grow white currants on the netting, with battens or sticks fastened to it as a protection from the heat of the zinc wire, which is fatal to everything. The trees are now all whitened with a preparation of lime, which is distasteful to the birds and insects. After all this, I shall indeed be disappointed if my crop of small fruit is not larger this year. However, a late frost may still defeat us altogether.

Mr. Wright, in his book 'Profitable Fruit-growing'

(171 Fleet street, London), has a sentence on the purchasing of fruit trees, which is so good I must copy it: 'First look to the character and position of the vendors, and deal with those who have reputations to maintain. They cannot afford to sell inferior trees or, what is of vital importance, distribute varieties under wrong names. It is a very serious matter to grow fruit trees for some years, then when they bear find they are not the sorts ordered, but inferior. Time thus lost cannot be regained. Order early in October, and the sooner the trees arrive and are planted after the leaves fall, the better they will grow.' He goes on to say, what is equally true, that the best trees are spoilt by bad planting, and it is deplorable to see how roughly the work is often done through lack of knowledge. Every kind of instruction is clearly given by Mr. Wright in this excellent, inexpensive little book, and if read carefully and followed, things must go right. I have fallen this year into the so common fault of ordering the little I meant to have too late; but, as they are only a few hardy Damson trees, I hope they will forgive me and do well all the same. Damsons are certainly not cultivated enough, and yet, after Morello Cherries, they make the best of jams and no fruit tree gives such big crops for so little outlay. The trees enjoy full exposure and need hardly any attention, but it is well to remember to stake them securely, to prevent strong winds blowing them about and straining the roots. Our only trouble is the birds, who eat out the buds before they even blossom. Some buds we could spare, but that is not Mr. Bully's way; if he begins on a tree he completely clears it, as the missel-thrushes do the Rowan berries of summer. Last year they fixed on a Pear tree that was covered rather early with buds, and in one week every trace and promise of blossom was gone.

December 14th.—I have a large field in which we have generally grown the coarser kind of vegetables—Potatoes, Cabbages, Jerusalem Artichokes, etc., and such things that do best in a very sunny, open place. Finding that now, as I do not go to London, I do not require such a large supply of vegetables, I am going to sow and grass over half the field. It is between this and the vegetable part that I have been planting the row of Damson trees—half common and half cluster, by way of experiment. The Bullace, a true cottager's fruit, is a variety of the Damson, and not to be lightly regarded for both preserving and pies. It ripens soon after other Damsons, and so a succession is made.

December 15th.—I am told some people have tried and approved of my suggestion of arranging greenhouse Chrysanthemums in groups of colour instead of dotting them about all mixed, one injuring the effect of the other. But I have not yet had the pleasure of seeing a large greenhouse so arranged, and I have not room for a great number myself. One of the very best is Abraham Lincoln, with its bushy habit, its grand bluish leaves, and its strong yellow flowers, which remain a good yellow at night. A charming small, but most decorative Chrysanthemum is called 'Mrs. Carter.' It is pale yellow, white at night, and its growth and appearance are just like those of a Sweet Sultan.

I saw the other day a little Geranium (*Pelargonium*), called 'New Life,' that was new to me; the petals were white and red mixed. Growing on the plant, it was not especially pretty; but picked and mixed with some light green it had quite an uncommon appearance. I thought on first seeing it that it was a double Bouvardia. 'Mrs. Leopold Rothschild' is a most beautiful pink Carnation.

Just now I have several pots in full flower of an orchid that never fails year after year, *Lygopetalum mackayi.* It does not require much heat, and lasts a long time, either on the plant or in water. It throws up long flowering stems, has a most delicious perfume, is quiet in colour — yellowish green and brownish purple — and very refined in shape. I find it a most useful plant for the time of year, and we have many more pots than we had, so it is not very difficult to increase.

In the corner of the greenhouse there is a good group of *Poinsettia pulcherrima.* Some people say they do not like these rather curious plants. They are useless for putting into water, but I think they look very bright and cheerful on these dark days. They do best if grown every year from cuttings.

December 19th.— We have been more successful this year with the forcing of bulbs — Roman Hyacinths and Paper-white Narcissus — than ever before, and I think it is a good deal owing to having carefully obeyed the instructions given in a little pamphlet, 'How I came to grow Bulbs,' which I have mentioned before. Mr. Robert Sydenham is as instructive about pot culture as he is about outdoor culture. He gives exactly the information required ; and if this is carefully read there can be no confusion as regards the different treatment required by Narcissi, Tulips, and Hyacinths. A great many nurserymen profess to sell the Chinese Lily, really a Tazetta Narcissus with a yellow centre, which grows with extreme rapidity in bowls of water; but instead of the true thing they often send out the Paper-white Narcissus.

Late though it is, I have been moving pieces of *Kerria japonica* and planting them against the bare stems of moderate-sized trees. They do admirably, and look so gay and bright in spring. They can be tied to the trunk for support, and the branches of the tree above protect them from spring frosts. They are most amiable plants, and in no way resent being moved about. The single and variegated Kerrias are not such strong growers as the double. If the latter get to look untidy, they can be removed after flowering.

I saw a curious account in a newspaper lately about the colour of glass greatly affecting the growth of plants. The discoverer of this theory is Camille Flammarion, the French astronomer. He has found that plants grown in a red hot-house become, in a given time, four times as big as those exposed to ordinary sunlight. The poorest development, practically amounting to failure, was under blue glass; and lettuces grown under green glass did badly. It would be interesting to try experiments. I wonder if it would answer to colour red the stuff sold for painting the glass of greenhouses as a shade in summer?

We have done a great deal of pruning this year of our old Apple trees, sawing out large branches in the middle to let in air. The trees have been shortened back so much that they bear far too many apples, and none come to any size.

December 18th.—We have never been very successful here with the growing of Mushrooms. We have no Mushroom house, and have to try what can be done in various sheds and outhouses. I am told that the most essential point to remember is that the horses must have no green food or carrots during the time that the droppings are being collected. My own belief is that our beds have been kept too dry, and that this is the reason of our failure, in spite of making up the beds with the greatest care, according to the directions in the excellent little books which are sold everywhere, and which always represent Mushroom culture as the easiest thing in the world. Also, it may be that when the beds were watered it was not with rain-water. Our soil is so sandy that even when mixed with anything that is put to it, it dries more easily than any ordinary garden soil. This winter my gardener has tried, with marked and satisfactory success, a bed under the greenhouse stage. It is made up in the ordinary way, and darkened and saved from the drip of the plants above by a sheet or two of that invaluable corrugated iron, which I mentioned before, and which I find more and more useful for protection at night, protection for pot-plants in spring, keeping the wet out of sunk pits, shading summer cuttings effectually, and so on. It also makes an excellent, though ugly, paling instead of a wall. Even Peach trees will grow well against it if the plants are tied to pieces of batten or sticks — some stuck into the ground and the branches tied horizontally from stick to stick, and some put across the zinc — as then the plant, be it Peach or Vine, enjoys the heat radiated from the zinc, which yet cannot burn or injuriously dry the bark in summer. In winter it is still more important that air should be between the plant and the zinc, which gets extremely cold in frosty weather. This, of course, applies equally to covering zinc houses or sheds with creepers.

This is a long digression from the Mushroom bed. We have already had several excellent and useful dishes off it from this the first experiment. Our outer cellar is too cold here to grow Mushrooms in winter, though it does well to grow the common Chicory for the *Barbe-de-Capucin* salad, and also protects from early autumn frosts the Broad-leaved Batavian Endive, which does so infinitely better here than the Curled Endive. We grow this in large quantities. It makes by far the best late autumn salad, and is also quite excellent stewed. (See 'Dainty Dishes.')

We have not yet succeeded here with the vegetable now so much sold in London in early spring; viz.,

Witloof or Large Brussels Chicory, but I mean to try this next year.

I went to lunch to-day with a neighbour, whose house is full of things recalling memories which belong to other days. As we sat at luncheon I began to gaze, as I invariably do, at whatever hangs on the walls, and I am always thankful when I have not to look at photographs. I have plenty of these myself, but they are the least decorative of furnishing pictures. On the wall opposite to me was rather an uncommon print of the Duke of Wellington, looking more than usually martial and stand-upright, and with an extra severe thundercloud behind him. It was from a picture by Lawrence, I expect, and a fine thing in its way. As a *pendant* to this was another print of a soldier. I turned to my hostess and, pointing to it, said: 'Who is that?' My friend answered, with rather a marked tone: 'Why, that is Lord Lyndoch,' as if most certainly I ought to have known. Now, frankly, I had never heard of Lord Lyndoch, so I said rather humbly and inquiringly: 'Peninsula, I suppose? But I am very badly read; who was he?' And then she told me: 'Why, the Grahame who went to the wars after his wife's death, as you describe in your book in speaking of young Mrs. Grahame's picture in the Edinburgh Gallery.' She added: 'He was on Sir John Moore's staff and standing close by his horse when he was wounded at Corunna, and Sir John Moore was carried into Mr. Grahame's tent or hut, where he shortly died, and the poor young man was so utterly exhausted he lay on the floor by his dead friend and slept.' She told me that Lord Lyndoch was a known feature in society and a visitor in country houses in her youth, and she remembered him well at her grandmother's house in Hertfordshire.

December 19th.—The weather has been so astonishing the last few days one cannot realise it is the week, not of the shortest days, but of the shortest afternoons of the whole year. This sentence brought about a fearful coolness between me and my dear secretary, who asked for an explanation of the statement, and, when I tried to give it, failed to understand. We agreed to refer the matter to an authority that we both believed in. The next day brought the following reply: 'The explanation you require is, I think, hardly suited to "*Pot-Pourri.*" I should put it somehow thus, "that week in which the almanack tells us the days are growing shorter, though the sun sets at a later hour." Of course the after*noon* does not grow longer. Noon is the moment at which the sun crosses the meridian, and it then attains its highest point for the day; and, of course, if it rises later, it also sets earlier. The apparent anomaly occurs thus—the solar day, which is measured from the time the sun crosses the meridian on one day to the time it does ditto on the next, is not of uniform length. The reasons—which you need not read—are: (1) The path of the sun does not lie in the equator, but in the ecliptic; (2) owing to the earth's orbit not being circular, its motion in the ecliptic is not uniform. Now, it would manifestly be very uncomfortable to have days of varying length; therefore, an imaginary sun has been invented which is supposed to behave in a decent and orderly fashion; the time by him is called "mean time," and is that shown by a watch. The time shown by the real sun is called "apparent time," and is that shown by a sun-dial. The difference between these two times is as much as sixteen minutes at certain seasons of the year. Now, on the shortest day the sun crosses the meridian nearly two minutes before twelve o'clock. He was earlier the few days before; therefore, his time of setting was earlier too. Suppose that on December 21st apparent noon is at 11.58 A. M., and the sun sets at 3.51 P. M., and on December 14th the apparent noon is at 11.55 A. M., and the sun sets at 3.49 P. M. Now the afternoon on December 14th is one minute longer than on December 21st (3 hours 54 minutes to 3 hours 53 minutes), and yet the sun has set two minutes earlier (by our watches).'

December 20th.— Another beautiful afternoon. Such clear yellow skies ! To me the top twigs of Holly bushes against a primrose sky recall, oh ! so many winter days in the past ; long walks through bare woods and rustling brown leaves beneath our feet ; the closing-in of curtains in the warm fire-lit rooms where we grew up, which in old age I see as plainly as if I had never left the house where I was born. But to return to the weather of this year, the following was in a newspaper a day or two ago : 'A beautiful yellow butterfly was seen disporting itself in the sunshine of yesterday.' I did not see a butterfly here, but Chrysanthemums still linger, Violets are out, and the yellow *Jasminium nudiflorum* is in unusually full flower.

I have no Mistletoe here, but I presume I might have it if I cultivated it. It no doubt has become so much rarer from being always cleared out of orchards, the pretty pale-fruited parasite being no friend to the Apple trees. If one wishes to cultivate the Mistletoe, select a young branch of Willow, Poplar, Thorn, or an old Apple or Pear tree, and on the underside slit the bark to insert the seed. The best time to do this is in February. One may merely rub a few seeds on the outside of the bark, but that is not so safe as inserting them actually under the bark. Raising Mistletoe from seed is better than either grafting or budding.

This is a good time for planting Ivies. There are

many different kinds, and they will grow in such a satisfactory way in such bad places. In London gardens or back yards Ivy can be made into quite a feature. As Curtis says, in his 'Flora Londinensis': 'Few people are acquainted with the beauty of Ivy when suffered to run up a stake, and at length to form itself into a standard; the singular complication of its branches and the vivid hue of its leaves give it one of the first places amongst evergreens in a shrubbery.'

My Lancashire friend sends me a list of a few Roses and annuals. Lists are always so useful to all gardeners, as it is interesting to know what one has got and what one has not, that I give his list as he wrote it: 'To begin with Roses. Kaiserin Augusta Victoria, Allister Stella Gray (climber), Gustave Regis, Maman Cochet, have done best with me. *Adonis autumnalis*, *Alonsoa Warscewiczii*, and *Kaulfussia amelloides* are three annuals new to me. *Acis autumnalis* is a small South of Europe bulb, rare and supposed to thrive out of doors in sandy soil. *Cimicifuga racemosa*—I think all borders ought to have this tall-growing, handsome herbaceous plant; *Dictamnus fraxinella* and its white variety, *Eupatorium purpureum*, *Gypsophila prostrata*, *Phygelius capensis*, *Polemonium Richardsoni*, *Rudbeckia purpurea*, *Spigelia Marilandica*, *Styrax japonica*, *Thalictrum flavum*. *Withenia origanifolia* is a new, very highly praised creeper which I shall try.' I cannot find this creeper mentioned in any of my gardening books. *Phormium tenax* (the New Zealand Flax) makes a very handsome tub plant for a bare entrance drive or large terrace. If treated like the Agapanthus, in full sun, it flowers.

Two or three years ago, when I knew nothing about Roses, a very clever Rose grower, who had devoted his life to them, wrote me out the following list. with the assurance that every one of them was worth having: 'A selection of Roses which, in ground well dug and liberally fed with farmyard manure, sheltered but not overshadowed, like Phyllis, "never fail to please." **Hybrid Perpetuals:** Duke of Edinburgh, Etienne Levet, General Jacqueminot, Her Majesty, Jules Margottin, Margaret Dickson, Mrs. John Laing, Merveille de Lyon, Paul Neyron, Ulrich Brünner. **Hybrid Teas:** Captain Christy, Grace Darling, Gustave Regis, Lady Mary Fitzwilliam, La France, Viscountess Folkestone, Caroline Testout. **Teas:** Anna Ollivier, Bouquet d'Or, Homère, Madame de Watteville, Madame Falcot, Madame Hosté, Marie Van Houtte, Perles des Jardins. **Polyantha:** Cécile Brunner, Perle d'Or.'

I have a near neighbour who is a most successful Rose grower. Walking through his beautifully kept beds the other day, I noted that the centre parts of the plant, both in standards and dwarfs, had some bracken twisted into them. This is a great protection against the coming frosts. For anyone who cares about the choicer Ferns, it is a protection to them, too, to have their own leaves twisted round them in the shape of a knob of hair on a woman's head, firmly tucking in the ends so that the winds of March may not untwist them.

December 21st.—The perennial and ever-recurrent aspect of the London streets at this time of year always reminds me of the old happy Christmas holidays and of long walks with three young gentlemen lately returned home, who then considered it my chief defect that I had not three arms. The mental attitude which I tried to instil into them was to enjoy looking in at the shop-windows rather than to admire or, above all, wish to possess the extraordinary amount of rubbish displayed inside, which, though it looked well enough arranged in redundant heaps, would, I thought, seem to them mere money wasted in poor, useless stuff if they brought it home. I dare say I am prejudiced in these matters, having always had a very great dislike to wholesale present-giving at fixed anniversaries, whether birthdays, Christmas, or New Year.

I think that while children are quite small — say, up to the age of ten or twelve — we might leave the matter as it stands at present, as the said redundant heap on the nursery floor may give a peculiar pleasure of its own. But this is quite different from an obligatory present-giving to all sorts of people — servants and dependents, grown-up children, fathers, mothers, and old grannies. We all know houses where this kind of thing is much practised, and where, year after year, it is an immense toil to the givers, and but very little appreciated by the receivers. It is almost laughable, the way that people who are apparently the greatest supporters of this custom of present-giving at stated times groan over the trouble and expense it entails, and congratulate themselves and each other when the terrible Christmas fortnight is at an end.

This fashion of giving presents to all sorts of promiscuous people at special times has immensely increased since my childhood, when it was only beginning — imported no doubt, as far as Christmas is concerned, from Germany. The French, who keep their rubbish-giving for the New Year, confine themselves almost entirely to flowers and bonbons, which, if equally useless, have at least the merit of passing away and of not crowding up our chimneypieces and writing-tables. The turning of every shop into a bazaar; the display of meat, game, and turkeys on the outside of shops; the spending of a disproportionate amount of money on feasting — all this is comparatively recent. I can quite well remember, as a girl, the excitement of first decorating a church. This developed into a fashion with the High Church party, and is not an old custom. I know one old clergyman who to this day refuses to allow any Christmas decorations, and says : 'Why desecrate my church with evergreens ?' If it has any antiquity it is a Pagan revival, like flowers for the dead. It may be pretty and desirable, or the contrary, but it is not Old English, though the Druids may have been as fond of mistletoe as they were of oaks.

To return to present-giving at anniversaries. I am more than willing to admit, as I have already said, that quite young children get considerable pleasure out of this custom, but even in their case it has distinct drawbacks. When children receive too many presents at the same time, it is apt to encourage criticism and ingratitude ; and having to thank for what they do not want or already possess is too early a training in what might seem to a child hypocrisy. Not to look a gift horse in the mouth is excellent and reasonable to those who understand it, but neither in word nor idea does it convey anything to a child's mind. I heard two delicious child anecdotes last winter. One was of a village schoolboy helping to decorate a Christmas tree for himself and his schoolfellows. He made a touching appeal to the kind but tired lady who was doing the same : 'Please, teacher, if you have anything to do with it, will you see that I get something that is not a pocket handkerchief ? I've got seven already !' Sad to say, his eighth pocket handkerchief had been assigned to him, and he had to put up with it. The other story was of a rich little lady who was taken to a neighbour's Christmas tree. On receiving a new doll, she said to her mother : 'Really, I don't know, mother, what I shall do with this doll. I have so many already, how *can* I find room for her ?'

It goes against my sense of the fitness of things to put either charity or affection into a treadmill, and force people to give presents at a particular fixed time. Do we not all know the phraseology so often heard in the shops : 'Will this do ? Does it look *enough* ? It won't be much use, but that doesn't matter. Oh! here's a new book that will do for So-and-so.' I heard of a wretched lady, with rather well-known tastes in one direction, who last Christmas received seven copies of one book. Then there are the presents for dependents, which are chosen in imitation of the luxuries of the master and mistress,—the sham jewel brooch or the shoddy Gladstone bag, which costs fifteen shillings and is supposed to 'look like thirty.' All this kind of thing seems to me false, and many people I know are ready enough to acknowledge what a slavery it is and how undesirable. Some reconcile themselves to the folly by saying : 'Well, it can't be helped, and it's good for trade.' Even if this kind of artificial demand is really good for trade, which many doubt, this has nothing to do with whether it has a good or a bad effect on ourselves, on our children, and on those who surround us.

The giving of wedding presents, though it is continually referred to as a tax, is so essentially useful to the receivers when judiciously done that I not only say nothing against it, but *think* nothing against it. I remember, in the early 'sixties, a cousin who was the victim of twenty-seven ormolu inkstands; but the practicalness of the present day solves the difficulty of duplicates, as the young people, without the smallest concealment, sell or exchange what they do not care about.

Though few people may agree with my abuse of wholesale present-giving at anniversaries, I think no one will deny that it tends to destroy some of the most delightful outward expressions of feeling that can exist between civilised human beings. To take the trouble to find out what somebody really wants; to be struck by something beautiful, and to know to whom to give it; to supply a real want to those who cannot afford it for themselves; to give anything, however trifling, as a remembrance— all these are the gentle sweeteners of life, and need none of those goading reminders which come with the return of anniversaries. And to come to the more selfish aspect of the question. Instead of the callousness, and almost fatigue, in consequence of receiving a great number of presents at once, is there not a delight that lasts through life, until we are quite old, at suddenly receiving a sympathetic and unexpected gift?

A great many people use holly and evergreens at Christmas-time to stick about the room in empty vases, round pictures, etc. But they hardly ever take the trouble to peel their stalks and put them in water, though—especially with holly—this makes all the difference as regards the retaining of its freshness; and if arranged in a glass, not too thickly, it looks much more beautiful, and does not acquire a dusty, degraded appearance before New Year's Day. I cannot bear to see the poor evergreens shrivelling in the hot rooms. We used to have hardly any Holly berries in the garden here, but by judicious pruning in February we now get quantities of a very fine kind.

One of my many correspondents wrote: 'If you are interested in the lighting of country houses, I can recommend the acetylene gas which our gardener makes for us. We have used it for over a year, and find it quite charming—a brilliant light, delightful to read by, cool, clean, and harmless to silver, flowers, and clothes, and safe, so far as our experience goes. Ours is the "pure acetylene," made by Raol Picket's patent, and not the explosive kind.'

December 22nd.—After all the fine, mild weather I have been mentioning, it suddenly began to freeze, with hard, cold, moonlight nights. So to-day I thought of my little birds. I now find it prettier and less trouble, instead of hanging the string with cocoanut and suet from a window or a stiff cross-bar, to arrange it in the following way: I cut a big branch, lopping it more or less, and push it through the hole of a French iron garden-table, that I happen to have, which holds an umbrella in summer. On the other side of the house I stick a similar branch into the ground. On these I hang, Christmas-tree fashion, some pieces of suet and a tallow candle—the old 'dip'—a cocoanut with a hole cut, not at the bottom as I recommended before, but in the side, large enough for the Tom-tits to sit on the edge and peck inside, and yet roofed enough to prevent the rain-water collecting in it. They seem to have remembered the feeding from last year, as they began at the piece of suet at once. On the table below I used to put a basin to hold crumbs and scraps from meals—rice, milk, anything almost, for the other birds who will not eat either the fat or the cocoanut. But I found this was such a great temptation to the cats and dogs of the establishment, who became most extraordinarily acrobatic in the methods by which they got on to the table, that I had to devise wiring the saucer of a flower-pot and so hanging it on to the most extended branch, out of reach of the cleverest of Miss Pussies. If once it freezes very hard, I put out bowls of tepid water. This the birds much appreciate.

December 23rd.—I have been out for a walk long after dark—or, rather, long after sunset, for the moon was shining bright in the cold indigo sky. At all times of year walking by moonlight gives me exquisite delight. Is it because I have done it so rarely, or because of the great beauty and mystery of it all! I went along our high road, the road along which Nelson travelled to Portsmouth on his way to Trafalgar, never to return. This evening it shone white and dry in the moonlight, and the tall black telegraph-poles — double the height and strength of those they replaced a few years ago, and which I have always hated for their aggressive size by daylight — in the winter moonlight only seemed to me straight and strong, and as if proud to support that wonderful network of wires which now encompasses the entire globe, annihilating time and making the far and the near as one, ceaselessly carrying those messages of happiness and despair, life and death, which, in the space of a moment, in the opening of an envelope, bring sorrow or joy to many a home. Something of the mystery of it all the wires sang to me to-night, with Æolian sounds different from any I have ever heard, on this one of the last evenings of a year that is nearly gone. By my lonely fireside, this poem came to my recollection:

The old friends, the old friends,
  We loved when we were young,
With sunshine on their faces
  And music on their tongue!
The bees are in the Almond flower,
  The birds renew their strain;
But the old friends once lost to us
  Can never come again.

The old friends, the old friends,
  Their brow is lined with care;
They've furrows in the faded cheek
  And silver in the hair;
But to me they are the old friends still,
  In youth and bloom the same
As when we drove the flying ball
  Or shouted in the game.

The old men, the old men,
  How slow they creep along!
How naughtily we scoffed at them
  In days when we were young !
Their prosing and their dosing,
  Their prate of times gone by,
Their shiver like an aspen-leaf
  If but a breath went by.

But we, we are the old men now;
  Our blood is faint and chill;
We cannot leap the mighty brook
  Or climb the break-neck hill.
We maunder down the shortest cuts,
  We rest on stick or stile,
And the young men, half ashamed to laugh,
  Yet pass us with a smile.

But the young men, the young men,
  Their strength is fair to see;
The straight back and the springy stride,
  The eye as falcon free;
They shout above the frolic wind
  As up the hill they go;
But though so high above us now,
  They soon shall be as low.

Oh! weary, weary, drag the years,
  As life draws near the end;
And sadly, sadly, fall the tears
  For loss of love and friend.
But we'll not doubt there's good about
  In all of human kind;
So here's a health, before we go,
  To those we leave behind!

December 24th.—It is so curious after a full life to be alone on Christmas eve. But, of course, it was my own choice, and not necessary. I could have gone away, but I love these winter afternoons and the long evenings at home. It is also, I think, essential wisdom that the old should learn to live alone without depression, and, above all, without that far more deadly thing — *ennui*. I have no doubt that training for old age, to avoid being a bore and a burden to others, is as desirable as any other form of education. The changes brought about by circumstances mean, in a sort of way, a new birth, and one has to discover for oneself the best methods of readjusting the details of one's life. I find this poem written in one of my notebooks many years ago by a man whom I had known from childhood. Though he was not the author, the poem represented his feelings rather than mine. It has truth in it, but it has also a touch of bitterness, which appealed, no doubt, to a man who had reaped nothing but life's failure. He had always lived up in balloons of his own imaginings, believing in ultimate wealth, and having the power to draw forth money from others, merely to lose it. He died in old age and poverty, in a garret at Venice. Do we reap as we sow? Very often; not always. I am sure that, up to now, I have never got back in mushrooms what I have spent in spawn. Of course the fault is mine; I know that.

> Laugh, and the world laughs with you;
> Weep, and you weep alone,
> For this brave old earth must borrow its mirth —
> It has sorrows enough of its own.
> Sing, and the hills will answer;
> Sigh, it is lost in air,
> For the echoes bound to a joyous sound —
> They shrink from the voice of care.
>
> Rejoice, and men will seek you;
> Grieve, and they all will go,
> For they want full measure of all your pleasure —
> They do not heed your woe.

Be glad, and your friends are many;
　　Be sad, and you lose them all,
For none will decline your nectared wine —
　　Alone, you must drink life's gall.

Feast, and your halls are crowded;
　　Fast, and the world goes by;
Succeed and give; it will help you live —
　　No man can help you die.
There is room in the halls of pleasure
　　For a long and lordly train,
But one by one we must all pass on
　　Through the narrow aisles of pain.

I like 'Bethia Hardacre's' song better, and to me the spirit is truer:

Bring me the book whose pages teach
The fortitude the Stoics preach;
Bring me the tome within whose scope
There lies the quickening of dead hope;
Bring me the comfort of a mind
That good in every ill can find,
And of a heart that is content
With its desire's relinquishment.

RECEIPTS

A kind friend sent me to-night half a pumpkin — a real French pumpkin. (See Vilmorin's 'Vegetable Garden,' *Potiron jaune gros*.) It was grown near here, and had kept perfectly. It was moist, and a beautiful apricot colour inside. I wonder always why the only pumpkin grown in England is the vegetable marrow. Sutton feebly recommends others in his book, but hardly makes enough of them as useful winter vegetables. Here is a true French receipt for **Pumpkin Soup.** Cut up the slices of pumpkin (say, about half a large one), and boil them in water. When well cooked, strain off the water

· and pass the pulp through a sieve. Boil half a pint of milk, add a piece of butter, very little salt, and a good tablespoonful of castor sugar. Pour this boiling milk on to the pumpkin pulp. Let it boil a few minutes. The soup must be thick, and small fried crusts should be sent up with it. This receipt is enough for two people. Dried vegetable marrow is not supposed to be so good, but I had some soup to-night, prepared exactly in the same way, from a large dried vegetable marrow, and it was excellent, though it had not quite so much flavour.

All through the last month my salads have been nearly as good as in summer, from tarragon and chive tops being forced in the greenhouse. Parsley and chervil are still good out of doors. When once one has become used to the herbs in salad, it does seem so tasteless without them.

Lentil Toast.—Four to six ounces of lentils, one ounce of butter, water, and slices of buttered toast. Look over and thoroughly rinse the lentils, and put them into a small saucepan with enough water to well cover them. Cook slowly till they are tender and the water all absorbed (ten to twenty minutes). Add butter, pepper, and salt; spread thickly on the hot, buttered toast, and serve with mint sauce. Suitable as a supper or breakfast dish.

Green and White Haricot Beans.—Soak in cold water for twelve or even twenty-four hours, then put them into boiling water, with a little salt and two minced shallots. Cook till tender, but not mashed. They will take from two to two and a half hours, and must be watched. A bunch of herbs and a bacon bone, or a little raw bacon, greatly improve the flavour, but can easily be omitted. Before dishing up, toss them in a little butter and serve very hot. Thin English melted butter, with chopped parsley, can be used as a change.

It is worth while to know that with all hard vegetables—peas, beans, lentils, etc.— if they have not been soaked the day before, the way to boil them slowly is to add every now and then a tablespoonful of cold water. The same thing applies to dried fruit.

To Roast a Fine Large Volaille (Chicken or capon or young turkey).—Take some very fat bacon or a good tablespoonful of good grease (clarified fat of beef or pork kidney, half and half). Dissolve it in a very deep copper stewpan, and let it get hot, but not very hot. Put the chicken into it, having previously well trussed it; chop up the liver and gizzard with some unsmoked raw bacon, and insert this in the bird. Put the lid on, and let it braise gently, on top of the hot-plate, by a slow fire. The chicken ought to produce enough moisture by itself to prevent it from roasting too fast. Should this be deficient, add a very little stock. After from thirty to forty minutes turn the fowl over, with the breast to the bottom of the pot, so that it gets a little coloured in its turn. The largest fowl takes an hour and a quarter. When done, remove it on to a dish. Add a little stock to the brown glaze that adheres to the stewpan, having previously removed the grease with a spoon. Pour it round the fowl or into a sauce-boat, and serve with the fowl.

An excellent way of making a next-day dish out of roast turkey is one I saw many years ago in a French restaurant.

Ailerons de Dinde aux Navets.—Take the wing-bones and a portion of the legs of a roast turkey, and divide them into reasonable-sized pieces. Take some cold stock which has been already well flavoured with vegetables, and add a little more onion, cut fine. Stew by the side of the stove till the meat is tender, not broken away. Add a good, large quantity of turnips, cut into small dice, and a very small amount of burnt sugar, pepper, and salt. Stew all together till the turnips are quite cooked (which depends a good deal on the quality of the turnips) and the stock reduced. Serve in a hash dish. The whole can also be cooked in a small fireproof *casserole*, and served in that, with a clean napkin round it. The excellence of this dish depends on the goodness of the stock and very slow cooking.

Raw Liver of Chickens, chopped up with a little bacon fat and fried, then put onto toast with pepper and salt, is a good breakfast dish or savoury.

JANUARY, 1899

Difficulties of growing *Daphne indica*—Journey last year to Ireland —Cutting down and re-planting trees—Apples—Skimmed milk —Manure heaps—Winter Honeysuckle—Botanical Gardens in Dublin—Botticelli's drawings—Tissot's Bible—Rippingille's patent stove—Blue flowers—'Snowdrop-time'—'The Sun-children's Budget'— Floral notes from 'The Scotsman'—Receipts.

January 5th.—After a white frost in the morning, we have had a day which, except for its shortness, we should be satisfied with and think beautiful in early spring. These mild, sunny winter days do great harm in prematurely forcing growth, but I know few things which it would be more difficult to wish non-existent. They make up to me for so many of our winter trials— fog and cold and darkness. I would not change them for the 'sunny south,' where sunshine is a right, while here it comes as a most gracious gift—all the more appreciated because it appears unexpectedly and lasts such a short time.

I have a plant of *Daphne indica*, one of my favourite winter flowers, in my greenhouse now. It is in flower and smelling deliciously, but does not look at all satisfactory, although it was only bought last year. It was put out of doors last summer, as it ought to be, but was allowed to get dry. It made no growth; it is leggy, drawn up, and the leaves are yellow, which, with hardwooded plants, generally means over-watering in winter. I have tried for years to grow these Daphnes, but they are difficult to strike, difficult to grow, and have a quite extraordinary love of dying without any very obvious reason. I must devote myself to finding out, if possible, what the reason is. I see that Mr. Smee, in his book 'My Garden,' says they did the same with him.

I have just gathered three beautiful, full white buds off a *Niphetos* Rose in the conservatory next the drawing-room. It is blooming extra early this year.

January 6th.—Fate caused me to go to Ireland about this time last year. I dreaded the long night journey and the arrival on the gray winter morning. But were the steamers far less splendid sea-boats than they are, and the waves every day as stormy as they sometimes are, I think it still would be well worth while for any garden-fancier to visit Ireland in January, if only to admire and enjoy the luxuriant green of the evergreens and the beauty of the winter-flowering shrubs. I had never seen *Garrya elliptica* in full beauty before. It had catkins six or seven inches long, flowering from end to end, one little flower growing out of the other like a baby chain made with cowslips. The *Jasminum nudiflorum* was not a flowering branch here and there, as in England, but one sheet of brilliant yellow flowers. This beautiful plant is very easy to propagate by laying some of the branches along the ground and covering them with earth. In six or seven months they will have made good root, and can be taken up and planted where desired. One house I saw in the neighbourhood of Dublin was covered on its southern side with the *Clematis cirrhosa*, or winter-flowering Clematis, from Algiers. The house was an old one, much frequented by John Wesley and mentioned in Southey's Life. On one of the thick, strong walls, inside, was the following inscription (translated, I believe, from the German):

The Angels, from their throne on high,
Look down on us with pitying eye,

That where we are but passing guests
We build such strong and solid nests,
And where we hope to dwell for aye
We scarce take heed a stone to lay.

There is a strong, practical common-sense in the lines which would have appealed to Wesley's instincts.

I saw at Howth a beautiful plant of the *Desfontainea spinosa*, with its foliage so like the Holly and its handsome flowers in the form of a tube, bright scarlet, tipped with yellow. This I had never seen flowering before, and one is not likely to come across it except under circumstances as favourable as those which belong to the Irish climate or to the west coast of Lancashire and Scotland. It seems almost a platitude to say that it is worth while going to Ireland to see the great beauty of the Irish Yew, one of the forms of the Common Yew, *Taxus fastigiata*. In old days in Ireland, I am told, it was called the Florence Court Yew, from Florence Court, where it was raised from seed about 1780. Seeds of this variety produce for the most part only the Common Yew, though some vary in form and tint. All the plants in cultivation are of the female sex, according to Loudon.

Whatever may be the climatic disadvantages of Ireland, such as sunlessness and damp, the air remains clear and pure, the soil is unexhausted, and it is free from many of the agricultural difficulties of other countries. In the south, at any rate, there are no manufactures, no smoke, no coal-mines, none of those things which injure the atmosphere in parts of England, and make the cultivation of vegetables and flowers difficult or even impossible. As, in the troubles of individuals, few things help more than sympathy with and an effort to understand the trials of others, so it is, I think, among nations. If Ireland could turn her attention to the trials England has gone through at various epochs of her history, of a kind which Ireland, through the very nature of circumstances, has escaped, there would be less of that one-sided judgment which inclines to think that all the woes of Ireland are peculiarly her own, yet solely due to the rule of the English. Troubles and difficulties come to all nations alike, and certainly England herself is in no way exempt. Witness, for instance, the terrible misery produced by the introduction of machinery, the cotton famines, and even the legislation of recent days which stopped the importation of rags for fear of the cholera. Let those who care for a vivid picture of such times read an old, forgotten novel by Benjamin Disraeli, written in the early part of this reign and called 'Sybil.'

During a short excursion into the country by rail, I was shocked to see how the trees, already less plentiful than they ought to be, proclaimed that sure sign of neglect—they were almost invariably covered with Ivy. This beautiful semi-parasitical plant is very picturesque, and many people have a sentimental love for it from its greenness in winter; but it destroys the trees, and, though it may hasten the end of very old trees to cut the Ivy down suddenly, it should always be killed on young trees—by cutting it through the stem at the base and allowing it to perish and fall away. I am told that one of the curious effects of the last Land Act is that the proprietors of land imagine they have an unlimited right to cut down their trees, without considering the evil effects this will have on the future climate and wealth of their country. As it is, Ireland has been far too much deprived of her forests in the past, and I, with the tyranny of one who imagines that she understands everybody's affairs better than they do themselves, should make the cutting down of trees penal. The wise old Dutch settlers at the Cape understood this subject well. They made a law which enforced that every man who cut down one tree should plant two in its stead. Everybody who has a little plot of land should never fail every autumn to plant some acorns, beech-nuts, chestnuts, etc. Many trees will also strike from cuttings in spring, notably all the Willow tribe, which grow the moment they are stuck into the ground. If I were a young Irishman, I should delight in thus renewing the woods and copses of my country. We know how the Irish love the soil, and the feeling is not badly expressed in this little poem, which I copied from an English newspaper :

> Often I wish that I might be,
>   In this divinest weather,
> Among my father's fields—ah me!
>   And he and I together.
>
> Below the mountains, fair and dim,
>   My father's fields are spreading:
> I'd rather tread the sward with him
>   Than dance at any wedding.
>
> Oh, green and fresh your English sod,
>   With daisies sprinkled over,
> But greener far were the fields I trod
>   That foamed with Irish clover.
>
> Oh, well your skylark cleaves the blue
>   To bid the sun good-morrow!
> 'Tis not the bonny song I knew
>   Above an Irish furrow.
>
> And often, often, I'm longing still,
>   In this all-golden weather,
> For my father's face by an Irish hill,
>   And he and I together.

One of the most beautiful colour-effects I saw in Ireland was a small lake planted with great clumps of Dogwood, with its crimson branches beside the bright yellow of the Golden Willow.

A great deal might be done by a study of the most suitable Apple trees to grow in Ireland. There seemed to me no reason why they should not do as well there as in Herefordshire or Normandy, but I have been since told that the want of sun does interfere with their ripening. This, however, only means that extra study must be given as to which kinds should be planted. The chief requirements of Apple trees are slight pruning in the winter and tying round the stem in October a band of sticky paper, to prevent the female moth, who has no wings, from crawling up and laying her eggs in the branches, to come to life the following spring and devour leaves and blossoms. Apples are most excellent, wholesome food. An Apple is quite as nourishing as a Potato, and a roast Apple, with brown sugar, is a far more palatable dinner for a sick child. Apples very likely might be plentiful in seasons when Potatoes did badly, and in districts near to markets they would fetch a much more fancy price. The following I must have copied out of some old book or newspaper : 'Chemically, the Apple is composed of vegetable fibre, albumen, sugar, gum, chlorophyll, malic acid, gallic acid, lime, and much water. Furthermore, the Apple contains a larger percentage of phosphorus than any other fruit or vegetable. This phosphorus, says the "Family Doctor," is admirably adapted for renewing the essential nervous matter, lethicin, of the brain and spinal cord. It is perhaps for the same reason, rudely understood, that old Scandinavian traditions represent the Apple as the food of the gods, who, when they felt themselves to be growing feeble and infirm, resorted to this fruit for renewing their powers of mind and body. Also the acids of the Apple are of great use for men of sedentary habits whose

livers are sluggish in action, these acids serving to elimi-
nate from the body noxious matters which, if retained,
would make the brain heavy and dull, or bring about
jaundice or skin eruptions, and other allied troubles.
Some such experience must have led to our custom of
taking Apple sauce with roast pork, rich goose, and like
dishes. The malic acid of ripe Apples, either raw or
cooked, will neutralise any excess of chalky matter en-
gendered by eating too much meat. It is also the fact
that such fresh fruit as the Apple, the Pear, the Plum,
when taken ripe and without sugar, diminish acidity in
the stomach, rather than provoke it. Their vegetable
salts and juices are converted into alkaline carbonates,
which tend to counteract acidity. A ripe, raw Apple is
one of the easiest vegetable substances for the stomach
to deal with, the whole process of its digestion being
completed in eighty-five minutes. Gerarde found that
the "pulpe of roasted Apples mixed in a wine quart of
faire water, and labored together until it comes to be as
Apples and ale—which we call lambes-wool—never fail-
eth in certain diseases of the raines, which myself hath
often proved, and gained thereby both crownes and
credit. The paring of an Apple cut somewhat thick,
and the inside whereof is laid to hot, burning, or running eyes at night, when the party goes to bed, and is
tied or bound to the same, doth help the trouble very
speedily, and contrary to expectations — an excellent
secret." '

Many people must have asked themselves how, in the
old days long ago, before the Potato came from America,
even the sparse population of Ireland fed itself. I feel
no doubt that the good monks who brought the art of
illuminating and of making the lovely old carved crosses,
also grew their vegetables, and did not find the climate
unfavourable. Probably, however, no other vegetable

will ever now take the place, as an article of food, of the much-loved Potato; nor is this in any way to be desired. Curiously enough, the other day a great London physician remarked to me, quite independently of Ireland and its troubles, that in his estimation the ideal food for the human race was Potatoes and skimmed or separated milk, all the nourishing properties of milk being there, the cream containing nothing but the fat, which stout people are better without. It is quite curious how few even educated people know or believe this. Skimmed or separated milk is constantly thrown away as useless, or given to the pigs; whereas it is very much better for adults than new milk, if they are eating other foods.

Modern science has made it quite easy, by using preventives in time, to keep down the Potato disease; but, in spite of all this, certain losses of crops are sure to occur, and the all-important thing is to cultivate the vegetables which would probably succeed best in the mild, wet autumns so dangerous to the Potato crop.

Where land and manure are forthcoming, seeds — which should be of the best — represent the principal outlay in the growing of vegetables. It is much more prudent to make many sowings in succession than to sow a great quantity at once. It is said that a Cabbage may grow anywhere and anyhow, that it will thrive on any soil, and that the seed may be sown every day in the year. All this is nearly true, and proves that we have a wonderful plant to deal with, and that it is one of man's best friends. Linnæus, the great botanist, mentions that he found it the only vegetable growing on the borders of the Arctic Circle. The Cabbage has one persistent plague only, and that is club or anbury, for which there is no direct remedy or preventive known; and the best indirect way of fighting the enemy is our old friend elbow-grease, or hard work. The crop should constantly

K

be moved; never grown twice in the same place, either
as a seed-bed or planted out, without well digging or
tilling the ground, putting it to other uses and well manuring it. All the Cabbage tribe are great consumers,
hence the need for abundant manuring. Wherever there
are manure heaps near houses or stables, or in farm-
yards, it is very desirable to sink a tub in the ground on
the lowest side of the heap, where the manure has a tendency to drain, cutting out a nick in the tub to guide in
the liquid, which can be constantly emptied out with a
can. This liquid makes very valuable nourishment for
young vegetables, pot-plants, and, in fact, all garden
produce—strength in youth being naturally a great help
to the whole crop. Besides its usefulness, this prevents
the untidy wasting of a manure heap.

I am very ignorant of Irish affairs in general, but I
listened with extreme interest to all that I could hear of
the coöperative movement now being carried out by so
many farmers in Ireland. I have since kept myself
informed in the matter by taking in that excellent
little weekly paper 'The Irish Homestead.' Mr. William
Lawler, in a long poem in the 'London Year-Book' for
1898, begins a paragraph on Ireland, of which the first
lines, at any rate, do not inappropriately express my
wishes and my hopes for the coöperation of Irish
industries :

> Oh, Ireland, when your children shall abate
> Their love of captious things to study great ;
> When you shall let your aspirations lie
> Far less in Statecraft than in Industry;
>
> .   .   .   .   .   .
>
> Then shall your people prosper and advance.

A charming shrub, and new to me, is *Escallonia
pterocladon*, which I saw growing on the walls of a

house in Ireland; it was covered in this midwinter time with white flowers rather like a large Privet.

I saw a pretty dinner-table decoration consisting of a quantity of *Jasminum nudiflorum*, picked and put in small glasses with leaves from greenhouse plants. Also an effective decoration was of Geranium flowers (Pelargoniums, red or pink), arranged in saucers full of moss and—in between these—narrow, pointed glasses with branches of pink Begonias. A little winter-flowering Begonia, called *Gloire de Lorraine*, has lately come into fashion. What a term for a flower! But it is true, and plants of this Begonia make a charming table decoration at a time of year when flowers are scarce. They look best growing in pots. Roman Hyacinths in glasses could be placed between, and pink shades used for the candles; or, for a small table, one plant in the middle would be enough. The colour, the growth, the shape of the leaves, all make it charming. I do not yet know if it is difficult to grow, as I have only lately bought a plant.

I did not see it in Ireland, but a shrub that should never be omitted from any garden, small or large, is *Lonicera fragrantissima*. It begins to flower in January, and continues through February and March. Like every flower or shrub I know, a little care—such as pruning and mulching—improves its flowering powers. I had it here in a neglected state in a shrubbery for years. I only knew its pretty green leaves, and never guessed what it was or its early-flowering qualities. But my gardening ignorance in those days was supreme.

In spite of the time of year, I had pleasant days in Dublin at the College Botanical Garden, and also at Glasnevin, the 'Kew of Dublin.' The little Irises, *Stylosa alba* and *speciosa*, were flowering well. They must be starved; for if their foliage is good, it means no flowers. Many kinds of Hellebores were coming into bloom, some of which I had never seen before. The warm, damp winters are very favourable to January-flowering plants, and we can scarcely expect to copy them in Surrey. The rather rare and interesting *Daphne blagayana* was growing to a great size, and covered with flowers, at Glasnevin. Mr. Robinson describes it as a 'beautiful, dwarf Alpine shrub of easy growth.' I have not found it at all easy; in fact, two out of the three plants I had have died, and the third looks rather ill. But I think I tried to grow it too much in the sun; it also wants pegging down every year after flowering.

In a country house in Ireland, I saw last year for the first time the reproductions, sanctioned by the Berlin Government, of Botticelli's illustrations of Dante. I never knew before that such things existed, or that out-line book-illustration of that kind was so old. The original drawings had belonged to Lord Ashburnham's collection, and we in England allowed them to be bought at his sale by the German Government for 25,000*l.*—an unfortunate result of the law, which never allowed the authorities either of the Print room in the British Museum or of the National Gallery to keep any money in hand. These drawings are curious rather than very beautiful, and many of them are unfinished. In the illustrations of Hell and Purgatory, Botticelli glories in detail; but the 'Paradiso' is left almost entirely to the imagination. Dante and Beatrix surrounded by a circle, he himself appearing often blinded by the rays of light, the whole surrounded by more circles; this is all he seems to have dared attempt.

In this same house, I was able to turn from these lineal illustrations of the fifteenth century, with their delicate, though meagre, draughtsmanship, to the latest and richest of modern illustrations, the finest colour-printing that France has been able to produce—the Tissot Bible. It was not otherwise than satisfactory to realise that, however much art may have in some respects deteriorated, these illustrations, artistically and mechanically, surpassed those particular drawings of the Middle Ages, though the comparison is an unfair one. It would be immensely interesting to know what will be thought of this Tissot Bible in a hundred years.

January 6th.—I always order all the kitchen garden seeds during January. My method is this—the gardener marks Sutton's list, and then brings it to me to alter or add to it any out-of-the-way vegetable. It is most important to go through the catalogues, and order seeds early in this month. This enables you to get first choice, and you are then prepared for any kind of weather, and can sow early if desirable. Also it is easy to make up omissions later on, while still not too late. For all the flower seeds that are the result of careful cultivation—such as Sweet Peas, Mignonette, Asters, Salpiglossis, and so on—the great nurserymen cannot, of course, be surpassed in excellence. But for small people who grow a variety of flowers they are very expensive, as they only sell large packets of seeds, have few things out of the common, and hardly any interesting perennials at all. I said before and continue to say that, for all uncommon seeds, there is one man without any rival so far as I know, and that is Mr. Thompson, of Ipswich. His catalogue alone is most descriptive and instructive. It is the only catalogue I know arranged simply and alphabetically, with a column telling whether the plants are hardy or half-hardy, tender or perennial, greenhouse, stove, etc. It also is the only catalogue which gives the approximate height that the plant ought to reach when grown to perfection. But, of course, this varies immensely, as he says himself, with the character of the soil and situation in which they are cultivated, especially if grown in pots. With this list and a careful reference from the things named to the more detailed accounts in the 'English Flower Garden' or in Johnson's 'Gardener's Dictionary,' the requirements of all the plants that are grown in English gardens can be arrived at. The books will tell you better than the catalogue which are the things best worth growing from seed. But a certain amount of experience and natural intelligence can never be left out of this kind of study. Mr. Thompson is also exceedingly obliging about procuring the seeds of certain wild plants which may not be in his catalogue, but which are very desirable to grow in rather large gardens where there is room, such as *Tussilago fragrans* and *Iris fœtidissima*. What amateurs find most difficult in arranging herbaceous borders—even more difficult than colour itself—is to acquire sufficient knowledge of plants to judge of their strength and robustness, and, above all, of their relative height. Putting Mr. Robinson aside, the only book I know that is full of instruction, particularly in this respect, is the one I named before with great appreciation, 'The Botanic Garden,' by B. Maund.

Gardeners and amateurs who are really interested in the subject are beginning to discover that to grow many plants successfully, especially in light sandy or gravelly soils, you must grow them from seed in the same air and soil in which they are expected ultimately to succeed. For this you must have three or four small pieces of ground given up to the purpose—some dry, some wet, some sunny, some shady, and which will require nothing but weeding and thinning. Seed-sowing, like all other planting, requires a great deal of thought and consideration. Some grow up in a few days and, every seed having germinated, require much thinning, however much you may imagine you have sown thinly enough. Some seedlings will transplant perfectly, and not suffer at all in the move; others must be sown in place at all risks. One seed-bed is required that can be left entirely alone for (say) two years, except for just breaking with a handfork and weeding, as some seeds germinate very slowly. Where this is known to be the case, with large foreign seeds it is well before sowing to soak them for twenty-four hours in warm water and a little oil—or even to puncture the hard skin, as with Cannas. For instance, I shall certainly soak the seeds of the little *Zucche*, a kind of Vegetable Marrow that I brought from Florence last year, as it is a plant that in England has to do much growth in a short time, and it is desirable to get it well grown on in good time to plant out at the end of May. The exact time of putting out must depend on the season, and must be decidedly after that late May frost which comes every year without fail, and which in some years does gardens so much harm, though we all know how this may be guarded against by a little protection.

I think the multiplicity of nurserymen, small and great, and the gardeners' sympathy with the trade, have had much to do with the fact that the sowing of seeds, except in the case of annuals, has gone so out of fashion. No matter where I go, it is not one garden in a hundred that has these permanent small nurseries for seeds or even for cuttings, or a reserve garden as described before. And yet I am sure many of the best perennials cannot be grown at all in a light sandy soil unless they are grown from seed on the spot, and a great many more are only to be seen in real perfection if they are treated as annuals or biennials. The growing of seeds is a work which an amateur gardener can see to himself—or, indeed, herself—and I am sure gardening is the healthiest occupation in the world, as it keeps one much out of doors. Instead of lolling indoors in comfortable chairs, one moves about, and with the mind fully occupied all the time.

They sell at the Army and Navy Stores an admirable little lamp-stove (Rippingille's patent) for heating small greenhouses. This will keep the frost out of a small house, and is far easier to manage, for an amateur with a gardener who goes home at night, than the usual more expensive arrangement.

There are also small forcing-boxes to put inside a greenhouse or in a room for bringing on seeds in early spring.

Greenhouse Cyclamens are always useful, and should be sown early in the year (February or March) in heat. They should be grown on steadily under glass all the summer, and kept well watered, then they will flower all through the next winter. Mr. Thompson sells Cyclamen seed of the sweet old-fashioned kind, which is rather difficult to get from other nurserymen, who all go in for the giant sizes, and are now spoiling this lovely flower by doubling it. It is best to grow them every year from seed; but if the old plants are sunk out of doors and kept moist through the summer they flower very well. I have a large old plant this winter in a hanging basket, and its appearance is very satisfactory. Some gardeners dry the bulbs on a greenhouse shelf; that also answers.

I would advise everyone to try and get the old Prince of Orange Pelargonium. There is nothing like it, but it is not easy to get, as gardeners do not understand that it requires to be treated like an ordinary flowering Pelargonium, rather than like the hardier sweet-leaved kind. It wants well cutting back at the end of the summer, and then growing on in rather more heat than the ordinary sweet-leaved Pelargoniums. This little care and constantly striking young plants in the summer will prevent its dying out. Out of the fifteen to twenty kinds of sweet-leaved Geraniums which I possess, I consider it the most valuable and the best worth having.

Cuttings of the best French Laurestinus, struck in May and grown on to a small standard, make excellent filling-up plants for a greenhouse now, and if judiciously pruned back after flowering, and stood out in half shade all the summer, they are covered with large white flowers at this time of year. When they get too large for pots or tubs they can be planted out in shrubberies; if a little protected by other shrubs, they flower as freely as the common one, and the flower, even out of doors, is larger and whiter.

After marking Sutton's list I mark Thompson's, as some of the flower seeds are best sown early in January. The difficulty about sowing seeds early is that they want care and protection for a long time after sowing and before they can be put out. We are able to sow the hardier annuals here by the middle of March, especially Poppies, Corn-flowers, Love-in-the-Mist, Gypsophila, etc. I am sure that, in this light soil, the second sowing in April never does so well for early-flowering annuals. Autumn things, on the contrary, are best not sown till May, or they come on too early. I never sow Salpiglossis or Nemesia out of doors and in place till the beginning of May. In favourable weather Sweet Peas may be sown, like Green Peas, in a trench out of doors very early in the year.

One of my kind correspondents said she observed I was not so rich in blue flowers as was desirable, and named the following (I mean to get all those I do not already possess): *Commelina cœlestis, Anchusa italica, A. capensis, A. sempervirens, Parochetus communis, Pha-*

celia campanularia. **Commelina cœlestis** does very well
in a dry back garden of a London house. *Browallia
elata* is a most useful annual, and there is a good picture
of it in Curtis' 'Botanical Magazine.' *Catananche cœru-
lea* is an old border perennial, and I have it. *Linaria
reticulata* is a pretty, small annual; so is *L. aureo-pur-
purea* and *L. bipartita.* *Omphalodes luciliæ* I have tried
to get, but failed, and mean to grow it from seed.

January 8th.—I have read once or twice in the newspapers that butterflies have been seen from time to time
this mild winter, and now this morning I have caught
sight of one of these press butterflies, a beautiful
large yellow one, floating over the field as if it were
summer.

To-day we have been sowing, in shallow ridges in our
most favoured border, two or three kinds of early Green
Peas. How this kind of thing draws the seasons together! I dare say we have much that is disagreeable
before us; still, when these Peas are ready, it will be
leafy June, and spring will be over.

January 9th.—The Iberis that ornaments French cottage windows, and that I called '*Gibraltarica*' in the first
book, is not that at all, but *I. sempervirens.* I have one
in the greenhouse that was cut back all the summer and
potted up in October. It has been in flower three weeks
now, and will go on for a long time. In the spring I
shall cut it well back and plant it out in the reserve
garden. It grows easily from cuttings, and Mr. Thompson, of Ipswich, keeps the seed. It is, of course, not a
choice plant, but it is an attractive and useful one for
those who have not much convenience for forcing on
winter-flowering things in December and January. Like
many of the commoner plants, I have never seen it
grown as a window plant in England, though it would
do well.

January 12th.—The first little Aconites are out to-day! This is early. Going through January without cold is rather despairing. I find that even in this dry soil the Aconites do much better under evergreens and at the edges of shrubs than in the borders which are manured and mulched. The borders are too good for them, and they increase better if not disturbed. I mention this, as I was so stupidly long in finding it out myself. The more the uneducated gardening mind cares about a plant, the more it turns to manure and mulching; but in many cases it does more harm than good — notably with Aconites, Daffodils, Scillas, etc. What they all want is moisture and protection at the growing time. Drying ever so much in the summer does them good rather than harm, and they never do well in a bed that is hosed or watered to suit other things. With the Aconites, our first outdoor friends, come a few Snow-drops. They have never been planted here in any quantity, and have a tendency to diminish rather than increase: perhaps mice are especially fond of them. I am more than ever determined to plant a large quantity next year; enough, if possible, for me and the mice too. This little Snowdrop poem has such an echo of 'The Baby-seed Song'—a great favourite in my other book—that I copy it out of a recent 'Pall Mall Gazette':

SNOWDROP-TIME

'It's rather dark in the earth to-day,'
    Said one little bulb to his brother;
'But I thought that I felt a sunbeam ray —
We must strive and grow till we find the way!'
    And they nestled close to each other.
Then they struggled and toiled by day and by night
Till two little Snowdrops, in green and white,
Rose out of the darkness and into the light,
    And softly kissed one another.

In the greenhouse have now been put the first pots of the lovely double Prunus, with its delicate whiteness of driven snow; no plant forces better. I said this, or something like it, before. Never mind; with some plants it is worth while to repeat myself. In the country I do not now care to grow India-rubber plants or Aspidistras, except to give away. They only remind me of towns, and take a good deal of room.

I have in the greenhouse several pots of a white Oxalis—I do not know its distinguishing name—with a long growth of its lovely fresh green leaves, which can be picked and mixed with delicate greenhouse flowers, as they last well in water. It has a white flower in spring, and the whole plant is very like an improved version of our Wood Sorrel, *Oxalis acetosella*. The more I look at my beautiful old 'Jacquin' Oxalis book, the more I feel how much interesting greenhouse cultivation is to be had out of growing several of the best Oxalises. Almost all are natives of the Cape of Good Hope, which means easy greenhouse cultivation, and winter or early spring flowering. I shall certainly try to increase my stock, though one very seldom sees any of them catalogued.

Tradescantias, that I used to grow in pots for London, I find equally useful here. The common green one is all but hardy, and flourishes outside by the greenhouse wall. This, picked and put into a flat glass, grows without roots in the water in the most graceful manner for weeks together. A few bits of flower stuck in—such as, for instance, the *Sparmatia africana*, which continues to flower better if constantly picked down to where the fresh buds are forming—and you have a lovely winter flower arrangement at once: grace of form in the growing leaves, contrast in the starry white flowers, colour in the brilliant yellow shot with red stamens. 'Munstead' flower-glasses, as designed by Miss Jekyll (very cheap, and all kinds of useful shapes), are still to be got at Green & Nephews, Queen Victoria street, London, E.C.

The variegated gold-coloured Tradescantia and *T. discolor* are useful and pretty, and should never be allowed to die out or get shabby. They grow so easily at every joint that they are to greenhouses what certain weeds are to gardens.

Mr. Smee, in his 'My Garden,' recommends *Forenia asiatica* as a good stove-plant. I have not yet got it, but mean to do so.

January 13th.—A tall greenhouse grass called *Cyperus laxus* I find easy to grow. It is very pretty picked in winter and stuck into a bottle behind some short pieces of bright-coloured flowers. It looks refined, and if against or near white paint or a white wall its shadows are pretty, thrown by the lamp through the long evenings. A greenhouse evergreen called *Rhododendron jasminiflorum* is worth all trouble. It is in bloom now, sweet and graceful, and not at all common. All these half-hardy hard-wooded plants I find rather difficult to keep in health, but I am going to pay much more attention to their summer treatment. They want to go out for a month or two; but, to prevent their getting dry, they must be either sunk in cocoanut fibre, or surrounded by moss, or covered with straw. If sunk in the earth, worms are apt to get in. I think they are best replaced towards the middle of August into the cool house, where they can be watched. Sinking the small pot into a larger with some moss between is the best help of all. There is no fun in growing only the things everyone can grow, and nothing vexes me like seeing a plant which came quite healthy from a nurseryman, and in a year not only has not grown, but looks less well than when it first came.

The *Choisya ternata* cut back in May is flowering

splendidly. I wish I had room for eight pots of them instead of only two. There are several pots with *Epiphyllum truncatum* in full flower. The flowers are very pretty when seen close, and look well gathered and put into small glasses; but the colour is a little metallic and magentary. Most greenhouses have them, but few people manage to flower them well.

Ficus repens is a little, graceful, easily cultivated greenhouse climber, which hangs prettily in baskets or creeps along stones in a greenhouse border.

Every year we grow various Eucalyptuses from seed —some for putting out, and some for retaining in pots— especially the very sweet *Eucalyptus citriodora*, which is in the greenhouse now and is a great help, as it looks flourishing; while the sweet Verbenas will have their winter rest, as they are deciduous, whatever one does— at least, so far as I have been able to manage up to now. But I am not sure that autumn cuttings, grown on in heat, might not remain growing at any rate for part of the winter. Life is always rather unbearable to my luxury-loving nature without Lemon-scented Verbena, and I miss it so in the finger-bowls at dinner, partly because those few leaves supply what one wants without much trouble. But a little bunch of Violets carefully arranged, and one Sweet Geranium leaf, especially the Prince of Orange, make a combination that pleases everyone, and they are always at hand at this time of year.

January 14th.—In the January number of a charming little periodical called 'The Sun-children's Budget,' intended to teach young children botany easily and amusingly, there was an account and an illustration of a rare English wild flower, *Pæonia corallina*. The coloured print of it gives the idea that the red may not be of a very pretty hue; but this would not matter, as the chief charm of the plant is the seed-pod. This slightly resembles in shape the seed-pod of that other charming wild flower, the *Iris fœtidissima*, also much less grown than it should be in semi-wild, damp places, with its beautiful coral-red seed and strange-shaped, gaping capsule, so decorative in a vase in winter. The seed-covered branching growth of Montbretias mixes well with the twiggy flower-stems of the Statice (or Sea Lavender). *S. latifolia* is the best for winter decoration. To return to *Pæonia corallina*. I have been able to get some plants from Mr. Thompson. He says it is a greedy feeder, that the seeds germinate slowly, and that the plant grown from seed is long in coming to its flowering time. It flowers in May and June, and in the autumn the brown, downy pods open along their inner side and display the seeds. It seems to be a most rare wild flower, growing on an island in the Severn. Sir William Hooker says it is to be found at Blaize Castle, near Bristol. Gerarde mentions it, and says that he found it in a rabbit warren at Southfleet in Kent. But in my edition the editor, Thomas Johnson, is sceptical, and adds severely: 'I have been told that our author himself planted that Peionie there, and afterwards seemed to find it there by accident; and I do believe it was so, because none before or since have ever seen or heard of its growing wild in any part of this kingdom.' The origin of the botanical word 'Pæonia' is from one Pæon, the physician of the Olympian gods, who used the leaves for healing, notably in the case of Pluto when he was wounded by Hercules.

January 16th.—Last January someone sent me a cutting out of 'The Scotsman'; it was called 'Floral Notes from the West Coast of Ross-shire.' The writer begins by showing himself extremely proud, as is only natural, of flowering his *Lilium giganteum*, nine feet high and with nineteen perfect blooms on it. He also praises, what I recommend to everybody, the biennial *Michauxia campanuloides*. He says everyone used to exclaim on seeing it, 'Oh! what a charming white Lily!' The only way, as I stated before, is to grow it from seed. *Watsonia marginata*, according to him, is a lovely plant which in Scotland can be classed as a hardy perennial. It a good deal resembles the *Sparaxis pulcherrima;* in fact, much more so than it resembles the other Watsonias, which, he says, are shy bloomers. He speaks of another little favourite of mine, *Linaria repens alba*, and describes it — as I have always done — by saying it reminds him strongly of a Lily-of-the-Valley. It is very easy to grow, and well worth having. It is seldom found in flower lists, and he says he got his from Amos Perry, of Winchmore Hill, Herts. He mentions a pure white *Iris kœmpferi* in full bloom, and below it a mixed mass of those new Tigridias (*Aurea* and *Lilacina grandiflora*) and brilliant blue Commelina. This mixture was hard to beat. Also the trimming round the base of the Michauxia, already described, consisted of a variety of Platycodons or Japanese balloon-plants, in different shades of blue, mixed with white Swainsonia. All these last-named, with the exception of the Swainsonia, came from Roozen's. Then he says: 'I think I have told you all that I can remember as being particularly good in 1896.' I thought he gave such a creditable list that it might interest others who did not see 'The Scotsman' — good combinations being so difficult to get in herbaceous and bulb gardens. He goes on to say: 'The most striking flowers grown here in 1897 were a collection of Calochorti. I had tried them previously on a very small scale, with very small success; but, knowing them to be quite a specialty of the Messrs. Wallace of Colchester, I corresponded with them, and they sent me a collection of Calochortus bulbs which they thought would suit, and suit they certainly did, for they gave us the very greatest pleasure and were the envy and admiration of everyone else who saw them.' He put his Calochorti into a border with all the best mixed make-up soils he could find. Planting them in November, they flowered the following June. The only trouble from which they suffered in their infancy was slugs. But slices of Potato and Turnip acted as counter-attractions, and the plague was stayed. He says : 'There were about seven varieties of the Calochorti, and I don't think that in their own Californian forests they could have done much better. Anything more perfectly fascinating than a vaseful of Calochorti it would be impossible to grow in a British garden ; and they last such a long time in water.' He names, without describing them, two other favourites, the first of which I have, *Dracocephalum argumense* and *Vancouveria hexandra,* 'both gems in their way.' He goes on 'For those who are fond of rare Tulips, I must not forget to recommend *Tulipa Kaufmanniana,* which I bloomed for the first time last spring, and which is quite equal in its way to *Tulipa Greigi* and several other Tulip species which I have had from time to time from my aforementioned Dutch friends. After the Calochorti, perhaps a bed of Ixias from the same Haarlem firm was the next best thing my garden produced in 1897. I find Ixias the very easiest plants to grow, and this year they were all but as good as I have ever seen them in Italian gardens. So marvellously brilliant were they as to be quite dazzling to the eyes on a sunny day. They have only one fault ; viz., that, after flowering in June and ripening off, they begin their next year's growth in October, and so their young leaves are rather apt to get punished by the black frosts of spring. The fact is, they suffer from insomnia, and so by rights they should be lifted in July and made to sleep, in spite of themselves, on a dark shelf till planted again in March; but they do wonderfully well here even if left to take care of themselves.' It is quite a relief to hear this wonderfully successful amateur has difficulties with Lilies. All the same, the description he gives of his own seems to me very like success. He speaks of the White Martagon (a Lily I am now trying to grow) and *Lilium testaceum* as being great favourites with him. He was struck at Torridon by another plant which he says does so much better there than with him; viz., the scarlet and green *Alstrœmeria psittacina*. The clumps were almost as strong as sheaves of oats. 'I have a new variety,' he writes, 'of this parrot flower—a deep crimson one— which was very good here at the end of November.' But if I go on I shall end by quoting the whole of this most interesting gardening letter. I hope the anonymous writer, who dates from Inverewe Poolewe, where the climate must be such as to make any gardener jealous, will forgive this long quotation extracted by a sincere admirer, though unknown fellow-gardener.

Since writing the above I have been sent another letter from a January 'Scotsman' of this year (1899). The opening sentence is so original and suggestive for anyone who has a garden capable of being easily extended that I quote it as it stands: 'My garden having become quite filled up, I have for the last few years taken to enclosing bits of rough ground inside the policies (or the domain, as they would call it in Ireland), and have gone somewhat enthusiastically into shrubs. I have now three of these small enclosures, and each one seems more or less to suit some particular class of plant. My "Fantasy" is hard and gravelly, and suits the *Genista* and *Citisus* tribes very well. My "Riviera" is very sunny and with good soil, and in it I grow my rarest exotics; and "America," my latest

creation, being more peaty, damp, and shady, like a
wee bit of the backwoods, has been given over to the
so-called American plants—Rhododendrons, Azaleas,
Andromedas, Kalmias, Heaths, and, besides these,
Magnolias, Bamboos, and very many other things; so
many, indeed, that besides the sixty Azaleas which fill
a bed in the centre, there are a hundred and seventy
kinds of rare plants in it, gathered from most of the
Temperate portions of our globe; and, with one or
two exceptions, I must say they appear very promis-
ing, considering my little "America" was only colonized
in April last.' He then details his triumphs: 'My
greatest this summer was my flowering abundantly the
rare and beautiful Chilian shrub, the *Crinodendron
hookeri*. I got it from Mr. Smith, at Newry, and
planted it in my "Riviera" in the spring of 1897; it
stood last winter well, and early in June it blossomed
freely. We have but few shrubs with crimson flowers,
the blooms of so many of them being either white or
yellow. But the Crinodendron is a grand exception.
Its nearest neighbours on each side of it consist of
plants of the *Abutilon vitifolium* and *Carpenteria californica*, both of which stood the winter; and the
former, from having come on so well, will be bound
to flower next season. It has a great name now, especially in Ireland, for hardiness and for its beautiful
blossoms. I possess in my "Riviera" a number of
things, of which I know little or nothing, with queer
names, such as Coprosmas, Callistemons, Aristotelias,
Pittosporums, Raphiolepis, Agalmas, Styrax, Indigof-
eras, etc.; and, in spite of their names, I must say
they look happy.'

As from the other letter, I only extract what seems to
me most interesting: 'I must now tell the contents
of my Azalea bed, already referred to, all of which

from M. Louis van Houtte, of Ghent. There are sixty plants, in sixty different varieties or species. There are single and double hardy Ghent Azaleas, and single *Azalea mollis*, and double hybrids of Mollis. They occupy the bed, with the exception of a clump of *Phyllostachys viridi glaucescens* and *Phyllostachys mitis* (Bamboos) in the centre, and I can truly say there was not a bad plant or a bad variety among the lot, and everyone of them was full on arriving. If anyone wants a brilliant edging to a Rhododendron bed, let me commend to them Azaleas *Fritz Quihou* and *Gloria Mundi;* the former is of an extraordinarily dazzling crimson. Many people are of the opinion that the flowering season of Azaleas is short and soon over, but this would not happen if they got a good selection from M. van Houtte. I see from my diary that the first Azaleas expanded with me on May 18th, and they did not finish till July 24th, so that they lasted more than nine weeks. About the last to open were the pink and the crimson doubles, *Bijou de Gendbruggen* and *Louis Aimé van Houtte*, and the lovely species *Sinensis flore alba* only began to expand on July 16th. For those who like species, Azaleas *Occidentalis and Arborescens* are both very interesting. . . .

'I have a great love of Heaths, but have not got many of them. After considerable trouble, I got some good plants of *Erica arborea* from Newry, which we had so much admired on the hillsides of Corsica. They seem to do very well here, and two of them bloomed this summer; but whether they will grow into trees in my "Riviera," as they do on the shores of the Mediterranean, I cannot yet tell. *Erica australis, Erica mediterranea*, and the Cornish Heath (*E. vagans*) are, like the Hydrangeas, delightful in late autumn, and so is the white Irish *Dabœcia polifolia*, of which we can hardly have too much. . . . . .

'I have, I think, merely alluded to the Genistas, and most people know, besides the common yellow, the White Portugal and the Yellow Spanish so-called Broom, which is, however, not really a Genista, but a Spartium, though it looks so like a Broom, and is very showy late in the season, when the common Broom is over. The low-growing real *Genista hispanica* is a very useful little plant. Those who have not got the Broom with the crimson lip (*G. andreana*), nor the cream-coloured hybrid (*G. præcox*), should not fail to get them both, as they are an immense acquisition to our hardy flowering shrubs.

'To-day I have been reminded of a nice plant of *Eugenia ugni*, a kind of Myrtle which has stood out some years against the terrace wall of my garden, and which bloomed and ripened its fruit so well that I have lately sent a sample of its fragrant berries to a friend in Switzerland. The scent and flavour remind one of both Strawberries and Pineapple, with a slight mixture of Bog Myrtle.' I hope no one will confound this description of a Scotch garden with what I am able to do in dry Surrey.'

January 20th.—It is a constant disappointment to me that I cannot get the *Tussilago fragrans*, called Winter Heliotrope, with its delicious fragrant spikes of flowers, to bloom here. It is quite hardy, and a weed supposed to grow anywhere, but I never get anything except a few leaves. This, of course, is in consequence of the dryness, the poorness of the soil, and the want of shade, as it has such a weedy growth I cannot put it into any good border. It is a distinct loss, not getting these flowers in midwinter. I should recommend everyone who has a damp corner to try and grow them. They are not showy, but when picked their delicious scent will pervade a whole room.

Rue, which is sometimes grown in kitchen gardens, though I think seldom used now in cookery, is hardly ever grown in shrubberies, where it makes in winter a charming feature. I find few people know that the French name for the plant is exactly the same as in English. Some people think the strong odour disagreeable, but I myself think it delicious. It is very useful to pick for winter bouquets, and the beautiful gray-blue of its foliage contrasts well with ordinary evergreens. If picked hard, that is as good as cutting it back, and only promotes its growth. It is very easy to grow— either from cuttings, divisions of the tufts, or seeds. Dryness, though making it look rather poor in summer, does it no harm for the next winter. Another plant that does admirably here in the light soil is Santolina (Lavender Cotton), and should always be grown for its pretty hoary foliage. It mixes well with some flowers, and is one of those plants that surprises one by its absence from any garden.

The lower part of the stage in my larger greenhouse —I do not mean my little show one near the drawing-room—has been a veritable widow's cruse for me this winter. We have constantly had Mushrooms from our bed, covered with its sheet of corrugated iron, that I mentioned before.

Lately we have had lots of Sutton's winter salad, Tarragon, Chives, etc., Cress—I do not like Mustard— Rhubarb, and Sea-kale. The Watercress in boxes, described before, has done admirably in the frame. My gardener is getting extremely clever at forcing things in this way through the winter. Early in this month, lunching with a neighbour, we had an excellent dish— the best I have ever seen—of forced green Asparagus. I think next year I must try and grow this too.

In my opinion, Leeks are far too little used in general

by English people. Most English cooks only use them as a flavouring for soup or boiled beef. They are really excellent stewed, and very good raw, cut up with beetroot, especially if not the large, coarse kind recommended in most of the English catalogues. The Long Winter Leek (*Poireau long d'Hiver de Paris*) is quite distinct from all other kinds. It is very delicate, quite small, withstands the winter well, and is the only kind that produces those fine, very long, slender Leeks which are seen in bundles early in the year in the Central Market at Paris. In France, gardeners help nature a little by earthing up the plants while they are growing. It can be chopped up fine with other salad herbs when Chive tops are not to be got unless they are forced. The wild Leek (the *Allium ampeloprasum*) still grows, I believe, in parts of Wales, and is, as to form and tint, beautiful and decorative. It is, of course, well known as the Welsh emblem.

January 27th.—I have on my flower table a shrubby Begonia, in a pot, with small, pointed, spotty leaves and hanging white flowers. They are easily reared from seed, and I do think they grow so beautifully and can be pruned into such lovely shapes! They are far more beautiful than those great, flat, floppy, opulent, tuberous-rooted ones that flower in the summer. The parent of my plant (mossy green leaves, spotted silvery white) must have been called *B. alba picta*.

The white Arums, which were laid on their side all the summer in the pots and well dried, are handsomer plants, and throwing up more flowers than I have ever had before when they were planted out in summer.

In this dry, frosty weather we thin and prune out the shrubberies. Every plant is given a fair chance or else cut down. Taking all suckers from the Lilacs improves them immensely. How seldom it is done!

January 28th.—There is nothing like a date and a detailed account of the weather for accentuating a garden fact. We have had lately several days of frost, and we had to-day for luncheon so excellent a green vegetable that both gardener and cook had immediately to be interrogated as to details. The gardener said it was grown from Sutton's hardy-sprouting Kale called 'Thousand-headed,' and I see in a note to the catalogue that 'the Borecoles thrive better in poor soil than most vegetables.' This naturally accounts for their being good-tasting here. In Vilmorin's list, they are described as a cattle-feeding plant of large size, and bearing frost extremely well. The cook informed me that she had cut the green of the leaf carefully off the stalk, and then cooked it exactly like Spinach. I give my cook the credit for cutting it off the stalk, as I had never suggested it. The result was most satisfactory.

RECEIPTS

An excellent way to improve northern or frozen game, of which a great deal is now sold, is to lay the birds in a bath of milk for twenty-four hours, changing the milk twice. They are then roasted in the ordinary way, and are excellent.

A good way of cooking potatoes in winter is to steam them without their skins. Then melt some very good fresh butter in a small iron saucepan, and to this add a good lot of onions shredded very fine, and fry till a good mahogany brown, not black. Put the potatoes in a very hot fireproof dish, and pour the hot butter and onions over them just before serving.

Parsnips.— Everybody grows parsnips, so far as I can make out, and hardly anyone ever eats them ; except now and then with boiled pork and with salt cod on

Good Friday. They are very good in England, as our mild winters enable us to leave them in the ground, which makes them much better than if they had been stored in sand or ashes. Here is a receipt for anyone who does not dislike parsnips and does like curry : Boil some fine parsnips whole, without cutting them, wash and brush them, and put into just enough boiling water to cover them. Simmer till tender and till the water is nearly evaporated—about one hour and a half. Tear the parsnips into fine shreds with two forks. Sprinkle with cloves and a little dusted sugar. Have prepared apart a curry sauce. (See p. 252, '*Pot-Pourri*'.) Pour this over the parsnips, warm up together, and serve with boiled Patna rice in a dish apart.

Mutton Cutlets à la Russe.—Braise the cutlets. The sauce is made as follows : One stick of horseradish (scraped), four shallots, one bay-leaf, a little thyme, a little raw ham (chopped), a little nutmeg, pepper and salt, one dessertspoonful of sugar, a tablespoonful of vinegar, the same quantity of sherry, and one ounce of butter. Simmer it over a slow fire for twenty minutes, then add a little white sauce, the yolks of two eggs, and a little cream. Stir over the fire until it begins to simmer ; then pass it through a hair-sieve and spread on one side of the cutlets. Strew on a little Parmesan cheese, and brown the cutlets in the oven. Dish them up with a little good gravy.

Open Apple Tart.—For this it is necessary to have a small, round, iron plate, flat, with a very narrow rim, as used abroad. In the country you can have them made, and in London you can buy them at the good shops. They must not be made of tin. Line this with a puff-paste, and have a deep rim of paste all round. Prepare a compote of good, rich apple, reduced till dry enough to mix in a small quantity of fresh butter. If at all lumpy, the apple must first be passed through a sieve.   Pour this on to the pastry, then peel and cut a quince into very thin, neat slices.   Lay these on the apple in circles till you nearly reach the middle.   Bake the *purée* in the oven till the pastry is cooked without burning.   Serve very hot, or quite cold.

Last year, in February, I wrote a little article on mistresses and servants in the 'Cornhill Magazine.' It was called forth by the report of a case in the Divisional Court which seemed interesting at the time. The point at issue was whether a servant was entitled to give notice at any time within the first fortnight of. her service, so as to enable her to leave at the end of the first month. The judgment did not settle the law of the case. My friends complained that I more or less put forth the difficulties of the present day with regard to mistresses and servants — especially the difficulty of the insufficient supply of servants — but that I suggested nothing new by way of a solution. As the question is one of very general interest, I think I will quote some part of the article, adding a few practical suggestions which have occurred to me since.

Servants may, and often do, get into situations which turn out to be entirely different from what they have been led to expect. It may be even that they find themselves in a 'bad' house; or with a drunken mistress; or, what is still more common with a young girl, under a drunken cook, whom the mistress still believes in; or under a foreign man-cook whose manners are disagreeable to her, but who gets very angry at her insisting on leaving when he wants to keep her. He then abuses her to the mistress, who is angry and put out at her wishing to go, and refuses to give her a character or pass on the one she received with her. All these, and many similar cases, are very hard on servants, who, as a rule, cannot afford to bring the case before the county court judge, and who would probably have little to adduce as proof, even if they could ask for help and protection. We all suffer from the well-known faults of servants, but we are apt often to forget how much there is to be said on the other side. With us, it is a case more or less of expense and inconvenience; with them, it is their actual livelihood.

I shall, I believe, be accused of seeing the question too much from the servants' point of view. But have we not all from our youth up heard of the selfishness, the ingratitude, the wastefulness, the idleness of servants? And each generation pronounces them to be worse than they ever were before. I can remember the time when servants were first expected to be clean, but baths were not provided; and to use the bathroom, which was done on the sly, was thought as great an impertinence as if they had asked for dessert every day after dinner.

Customs change, but the big fact always remains the same — that the relation between master and servant is, and must always be, one of self-interest. Within limits, each tries to get the best of the bargain. One pays to command; the other receives to obey. The most self-denying Christian principles are of no avail. Carried to a logical conclusion, these principles would lead to the Christian mistress doing the work and the idle maid going to bed; or, the humble Christian servant declaring that her work was a pleasure, and that she could not possibly take her wages. No, we are — on both sides — just as selfish as we dare be. And this self-interested bargain between masters and servants can only be settled on each individual case. The merits on each side must, according to one of the oldest of symbols, be placed in the scales, and the noble, majestic, upright figure of Justice must hold out her arm and adjust the balance.

We never get beyond this, and it is the only escape from the greatest of tyrannies — the power, either by gold or by force, of one human being over another. This power it will ever be the business of civilisation to rule and to diminish. This, in our day, is the business, first, of the master of a house; or, when he has the chance, of the county court judge.

The temptation to give false or partially false characters is a very great one to young and kind-hearted people. As in so many other cases, the public themselves are responsible for this — so many people like being deceived, and look upon truth as naked and barbaric. If a mistress gives an honest character, not all praise, in nine cases out of ten the servant fails to get the place. This state of things is unreasonable and ridiculous; and if those about to engage a servant would ask for the chief failing of the person they are going to admit into their families, they would be better able to judge if the servant were likely to suit them or not. I remember, many years ago, being asked if I knew of a young nurse who was to have every good quality under the sun. She was to be strong, she was to ask for no holidays, she was never to leave the children to associate with the other servants, her temper was to be perfect, and so on. I wrote back that such a combination of good qualities as was expected for twenty pounds a year I had never yet met with in any young mother. A corresponding story is of a lady who wrote to a French friend for a holiday tutor. He also was to be a lump of perfection. The Frenchwoman wrote back: 'Je ferai tout mon possible, mais si je trouve ton homme je l'épouse.'

A wit of fifty years ago used to say: 'I marry my wife for her money, I engage my footmen for their looks, as those are the only two things that can possibly be known beforehand.' As is common enough with a cynical remark, there is a good deal of truth in this.

Now we come to what I consider to be one of the greatest changes that has occurred of late years ; viz., the extreme facility for women getting employment without any character at all; that is to say, without any prying into the private conduct or personal characteristics of any individual. For example, all shops and stores, laundries and many other houses of business, engage their employés from their general appearance and the account they give of themselves. If they do not do their work, if they are insubordinate or unpunctual, they are dismissed on Saturday night — sometimes even without the usual week's notice and without any reason being assigned. This often appears a great hardship, but my point is that one of the chief objections to domestic service is that, from the very start, some sort of recommendation is required from someone who is supposed to be in a responsible position. I do not say this is not necessary, but I do think the custom might be considerably relaxed, with advantage to everybody. The usual characters given are often clever skating on very thin ice, and convey little real knowledge of the servant's faults or merits. Servants, like other people, have undoubtedly the defects of their virtues, and the wise way is to make up our minds what we are prepared to give up. If we go in for youth and good looks, we can scarcely hope for the qualities we may expect to find in age and ugliness. In considering the merits of a situation, the more educated mind should not fail to look at it from the point of view of the servant.

After leaving school, village as well as town girls, in a great number of cases, are kept at home for a few years by their mothers. This gives them a love of freedom and amusement which singularly unfits them for the discipline of domestic service. It might be a possible bridging of the difficulty if it became usual for each family, according to its position, to keep fewer permanent servants and give, as a matter of course, more outside help, each of a specialised kind, to be got from girls who have lately left school, and whose mothers would probably not at all object to their earning a little money and doing outside work — let us say, up to two o'clock. A girl who was a good needlewoman at school might be used once a week to repair linen, or to do any other casual mending. I heard lately of a young housekeeper, tired of boys who did their work badly, having obtained excellent assistance from a schoolgirl of sixteen, whom she trained to clean boots, knives, and lamps every morning. A beginning of this kind might, I think, greatly increase the much-needed supply, and, above all, create a means of direct communication between the poor and rich, which is still one of the great wants of the day, in spite of all the charitable ladies. Some people would suggest that it might bring infection into the house; but I really think that the risk is no greater than with everything else in London. There is always a proportion of risk — in the street, the 'Underground,' the omnibus, the Zoölogical Gardens, the bread, the meat, and, above all, the milk.

A proof of the exceeding difficulty that many have in getting employment is to be seen in the large numbers that exist of those terrible harpies called Registry Offices, the very maintenance of which depends on robbing the poor girls who seek employment just at the moment they can least afford it. I could quote story on story of how six, seven, or eight shillings are taken from a country girl without the smallest return to herself ; indeed, in some cases they simply retain any written references which she may have given into their charge at their request. I believe an effort is being made to meet this difficulty by an association called 'The Guild of Registries,' and it certainly appears to be sadly wanted.

A new agency has been lately started on rather different lines in Derby street, Mayfair, and conducted by three house-stewards, who have lived many years at the head of large households. Their idea is that they are perhaps better judges of the kind of servants applying for situations than those with less experience can be. Also they mean to get introductions to clergymen and the heads of schools all over the country, so as to help girls from villages who wish to go into service. The experiment seems to me an interesting one.

Things must still be very wrong when the proportion of people who keep servants is so very small, and that of the poor population so very large, and yet we continually meet with the complaint that servants, especially under-servants, are so difficult to find.

As we get older, we, most of us, step into shoes we should have vowed in our youth we never would put on, and each one in his generation sees some progress in civilisation which has ruined servants, and feels that good servants are far more rare and difficult to find than they were twenty, thirty, or (say) fifty years ago. Good servants—by which I mean unselfish, devoted human beings — are never likely to be a great glut in the market. But then are extra good, judicious, sensible masters and mistresses so very common?

Of all the deadly-dull subjects of conversation among women, the deadliest is the abuse of servants; and few seem to realise that it is practically self-condemnation, as, in the long run, bad servants mean bad mistresses, or, at any rate, mistresses with unsympathetic natures and without the talent to rule firmly but not tyrannically.

When we think of servants' homes and training, and how their youth has been passed, especially in large towns, and how they are suddenly brought to face unaccustomed luxury and high feeding, and to live an exciting life of society among themselves, the ceaseless wonder to me always is that servants are as good as they are, and keep as 'straight' as they do, more especially as they are very often set a bad example by the people they serve. In large households where there are many — and consequently idle — menservants, keeping up a high standard of morality is hopeless, or at least very difficult. The constant absence from home so common to-day is one of the great causes of unsatisfactory establishments.

Under-servants in moderate-sized houses are the ones that excite my pity. It is always 'the girl' who is to do this and that, the half-up and half-down drudge who has two or three people who think they have an absolute right over her; or 'the boy' who is to have all work and no play. It is on the same principle, I suppose, as the 'fag' at school. 'I had to do it once, so now I will make someone else do the same.' Petty love of power and cruelty is so inherent in human nature! As was recounted some time ago in the 'Spectator,' 'I'll learn you to be a toad!'—the remark of a small urchin as, stone in hand, he eyed the offending reptile.

M

One of the many causes of disappointment about servants is, that those people who treat them with kindness and consideration expect in return more gratitude than the circumstances admit.

I remember a friend who had been good to a little Swiss nurserymaid, and reproached her for leaving her to go to another situation with slightly higher wages. The girl put out her hands, shrugged her little shoulders, and said : 'Mon Dieu ! madame, que voulez-vous ? J'ai quitté ma mère pour cela !' How true it was ! And not only her mother, but her green Swiss valley, with the beautiful sunlit mountains all round — to live in London, with its smoke and its darkness ! My friend was convinced, and said no more.

Servants stick very closely to what they consider their own duty, but I have never found servants object to anything if told of it beforehand. They do not like unexpected duties sprung upon them, and this is merely a safe rule for their own protection. But the mistress of a house must reserve to herself the right to ask a servant to do anything, and if the refusal is at all impertinent, there is nothing for it but to part. There is reason, too, for this irritating attitude of servants declaring they will not do work they have not been engaged to do. The common-sense of the matter protects them from each other, as one masterful, selfish servant would get all her work done for her by another (as boys get their lessons done at school), if public opinion amongst themselves were not strongly against such a shuffling of duties.

Servants almost always behave admirably when their common humanity is affected. At times of sorrow or joy, births and deaths, or any sudden change and loss of fortune, they are shaken out of their attitude of habitual selfishness. But, as time goes on, they resent the position being different from what they undertook when engaged, and think it better to make a change.

One of the things that seems a remnant of other days, and strikes servants themselves as being particularly tyrannical, is being expected to attend family prayers, whether they like it or not, and that, too, in the midst of their morning work. But the attitude of mind and the ways and customs of servants are as incomprehensible to us as are those of the gipsies; and to worry and hurry people who have not our views, whose laws are not ours, whose morality is not ours, whose customs are not ours, is a most useless tyranny, be it directed against gipsies or against servants. These manners and customs have grown up and are repeated by servants over and over again, in a way that they themselves often do not understand. One of their invariable rules, which is often commented on, is that servants — almost without exception — refuse to eat game. It is generally supposed that this is because game does not cost their masters and mistresses actual money. This is so foolish a reason I cannot believe it to have been the origin of the objection. I feel it is far more likely that in the days before railways, when game travelled slowly, it was the fashion for everybody to eat high game; but when it got past sending to table — unbought luxury though it was — the thrifty housekeeper suggested to the cook that the servants might have it. They had far better opportunity than the master upstairs of judging what state it was in, and I confess I am not surprised that, as a body, they declined to make their dinner off it. And so that mysterious thing—a custom—grew up for servants not to eat game.

Servants, even the best and most devoted, will not 'tell of each other.' It is useless to expect it: just as useless as a master expecting boys to tell tales at a public school. And, on the whole, this is a good rule even for ourselves. If a system of tale-bearing could be established, it would make life unbearable for all of us.

An eternal complaint against servants is about early rising. I believe a number of people have no doubt that fifty or sixty years ago (which is, I fancy, the time when rather young people think old-fashioned servants lived) they all got up early. We are certainly not the worst among the nations, but I do think that late rising amounts almost to a national fault. These things are greatly the result of climate; but to insist on maids getting up in the dark, when there is very little to do, and to give the order that the kitchen fire is to be lit at 6.30, when the family do not breakfast till nine or half-past, seems to me almost tyrannical, though we have a perfect right to expect that the water should be hot and the breakfast ready at whatever time we choose to order it. For two months in the winter I always postpone the breakfast hour from eight to half-past, and I always use — for health reasons — cold water all the year round; but I never have the slightest difficulty in getting breakfast punctually at eight, though I feel quite sure of one thing, that if I did not get up early no one else would. It seems a relief to some people's consciences to insist on the early rising of others, when they lie in bed late themselves. Servants are the first to remember that they can go to bed early, when very often their masters and mistresses cannot. I think all of us shorten our living hours by taking more sleep than is at all necessary. As an example of the strength of some men, Mr. Max Müller mentions that the great Baron Humboldt complained that as he got old he wanted more sleep — 'four hours at least. When I was young,' he continued, 'two hours of sleep was enough for me.' Mr.

Max Müller ventured to express his doubts, apologising for differing from him on any physiological fact. 'It is quite a mistake,' said Humboldt, 'though it is a very widely spread one, to think that we want seven or eight hours' sleep. When I was your age I simply lay down on the sofa, turned down my lamp, and after two hours' sleep was as fresh as ever.'

Of all servants that I have known in my life, the ones I have admired and respected most are the children's nurses. The love and devotion they give to children not their own is extraordinary. The highest life which George Eliot could imagine for 'Romola,' after the disappointment and failure of her own life, was to attend and minister to the children of others. Nurses will often refuse to leave children, even when it is for their interest to do so, knowing all the same, quite well, the time will come when the children will leave them, as an animal leaves its mother when it no longer wants her. I asked a nurse of this type once, when she was getting old, why she had never married. 'O' m'um,' she said, 'can't you guess? I had passed my life in the nursery amongst ladies and gentlemen ; my own class who wished to marry me were distasteful to me, and I was too proud for anything else.' This last half-sentence, with its faint allusion to having once loved someone above her, touched me supremely. Servants must so often pass through a temptation of the kind — pride in those they love being such a great stimulus to the affection and constancy of women. I think it is very desirable that children should early come downstairs for their meals, and the nurse go to hers with the other servants. She does not very often like this; but it is for her good, and much more for her own happiness, that she should not lose touch with her class and isolate herself on a slightly raised position, which, from the very nature of the circumstances, can only lead to unhappiness.

Nothing is of more importance than to help servants with their money affairs. They are very ignorant and very improvident, though often very generous. The extravagant servant will listen to no reason about putting by for the 'rainy day,' and the best among themselves constantly help to support some of their own relations. If they are willing and the mistress is tactful, talking over their affairs is often of great use, especially in giving them an idea what to do with their savings, if they have any; as, like other classes, they constantly lose their money in unfortunate investments offering high interest, and sometimes are even attracted to do this by 'big' names on the prospectus, often those of connections of their employers, which they look upon as a guarantee for security.

Whenever depression comes upon me from associating with those who are complaining about the ways and fashions of the time they live in and the ruin of their own generation, whether in the classes above or those below them, I fly to some of the books of the eighteenth century, and never fail to get the consolation I require. What has received the greatest abuse in my time is the Board School education and the destruction it has wrought amongst those who become domestic servants. I myself totally disbelieve this. First of all, those who go into the higher schools are very few in number, and nothing is so important in a free country as that all should have the power to rise, if their talents fit them for it. Here is a sentence of Oliver Goldsmith's, in one of his essays. In his time it was a higher class that met with his disapproval, but it reminds me of remarks that I am constantly hearing now about those who used to be called 'the uneducated':

'Amidst the frivolous pursuits and pernicious dissipations of the present age, a respect for the qualities of the understanding still prevails to such a degree that almost every individual pretends to have a taste for the Belles-Lettres. The spruce 'prentice sets up for a critic, and the puny beau piques himself on being a connoisseur. Without assigning causes for this universal presumption, we shall proceed to observe that if it was attended with no other inconvenience than that of exposing the pretender to the ridicule of those few who can sift his pretensions, it might be unnecessary to undeceive the public, or to endeavour at the reformation of innocent folly productive of no evil to the commonwealth.'

Spending youth in school may prevent a young servant from knowing her duties as a servant so well as if she had been brought up at home; but, on the other hand, being moderately well educated makes it far easier to learn, and I maintain that, with a very little practical teaching, the modern schoolgirl makes an excellent servant. But no one can have a well-ordered house on a small scale who is constantly leaving home or constantly changing servants. An indifferent servant who knows your ways is better than the good servant who is quite fresh to the work in your house. Leaving home often means a badly kept house, of that I am sure, unless many members of the family remain at home and give plenty of employment to everybody. Then, perhaps, the real mistress of the house may be very little missed.

The fulness of life, the selfishness of life, often prompt the modern housewife to throw up the sponge, to rush away to the idleness of the hotel or the lodging; but it is a cowardly wish — a wish, except in real bad health, to be ashamed of. Our troubles and sorrows, be

they real or imaginary, go with us, and our only usefulness is at home.   Here is a poem written by one of that
brave trio, the Brontë sisters — Ellis Bell (Emily Brontë)
— which, if not so subtle as Lionel Tennyson's 'Sympathy,' has a strong ring about it — that hand-shake in
life's way which helps so many:

SYMPATHY

There should be no despair for you
  While nightly stars are burning,
While evening pours its silent dew,
  And sunshine gilds the morning.

There should be no despair, though tears
  May flow down like a river.
Are not the best beloved of years
  Around your heart for ever?

They weep, you weep; it must be so:
  Winds sigh as you are sighing,
And winter sheds its grief in snow
  Where autumn leaves are lying.

Yet these revive, and from their fate
  Your fate cannot be parted.
Then journey on, if not elate,
  Still *never* broken-hearted!

I am told by young married women that so very
much attention has been given to cooking of late that
most girls of the leisured classes now know something
about it, or, at any rate, turn to books or go to some
school of cookery to learn; but that they are quite ignorant
about training servants in other work, especially inexperienced girls who have done more schooling than
cleaning in their childhood, and who think anyone can
be a housemaid.   There is excellent instruction on many
points in that book I named before, 'How to be Happy

though Married.' It dwells, however, rather on management of husband and house than actually on teaching
the servants their duties. A really well-housemaided
room requires but very rarely that terrible turning-out
— when everything is upside down for a day, and things
are mislaid, and some things are never found again —
which is the terror of all masters and mistresses. Two
things are essential in a well-kept house, and, unfortunately they war against each other; one is continually
having plenty of open windows, and the other is a prevention of any accumulation of dust. This can only be
fought by continual wiping and dusting. When the
mistress of a house is looking through cupboards and
larders, and insisting that they should be well aired, the
servant's view is that then 'so much dust gets in.' And
yet, by a 'cussedness' peculiar to themselves, they constantly leave ice-safes open, which of course — to act
properly — should be kept tightly closed, and never
opened at all except for the minute when things are
taken out or put in. When the ice is melted, they
should always be carefully cleaned out. The following
is, I consider, a good way of keeping things from dust
in a larder without shutting the windows: Instead of
the usual perforated tin covers, which get rusty and
shabby and cannot be cleaned, I have neat covers of all
sizes (made at home) of rather thick zinc wire, and then
I cover these with clean butter-muslin, which can be
renewed or washed directly it gets dirty. They should
have a twisted zinc wire handle at the top, to lift the
cover on and off quite easily. The principle is the
same as the outdoor covers for keeping off spring frost
on young plants, recommended in my former book.

The real fault of all the houses I go into to-day, my
own included, though less so than some, is that they are
far two full. Things are sure to accumulate. Avoid

rubbish, frills and valances, draperies and bows, and all
the terrible devices of the modern upholsterer. They
all mean dust and dirt in a very short time, especially in
London, and a labour to keep clean — which, in fact, no
one carries out, and which is only very temporarily
rectified by the spring cleaning once a year. I have a
French domestic book which I think fascinating and
instructive, just because it is French, and much less
showy and more primitive than English books of the
same kind. It is in two volumes, is called 'Maison
Rustique des Dames,' and is by Madame Millet Robinet.
It has had an immense sale in France, and all the little
details of household life seem more dignified and less
tiresome when read in excellent French.

I will translate one receipt for the destruction of flies
that seems to me good, and I wish I had known of it
when travelling abroad in hot weather and staying in
small hotels : 'Half fill a tumbler with soapy water.
Cut a slice of bread half an inch thick ; cover the under
side with honey, sugar, jam — anything that attracts
flies. Cut a small hole in the middle, larger at the top
than the bottom ; fix the piece of bread in the top of the
tumbler. The flies crawl in after the sweet jam, and
are quietly suffocated.' The book abounds in useful
hints of all kinds.

In my youth, tea-leaves were always used for sweeping carpets. Then came the idea that they stained and
injured the colour of light carpets. This is to be rectified by rinsing the tea-leaves well in cold water and
wringing them out before they are used. There is no
magic in the tea — it is the damp substance of the leaves
that gathers the dust. There is an excellent thing now
sold, called 'carpet soap,' which really revives the
colour of dirty rugs and carpets. To sweep without
using something moist merely diffuses dirt. Covering a

broom with a wet cloth is the best way of cleaning under beds, wardrobes, etc.— anything to prevent the dust flying.

If every room is taken in turn and extra cleaned once a week, the necessity for the complete 'turning-out' is obviated. Most people will say, 'Everyone knows that'; and yet it is astonishing how one has to remember to tell the same things, over and over again, to each fresh young servant that comes. And one often lives a long life without knowing most commonplace things oneself. I never knew till the other day that black-leading fire-brick destroyed all its qualities for radiating heat and made it like iron. It ought never to have been black-leaded at all.

Tin jugs are excellent for hot water, but they must be cleaned inside with sand-paper, or they rust and spoil.

It is almost despairing how even excellent and ex-perienced servants forget that no crockery can or will stand boiling water being poured into it suddenly, espe-cially in cold weather; the quick expansion makes all glass and china fly. But the same thing goes on, over and over again, in every household, from expensive dishes or dairy-pans to servants' jugs and tumblers, and partly one is oneself to blame for not having explained the simple fact to each new girl who comes.

In the chapter on Furnishing, in my first book, I recommended that young people should go to sales instead of buying rubbish at wholesale furniture ware-houses. Commenting on this, the excellent and amusing writer of 'Pages from a Private Diary' reproves me and says: 'Why drive good taste into a mere fashion, and so quadruple the price of pretty things for those who can appreciate them?' This was not my intention, though I admit it may be a result of my advice. But I only wish someone had given me the hint when I was young. However, if it does improve taste, and if it does raise the price of pretty things, surely one's sympathies in such matters are rather with those who have to sell the things they value than with those who can afford to buy them. My one object, both in this book and the last, is to give everyone—so far as I can—anything I know or have learnt in a long life. And in writing the first book, under the impression that it would be an absolute failure, I used to console myself by saying: 'Well, if it helps ten people just a little, that makes it worth while.'

Old Sir Thomas Browne, in his quaint and self-opinionative way, puts pretty strongly what I feel: 'It is an honorable object to see the reasons of other men wear our Liveries, and their borrowed understandings do homage to the bounty of ours; it is the cheapest way of beneficence, and, like the natural charity of the Sun, illuminates another without obscuring itself. To be reserved and caitiff in this part of goodness is the sordidest piece of covetousness, and more contemptible than pecuniary Avarice.'

February 2nd.—I have been reading lately two fascinating books on natural history by George D. Leslie, the painter—one is called 'Letters to Marco' and the other 'Riverside Letters'—descriptions of his own home on the river. The little illustrations have a great deal of artistic individuality, and are to me, though slight, very superior to the ordinary photographic reproductions. His description of cultivating the difficult 'Iris Susiana' is so good that I think I will copy it:

'As ill-luck would have it, I missed the first burst into bloom of an Iris Susiana, to which I had been looking forward with great eagerness. This Iris is very difficult to manage in our fickle climate. It is six years since it bloomed with me, then it did so in the open garden; but I have never succeeded in repeating this triumph in the open air, and this is the first success, after many failures, under glass. This Iris is in its native land (Levant) generally covered with snow during the short, sharp winter, and makes its extremely rapid growth during the short spring which follows; after blooming, it endures the long, baking drought of summer, which ripens the tuberous roots thoroughly. Of course, in our country, such an arrangement in the open ground can hardly be expected, and though, when planted in the open, the tubers thrive and grow amazingly, they make in our damp autumns far too early a start, throwing up a number of strong green blades, which are almost always doomed to destruction by the last frosts of winter without showing the least sign of bloom. The books say that they require some protection, such as a hand-light, in the winter, but I have tried it, over and over again, without the slightest success. In my little greenhouse, however, I think I have mastered the difficulties of its culture at last. My method is to defer planting until very late in the autumn. I put the tubers into rather a small pot of nearly pure river sand. This pot I place inside another larger one, and plug the space between the pots with dry moss. I place the pots on a shelf in the sunniest part of the greenhouse, and give no water at all until some time after Christmas. Strange to say, the green shoots begin to show before the plants have received a drop of water. I give the water very liberally at first, but in great moderation as the plants shoot into growth. I let it have all the sun that shines, and, if the frosts are very severe at any time, I take the pots into my studio whilst the extreme cold lasts. This year my treatment has been quite successful, and the plant burst into bloom on the 4th of April.'

This receipt will be extremely interesting to many gardeners, and especially those—and they are not few—who are striving to produce flowering Irises from January to August.

I believe I mentioned before Mrs. Brightwen's 'Guide to the Study of Botany.' I should recommend every amateur gardener to get it. It is a clear, cheap, popular book, and any grown-up person or child who wishes to understand the rudiments of the mysteries of botany could not do better than to have this book as a companion.

Through the year, books on natural history and gardening must be our constant companions to be any real good. We must verify for ourselves what the book tells us. This greatly increases the interest of life in the country, and no one is ever dull or bored who can learn about plants and insects. I know, alas! that to those who really love to dwell in towns it is no use speaking of such things. The poetry of life is never to be seen by them out of the streets; and children brought up in large towns rarely acquire a love of the country, I think. I remember when we were children, a friend who came from London to see us used to tell us she could not say her prayers in the country—it was so dreadfully still! Fancy missing to that extent the city's noise, the rattle of the cabs down the street, or the measured tread of feet along the pavement! It is lucky, perhaps, that what we are used to is what we like best.

A collector of old books objected to my great praise of 'Les Roses,' by Redouté. He says: 'I do not attach the same value to it that you do, and have never found it of much use, as nearly all the Roses are hybrids and varieties many of which have passed away.' I was no doubt mistaken, but my impression was that the lovely illustrations represent in many instances the wild Roses of the world which have ceased to be cultivated, but which could easily be produced again from seed by those who took the trouble. This, I believe, Mr. Paul is doing. I think, as I said before, that in a soil where Roses grow easily a collection as large as possible of these same wild Roses would be exceedingly interesting. My correspondent goes on to describe a book — which I had never seen — that treats of all the wild Roses of the world. He says: ' You should get a coloured copy of Lindley's "Monograph of Roses," 1819. It is an excellent book, both as to plates and descriptions, and, though not common, is cheap. You can see them all at Kew. As you do not mention it, I fancy you cannot have the true York and Lancaster — Shakespeare's — a very different plant from the one with the splash petals. This difference is so well described in a page of Canon Ellacombe's endlessly interesting "Gloucestershire Garden" that I give it to you :

' "A second favourite double or semi-double Rose is the York and Lancaster, of which there are two kinds ; one a very old Rose in which the petals are sometimes white and sometimes pink, and sometimes white and pink in the same flower. This is without a doubt the ' roses damasked, red and white' — the rose ' nor red nor white, had stolen of both ' — of Shakespeare, and it is the *R. versicolor* of the old botanical writers. In the other sort, the petals are a rich crimson flaked with white ; it is a very handsome Rose, comparatively modern, and is the *Rosa mundi* of the ' Botanical Magazine,' 1794." ' I have lately seen a double *Rosa lucida*, a great improvement on the single one ; also a double white *Rosa rugosa*.

Since writing the above, I have succeeded in procuring through my Frankfort friend a coloured c‹

'Rosarum Monographia,' by John Lindley (London, 1820). On the title-page is this nice little motto :

> E guadagnar, se si potrà, quel dono,
> Che stato detto n' è, che Rose sono.

The letterpress is far more interesting and instructive, but the actual artistic treatment of the plates is less beautiful and delicate than Redouté's.

February 9th.—Where people suffer much from the birds eating out buds, as I do, I strongly recommend picking some of the branches of *Prunus Pissardii* when in bud, and sticking them into Japanese wedges or into ordinary glass vases. This, in so far as house decoration is concerned, defeats the bullfinches, and the buds come out very well in the room. This is the same with all the early-flowering blossoms. The pink Almond and *Pyrus japonica* are far more lovely flowered in water in a warm room than left on the trees exposed to the cold nights and the nipping east wind.

February 10th.—On this day last year, I went to one of the Drill Hall Horticultural Shows, and was especially delighted with *Amygdalus davidiana;* it is one of the earliest of the flowering shrubs. I immediately bought a plant, and on my return this year I found it in full flower, every branch wreathed with the lovely delicate white flowers. I only wish I had bought three or four plants instead of one. I shall certainly do so next autumn. The branches I ventured to cut have lasted over ten days in the room in water, and those left on the plant have turned brown from the frosty nights.

I went to a neighbour to-day, and found the house filled with pots of *Genista præcox.* They came from Waterer's, and a more charming effect in a large room I never saw. The plant was beautifully grown and one mass of pale lemon-coloured bloom—sweet-smelling, too. I have long had it outside, and it does very well; but it seems difficult to strike, though I think it could be managed just before it is in full bloom. I expect what I saw was grown from seed, but it is not in Thompson's list.

February 20th.—I returned home to-day, after staying some little time in London. Apart from other reasons, it is worth going away for the joy of returning. While in London I again went to the Drill Hall Show, on the 14th, some few days later than last year. Nothing struck me so much this year as *Amygdalus davidiana* did the year before; but it was an especially good show of flowers for so early in the season. Year by year the Cyclamens grow larger and finer in colour, but I do not think they are plants that have been greatly improved by increased cultivation and Brobdingnagian size. I prefer the pretty little, old, sweet-smelling types. Pans full of miniature Daffodils were very attractive, and Messrs. Hill & Co., of Lower Edmonton, had a lovely and most uncommon collection of greenhouse Ferns. *Nephrodium membranifolium* and an *Aspidium* struck me particularly, from the charm of their growth. The fashionable little, bright pink Begonia *Gloire de Lorraine* was in large quantities and most effective. The lovely *Iris reticulata* was also exhibited.

The London streets were more than ever full of beautiful flowers, none beating the showy branches of the Mimosa, *Acacia dealbata*, from the south of France.

I found at home that the Crocuses had made much progress, and the Daffodils, instead of only showing green spears, are all now in bud. The complete stillness is so delicious to me!

> How sweet, how passing sweet, is solitude!
> But grant me still a friend in my retreat,
> To whom I may whisper, ' Solitude is sweet.'

That is what the young feel. The old can do without companionship.

My little conservatory looked bright and full of bloom. Last year I had a lot of Daffodils in pans, and they did very well and forced easily. This year I have Hyacinths ; but, though they were not very good bulbs —some being successful, and some failures—still they look well and picturesque in the open pans ; far prettier than in pots. I have one little oriental slop-basin filled with the bright blue Scillas, which is very effective ; and the Freesias are always most satisfactory. Mr. Sydenham recommends buying them each year ; but I think, cheap as they are, that must be advice rather for the seller than for the buyer, as with us, treated as recommended before, they improve and increase, and, when there is so much to buy, that is what I call satisfactory. The common Lachenalias do the same. The *Lachenalia aurea* is more difficult to increase. Lachenalias do not require so much baking and drying as the Freesias do, and should be kept in half shade in a frame after the leaves die down, and not quite dry. Early re-potting in July is desirable for both.

To make variety in colour, and because they are such useful flowers for picking — their duration in water being almost endless — I have several pots of the Orchid *Dendrobium mobile*, and one fine spike of *Odontoglossum Alexandriæ* in full bloom. My large, old-fashioned, sweet-smelling white Azalea, which has been so faithful a friend for many years, has failed this year — either from mere fatigue of being forced, or from being over-dried and pot-bound last summer, which I think more likely. I have a young plant of the same which is now in full flower — *Azalea indica alba* it is called in the catalogues. But often other varieties are sent out under the same name which have no scent at all, and are consequently much less worth growing in a small green-house. My old plant had the most delicious, delicate, and yet powerful perfume. We have now broken it up and re-potted small pieces, with the hope that they may grow again. The large pots of Imantophyllums are looking glorious. They are rather handsomer varieties, both in size and colour, than the usual ones. I got them two or three years ago from Veitch, who has specially improved these most useful and showy of winter-flowering plants. A small, shrubby plant of the bright yellow Coronilla gives another spot of bright colour by the blue-green of the sweet-leaved Eucalyptus. We have brought the forcing of the *Polygonatum multiflorum* (Solomon's Seal) to most useful perfection; and, put back in a reserve bed after flowering, it is ready to force again after a year or two. It is the easiest and most effective of the hardy plants to bring on in a greenhouse.

February 22nd.—I brought back with me from Ireland last year several plants of the *Iris stylosa*. The white one has flowered, but not the blue ones, though these were put in two situations—some in good, rich soil, and some in poor ground. These latter, perhaps, may flower later. One of the reasons why Irises should be so much cultivated is that they have the merit, which can never be too much appreciated, of flowering admirably in water if picked in bud. A flower can hardly claim a greater merit for domestic purposes, and, for the same reason, they are well adapted for travelling.

February 23rd.—A treat has come for all of us amateur gardeners this month in the publication of a long-looked-for gardening book by Miss Jekyll, charmingly illustrated from photographs of her own. But, good as are these reproductions, in my opinion they can never compare with woodcuts or steel engravings, and they give but a faint idea of the unusual charm and beauty of her self-created garden. Her book is most truly called, 'Wood and Garden,' and is a never-ending lesson of how to lay out a piece of ground by using its natural advantages instead of hopelessly destroying them by clearing the ground to make a garden. In this case there can be no imitation, as, without the copse-covered piece of ground which she selected, no one could produce the same sort of garden. Nature must have had her way first. But the charm of the combination of nature and art as carried out by Miss Jekyll is very great. We always open these books at the month we are in, and she says: 'There is always in February some one day, at least, when one smells the yet distant, coming summer.' Such a day has been ours to-day, and I enjoyed it doubly in consequence of having so lately returned from London. And the forwardness of the spring — it really is more forward even than last year — makes one enjoy it more. Though everything is growing so fast, it is quite agitating for the gardener, giving the feeling that all the work is behindhand. I am told that in my first book many thought I recommended that things should be done too soon; but, in my experience, human nature rather tends to reversing the proverb, and acts on the principle of 'Never do to-day what can be done to-morrow.' And in all things about a garden, except when Jack Frost is to be feared, it is best to be early rather than late.

My January-sown Green Peas are coming up very well, but they would not survive except for the pea-wire coverings, as the sparrows would nip out the hearts. The black cotton strung about the *Prunus Pissardii* has answered. I have far more bloom than I have ever had before.

As I rush about the garden, and see how the Daffies

grow an inch each day in such weather, in spite of very
cold nights, and though I have the usual endless 'Mar-
tharish' bothers of life inside the house, I can indeed
say, with Thomson:

> I care not, Fortune, what you me deny;
>   You cannot rob me of free nature's grace;
> You cannot shut the windows of the sky,
>   Through which Aurora shows her bright'ning face;
> You cannot bar my constant feet to trace
>   The woods and lawns by living stream at eve.
> Let health my nerves and finer fibres brace,
>   And I their toys to the great children leave.
>   Of fancy, reason, virtue, nought can me bereave.

To appreciate Miss Jekyll's book in a way to profit
by it, one must read and re-read it. One more quotation I must make. In 'May' she says: 'The blooming
of the Cowslip is the signal for a search for the Morel,
one of the best of the edible fungi. It grows in open
woods, or where the undergrowth has not yet grown
high, and frequently in old parks and pastures, near or
under Elms. It is quite unlike any other fungus, shaped
like a tall egg, with the pointed end upwards, on a short,
hollow stalk, and looking something like a sponge. It
has a delicate and excellent flavour, and is perfectly
wholesome.' I have, alas! spent nearly all my life, and
I have never searched for the Morel! Have you, dear
reader?

February 26th.—I have been to-day planting large
quantities of the roots of the *Tropæolum speciosum* in
various parts of the garden. These were given to me
by a kind neighbour. He says the great secret (and he
is very successful himself) is digging the holes quite
four feet deep, filling them in with leaf-mould and the
light earth, and planting the roots a foot below the surface, and then they have two feet of loose soil to work

down into. I hope they may be successful; I do hate being beaten. At least some must succeed, one would think, planted in five different situations. They have to be labelled with large white labels, as the great danger, if one's back is turned, is of their being dug up.

Driving last year on this day, I find I noticed the Nettles were well up in the hedges and just ready for picking, and the catkins were hanging from the Hazel boughs. A little Celandine, on a moist bank, opened its yellow star in the sun. I have never seen it cultivated in gardens, which—weed though it is—seems a pity, and I think I shall try it in patches under some shrubs. No doubt it is rather its early appearance than its shining beauty that has made it so loved of the poets. Wordsworth describes it and its surroundings with grace and truth in the following well-known poem:

Pansies, Lilies, King-cups, Daisies,
Let them live upon their praises;
There's a flower that shall be mine,
'Tis the little Celandine!
Ere a leaf is on a bush,
In the time before the thrush
Has a thought about its nest,
    Thou wilt come with half a call,
Spreading out thy glossy breast,
    Like a careless prodigal;
Telling tales about the sun,
When we've little warmth or none.

Careless of thy neighbourhood,
    Thou dost show thy pleasant face;
On the moor and in the wood,
    In the lane — there's not a place,
Howsoever mean it be,
But 'tis good enough for thee.

I picked to-day and ate with great relish my first Dandelion salad. I can recommend it again and again to salad lovers; but it must be very carefully washed, as any grit entirely spoils it. Later on the leaves get tough and bitter.

February 27th.—The last few days have been very cold, but I have some most beautiful branches of Almond in full flower in the house. They were picked, as I have explained, whilst in bud, and put to expand in the greenhouse. This method defies the frosts and wind, and greatly prolongs the time of enjoying the blossoms.

About this time last year I cut away another bed of Laurels, which we had not time to do in the autumn, and it has made a nice snug corner for some newly-bought flowering shrubs—Lilacs which I had not got, such as Dr. Lindley and Charles X., and some white ones; a double-flowering Cherry, which is such a beautiful thing (though I fear it will never do well here, as it likes a strong, damp soil); a Cerasus, Pseudo Cerasus, Double Crimson Peach, *Hamamelis japonica* (which has died), *Eucryphia pinnatifolia*, and the before-mentioned *Amygdalus davidiana alba*. I have a great many Spiræas in the garden, but never till now the *Spiræa confusa*, which forces very well, and is a lovely thing. I have put it, for the present, with these new shrubs. I find it a distinct advantage putting new things in one place, as then one sees how they do, and what spreads and flourishes, and what is only a dry stick and a label the following year. It is mysterious why some plants die. I bought two beautiful Tea Roses in pots, which were planted outside and drawn through into the greenhouse—one a Maréchal Niel, the other Niphetos. Both flourished equally well through the summer. The next spring, without any apparent reason, the Maréchal Niel having made its leaves, turned brown and died—very provoking, as in this way one loses a whole year's growth. I think anyone who grows forced Tea Roses for picking will find they do far better and look more satisfactory in water if floated in large glass bowls than if only their stalks are in water.

I received a letter to-day from the Engadine, describing a phase of modern luxury which reads strangely to those who live quietly in country corners. My friend writes from San Moritz, and thus describes an episode in a fancy-dress ball : 'In the cotillon they had an enormous silver sledge, smothered in the most gorgeously lovely flowers—Imantophyllums, *Lilium speciosum*, Lilies-of-the-Valley with stalks eight inches long, white Lilac and Prunus. And all these looked as if they had just been freshly gathered ; yet the whole thing came from a flower-shop at Frankfurt-on-the-Main. I must say I never saw anything prettier, and in the sledge sat a lovely downy young English beauty, scattering bunches of flowers about, as they dragged her round the room. The whole thing seemed beautiful Fairyland, up here in this world of ice and snow.' I suppose it is no more luxury for those who can afford it than my humble little greenhouse, which also costs money ; yet one cannot help feeling sorry that these beautiful hothouse flowers should have been dragged up there for the wasteful enjoyment of one evening.

RECEIPTS

Poulet à la Valencienne.—Cut a good fowl into pieces. Wipe it dry, but do not put it into water. Take a saucepan, put in a wineglassful of olive oil, and add two cloves of garlic. Be careful that it does not burn ; for if it does, it will turn bitter. Stir the garlic until it is fried. Put in the chicken. Keep stirring it about while it fries, then add some salt, and continue to stir. Whenever a sound of cracking is heard, stir it again. When the chicken is well browned, which will take from five to ten minutes, stirring constantly, put in chopped onions, three or four chopped red or green chillies, and stir about. If once the contents catch the pan, the dish is spoilt. Then add tomatoes divided into quarters, and parsley. Take three tea-cupfuls of well-washed rice, and mix up well together. Then add hot stock, enough to cover over the whole. Let it boil once, then set aside to simmer till the rice becomes tender and done. The great art consists in having the rice turned out granular and separate, and not in a pudding state, which is sure to be the case if a cover is put over the dish, so that the steam is con-densed. It should be served up in the *casserole* in which it is cooked. Bits of fish, sausage, and chicken livers may be added; also a little saffron.

Chasse.—Ingredients: One onion, six tomatoes, three potatoes, a slice of ham, some grated cheese, red pepper, very little allspice. Fry the sliced onion lightly in some lard and butter mixed. Add the tomatoes and ham, both cut into small pieces. When they are well browned, add some water and then the potatoes, hav-ing first cut them in dice shapes. Let all cook until the potatoes are done; then, just before serving, mix in grated cheese, well flavoured with red pepper, until the sauce is 'ropy.' Have a very hot dish, pour the sauce on to it, and serve carefully poached eggs on the top. This makes a delightful breakfast dish.

Water Souchet.—Take six flounders, fillet four; put the fillets into a saucepan. The carcasses and the others put into a stewpan with some stock, a bit of parsley and a little carrot, which boil for an hour. Strain, and shred some carrot, also parsley root and a few sprigs of parsley. Boil for ten minutes more. Put the fillets into the oven to cook. When the souchet is dished, put in the fillets, and serve with brown bread and butter, and lemons.

Everything of the kind is now to be bought, but I think the following few receipts may turn out useful. In washing paint, so many do not know how injurious is soda or yellow soap or soft soap.

For Washing White Paint.—Shred common yellow household soap, and boil it down in a saucepan with sufficient whitening to make it into a thick paste. Put it in a jar, and use a little on a rag when required. It will clean the paint perfectly, and will not turn it yellow. Never use soda for paint; it spoils it and marks it at once.

Furniture Polish.—To clean, polish, and take marks out of furniture, 'Sanitas Furniture Polish' is excellent and not expensive; but the following is an old receipt and very good: Equal quantities of methylated spirit, vinegar, and linseed oil. The bottle should be well shaken before using, or the spirit remains on the top and will burn the polished surface of whatever it touches.

For Polishing New Brown Boots and Shoes.—I am sure many people will agree with me as to the extreme ugliness of new brown shoes; yet we all must have them new sometimes. An excellent way of correcting this ugly newness is to rub the leather three times in succession with vaseline. After that, clean them in the ordinary way with brown cream, and they will take the polish as if they were months old.

To Remove Fruit Stains.—Soak the stain in a glass of water in which you have put ten to twelve drops of sulphuric acid. Then wash with clear water.

To Prevent Lamp-wicks from Smoking.—Steep

the wicks in very strong vinegar; then let them dry completely before they are used.

A series of penny books, published as the 'Domestic Science Series,' is full of useful information. The only one I actually know, called 'Manual of Housewifery for Elementary Schools,' by Helena Head, to be bought at 4 Princes Road, Liverpool, seems to me thoroughly practical.

One thing I must copy out of Mrs. Roundell's most excellent 'Practical Cookery Book,' more especially as it is not a cooking receipt, but a cure for one of the most distinct worries that affect nearly every house in England, more especially if keeping down in the spring is neglected—and yet how few servants do not neglect it till it has become a plague!—I mean blackbeetles. Mrs. Roundell gives the following receipt, and we found it excellent in a new flat in London which swarmed with them :

'**To Destroy Blackbeetles.**—Not long ago the kitchens and bakeries of the Fir Vale Union Workhouse at Sheffield swarmed with blackbeetles, to such an extent that the Government Inspector feared the buildings would have to be pulled down. The insects even got into the soup and bread provided for the inmates, in spite of all vigilance and every remedy. The Board of Guardians, in despair, consulted the curator of the Sheffield Museum—Mr. Howarth, F.Z.S.—and he invented a paste which in a short time completely freed the workhouse from blackbeetles. This "Union" cockroach paste can be had in tins from Mr. Hewitt, chemist, 66 Division street, Sheffield. It never fails in its effect.'

'Keating's Powder' is also effectual if the beetles are swept up in the morning and destroyed.

MARCH

Confessions about diet—Cures for rheumatism—Effects of tea-drinking—Sparing animal life a bad reason for vegetarianism—The Berlin foot-race—Mrs. Crow in Edinburgh—Bagehot on luxury—A word about babies—German and English nurseries—Sir Richard Thorne Thorne on raw milk—The New Education Difficulty of understanding young children—Gardening—Cooking.

I feel at last the moment has come when I must make a confession. I am a non-meat-eater! I know that this will probably entail the loss of the good opinion of my readers, and I should never have dreamt of bringing forward so personal a matter, had I not felt compelled to do so in consequence of the numbers of letters I have received in which the writers deplore their loss of health, their gout and rheumatism, and the general ailments that prevent their going into the garden, etc. This strikes me as unnatural and wrong. There is no reason at all, unless there be actual disease, that sickness should, as a matter of course, accompany old age any more than any other period of life.

This chapter is not intended for the young or the healthy or the really sick, but for those chronic sufferers who are constantly appealing to the medical profession for 'something' that will cure their aches and pains, their sleepless nights, their stiff joints, and their neuralgias, and who put all their faith in drugs which, even when they seem to do good, turn out to be palliatives, not cures—that is, in the case of constitutions where the ailments are the result of gout and rheumatism.

(220)

Some years ago all these symptoms in various degrees were mine, and I fully expected that they would increase with age; but I was wrong—by gradual steps they all disappeared. Nothing, of course, makes the old young; but bad health, the chief dread of old age, I no longer have. I can work out in the garden with even greater impunity than I could have done twenty years ago. I take long journeys—say, of twenty-seven hours—without fatigue, and I sleep excellently. This all reads like an advertisement for a patent medicine, but it is nothing of the kind; in fact, for years I have taken no medicine at all. But if I am asked to account for this improvement, in one word it is—diet. I have become an ardent advocate of non-meat-eating, but without any of those sentimental feelings about the killing of animals which many people have who yet continue to partake of ordinary food; nor did it begin from the belief that meat is a frequent conveyor of poisons. I left it off at first simply as an experiment. I believe that meat, especially if eaten daily—the small quantities ferment the other foods—is on the whole deleterious to the health of the human race, and simply poisonous to the gouty, the rheumatic, or the neuralgic.

All through my lifetime there seems to have been the strongest belief everywhere in Europe, amongst all classes (especially those who are habitually over-fed), that if they feel weak or anæmic, or what is called 'below par,' therefore they must try and eat more, and cram themselves with stimulating food, such as meat-juices, beef-tea, or even raw beef, and—as with drugs or alcohol—for a time it often answers. The origin of this belief, no doubt, has come from the teaching of the medical profession, only disputed now and then by a solitary member. Surely this system is nearly on the level, and only one degree less harmful, than yielding to the request of the poor drunkard, who wildly cries for more of the very poison that is killing him. The immediate relief is actual and visible ; the after-reaction in both cases being the cause of fresh suffering.

My object as a propagandist in the cause of non-meat-eating is merely to give others my experience, with the ordinary human desire that they may try a cure which has been so beneficial to myself. When, some years ago, chronic rheumatism was gaining upon me, I resorted to the usual solaces of the well-to-do. I consulted doctors, I took drugs, I left off wine—which before the age of forty I had rarely taken, and after forty only in small quantities. I went to Aix-les-Bains. I got momentary relief from all these cures, but on the whole the malady gained upon me, and I looked forward to a cripply old age with great dread, knowing full well that it would prevent my enjoying my favourite occupation of gardening. My family physician summed up the case with : 'Well, Mrs. Earle, at your age this rheumatism which has settled in the hips is extremely difficult of cure.' I repeated this to a vegetarian friend, who lent me a book, called 'The Science of Healing,' by L. Kuehne, a German non-medical man who practises a strict vegetarian water-cure at Leipzig. In consequence of reading this book, I undertook to try and cure myself. The results have been simply wonderful, and I find the kind of food I eat, now that I am used to it, entails no self-denial at all. I carried out the cure strictly for many months—almost as strictly as Kuehne recommends, only breaking his rule by a small amount of milk and butter, and I was greatly the better for it. I took absolutely no animal food, and neither cheese nor eggs. If ever I relapsed into ordinary diet, after a very little time the old pains reasserted themselves. My friends declared I looked old and ugly, and most of my family thought the first illness would play the part of the legs in the epitaph :

> Two bad legs and a troublesome cough,
> But the legs it was that carried her off.

My own faith in the matter only grew and grew, but it has taken four or five years for me to be absolutely free of pain, and even to this day I occasionally feel twinges, which I immediately treat by diminishing in quantity what I generally eat. The result is invariably satisfactory, and unaccompanied by any feelings of weakness or fatigue. Last year I became the object of considerable jealousy to one of my friends, who could not understand why I had grown so much better. I, loth to encounter the anger of her numerous family by recommending my method, remarked—what I did not believe—that very likely my diet would not suit her. I am so tired of hearing that 'One man's meat is another man's poison' ! Seeing the marked improvement in me, and thinking the matter over after I had left, she telegraphed to her London doctor, saying : 'Who is the great authority in London at this moment on gout and rheumatism ?' He wired back : 'Dr. Haig, of Brook street.' She accordingly went to him. When next we met, one of her first remarks was : 'A most extraordinary thing has happened to me. I have been to a new doctor for my rheumatism, and his printed paper on diet is in all essentials what you practise, except that he orders more milk and cheese.' She handed me the leaflet, and from this I got to know Dr. Haig and his most interesting book, 'Uric Acid as a Factor in the Causation of Disease.' This book is rather medical for the ordinary public, who had better begin with his two-shilling book called 'Diet and Food considered in Relation to Strength and Power of Endurance, Training and

Athletics.' On Dr. Haig's recommendation, I deserted the extreme strictness of the German cure, and I have undoubtedly felt stronger for taking more skimmed milk (separated would be better) and a little cheese, though whenever I am less well I go back to the Kuehne diet. It was the greatest satisfaction to me to find a man whose years of study and scientific investigations entirely corresponded with my own groping experiences. If anybody now ever asks me about the matter, I say: 'Read Dr. Haig's books, and then consult him or not, as you like.' His tables of diet are so severe that I am afraid they may tempt a great number of people to agree with the late Lord D——, who, when sent a sample of sherry which was recommended to him as being essentially wholesome, wrote back that he found it so bitter and dry he much preferred the gout.

Although it is rare to find a doctor who will recommend strict dieting in chronic cases, I think it is becoming equally rare for a doctor to make any objection if the patient himself proposes it. He will not risk offending a patient by not giving him medicines and by greatly reducing his food. One can hardly blame a doctor for this, and it brings us to the conclusion that the initiative in matters of diet and abstinence must come from the patients themselves.

Not many people seemed to take any interest in the health allusions in my last book. Still, I received the following letter, which, in a chapter bound to be unpopular, the few who read it may find as interesting as I did:

'I have been specially interested in your health chapter, for if there is one subject more than another which ought to be thrashed out by the lay mind, it is health. On it depends, to a great extent, the future progress of mankind. As a rule, individuals lean to the idea that it is not a question for themselves to think on. They seem to imply that it is a question solely for the medical hierarchy. But these authorities are so hampered by the limitations engrained in them in their medical education that it is with difficulty any of them exercise a free mind on the subject. You have given examples, it is true, of some few; and I know a few more, both here and in America, who have broken away and have given full vent to their reasoning powers. All hail to them, but they want supporting. There is no doubt that if doctors were to take up the reforms honestly they would do good, inasmuch as there is a blind faith in them on the part of the majority of people. But when has a profession reformed itself? All reforms come from outside.

'There are two great assumptions on which medicos act, and on which they impel their patients to act. The first is, that it is positively necessary, under all circumstances, to eat every day in order to live. Dr. Keith, whose book I have just seen before I got yours, is an exception to this; and Dr. Dewey, in America, in his "New Gospel of Health," is another. They show clearly that not only is it not necessary, but under certain conditions of illness it is positively injurious to eat. I have seen, I am sorry to say, food violently forced down the throat of a patient by a medical man when nature was evidently telling the patient that food was no good, but, on the contrary, was adding to the troubles. This is quite irrespective of what is suitable food and what is not. All I maintain is, that at times no food at all is required, for it is then only by the absence of food that nature finds time to recuperate herself. The second assumption that the Faculty, as a body, insist on is, that meat is absolutely necessary for strength. Meat is no doubt a concentrated food, but concentrated foods are

o

not necessarily nourishing. On the contrary, the waste that comes from them is most trying to all the organs of the body, which, after a time, break down entirely. There are heaps of foods which are natural foods, which easily assimilate, and which in their waste are not unduly trying. Then, no doubt, in meat there is decomposition always going on, which, when it is eaten by human beings, may produce fermentation leading to serious diseases. Of course there are many other arguments against meat; but as long as it is considered a positively necessary food, there is no good using them. I find that with young people it is useless to preach against meat. They like it, they see everybody eating it, they are told that the Faculty consider it positively necessary, and, owing to their youth, they feel no ill-effects, except now and then a temporary derangement, which they attribute to something they don't like so much. The great thing with them is to urge abstemiousness, and even at times total abstinence, and, when they feel ill, simple starvation. The day may come when they will find it best for themselves to give up meat. I only wish that I had been brought up to rely upon my own reason in dealing with illness. Half the ailments that mankind suffers from could be cured by nature herself, if she were given time and were not forced. She is interfered with in every way by both doctor and patient.

'Power has been usurped by the Faculty. Very few men can stand power; they get to be assertive and dogmatic, and eventually become tyrants.'

So I hear of bad health here, sufferings there, and, what we used to say of old people when we were young, 'cases of fifteen mortal maladies and yet living on to a good old age.' They live long because their constitutions are good; they suffer much, in my opinion, because they eat what is not good for them, both as to quality and quantity, only adding to their ailments instead of diminishing them. The modern invalid always says: 'The doctor has ordered me to eat well,' and feels his conscience absolved. This reminds me of a rather good old story which a doctor told me, when I was a girl in Brussels, as having happened to himself. A bishop who was eating stuffed turkey with this doctor on Good Friday excused himself to a punctilious friend, who was shown into the dining-room by accident, saying: 'Le docteur me le commande, et moi je lui donne absolution.' But can one imagine anything more hopelessly exasperating for poor doctors, who have to make their living, than to find that loss of patients is the result if they venture even to ask in chronic cases what people eat and drink? We all know how they knock off food in cases of serious illness, though even then I think they still allow far too much. During convalescence it is often desirable for the patient to eat anything that he can digest.

I know it will be said that the next generation may suffer from the results of a low diet, as the doctors are perpetually telling us that we have all suffered from the port wine drinking and high living of our ancestors. Nothing but time can prove this.

In my youth, heaps of doctors, especially on the Continent, still believed in bleeding, particularly in fever cases. Now this is as unknown as if it had never been practised at all. Is this right or wrong?

I see even restaurants now advertise suppers which are not indigestible! An interesting pandering to the growing faith that good health comes far before good feeding.

I was asked the other day to give a lecture on the right spending of money. Oh! what a fraud these appeals to my knowledge or wisdom make me feel! I, who have so little knowledge of figures that I cannot even keep my own accounts! But most certainly, if I were to give a lecture, I should say to everyone, high and low: 'Spend far less in food and drink.' To the under-fed and poor: 'Live twice as well as you do, on what you have, by spending judiciously.' To the farmers: 'Grow more peas and beans for wholesome human food.' And to the seedsman: 'Sell these food-producing seeds much cheaper, and put the price on to something else.'

I have said nothing about the cheapness of the diet I recommend, as it is not cheap if it does not make you well. If it does, it is very satisfactory, I think, to spend so very little on food; and eating so much less at each meal is so delightfully comfortable! I could not have believed some years ago that it was possible to keep in excellent health on so little.

In Dr. Haig's little book 'Diet and Food,' he holds out a kind of millennium where cooks might cease to exist, and he gives a table of food requiring scarcely any cooking, and which yet contains what he considers a sufficient amount of albumen. This might prove extremely useful under exceptional circumstances.

A reform I should much like to see is that, when a doctor leaves a house at the end of an illness, he himself should burn his prescriptions; and that it might be made penal for chemists to make them up except by a doctor's orders. Doctors frequently give strong remedies in severe cases, but they themselves would be the first to regret these remedies being taken again and again on the smallest provocation by the patient. The insane desire to kill pain and to gain relief by narcotics and strength by tonics which pervades our modern society, from the youngest to the oldest, is, in my opinion, very likely to act more deleteriously on the constitution than the excesses of past generations. People become aware of the loss of health, but the mysterious ways in which remedies may have injured us are wrapped in as complete darkness as is the origin of most of the diseases from which all classes suffer.

I wonder if other people have noticed, as I have done throughout my life, that the families where medicines are least in use are those of doctors themselves. This want of faith in drugs on their part was one of the first things which, years ago, opened my eyes.

What strikes me is, how few people are really well! And if they could put side by side the pleasure of eating food which is harmless, and the better health and strength this would bring, compared with the pleasure of eating large dinners and the feeling of the following morning thrown into the balance, I believe the bird-in-the-hand pleasure would lose most of its attractions. It has been a real surprise to me, though apparently doctors know it well, how vast a number of people would much rather be ill, or even die, than be convinced that the food they like does them harm. The young, especially, seem to think that one of the chief pleasures of life would be removed if they did not eat what they preferred, quite forgetting that fruit and sugar and many other good things are quite harmless—nay, beneficial—to the non-meat-eater. What we do daily soon ceases to be the penance that abstinence once a week was supposed to inflict. It may be said that 'starving,' with many people, does not make them feel well. All I can say is, it is very seldom tried on the right lines; at any rate, not for long enough time to give it a chance.

It is curious how things repeat themselves. Sydney Smith says, in one of his letters: 'All gentlemen and ladies eat too much. I made a calculation, and found I must have consumed some wagon-loads too much in the course of my life. Lock up the mouth, and you have gained the victory. I believe our friend Lady Morley has hit upon the right plan in dining modestly at two. When we are absorbed in side-dishes, and perplexed with variety of wines, she sits amongst us, lightly flirting with a potato, in full possession of her faculties and at liberty to make the best use of them—a liberty, it must be owned, she does not neglect. For how agreeable she is! I like Lady Morley; she is what I call *good company*.'

The really difficult part of practising any form of diet, especially if you have gained immensely by the results, is the irritation it causes to the people who surround you. I was told the other day that having mentioned in a letter the fact that I had become a vegetarian was more than enough to account for my receiving no answer. If any sufferers feel tempted to follow my example of a strict diet, I strongly recommend them to do all in their power to make it as unobtrusive a factor in family life as possible. It will also be found a great advantage to those who go out in society to cheat; by which I mean, take things on your plate as a ' blind,' though you have no intention of eating them. The sympathy expressed lest you should kill yourself, and the terror lest your influence should prove the death of somebody else, make life a martyrdom for a very insufficient cause.

I never realised till this year that there is considerable danger in a sudden change of diet, especially in hot weather and to those who are most in need of it. One is always hearing of cases where abstention from meat answers for a few months, and then has to be given up because the patient finds himself less well, and attributes everything to his change of diet. Dr. Haig fully explains the reason for this. He may, of course, be wrong in his deductions; if he is right, it should lead to great changes in diet in this country through the conversion of the medical profession.

One of the great advantages of the non-sentimental over the sentimental vegetarian is that in case dislike of foods occurs, as it very commonly does, and with it a decided depression of the nervous system from the dropping of all stimulants, a slight return to ordinary diet for a time may be beneficial. Anything is better than producing a nervous irritation against the diet. Patients at any rate are then able to realise for themselves whether it does them good or not, and are able to remember how they benefited at first from the cure, and go back to it when they feel inclined. They must also remember that much that they suffer from is hereditary, and has to be continually fought rather than cured. To attribute every ailment to the new diet, when people have lived on meat and stimulants all their lives, and had constant attacks of illness, is, to say the least of it, unreasonable. In the case of vegetarians, Dr. Haig has told me that they often come to him insufficiently nourished. It is specially easy for vegetarians to over-eat and yet be under-fed.

I am the last to deny that many, and especially old people, have benefited from a purely meat diet (the 'Salisbury Cure') when very strictly carried out, though I never tried it myself. All that I feel, and I feel it strongly, is that health is more likely to be bettered by only taking food that clearly improves the blood than by depending for cure on alterative medicines and tonics which only relieve for a time.

True wisdom always brings us back to the old rule that moderation in all things is the best guide for everybody. The fact has long been known with regard to alcohol; but it has only lately been acknowledged that tea, coffee, and beef or chicken tea, are also stimulants and not food, and are injurious to the nervous system. Who would not have laughed, a few years ago, at the statement that tea-drinking in large quantities produces a form of *delirium tremens?* And yet the illness is now quite recognised as existing among the under-fed who drink tea in excess. The craving for stimulants of some kind is universal, especially when nourishment is insufficient. This proves, I think, that what is most wished for is not always best for us.

The law, and generally our own inclination, obliges us to leave the treatment of disease, once acquired, in the hands of doctors and surgeons, and this in spite of the many mistakes they make—often grievous mistakes, such as cutting people open and then merely sewing them up again because nothing is wrong, or leaving pieces of lint or even forceps inside after operations. Both these cases have come under my knowledge. Knowing of these things only depresses one and does no good. But the maintaining of health from babyhood upwards and the prevention of disease—for these, to my mind, all human beings are individually responsible, both as regards themselves and their children. The more the latest and most conflicting scientific theories on the subject are known by everybody the better.

For all who are interested in the subject of non-meat-eating, much general information (cooking and other) is to be got from 'The Vegetarian,' a weekly penny newspaper. It is, of course, written from the sentimental point of view of the non-killing of animals, the health of man being considered as only secondary. Everyone with any understanding must have his feelings aroused by the sufferings of animals, whether caused by man or by each other. The killing of animals comes under a different category. Anyone who keeps cows knows well the sad order that has to go forth for the slaughter of the beautiful little bull-calf, as even the most fortunate farmer cannot expect to breed only cows. Is not all or nearly all our complicated civilised life directly or indirectly mixed up with the killing of animals? No one can hate cruelty more than I do; no one can wish more than I do that legislation should be applied to control and rule the cruelty of man. But the most tender-hearted of old maids has to shut her eyes to the fact that superfluous kittens and puppies are put out of the way; and if we are told that the rats are devouring our beautiful black and white pigeons, the cruel rat-catcher is sent for to fight and kill the enemy, though, poor things! Mr. and Mrs. Rat enjoyed their spring life and their young families quite as much as the pigeons. Can vegetarians keep their kitchens full of blackbeetles or their Roses covered with greenfly? Do they give over all their Peaches to the wasps, or their nuts to the mice?

The wasteful redundancy of nature involves the whole question in a cloud of difficulties, and to my mind not one of these is removed, nor is any light thrown on the subject by the sentimental view that we should give up eating meat, not for our own good, but with the idea of sparing animal life.

Besides, such countless other products are dependent upon the killing of animals that, even if the whole world were non-meat-eating, hardly fewer animals than at present would be bred and slaughtered.

I myself believe it has to be proved that people who do not eat meat are less strong than those who do. The subject is receiving much attention in Germany. Last year I saw in the newspapers that a man left money to build a school for poor children, on condition that it was conducted on vegetarian principles. The trustees refused the bequest. On the other hand, last June a very interesting walking-match took place in Berlin which, the papers said, attracted the attention of the Minister of War. The course was over seventy English miles. There were twenty-two starters, amongst them eight vegetarians, and the distance had to be covered within eighteen hours. The interesting result was that the first six to arrive at the goal were vegetarians, the first finishing in fourteen and a quarter hours. The two other vegetarians missed their way and walked five miles more. All reached the goal in splendid condition. Not till an hour after the last vegetarian arrived did the first meat-eater appear, and he was then completely exhausted. He, moreover, was the only one, the others having dropped off after thirty-five miles. This does not look as if power of endurance were necessarily diminished by non-meat-eating, and a great many people who have tried non-stimulating food find, as I do, that their brains are immensely clearer, their capacity for work restored and increased, they are much less affected by changes of temperature, and their general powers of endurance are much greater than before. In short, my belief that wrong diet, in some form or other, is the cause of all the hundred and one complaints which are called by different names, and that they do not originate from external germs, is as great, and some will say of the same nature, as that of Mrs. Crow, the ghost-seer in the old story. This lady had unbounded faith that certain acts would make her invisible, and so went out into the streets of Edinburgh, with nothing on and a prayer book in one hand. A policeman rushed at her with his cape. She was not disconcerted, but said : 'What, you see me ? Then I must have put the book into the wrong hand.'

I have noticed before the fact of the extraordinary economy brought about by reduction in food, wine, etc.; but this is not necessarily an argument in favour of a simple diet. The money people have must go somewhere; and if they like meat and drink better than most things, but for the injury to the body it might as well go in that way as in any of the other luxuries of life which are not essentials. Much as I enjoy providing food for others, I now feel that it is anything but a true kindness to them. It is difficult to imagine the change that would come over civilisation if that most improbable of all miracles were to take place and the majority of people became non-meat-eaters. I have a note from one of Walter Bagehot's books, which points out the evil of reduction in luxury. I am not political economist enough to know whether his view is generally accepted now; it is in contradiction to that of other teachers. He says: 'We must observe, what is incessantly forgotten, that it is not a Spartan and ascetic state of society which most generates saving. On the contrary, if a whole society has few wants there is little motive for saving. . . . Nothing is commoner than to read 'homilies on luxury. Without the multifarious accumulation of wants, which are called luxury, there would in such a state of society be far less saving than there is. And if it be good for the poor that capital should be saved, then the momentary luxury which causes that saving is good for the poor.' I spend in fruit and on the garden what I should have spent under ordinary circumstances in meat and wine, with certainly more enjoyment to myself and, perhaps, less waste.

My nieces, I believe, look upon me as a kind of witch —meant no doubt as a subtle compliment—and, now that many are married and have babies, they say they want my opinion on the important question of how to manage them. I am very fond of babies and a great admirer even of large families, now so out of fashion. In a book lately published, I read the other day of a bishop at the beginning of this century who wrote to his young married daughter: 'Go on, my dear Eliza, and never fear hurting your constitution by honest child-bearing, since, for one mother that grows thin with this work, there are five hundred old maids that grow thin for want of it.' As a matter of fact, I have seen very little of nurseries of late years, but I never travel in railway carriages with babies, or look into the village perambulators, without being shocked by the universal use of those terrible modern inventions, sold by every chemist throughout the land, called 'baby comforters or soothers.' I cannot imagine any child's digestion not being weakened and injured by them. The suction is exactly the same as with the real bottle, and the waste of saliva must be excessive; so great that the flow must be much reduced when food is actually taken, and this of itself must begin the non-assimilation of food which modern children, especially those brought up by hand, suffer from so much. My objection applies to babies after they are three or four months old; before that these 'comforters' do not do much harm. But, the habit once acquired, few nurses or mothers have the courage to break it.

Every doctor I have asked has corroborated my view on this subject. A thoroughly conscientious doctor ought, I think, to refuse to attend the children of the rich where such things are used. The mothers and nurses say: 'It is such a comfort to the child, and prevents its crying, which is so dangerous.' This is the modern receipt for everything! Momentary relief and palliatives, at the cost of eventual good! What makes babies cry is not only dyspepsia and discomfort, but also spoiling; that is to say, responding to that natural appeal of crying for what they want. Many a child that has been too much held in nurses' arms from its birth cries when it is laid down. That does not mean that it is bad for the child to lie down, for, if it is quite loosely dressed, this does it only good. It cries, as a dog whines, merely to express, in the only way that it can, what it wants; and if taken up directly it cries, this teaches it, by the only way it can learn, to do it again next time.

I saw some years ago a most intelligently managed baby; it was half German, half French. I was also much struck with the superior common-sense of many of the arrangements in the foreign nursery that I visited, and was told that they were the general custom in that part of the world. All babies' cots from the very beginning are firm, never rocking — which must be better. And the little mattress is made of hard, firm horsehair, not wool. On the top of this is another mattress, made of strong linen, four or five inches thick, loosely filled with husks. The pillow is also loosely filled with the same material; viz., the husks of oats, well dried and cleaned of all dust. The husks can be got from a corn or forage merchant, and — to thoroughly clean them — they should be washed in water, left to dry for some days, then well shaken out in a thin muslin bag, and also well aired. The reasons for this kind of pillow are its cleanliness, and the fact that it is much cooler and wholesomer than either wool, down, or feathers. In Germany, children sleep on a husk pillow till they are seven or eight years old, and later in cases of illness. The coolness of this pillow and mattress is particularly essential, because the babies are never held in the arms of mother or nurse except when they are being fed. This is an important factor in the nursery management, especially in houses without many servants, as it makes the nurse or mother so much freer to do all that she has to do. Small babies are far too much nursed, as a rule, in England; a child is trained from the first by the monthly nurse to lie constantly on her knee, whereas, abroad, the first thing done from the very beginning is to train a baby to be perfectly content in its cot. And when the weather is fine and it goes out, it is never carried or wheeled about before it is seven or eight months old. It lies for hours in the open air as in a bed. It is very important that children of all ages should sleep on a hard, flat bed, and that mattresses should be re-made whenever they get hollow. I believe that neglect of this is the cause of many round shoulders and weak spines. A husk pillow (which can be made of dried and pounded bracken Fern if the husks of oats are not available) is also used for washing a baby, on a method which I think both safer and easier than our English way. There is a large, plain deal table, three sides of which are surrounded by a rim as in our wooden washstands. On the right and left of this table is placed everything the nurse is likely to require for washing the baby. On a little table next to this big one is a basket with the clothes. In the middle of the large table is placed the above-mentioned pillow, covered with a piece of mackintosh sheeting, over which is laid a large bath towel. On this is placed the little naked baby, and it is then the superior advantage of this system over the English one becomes apparent. No one can see it done without appreciating how much less experienced the mother or nurse need be, as both hands are left free to soap and sponge, and wipe and powder. After being soaped, the baby is dipped, as with us, into the bath, and immediately laid back again on the pillow, where it looks like one of the little Christian 'bambinos' in sugar or plaster, which used to be sold in Italy at Christmas time.

The child is wrapped in the bath towel and dried. The mackintosh and towel are then removed, and the really difficult process of dressing a very young baby is safely and easily performed on the pillow. I saw it done by a young and inexperienced nurserymaid of nineteen, who certainly could never have been trusted to wash a baby as we do it in England, and I came away greatly impressed with the merits of the chaff pillow.

A favourite trick practised by those who have charge of babies is to cover or nearly cover over their faces, so that the child breathes its own breath, which all educated people know is poisonous. When you expostulate, the nurse says : 'It makes the child sleep better'—which means the child is more or less asphyxiated by want of air. This excuse could be urged for anything, even for giving what, when I was in Canada, I saw advertised everywhere as 'Sirop calmant de Madame Winslow.' The wretched stuff acquires a new dignity when translated into French! Fresh air, night and day, is the great essential for health ; and, pretty as are babies' veils, I think the babies are far better without them. All the same, I saw a lovely little baby's hood last year, made in a close-fitting way, like an old-fashioned baby's cap, and over all was thrown a large square of net, hemmed and run with three rows of satin baby ribbon.

The public mind has been a good deal disturbed and exercised by the bill, passed in '98, enabling people who have 'conscientious objections' to be absolved from having their children vaccinated. I should like to see all vaccination voluntary, as it seems to me to be exceedingly likely that the last scientific word on the subject has not been said. But if it is really for the good of the community that vaccination should be universally enforced, then the 'conscientious objector' is a danger to the whole community, and should not be allowed to have his way. Anybody interested in this subject will find, in the twenty-fourth volume of the 'Encyclopædia Britannica' (ninth edition), an exhaustive article on vaccination, which, the writer says, is 'the result of an independent and laborious research.' To me it was interesting and most instructive. The public now have such glorious chances of learning the truth, instead of living on false tradition ; but how few avail themselves of them ! The statements at the end of the article about the epidemic of smallpox in 1870–71 are most curious, and certainly contradict many of the usual medical assertions.

To return to the babies. Anxious young mothers with delicate infants are nowadays very apt to get hospital nurses to look after them. I am sure that this is a mistake, and I have known two or three cases amongst my acquaintances where this was tried and answered extremely badly. The hospital nurse is apt to be over-clever, and try far too many things, such as changing the foods unnecessarily, and using medicines much too freely. A baby wants ordinary animal care, warmth, regularity of treatment, and the people who look after it to have the courage that comes with love. It does not want remedies which check ailments one day and reproduce them the next day with renewed force. Why does it never strike the mother or nurse, who gives a child — with absolute courage — a harmful drug, such as fluid magnesia, that they could try instead such harmless remedies as spoonfuls of orange-juice, or apples or prunes rubbed through a sieve ? A doctor told me the other day that a child brought up on fluid magnesia was bound to suffer from that troublesome, if not danger- ous, ailment too well known in most modern nurseries, chronic constipation.

If a child is very delicate, the mother nervous, and if no good, experienced children's nurse is to be got, then I would recommend a monthly nurse ; though, of course, they too are sometimes difficult to get. There is an institution now started, called the Norland Institute, 16 Holland Park Terrace, London, W., and the principal will send all information if requested. It is for the training of ladies as children's nurses on Froebelian principles. I do not know much about it myself, but it appears to be useful both for employers and employed. So many women, though willing enough, are unfit for any employment through want of training, and many a young woman would be an excellent nurse for young children who could never make a good governess or school teacher.

Nursery arrangements are much cleaner now than they used to be. A well cared-for baby has its little gums wiped out every day with a soft rag, which is then burnt. This plan is safer than the soft little bit of sponge sold for the purpose, as sponges are difficult to keep perfectly clean, even if well washed and dried. The following is the receipt for the mixture with which this should be done, and which makes the baby smack its lips: Mix one teaspoonful of powdered borax with two teaspoonfuls of cold water, and add three ounces of glycerine. Shake the bottle well, and the mixture is ready for use. In the case of a baby that has been neglected, and when the mouth has become really bad, it should be washed out with warm water several times a day after food.

There is still a strong prejudice in England against boiling and sterilising milk; but, in the face of the recent revelations as regards tuberculosis in cows, I trust this will become less and less. The German patents are to be got at all chemists'. Soxhlet's apparatus is one of the best, I believe, but new sterilisers are constantly being brought out; and, when once understood, the process gives no more trouble than any other careful preparation of babies' food.

To give children and invalids raw milk does seem a most cruel risk. I know many young people who say they would rather die than drink boiled milk. If they were brought up from babyhood on cooked milk, I am sure that this feeling would disappear. I copy the following extract on this subject of milk-sterilising from a lecture (published in the 'Journal of State Medicine,' January, 1899) on 'The Administrative Control of Tuberculosis,' by Sir Richard Thorne Thorne, Medical Officer of the Local Government Board, as it interests and concerns far more people than the mere management and health of cows, although this is the chief point of Sir Richard's clear and admirable lecture. The extract may seem rather long, but I feel compelled to copy it, as it may in that way reach homes where the more scientific periodical may never have been heard of: 'It is a somewhat curious fact that the inhabitants of the United Kingdom stand almost alone amongst civilised nations in the habitual use of uncooked milk as food. This is the more to be regretted because, by reason of this practice, human life, especially that of infancy and childhood, is being sacrificed on a scale which, to use the mildest term, is altogether deplorable. That this should be so is also altogether unreasonable in the face of the certain knowledge we possess, and which is set forth in the report of the Royal Commission of 1890 in the following words: "The most deadly tubercular material can be rendered absolutely innocuous, in so far as any spreading of infective disease is concerned, by the action of a temperature at which water boils." And again: "It is sufficient to state that boiling, for an instant even, renders the tubercle bacillus absolutely innocuous." Milk exposed to a temperature of 100° C., whether by boiling or other form of cooking, will not convey tuber-

culosis; and milk sterilised, as by placing it over the
fire in one saucepan, which stands in an outer one
filled with water, until it has reached a temperature of
some 80° C. to 90° C., *i.e.*, 176° F., or perhaps even
less, is an equally innocuous food. And yet, whilst
we have this knowledge at our disposal, and whilst we
know, still further, that some 7,000 persons, mostly
infants, are annually killed in England and Wales by
that form of tuberculosis called "labis mesenterica,"
besides some thousands more by tubercular meningitis
—a cause of tuberculous death which is on the increase
under three months of age, is undergoing no diminution at the next three months of life, and which exhibits substantial increase during young adult life—
and yet we find people apparently intelligent, including
even heads of young families, who discard the remedy
on the mere ground of "taste." And what is still
more striking and reprehensible is the fact that in
many of our hospitals, established for the cure of disease, no effort is made to avoid the chance of impart-
ing disease, merely because effort would cause some
inconvenience. The avoidance of all that is septic in
connection with surgical operations stands in striking
contrast with the courting of infection in the wards
by the use of uncooked milk. But even the taste
which attaches to boiled milk, and to which infants
become at once habituated, may be largely avoided if
the milk boiled after the morning delivery be stored
in the cool for use in the afternoon, and if the afternoon milk be similarly set aside until next morning.

'But some allege another objection. It is maintained
that cooked milk is less nutritious than raw milk. I
admit that there is an element of truth in this. Milk is
a fluid having a biological character; it is living fluid,
and this character is destroyed by boiling or sterilisa-

tion. From the purely scientific point of view, it is most desirable to bear this in mind, but in its practical aspect it is well to remember that the slight diminution in nutritive value which cooking brings about in milk cannot be named side by side with the immense gain in freedom from the risk of infectious disease and death which is thus insured. . . .' He ends by saying:

'The need for educating the public of this country as to the risks involved in the use of raw cows' milk, and as to the simple methods by which these risks can be effectually avoided, is a pressing one, and it can only be met by enlisting the active services of my own profes-sion. Our influence in such matters is necessarily con-siderable; our responsibility is correspondingly a heavy one.'

I should like to know the opinion of the Faculty on the dangers of butter, cream, and cheese, which I have never seen mentioned. Butter, however, is now often made from boiled milk.

Here is a receipt for boiling milk for butter or keep-ing: Let the milk stand for twelve hours in an open tin, then put it on the stove and let it just bubble round the edges. Take it off, let it stand another twelve hours, and then make the butter.

The popular impression is that separated milk is use-less as human food. Yet I believe it is now acknowl-edged by scientific investigators that the nourishing and life-giving properties of milk remain when the cream is taken off, the cream containing nothing but the fat. Of course, to children and many people fat is desirable, but can be obtained in many other ways.

The newspapers of the last few months have been so full of this most interesting question of tuberculosis in cows that it seems almost superfluous to allude to it. Yet nurseries are so under the power of women who,

however good and devoted, are uneducated, and therefore bigoted in their opinions, that it is as well to
caution young mothers not to yield to what might
seem to them the greater experience of the nurse. I did
it myself, having as my nurse one of the best of women,
who had brought up several babies. All the same, I
think now I was wrong; but in my youth the rules of
health were in the dark ages compared to what they are
now. To-day every young mother should learn for
herself what is the last and the most approved theory as
regards food and fresh air. On one subject science and
nature go hand in hand, and lead more and more to the
belief that the only really right nourishment for a baby
is what nature provides. In the 'upper classes' it has
become in my life-time rarer and rarer for young
mothers to nurse their own children. When I was
young the only women who were supposed to be good
wet-nurses were the Irish; and why was this ? Because
they were poorly fed; they came, too, of generations of
poor feeders, and before the days when they could obtain
either meat or tea except in very small quantities. In
France and Germany the wet-nurses always came from
the poor districts, where, as a rule, meat-eating was
unknown; and of late years these women are more and
more difficult to procure, though this may, of course, be
from many reasons other than nature failing to supply
what is required. I believe that if young mothers were
greatly to reduce their ordinary food during the time
before the birth of their children, they would not only
greatly reduce the common suffering which nature has
had to resort to, so as to lessen the food taken, but the
chances of the baby's health after its birth would be
infinitely greater. A large, heavy baby often loses
weight after its birth, especially when the mother cannot
give it natural nourishment. This should not be ; they

should increase in weight during the first month. I was always under the impression when young that a delicate mother, and especially one threatened with consumption, ought on no account to nurse her child. In the lecture from which I quoted before, Sir Richard Thorne Thorne says that 'there is no sterilising apparatus that can give results comparable with those provided by nature in the healthy female breast, and that tuberculosis in the human milk glands is a disease so rare that it hardly needs consideration in connection with the feeding of infants. At the child-bearing age it is all but unknown.' I extract this because I think it will help many a young mother to fight the opposition of perhaps both her husband and the doctor, who may be thinking, as is natural, more of what they consider good for her than for the child.

I heard yesterday, in our village, an excellent lecture by a young mother on what she called the 'New Education.' I agreed with every word, and had myself tried to carry it out many years ago. It is sad that what she propounded has made so little way these five-and-twenty or thirty years. Her recommendations were much on the lines of a book first published in 1868, called 'Essays on Educational Reformers,' by Robert Herbert Quick. I only did not mention this book before, much as it interested me years ago, and much as I admire it still, because I thought it was out of print and not to be got. Now it is republished by Longmans, Green & Co., in a cheap edition (2s. 3d.) and arranged on a clearer plan. Get it, you young mothers, and read it. It is the most comprehensive and illuminating book that I have ever seen on the all-important subject. It is far better known in America than in England. The chapter on Pestalozzi is perhaps especially excellent. Nature should be helped by art, and art should come to the assistance of nature. After showing how children can only learn in their own way, he ends with, 'Of course I do not mean there is no education for children, however young; but the school is the mother's knee, and the lessons learnt there are other and more valuable than object lessons.' He goes on to say: 'The mother is qualified, and qualified by the Creator himself, to become the principal agent in the development of her child . . . and what is demanded of her is a *thinking love* . . .' Is it not almost fearful how many children grow up without any *thinking love* at all? Is there anything more pathetic in three lines than these — by Blake — or more terribly true? Think of all the half-castes all over the world, not to mention our own cities!

> The Angel that presided o'er my birth
> Said, 'Little creature, formed of joy and mirth,
> Go, live without the help of anything on earth.'

It is the non-understanding of children makes the difficulty. The following poem by Mrs. Deamer will give a stab, I think, to many a young mother. Maternal love often wants cultivating, and does not come naturally to many young women; of this I am sure. And, though they learn many things, they seem to think being a good mother comes by instinct or not at all. This is not true. Besides, the apparently devoted mother may want quite as much training and self-cultivation as the indifferent one; perhaps more so, as she takes more responsibility on herself, and so, possibly, deprives the child of being looked after by someone else.

> I think the world is really sad,—
> I can do nothing but annoy;
> For little boys are all born bad,
> And I am born a little boy.

It doesn't matter what the game,
   Whether it's Indians, trains, or ball;
I always know I am to blame,
   If I amuse myself at all.

I said one day, on mother's knee:
  'If you would send us right away
To foreign lands across the sea,
   You wouldn't see us every day.

'We shouldn't worry any more
   In those strange lands with queer new toys;
But here we stamp, and play, and war,
   And wear your life out with our noise.

'The savages would never mind,
   And you'd be glad to have us go
There; nobody would be unkind,
   For you dislike your children so.'

Then mother turned and looked quite red,
   I do not think she could have heard;
She put me off her knee instead
   Of answering me a single word.

She went, and did not even nod.
   What had I said that could annoy?
Mothers are really very odd
   If you are born a little boy.

I could go on quoting for ever from Mr. Quick's book, but why should I, when it is within reach of all? His last sentence is: 'The duty of each generation is to gather up the inheritance from the past, and then to serve the present and prepare better things for the future.' How can there be a better motto for young or old?

The kindergarten system, when well carried out, seems to be the best method of teaching children under seven, and a kindergarten child has more thoughtful independence than other children. I once tried to make a boy of five clean his teeth, but he was rebellious that night, and, in an unguarded moment, I said he must. So after standing some time beside him, I said: 'I do not know how long you mean to keep me here, but I can't give in now I have said you must.' The child answered quite calmly: 'Well, it *is* odd, mother, you should say that, as it is exactly what I feel.' And then we came in some way to an amiable compromise which hurt no one's dignity. It is so idiotic, in the management of children, to give direct orders which they do not understand, and which appear to them as unreasonable tyranny. A mother had better command by example, not by authority. Subjection and blind obedience are all wrong, and result from quite a mistaken idea of the evolution of the universe. 'Every human being has a claim to a judicious development of his faculties by those to whom the care of his infancy is confided.'

Teeth cleaning of children used to be thought rather an unnecessary tyranny. It has assumed different proportions now, and it ought to be seen to in all schools. A great many people will be surprised to learn that often would-be recruits are rejected on the ground of bad teeth. It is no better with officers, and cases are common in which candidates, after an expensive preparation, have failed to pass their 'medical' on account of deficient dentures. In an examination of 10,000 of British children, of an average age of twelve years, eighty-five per cent required operative treatment. One more example that the ordinary food of the present day is not conducive to the health of the human race. Improvement in teeth and gums is one of the most marked and satisfactory symptoms experienced by people who take to the health-giving food recommended by Dr. Haig.

I find, among my old letters, this anecdote of a young mother trying to give religious instruction to a delicate little girl of two and a half: 'M—— is a sweetly good, dear child and in better spirits than usual, which is a good sign. I was trying the other day to convey some notion of a Creator to her mind. She started with pure atheism — that nobody made the trees, etc. Having made her understand her clothes must be made, and dinner prepared by somebody, she seemed to accept the notion of "God" with a long-drawn "Oh!" And when I said he was a long way off, in the beautiful sky, she said quickly: "What a bore!" I asked: "Why?" She answered: "Me like to *see* God, mamma." In short, she caught up some notion of a good fellow who made everything that was good and beautiful, and has told me ever since: "Dod made the trees, the sun and the moon, and all the pitty things." So I flatter myself she is on the fair road to deism. Christianity must dawn upon her mind by very slow degrees, poor little infant! But she is so loving and gentle she is no bad exemplification of "Of such is the kingdom of Heaven," and I am very dotingly fond of her.' I think if this fond mother had given the love without attempting the instruction, merely teaching the child to admire and notice and love, she would have been more sensibly employed in fitting it for its future life than in trying to explain and expound deism or Christianity at so early an age.

I knew, years ago, two conscientious young parents, both equally religious, who stayed away themselves from going to church, which they loved, in order, as they said, to break the temper of their little daughter, aged two and a half. As I said before, temper, which is inborn and hereditary, should never be fought, but always treated with love, gentleness, and tenderness, as an ill-

ness. Temper cannot be conquered, except from within.
To help the child to help itself, that is the only method.
I do not really believe that punishment ever does any
good to old or young, though self-mortification helps
many natures. Prisons rank with mad-houses; they
exist to protect the public, not to benefit the individuals
who suffer punishment. The only way with children is
gradually to get them to see what most helps themselves.
I admit that to understand the way children's minds
work is a humiliatingly difficult task, and one cannot be
too careful not to shock their feelings by either laughing
at them or letting them see any contempt for their most
natural ignorance. There is a well-known story of a
little girl who, having been naughty, was told to ask
forgiveness of the Almighty in her evening prayers.
The next morning, when questioned as to whether she
had done so, she quietly answered: 'Oh yes, but Dod
said: ''Don't mention it, Miss B———'''!

In a letter on some remarks about children in my
first book, a most kind and able woman wrote to me as
follows: 'The only point on which I do not quite agree
with you is where you say you cannot judge of a child's
character before twelve. When I look back to my early
childhood, I can see how exactly I and my brothers and
sisters were as little children what we are to-day. What
I *do* think is that, from about twelve to twenty-two or
three, or even twenty-eight, a certain deflection takes
place; but as one fully develops, one returns to what
one was as a little child. I know that I am to-day far
more like what I was at seven years old than what I was
at sixteen. The child is father to the man, not to the
youth. Of course you must be keen enough to read the
child's character. Children are such mysterious things
that few grownup people, even those who are keen readers of adult character, *can* understand them.'

So far as I understand what is called 'the new education,' it does not mean knowledge teaching at all, but the developing and fostering the good qualities that are born in a child, and so keeping under the evil propensities which are equally born in it. In fact, to make grow and develop what is actually there in the best way you can ; not try to cram in, as into an empty sack, what you think ought to be there.

Some years ago the 'Pall Mall Gazette' used, from time to time, to contain charming original articles on various subjects. Among my cuttings I find the following, so true to child life that I think it will rejoice everyone who cares to understand children. This study is really only just beginning to be approached, as it should be, with the humility that belongs to great ignorance and non-understanding :

'It has often been remarked that one half of the world does not know how the other half lives, but it is curious enough that this should be the fact about a half of the world who share our homes, who occupy our thoughts, and who possess our hearts, perhaps, more entirely than do any other earthly objects.

'The world in which our children really move and live is as remote and unvisited by us as the animal kingdom itself, and it is only now and then that a chance glimpse into the working of their minds makes us realise the gulf that separates us. They can come to us, but we cannot go to them ; nor are they, indeed, without that touch of contempt for us and our affairs which might naturally be considered the exclusive privilege of the elder and stronger beings. "Don't disturb poor father ; he is reading his papers," is a sort of counterpart to "Oh, let them play ; they are doing no harm." When we cast a reminiscent glance over our own childhood we realise how solitary were its hopes and

its occupations, shared at most by one of our own age —
a sister, a brother, or a friend. The elders appear from
time to time as the *di ex machina* of our existence, for
redress or for deliverance. We remember them as
teachers, as purveyors of pleasure, often as separators
of companions and terminators of delights, but rarely as
sharers in our most exquisite amusements. ''What will
mother say?'' had about it a half-gleeful anticipation of
disapproval, seldom destined to be unfulfilled; and that
not because of any severity on the part of the parent,
but from a radical want of sympathy with the first principles of enjoyment. Wet, dirt, fatigue, a very little
danger, late hours — all were in themselves positive
pleasures, and with some this flavour lingers till far on
in life; but, as a rule, you cannot depend upon a grown-
up person not really preferring to be warm and dull and
dry, to any discomforts you can offer him.

'Then what a strange twilight reigns in children's
minds! What dim mysterious associations of words
and phrases lost to us through the garish light of grammar, or of a clear and positive orthography! Now and
then across the years comes a memory of difficulties
never guessed at by anyone but ourselves. How surprising it was to hear of people with broken arms or
legs, which members nevertheless were not visibly sev-
ered from their persons nor lying on the floor, as in the
more rational world of dolldom! And what mysterious
and terrible fate did ''being killed on the spot'' signify?
What spot, or, rather, which spot? for we invariably
referred it to some bodily blemish of our own.

'Holy Writ, of course, offered countless problems to
the imagination, and so did the services of the church.
The collects were fraught with a meaning their authors
never dreamed of. ''The ills which the devil Orman
worketh against us'' referred, we knew well enough, to

the deadly practices of some bottled Jinn or Efreet;
and one companion has since confessed that the Pontius
Pilate alluded to by the congregation every Sunday was
for him the Bonchurch pilot, strayed into strange company, no doubt, but one with whom he had established
friendly relations during the week. "Keep thy servant
from consumptious sins," we said devoutly, for doubtless a consumptious sin was connected remotely with the
storeroom.

'What confusion must have reigned in the mind of
the white-robed infant we once heard murmuring at his
mother's knee the following invocation:

> Tiger, tiger, burning bright,
> Through the darkness be thou near me!

And how fortunate that prayer is not always directly
answered! The words our children use are generally
direct and picturesque, coined with a view to their
expressive value. We know few terms more felicitous
than "a sash-pain," by which a child (the sex is
evident) was in the habit of alluding to one of the ills to
which flesh is heir. A "rocking-bed" is a better name
than a hammock, and a "worm-pool" is evidently the
Early Saxon rendering of a whirl-pool, or why should
you be in danger of being sucked down by it? A "poor
wheeler" delicately suggests the moral inferiority of
square cabs to hansoms. What can be better than a
child's definition of drawing: "First you think about
something, and then you draw a line round your
think"?

'Sometimes their utterances betray character, as of the
little boy who, when the tiger's growls behind the sofa
had become too realistic for human endurance, burst
forth with "Mother! mother! don't growl so loud;
it frightens granny"; or the self-conscious infant who

rushed to leave the lion-house at the Zoo because, he said, "the lion is peeping at baby"—as if that wide-eyed majesty were conscious of anything nearer than some Libyan desert visible to his mental gaze. Often they are questions to confound the wise. "Mother, does anyone have to-morrow before us? and will they use to-day when we've done with it?" has a flavour of oriental wisdom about it difficult to meet. Most grandparents can supply you with genuine expressions and utterances drawn from nursery life, and they are willing to do so on the smallest encouragement; it is in them that children find their most intelligent sympathisers. We noticed two of the most distinguished men of the present day in deep and confidential discourse at a state entertainment in London the other season. To the superficial observer they appeared to be settling the affairs of the nation, but in reality they were capping stories about their respective youngest grandchildren, and their confidences lasted long and late.

'It seems strange that with an inexhaustible field of observation open to everyone, the children of fiction should not be more lifelike and less sentimental than is usually the case; but the subject is one that might be indefinitely pursued.

'Memory, it is true, is apt to play us false when we try to reënter the realms of our youth'; but few of us seem ever to have listened at the nursery door, or to have looked through the eyes of childhood into the make-believe world it inhabits.'

I knew a little boy once who used to go out into Hyde Park when the soldiers were exercising, and on his return give long and detailed accounts of the real battles he had seen. His elder and less imaginative brother would stand by in silent amazement at what seemed to him absolute untruths. The child, in a way, knew he had not seen what he described, and yet, as he had seen with the eye of imagination, it was real and true to him.

Here is a little child's song, the words by E. Nesbit, set to music by Liza Lehmann. I think it charming, and so illustrative of the kind of imagination children have, knowing quite well that what they think is not the actual fact, though true to them:

> When my good-nights and pray'rs are said
> And I am safe tucked up in bed,
> I know my Guardian Angel stands
> And holds my soul between his hands.
> I cannot see his wings of light
> Because I keep my eyes shut tight,
> For if I open them I know
> My pretty angel has to go.
> But through the darkness I can hear
> His white wings rustling very near.
> I know it is his darling wings,
> Not mother folding up my things.

I never refuse to name anything I like when I am told 'Everyone knows that,' for 'everyone' is a very limited London circle, where bright, pretty things come like beautiful bubbles, are seen by what is called 'everybody,' and are gone in a moment. I think of my kind unknown friends who are far away bearing the white woman's burden, and who have written to me saying they enjoyed the little breath of home my last book brought them. They may not have seen or heard what I have, and even here in Surrey I find that often the thing that 'everyone knows' does not even reach the next parish.

March 3rd.—This is the first year I have forced *Spiræa confusa*, and it makes a lovely pot-plant. We left it out in the cold till the middle of January. In forcing all hardy things, that is the great secret,—send them to sleep as early as you can by taking them up and exposing them to cold. All plants must have their rest; they are not like Baron Humboldt and his night of two hours. The leaves of this Spiræa are a blue-gray, and the branches are wreathed with miniature 'May blossoms.' Alas! they do not do well picked and in water.

I am sure, for anyone who wants to force coloured Hyacinths, only the very best bulbs are worth while, especially when single flowers are preferred, as in my case. They are so sweet in the house that I think they are worth the trouble of growing and the expense of buying annually. I got last autumn a larger and later flowering kind of white Hyacinth from Van Tubergen, called 'Italian Hyacinths,' single ones and quite cheap. They have come on splendidly. They are something like the early Roman ones, only far larger and stronger. They flower much later and are of an accentuated white, well worth growing, and I think they will do out of doors next year or the year after. Two newly bought *Staphylea colchica* are looking lovely now in the greenhouse, and also a bought plant of white Lilac is covered with bloom. We must cut them all back hard after flowering, plant them out, and give them a year's rest; then I hope they will do again. *Libonia floribunda* is also a very pretty little greenhouse plant at this time of year. This is the time to pot up some rested plants of Sweet Verbena, and put them into the warmest house to start their growth. They soon come into leaf, and are then best in the ordinary cool house. This gives plenty of Verbena for early picking.

March 8th.—The lion-like character of the weather is softening, and all the little spring things begin to come through. Each day makes a difference, but the delightful feeling of new life is already everywhere.

Q

Our reason tells us this is because nature has been asleep, not dead. There is no mistake about the poor really dead plants; we know them too well. Early spring here is not beautiful at all; it is dry and shrivelled and hard-looking, not like the neighbourhood of my old home by the Hertfordshire millstream.

The white Alyssum, the common Pulmonaria, and the Wallflowers are all coming into flower. I feel more and more sure that mixed borders ought not to be dug up in autumn, as gardeners—especially gardeners new to a place—are so fond of doing; in that way half the best things get lost. The best way is to replant, or dig out large pieces and divide each plant if it wants it after flowering and before they quite die down. The white Alyssum and the Pulmonarias both do better under the slight protection of shrubs than quite in the open border, where the cold winds catch them.

My two large old Camellias planted out last autumn, well under a Holly, and facing north, are doing well, and one has three bright rosy red blooms. It remains to be seen how they will do next year. It is a pleasure to think Camellias do better in London gardens than almost any other evergreens, and only want well planting in peat and leaf-mould, and well syringing and watering in the spring. But there also they must have the protection of other shrubs, to hang over their tops and keep off the spring frosts.

A semi-double Azalea for the greenhouse, called *Deutsche Perle,* was given me the other day, and is a charming greenhouse plant. The flower has something of the appearance of a Gardenia, but it has no scent.

I have had two real good days' gardening, and have tried to carry out some of Miss Jekyll's hints, even in this commonplace, every-day garden. I have pulled down some of the climbing Roses, to let them make low-growing bushes ; for it is so true that, as she says, when planted on a pergola all their beauty is only for the bird as it flies. In the lanes, too, I saw some of the wild Arum leaves, and got out of the carriage to get some. Having no garden-gloves or knife with me, I ran my finger down into the soft, leafy mould to gather them with the white stalk underground. I trust these will rejoice an invalid friend in London to-morrow. One gets almost tired of the mass of flowers in London now, and things that smell of ditches and hedgerows are what one values most.

March 9th.— *Odontoglossum Rossii major* is a charming little Orchid to hang up in a shallow pan in a greenhouse when in flower. I am getting to like Orchids more and more now that, instead of thinking of them in their hot glass palaces, the easy-growing ones are treated here like other greenhouse plants. They give me great pleasure ; the flowers. are beautiful and interesting to look into and examine. I must learn more about them. In all things concerning nature, it is only ignorance that makes us take likes and dislikes.

This is the first spring morning. How one appreciates the slightest rise in the temperature ! I quite pity those who have rushed south, and who cannot watch the slow development of our English spring, with all its many disappointments.

The bright yellow flowers of the improved Tussilago Coltsfoot, sold by Cannel, are now just coming out, and the gravelly corner where they grow is a bright mass of buds. These flowers that come before their leaves, like the autumn crocus, are attractive, though the size of their leaves, when they do come, puts one sometimes out of conceit with them, especially if crowded for room ; though it is astonishing how corners can be found in even small gardens for all sorts of things, if one gives the matter constant attention. Having everything under one's eye, one never forgets to notice how they get on ; the greatest danger for the beds and shrubberies is the forking-over in autumn. It is far better left alone, if it cannot be done with care and knowledge.

My little plant of the *Daphne blagayana* is now in flower, but none of the Daphnes do well here for long ; even the *mezereum* goes off after a year or two, and *D. cneorum* wants constant attention. *D. blagayana* has to be grown like *D. cneorum*, pegged down in peat, and with some low-growing plant to shade it. All Daphnes are well worth the care they need, but it is a hard struggle. I think the spring air is too dry for them.

The best gardeners tell me we ought to be able to get Irises during eight or nine months of the year, and that this is done by keeping back Japanese Irises with their toes in the water till October. I confess I have never seen any *Kæmpferi* in bloom after the end of July in this part of the world.

I have lately been given this most useful list for the blooming time of Irises : February and March, *Iris stylosa* (blue and white varieties), *I. reticulata*, *I. unguicularis alba*, *I. persica*, *I. histrioides* ; March and April, *I. pumila atropurpurea*, *I. pumila cærulea*, *I. backeriana*, *I. tuberosa*, *I. orchioides*, *I. assyriaca* ; May, *florentina* ; May and June, German and Spanish and *I. sibirica* ; July and August, English and Japanese.

I have had the ground prepared, and to-day I am sowing the Shirley and other Poppies and Sweet Peas. Early sowing of early summer annuals is most essential here. I see Miss Jekyll holds much to autumn sowing. I have tried it, and failed in some cases, but that is because I have done it too late in the autumn. Early sowing is the only plan of spring sowing that is at all successful here. This particular first week in March, 1899, is perfection for all gardening work. I never saw the ground in such a good state — pulverised by night frosts, without being too dry and dusty. The gardening papers say there has not been such a sunny February for thirty years.

The paper of instructions sent out by the secretary of the Royal Horticultural Society with the seed of the Shirley Poppy is so excellent, and such a help for many annuals, that I cannot do better than copy it. One of the reasons people fail with hardy annuals is, as I said before, from not sowing them early enough :

' 1. On as early a day as possible in February choose a plot of ground sixteen to eighteen feet square or thereabouts, give it a liberal dressing of rich dung, and dig it in well, and leave it to settle.

' 2. For sowing, choose the first fine, open day in March, free from actual frost, when the ground works easily, and rake the surface over.

' 3. Mix the seed with five or six times its own bulk of dry sand, so as to make it easier to sow it thinly.

' 4. Scatter the mixture thinly, broadcast, over the raked surface, and rake it again lightly.

' 5. When the seedlings are large enough to handle, if there should be any bare patches in the bed, move with the tip of a trowel a few tiny clumps from where they stand thickest.

' 6. As soon as the bed shows regularly green, stretch two lines across it parallel to each other, at eight inches apart and, with a Dutch hoe, hoe up all between the lines, sparing those plants only that are close to each line. Move the lines and so hoe all the bed, which will then consist of a number of thin lines of seedlings eight inches apart, and the hoed-up ones lying between.

' 7. About a week later stretch the lines again eight

inches apart, at right angles to the previous lines, and hoe again. This, when finished, will leave a number of tiny square patches of seedlings eight inches apart each way.

'8. A week later thin out the little patches by hand, leaving only one plant in each. Now every plant will have eight inches square to grow in.

'9. Directly the plant shows the first sign of running up to blossom, put a thin line of two-feet-high pea-sticks between every two, or at most every three, lines of the plants to strengthen them to resist the wind and rain. They will soon grow above and hide the sticks.

'10. In dry weather thoroughly soak the bed once a week. A little sprinkle overhead is no use.

'*N. B.*—Be sure the operation described in No. 6 is done early enough; otherwise the plants will have become "leggy" before your thinning is complete, and when once Poppies become "leggy," they are practically ruined.'

March 14th.—My garden is now full of the old wild Sweet Violet (*Viola odorata*) of our youth—before even the 'Czars' came in, much less the giant new kinds. I have an immense affection for this Violet, with its beautiful, intense colour and its delicate perfume. It grew all about the Hertfordshire garden under the hedges, and little seedlings started up in the gravel paths, looking bold and defiant; but, all the same, they were rooted out by the gardener when summer tidying began. At the end of March or early in April, when the rain comes, I divide up and plant little bits of these Violets everywhere, and they grow and flourish and increase under Gooseberry bushes and Currant bushes, along the palings covered with Blackberries, under shrubs—anywhere, in fact—and there they remain, hidden and shaded and undisturbed all the summer.

Where seedlings appear, they are let alone all the summer and autumn till after flowering time in spring. They look lovely and brave these cold, dry, March days ; but their stalks are rather short here, for want of moisture. If anyone wants to see this Violet to perfection, let him chance to be in Rome early in March, as I once was, and let him go to the old English cemetery, where Keats lies buried, and the heart of Shelley, and he will see a never-to-be-forgotten sight — the whole ground blue with the Violets, tall and strong above their leaves, the air one sweet perfume, and the sound (soft and yet distinct) of the murmur of spring bees.

Just at this time we rake off the winter mulching that has covered the Asparagus beds, water them well with liquid manure, and salt them when the rain comes.

March 16th. — As the seasons come round, the changes often recall to my mind certain verses in 'Bethia Hardacre's' volume. Such tender, loving versions of some of nature's facts are there, and I go out to verify them. The garden now is one mass of Crocuses, Violets, fading Snowdrops and bursting Daffies ; and this is how the flower-chain is described by her :

> Blossoms, meet to mourn the dead,
> On each season's grave are spread :
> Lilies white and Roses red
> O'er dead Spring are canopied;
> Roses, in their latest bloom,
> Blazen golden Summer's tomb;
> Stealthy showers of petals fall
> At still Autumn's funeral;
> But the darlings of the year
> Strew rude Winter's sepulchre..
>
> Scarce a flower does Winter own;
> Of four seasons he alone
> Scarce a bud does to him take —
> Barren for the future's sake,

Well content to none possess;
And Sweet Violets — faithfulness —
And White Snowdrops — innocence —
Are in death his recompense;
And these darlings of the year
Strew rude Winter's sepulchre.

March 20th.— Of all the many catalogues I receive, none, I think, are produced with anything like the attractive intelligence of the one sent out by Messrs. Ware, of Tottenham. This year one is tempted to say, from the pretty European-Japanese drawing on the cover, that nature made a mistake in not giving us sometimes an all-over pink sky instead of a blue! The soil at Tottenham is very heavy, and plants that flourish admirably there, from my experience, unfortunately decline altogether to grow when removed to a purer air and a lighter soil. I am sure that all amateurs who are interested in the rarer varieties of hardy and half-hardy plants had far better try and raise them themselves from seed. But a visit to Messrs. Ware's garden, near London, as well as constantly going to Kew, will show amateurs what can be done. The old-fashioned idea that a garden meant a place of quiet and repose is not the proper mental attitude for suburban plant-culti-vators. The drawings in the catalogue are excellent, though they perhaps rather represent the cultivator's expectations than the truth. Still, it is well to have high ideals, even in annuals and biennials. To return to my catalogue — no one can give time and study to it without being the wiser.

In spite of all my resolutions to stay at home, I have a very great longing to go once more to the 'Riviera,' and see some of the really good gardens which have grown up since my time, especially that of 'La Mortola, Italy,' belonging to Commendatore Hanbury. Last

year, with his help and permission, a little book came
out which was a great success, and quickly ran out of
print; it was called 'Riviera Nature Notes.' A book of
great interest to us who are only English gardeners,
what would it be to those who are his neighbours on
those sunny slopes? The first line in the book is:
'J'observe et je suis la nature; c'est mon secret pour
être heureux' (Florian).

Can we hear this truth too often in prose and poetry
and in all art? I have always thought one of the most
beautiful of Burne-Jones' early pictures is the one
which represents the wild god — Pan — lovingly receiving poor little Psyche, thrown up by the river that
refused to drown her. And does it not mean that nature
from all time has been the best comforter for one of the
greatest of human sorrows, unrequited love?

These 'Riviera Notes' are full of desultory but most
interesting information. How delightful to read them
in a dry Olive yard or under an umbrella Pine, with the
blue sea behind the tree's rich stem! Or, when too
warm to walk so far, to sit below the Orange trees,
whose tops above one's head are masses of golden fruit
and sweet-smelling flowers! At the end of the book are
chapters on birds, insects, and the 'Riviera' traces of that
individual — apparently so much alike in all countries —
prehistoric man. Were they happy, those dim mysterious multitudes of the Old Stone and New Stone ages?
This little book must have delighted many, as it
delighted me; and it is not too difficult for anyone as
ignorant as I am to understand. As it bears on my
favourite topic, I must quote from this book the fact that
'polenta,' or Indian corn porridge, is the chief food of
the Piedmontese, and I observe it is also stated that they
do the hard manual labour at 'La Mortola.' They work
all about the country as navvies, porters, and so forth,

which proves that, at any rate, this food does not make them unmuscular. They are powerfully made men, and the Niçois are ludicrously afraid of them, for they consider them capable of any act of violence. It is also said that these Piedmontese suffer from a disease called the 'pellagra,' caused by living on this polenta, 'one of the least nourishing of the farinaceous foods.' May it not be the food mixed with some form of alcohol ? It appears as if some disease belonged to every kind of food eaten without variety and in large quantities.

Mr. Barr gave me, two years ago, some small bulbs of *Crocus tommasinianus*. I thought at first they were going to do nothing ; but this year they have flowered beautifully, and are of a very delicate pale lavender colour. He says they will come up every year, and I think they are really far prettier than the large, strong, cultivated Crocuses. I have often been asked, What should be put into Rose beds to enliven their dull branchiness for early spring ? Strong clumps of winter Aconites planted very deep, to be succeeded, when the Aconites are only bright green tufts of leaves, by large, pale Crocuses, white and light lavender, are as good a combination as I know; and when they die down a fresh top-dressing can be lightly forked into the Roses without hurting the bulbs.

A correspondent noticed that I did not mention *Anemone Pulsatilla*. It is quite true I have not got it. In my ignorant days I bought it once or twice, and it quickly died ; and I have not yet tried to grow it from seed, but shall do so this year. This correspondent writes from Gloucestershire, where he says it grows wild, and that, when well grown, 'it is the most beautiful native plant we have.' His letter is dated March 9th, and he adds : 'I have one now in a twelve-inch pan, taken up about three weeks ago, which has about 150 flowers and buds on it. Like Lilies-of-the-Valley, it grows in the poorest and dryest lime soil. But it likes good feeding. I think that description sounds as if it were worth trouble to produce. Of course he meant, when he took it up, that he grew it under glass.

Two years ago I bought a plant of *Holbœllia latifolia*, and planted it in the ground in my cool greenhouse, where it is doing quite beautifully, and is now covered with buds. It is a delightful plant for a cool greenhouse creeper, as the fragrance of its white flowers is delicious, almost exactly like Orange flower; and it is so nearly hardy it will do out of doors against a wall in many parts of England. I shall try it here when I have struck some cuttings. It is often called, erroneously, *Stauntonia latifolia*.

I have just brought into the conservatory next the drawing-room from the cool house in the kitchen garden an interesting panful of one of the Moræas. They seem a large family; all from the Cape of Good Hope. A piece was given me by someone who called it *M. fimbriata*. It has not been touched for two years, and was well baked all the summer, is now healthy and growing, and has four bloom-spikes; last year it only threw up one. The flower is like a small, delicate Iris, of a lovely cold china-blue colour. The growth is quite different from that of an Iris. The stalk has a graceful bend, and a branching end with several buds, as is the case with so many of the Cape bulbs. The buds open one after the other as the flower dies. They will do when picked and in water. My *Crinum Moorei* I have had for three or four years in a large pot. It makes its leaves in February, and throws up without fail its enormous brown flower-stem. It is beginning to open now its lily-like flowers; these, like the buds of the *Moræa fimbriata*, flower in succession, but, as each one lasts

about a week in bloom, the flowering period is extended
for a considerable time.   It is well fed, while growing,
with liquid manure.   Its healthy, strong appearance and
delicate scent give me a great deal of pleasure year by
year.

Mustard and Cress, much grown in boxes in early
spring, and which is so delicious at five o'clock tea or
with bread and butter and cheese, many people will not
eat because it is so often gritty.   This certainly makes it
horrid ; and if the Cress is washed it makes it very wet,
often without getting rid of the grit.   The best way to
grow it is to make the earth very damp before sowing,
press it down flat, and then sow the seed very lightly on
the top, making a division between the Mustard and the
Cress.   Cover it with a tile, or something else to make
it dark, till it has sprouted, and then cut it carefully,
straight into the plate or small fancy basket in which it
is to be served, without washing it at all.   If grown in
this way and carefully cut, there will be no grit whatever.   I find small, low, round Japanese baskets of various sizes (from Liberty's) are most useful in a house
with a garden.   They are beautifully made and very
pretty, and fruit can be picked into them at once, and
served either at breakfast or luncheon without any fin-
gering in the pantry or kitchen.

March 28th.—Towards the end of this month, or
quite the beginning of next, it is most important to erect
shelters under walls or trees, where the sides can be
protected from wind and the top covered up on cold
nights, as now is the time it is so important to clear out
greenhouses, both for the sake of the hardier plants that
are going out, and the more special ones that remain
inside.   When they are moving, feeling the spring in all
their fibres, that is the time they begin to get weak and
drawn up if not given room and air.   This is especially

the case with the large old Geraniums that are in the greenhouse, Carnations, Abutilons, not to mention all the forced things that have done flowering. Putting them out under these shelters hardens them off well before they are planted out in the open. Nothing is more distressing to a real plant-lover than to see bulbs and Spiræas and Azaleas lying about untended, just after they have done their work so valiantly for us early in the year. If a plant is not worth care, it is not worth keeping. Throw it away at once, where it goes to make food for future generations, and the pot is useful when many pots are wanted. As I said before, but remind now, pieces of corrugated iron come in most usefully in making these temporary pens and shelters. For some plants, a sunk pit with a raised rim of brick or turf answers well. On this the sheets of iron are laid at night.

March 30th.—At this time last year I wrote in my notebook that the cold and tempestuous weather, which had lasted the whole of March, moderated a little, and so I drove to the lovely wild garden in this neighbourhood, which is always so full of interest to me the whole year round.

One of the most striking things in the garden was a plant of *Daphne blagayana*. I asked how they managed to flower so well what I found so difficult, and was told this Daphne had been protected with a wire hencoop covered with green canvas, which keeps out six or seven degrees of frost. The *Adonis vernalis* was out much earlier than mine, but the garden is damper and more sheltered. *A. vernalis* is a beautiful spring flower, but it dislikes being moved. There must be some difficulty, I suppose, about its cultivation, as one so seldom sees it. The *Chionodoxas* were the finest and largest I have ever seen, and were called *Allenii*. The true *Anemone fulgens grœcii* was a more brilliant colour than the ordinary one. I imagine it is rather difficult to get. A blue Chilian Crocus I had never seen before (*Tecophilœa cyaneo*) is slightly tender and requires protection. It was out of doors in this sheltered wood, and had only been protected with a handglass. *Forsythia intermedia* is one of the best, and was flowering well. For anyone who has a damp, shady wood, there are no shrubs more beautiful than the various Andromedas. Yards of ground in this wood were covered with the Pyrola (Winter Green). Its small red berry was still on, and spring flowers and bulbs of all kinds were growing up through it. A more beautiful covering for the ground, where the soil is leafy and the moisture sufficient, does not exist.

A good rockery label, as it shows very little, is a small stick with the bark left on, but for a flat piece cut off at the top, which is painted white, to receive the name.

RECEIPTS

Turbot à la Portugaise.—Cut into Julienne strips equal quantities of carrots, onions, turnips, and celery. Fry lightly in butter till a good colour. Add fresh tomatoes, peeled, and with the seeds taken out. Cut them in slices before adding to the other vegetables. Moisten with a glass of white Sauterne wine and a little German sauce (see 'Dainty Dishes') to bind the vegetables, a little veal gravy, a little salt, a pinch of sugar; and leave the whole to cook for twenty to twenty-five minutes, till of a good consistency.

Meanwhile take the fillets of a moderate-sized turbot without bones or skin. Butter freely a rather shallow sauté-pan, place the fillets in it, season with salt and white pepper, moisten with one or two glasses of

Sauterne wine, and bring to the boil on the fire. Cover with a round bit of buttered paper, and finish cooking them inside the oven. Baste them constantly, so that they should not get dry. They will take from twenty to twenty-five minutes to cook.

Serve the fillets in a silver dish—whole or in slices. Add to the vegetables the gravy of the fillets of turbot which remains in the sauté-pan. Cook these to a turn, add a good bit of fresh butter and a little Hungarian 'paplika'; in default of which a little cayenne pepper can be used. Pour the vegetables over the turbot, to hide the fillets. Place for a few moments in a hot oven, and serve.

When mushrooms are small or not very fresh, they are best chopped fine, warmed up with a little butter, pepper and salt, and poured on to some squares of hot toast. The yolk of an egg is an improvement for non-vegetarians. For broiling mushrooms in the oven, they are much better if done in bacon-fat instead of butter.

Sutton's winter salad is now getting rather old. If it is cut up in small shreds, and a raw leek and beetroot added (also shredded fine), and the whole mixed together with a little half mayonnaise sauce or plain oil and vinegar, it makes a very good salad.

We get the seedling lettuces in boxes a little earlier year by year, as it is such a pleasure to get back to a really fresh salad. It always recalls to me the young spring salads the monks used to bring to my mother at Cimiez, and which she attributed to some mysterious monkish secret. The fact is, the climate there enables lettuces to be sown out of doors very early.

It is well to know that rhubarb can be made to take the flavour of anything you cook with it; but with forced young rhubarb, when the flavour is delicate, it is a mistake to put in anything except a little sugar. Cooks can be reminded at this time of year, when dried fruits are so useful as compotes—apricots, prunes, apples, etc. —that it is a great improvement in the stewing of them to add occasionally a tablespoonful of cold water, to prevent their cooking too fast. Bleached almonds are a pleasant addition as a change in these compotes.

I read with regret the other day in a leading evening newspaper of the authoritative revival of the notion that eating tomatoes is the cause of the increase of cancer. This theory seems likely to deprive the poorer public of one of the best and cleanest blood-purifiers within reach of the inhabitants of our towns. It seems to me on a par with Swift's idea that his life-long headaches were in a great measure due to a surfeit of fruit consumed when very young at Moor Park, and which, naturally enough, brought on the first attack, as a dish of strawberries will upset a meat-eating and gouty patient—this state of the blood being produced by eating, not too much, but too little fruit. The population of the whole south of Europe has eaten tomatoes from time immemorial. Would it not be far more sensible to look for the cause of cancer in the great increase of meat-eating, especially in towns, the over-fed and diseased cattle, tinned and other preserved animal foods, and the much consumed modern stimulant, beef-tea?

I do not vouch for the absolute correctness of the following statements, but I find them among my notes, and I think there is some truth in them :

Lettuce is calming and beneficial to anyone suffering from insomnia.

Honey is wholesome, strengthening, cleansing, healing, and nourishing.

Lemons afford relief to feverish thirst in sickness,

and, mixed with hot water, are a help in biliousness, low fever, colds, coughs, rheumatism, etc.

In cases of diseases of the nerves and nervous dyspepsia, tomatoes are a powerful aperient for the liver, and are invaluable in all conditions of the system in which the use of calomel is indicated.

Onions are useful in cases of nervous prostration, and will quickly relieve and tone up a worn-out system. They are also useful in all cases of coughs, colds, and influenza.

Apples are nutritious, medicinal, and vitalising. They aid digestion, clear the voice, and correct the acidity of the stomach.

April 1st.—This book is the last bit of work of the kind I shall 'ever do, and I am anxious to state, as I think of them, any views I may happen to have on various matters.

I am deeply interested in watching the gradual development of public opinion on cremation. I casually alluded to this before, in reference to Mr. Robinson's well-known book on the subject. So far as I can judge from the newspapers, cremation is making a little way among the rich and well-known, who alone seem in this country to have the power of influencing the majority. But if what I read is true, a terrible fashion is growing around this excellent, clean, practical way of being dealt with after death, and that is that instead of one funeral there are to be three—one the cremation, another the funeral service in London, a third (and worst of all) the burying of the ashes. The newspapers gave an account of a cremated peer who, by his own wish or his family's, had the box with the collected ashes deposited in an ordinary-sized coffin, in order that the tenantry might have the honour of carrying the coffin in the usual way to the vault. This kind of thing, I think, tends to make the process ridiculous. And as only those are cremated who wish it, detailed directions might be left that the ashes should be spread under the sweet vault of heaven, and a memorial erected, useful or otherwise, in church or street, as seems good to the family. That alone, in my opinion, gives dignity to the whole proceeding ; the burying of box or urn is meaningless and almost puerile. How dogmatic it reads in print, to say simply what one feels ! But I mention my view of the question because, in talking with people, I so often find they have done such and such a thing merely because they had not thought of the other way. The old world, it is true, collected the ashes. But we know that in later days they were used by the Roman washerwomen, so long as they could get them, as we use soda, for the purifying alkalies they contained. I see no need for us to provide alkaline matter for future generations.

April 2nd.— I have been lately to some of my Suffolk friends, in whose gardens I always learn so much. In a bowl of mixed flowers in my room I quickly detected a flower I did not know, a pale lavender double-daisy-shaped ball, many on a branch, and yet not crowded or thick. This turned out to be double Cineraria, grown from seed sent out by Veitch. I can see the horror of many of my good-colour-loving, bad-colour-hating friends, who dislike the ordinary finely-grown gardener's Cinerarias as much as I do. These double ones have the advantage of doing exceedingly well picked, and are one of the few plants which I really think are prettier double than single, though I afterwards saw that some of the plants were very crude and hard in colour.

Dimorphotheca eclonis is a very pretty-growing, long-flowering pot-plant from Africa. It is of the same family as Calendula (Marigold), and very like *Calendula pluvialis*, figured in Maund's 'Botanic Garden,' that never-to-be-too-much-praised book. The whole family

of Calendulas close on dull, damp days.   Maund says of
these plants : 'The Latin *pluvialis*, which pertains to
rain, is used in reference to the influence which rain or
dew has on the opening and closing of the blossoms of
our present subject.   All flowers, we believe, which
close in rainy or cloudy weather have the property of
closing at night.   The same object, protection from
moisture, is attained in each instance.   This peculiarity
is prettily alluded to in the following lines, which I
copy from Dr. Withering's arrangement :

> The flower enamoured of the sun,
> At his departure hangs her head and weeps,
> And shrouds her sweetness up, and keeps
>   Sad vigils, like a cloistered nun,
> Till his reviving ray appears,
> Waking her beauty as he dries her tears.

The seed of this *Calendula pluvialis* may be sown in
the open ground in April.

I have never seen Messrs. Backhouse's gardens at
York ; but so far as I can judge, from seeing various
rock gardens they have made and planted, no one is half
so good as they are for all Alpines.   They have so improved the actual plants that they are scarcely to be
recognised as the same which grow in their mountain
homes.   Many will say : 'What a pity !'   But that
applies to all rock-gardening.   If one tries to grow
Alpines, one wants them to be strong and to live.
Saxifraga oppositifolia is, for instance, really like what
Mr. Backhouse describes in his catalogues and David
Wooster illustrated in his book on Alpine plants.   *Saxifraga sancta* blooms in profusion as early as this, and is
a bright, pale yellow.   All these plants require either to
be divided or else to have some handfuls of light earth
thrown over them after flowering.   *Saxifraga bur-*

seriana is also very early, and has a pretty flower. But all these plants cost money, as they make no effect except in large clumps; and, to do well, I fear they want stiff, moist soils.

Those who live near the coast may be interested to hear of an experiment which I saw being tried for growing Asparagus in a wild state on the sandy shore of Suffolk. The gardener wrote me the following description of what he had done:

'In the spring of 1896, some yearling Asparagus plants were planted on the lower portions of some raised banks close to the sea. There was no attempt at preparing the ground; it was not even properly cleared of weeds, or sufficient care exercised to plant the plants far enough apart to give them growing room. But the result far exceeds what might have been expected from such rough-and-ready treatment, for one can almost say they have grown wild. As regards the soil of which these banks are composed, the only remark one can make is that it is of a very questionable character, although of three classes: No. 1, pure, fine drift sand; No. 2, drift sand crag and river mud mixed; No. 3, river mud. The plants in No. 2 mixture have given the best produce, No. 3, river mud, being very close; whilst the produce of No. 1, from the fine drift sand, is very poor. There has been no attempt to give cultural aids in the way of manure up to the present. In summing up the result of the above experiment, it is quite evident that our home-grown Asparagus supplies might very easily be largely increased, and it is to be hoped the idea may be taken up as a means of profit by working men who are holders of land by the sea.

'It will be necessary, if success in the production of the first-class article is to be arrived at, to observe clearly at the onset three things of the utmost importance. First, thoroughly clean the land to be planted with Asparagus of all such weeds as Docks, Spear-grass or any other perennial weed, as if done at the first it is done for good, leaving the land free to be taken possession of by the Asparagus roots, and doing away with any after-necessity of forking about them. Second, plant good, strong yearling plants not nearer together than two feet, better still if the distance is increased to three or four feet, marking the spot where each plant is planted with a stout stake, so that their position can be known. Third, the land must be kept free of weeds, and a dressing of manure, or any form of liquid manure, may be given occasionally during their season of growth.'

I may add that, even in inland sandy places, I am certain a very fair success is to be obtained in growing Asparagus by planting them in odds and ends of places, even amongst shrubs, or anywhere in suitable corners. The difficulty is to mark the place clearly enough in winter, so that when a new hand comes in the roots may not be dug up. The Asparagus plants that annually bear a quantity of berries are by no means so large as those that are unfruitful, and great numbers of gardeners now discard them at planting time where they are known to exist. This, no doubt, is a step in the right direction. I believe this excessive seeding of some plants is the result of check in growth in young stages, such as severe root-injury, overcrowding in the seedbed, and poverty of soil. It is well to add that in all exposed places it is necessary to secure by staking the summer's growth, as it is very important that this should be preserved from being broken down, and it should not be cut down till quite late in the autumn.

April 4th.—Returned home to-day. It is incredible

the difference a little warm rain makes. The whole garden looks so changed from when I went away, four or five days ago!

I have in the entrance drive a large Balsam-bearing Poplar—or Tacamahac tree, as I believe it to be correctly called. Mr. Loudon, in his 'Arboretum,' describes it exactly. Every garden of a certain size would be the better for having one of these trees, because of the exquisite smell of the long catkins produced in April. If one passes near the tree in showery weather, the air reminds one of a greenhouse filled with Cape Jessamine or Gardenia. The scent does not last very long, but while it does I know nothing sweeter.

April 5th.—Years ago I had the great pleasure of going to D. G. Rossetti's studio. He was working at the small replica of his beautiful big picture now at Liverpool—Dante's dream—from the 'Vita Nuova.' In the picture Love holds his hand and gives Beatrice—dead—the kiss that Dante never gave her living. It is a poem which can be interpreted in a hundred ways, according to the mind and heart of those who look. To most people I suppose it is the glorious interpretation of a very common mental attitude—what we have not had is to us what is most precious and most beautiful and most lasting. When Rossetti ceased to be among us, and with the memory of that afternoon at his studio strong upon me, I went to his house in Cheyne Walk on the 'private view' day before the sale. I tried to buy one or two of his things, but they went at very high prices, and I got nothing; still I have always remembered what struck me as a lovely and original firescreen. I have had it copied several times, and it has given pleasure to many; so I will describe it here, that it may give pleasure to a few more. It was a little Chippendale plain mahogany screen, consisting of three narrow

leaves. The surface of each of these was entirely covered with the eyes of peacock feathers stuck one over
the other, like the scales of a fish, each eye having the
long feathers round it cut off. The other side of the
panel was gilt, and I have lately found that thin oak
takes the gilding best. I think in the original Rossetti
screen it was gilt paper or leather. On this, long peacock feathers, split at the back to make them lie flat,
were arranged in groups of three or five or six, at
various heights, according to fancy. They look best if
the stalks nearly meet at the bottom. The panels are
glazed on both sides. A square firescreen can be arranged in the same way. The effect is most satisfactory, and it has that great merit in furniture—unchange-
ableness. The colours, being natural, never fade ; and
the glass preserves the feathers from perishing.

The following is a receipt for varnishing plaster
casts, given me many years ago by Sir Edward Burne-
Jones :

Quarter of an ounce of gum elami, two ounces of
white wax, half a pint of turpentine ; add a small
squeeze from an oil-paint tube of raw umber when a
small quantity of the varnish has been poured into a
saucer ready for use. Apply with a brush, and spread
quickly and evenly. This has to be done three times,
with a day between each coating, and rubbed hard with
a silk handkerchief between each painting. It gives
casts and plaster figures the colour of old ivory, and
makes them useful and decorative in a way they can
never be without it. The varnish on the casts lasts for
ever, never becomes dirty, and the dust can be rubbed or
even washed off quite easily. The best place in London
for plaster casts is Brucciani's (40 Russell street, Covent
Garden). I know few decorations more satisfactory—for
those who appreciate them and in certain rooms—than

these casts, either from Greek friezes or (best of all) the low-relief reproductions of Donatello's almost divine work.

Dinner-tables in country houses are often a great puzzle. I know nothing so dreary as two or three people sitting down to a large, empty table at breakfast or dinner, because it is not worth while to change it, as a few more are coming to luncheon. When we first came here, even our family party varied so much in numbers that I thought it most desirable to find something that would suit my notions, and be easily and quickly changed from little to big and *vice versa*. I hunted the old furniture shops with no success, and at last decided something must be made to carry out my intentions. We got three oak tables made of exactly the same size, the top of each being forty-five inches square. It was impossible for these tables to have four legs, as when put together, which was my plan for enlarging, they would be much in the way. The top was not very thick, so had to be firmly supported. This was done by two pieces of wood placed underneath the top and resting on four wooden columns (after the manner of Chippendale's round tables) fitting into a piece of wood fourteen inches square and eight inches from the floor. From the four corners of this spread out four feet, almost but not quite to the outside edge of the table above, thus making it quite firm. This table is equally suitable for two or four people. In order to make it comfortable for six, we lay a false top upon it a few inches longer at both ends. When guests are more numerous, two of the tables are put together, and for a still greater number the third can be added. They remain perfectly firm and level if made of seasoned wood, and need no fixing or machinery to join them. The oak can be varnished or left plain, smoked or stained green, according to taste. Mr. Watson, of 11 Orchard street, London, makes them to order. For breakfast or luncheon we use the small tables apart, even when our party is complete. But at dinner this gives so much more trouble in waiting that we put them together.

April 8th.—This year gardening knowledge is given to the public cheaper than ever. There is a new penny handbook on gardening to be got at any railway station (Ward, Lock & Co.). It is quite good, giving all the elementary instruction necessary.

The uses of petroleum tubs in a garden are endless. I get my oil now from London, and so do not return the barrels. Mr. Barr told me the other day he was knocking the bottoms out of some, sinking them, one below the other, with a pipe in between, and puddling them with stiff clay at the bottom; then he was going to plant them with specimens of the beautiful new French Nymphæas (Water Lilies), M. Marliac's hybrids being the most beautiful perhaps of all. A full, excellent, and detailed account of the cultivation of these Water Lilies is to be found in Mr. Robinson's last edition of 'The English Flower Garden.' As is natural at my age, I have a most elderly affection for types and parent plants, because, as a rule, they are less expensive to buy, and much more willing to be managed when one has got them. But I do not say this without from my heart giving all honour to cultivators of hybrid plants.

Tub arrangements can be made of endless use even in the smallest gardens and back yards, if sunny—never forgetting the precious rain-water, which every slight slope in the ground makes it easy to collect if the tubs are sunk level with the ground. I mention things again and again, knowing well in our full modern lives how useful it is merely to remind. This year I have sunk a tub under every tap I have in the garden, as exposing the water to the sun and air prevents its being so hard and cold as when it comes straight out of the pipe.

We have just had, what we always feel to be doubly precious in our sandy soil, a good shower of rain. Mr. Stephen Phillips, in the 'Saturday Review' last year, had a poem which describes this kind of shower beautifully and originally:

After rain, after rain,
Oh, sparkling Earth!
All things are new again,
Bathed as at birth.
Now the pattering sound hath ceased,
Drenched and released,
Upward springs the glistening bough
In sunshine now;
And the raindrop from the leaf
Runs and slips;
Ancient forests have relief,
Young foliage drips.
All the earth doth seem
Like Dian issuing from the stream,
Her body flushing from the wave,
Glistening in her beauty grave;
Down from her, as she doth pass
Little rills run to the grass;
Or like, perhaps, to Venus when she rose
And looked with dreamy stare across the sea,
As yet unconscious of the woes,
The woes, and all the wounds that were to be.
Or now again,
After the rain,
Earth like that early garden shines,
Vested in vines.
Oh, green, green
Eden is seen!
After weeping skies
Rising Paradise;
Umbrage twinkling new
'Gainst the happy blue.

God there for His pleasure,
In divinest leisure,
Walking in the sun,
Which hath lately run;
While the birds sing clear and plain,
Behind the bright, withdrawing rain.
Soon I shall perceive
Naked, glimmering Eve,
Startled by the shower,
Venture from her bower,
Looking for Adam under perilous sky;
While he hard by
Emerges from the slowly dropping blooms
And warm, delicious glooms.

April 10th.—This is a time when I always find it a little difficult to keep the conservatory next the drawing-room gay. The large Crinum is going off, and the Azaleas are rather a bad metallic colour, which kills everything else. *Primula farinosa* is a pretty thing if well grown ; *Cineraria cruenta* is in full bloom, but I must get some fresh seed, as the flowers have all become one shade, which they were not at first. A charming, sweet little shrub which looks something like a white Daphne is *Pittosporum tobira ;* it comes in usefully at this time. We have had in succession since January pots of Polygonatum (Solomon's Seals), and they all go out into the reserve bed to be taken up another time, so are not at all wasteful. I have never had *Forsythia suspensa* so good in the garden as this year. The shrub is one golden mass, and when picked in long branches and peeled it is quite admirable in water. I suppose its being so good is partly an accident of the weather, partly that after flowering last year it was cut back hard, and partly that we twisted black thread about it to prevent the birds eating the buds in February, which they invariably do here, both with this plant and with *Prunus Pissardii. Spiræa Thunbergii* responds in the most delightful way to constant pruning. The more the dear little thing is cut, the better it seems to do. That is the real secret of all these early-flowering shrubs; they do not exhaust themselves then with leaf-making and growth. Under those shrubs where there are no Violets and no white Arabis, the common Lungwort (Pulmonaria) makes an exceedingly pretty ground-covering; for instance, under a Lilac bush or any deciduous shrub. This kind of spring gardening is only trouble, not expense, as all these plants divide into any number after flowering, and take away the bare look of a spring garden on light soils. When the leaves are out, the place they are in wants nothing and would grow nothing else. In fact, in these kinds of gardens the more the earth can be kept clothed and covered with light-rooting dwarf plants the better, as it saves weeding—always such a terrible business.

Nothing, I think, tempts me so much to neglect all duties and to forget all ties as gardening in early spring weather. Everything is of such great importance, and the rush of work that one feels ought to be done without a moment's delay makes it, to me at least, feel the most necessary thing in life. A friend wrote to me once: 'The best thing in old age is to care for nothing but Nature, our real old mother, who will never desert us, and who opens her arms to us every spring and summer again, warm and young as ever, till at last we lie dead in her breast.'

And another wrote: 'Serenity, serenity, serenity and light! Surely this is the atmosphere of Olympus; and if we cannot attain to it in age, in vain has our youth gone through the passionate toil and struggle of its upward journey to the divine summits.'

These thoughts fit better the solitude of bursting woods in the real country than the cultivating mania in a small garden, where we are all tempted to fight against Erasmus' assertion : 'One piece of ground will not hold all sorts of plants.'

A great deal of pleasure is to be got by striking cuttings of Oleanders in heat, and growing them on in a stove or greenhouse till the small plant flowers. I saw the other day a cutting of double pink Oleander struck last summer, with the largest, finest blooms, both for colour and form, I have ever seen. It had been brought forward, of course, in considerable heat. Oleanders are now to be had of all colours, from the deepest red to palest pink and pure white. They strike easier in summer if the stalks of the cuttings are stuck in water for a few days before they are planted.

I have lately been able to procure a book called 'The Insects of Great Britain,' by W. Lewin, 1795—an ambitious and comprehensive title indeed, and only one volume of the series ever appeared. But Mr. Lewin began with the most attractive and showy of the insects ; viz., butterflies. His plates are most beautiful and careful, even for that excellent period of hand-coloured illustration. I suppose that everyone knows the easy way to distinguish between butterflies and moths. In butterflies the antennæ, or what children call 'horns,' are always knobbed, and in moths they are the same thickness to the end. When I was in Florence I saw an old fireplace decorated with most lovely tiles. I am not knowing enough to say if they were Dutch or Italian, but they were very pretty. There were lines, brown and yellow, round each tile, the inner lines cutting off the corners ; then a dainty little wreath of Olive branches and inside it a butterfly, the butterfly on every tile being different. The ground-colour of the tile was a creamy white. This book would render the remaking of such tiles comparatively easy.

Last summer (1898) a little book appeared called 'Where Wild Birds Sing,' by James E. Whiting, published by Sydney C. Mayle, 70 High street, Hampstead. The writer is a real nature-lover. The motto of the book is from a speech by Gladstone, who said: 'I think the neglect of natural history was the grossest defect of our old system of training for the young; and, further, that little or nothing has been done by way of remedy for that defect in the attempts made to alter or reform that system.' It is as a slight help in that direction that I name these charming modern natural history books, full of observation and love of nature, told in the most simple way. This pretty little 'Invitation,' at the beginning of the book, seems to be written by a relative of the author, as it is signed 'S. Whiting':

> Come, leave the city's toil and din,
>   The weary strife,
> The cankering cares and sordid aims,
>   That deaden life.
>
> Come, leave behind this restless rush,
>   This anxious strain;
> Dame Nature tenders healing calm
>   For tired brain.
>
> Come, by yon grassy, shady lane
>   Rest tired eyes
> On yonder meadows vernal green,
>   On cloudless skies.
>
> Come to the woods, where Oak and Beech
>   Their shadows fling.
> Come, weary toiler, rest awhile
>   Where wild birds sing.

I cannot understand anybody living in the country and not taking a special interest in birds—from the skylark, the smallest bird that soars, to the water wag-tail, the smallest bird that walks. The constant fight always goes on as to whether birds in a garden do good or harm. Nothing convinces my gardener that we do not suffer more than our neighbours from the non-killing of bullfinches. Poor little things! the harm they do is terribly more apparent than the good, which has to be taken on faith ; and this I do.

As I stated before, I have lately been growing Watercresses in pots and pans, with some measure of success. But I never feel my ignorance without looking about for some book which recounts an experience greater than my own. I have found a perfectly comprehensive little manual called 'Home Culture of the Watercress,' by Shirley Hibberd (E. W. Allen, 1878). Anyone interested in the subject should try and get this book. The reason of my comparative failure is that I did not stand the pans in receptacles that would hold water. Also Watercresses are much better grown from small cuttings than from seed. Mr. Hibberd says that, if kept sufficiently moist and grown in his way, in about twenty days or less one ought to be able to pick a nice dish of Cresses. There is no garden, however small or dry, if watering can be abundant, that cannot grow Watercresses in summer quite successfully as he recommends. The winter supply requires to be kept from frost.

From the point of view of a real Cactus lover, I am but a weak-kneed disciple. I confess that a greenhouse full of these plants in various stages of bumpiness and without a single flower, as is often the case, leaves me cold and rather depressed. But to grow a certain number is of very great interest to me. The power they have of clinging to life is shared by few plants. This accounts for the fact that some of the finest kinds may be seen occasionally in cottage windows. The most gratifying point about cottage-window gardening is that in it fashion is unknown. Plants are handed down from father to son, with a total disregard as to whether these are fashionable or not. For a lengthened period Cactuses havé been a neglected family. Just lately magnificent groups have been exhibited by London nurserymen, so they are fast coming to the front again.

Since writing my last book, I have learnt by experience a good deal more about Cactus culture. In this country they require a kind of double treatment, according to whether you want them to grow or to flower. If you want small pieces to grow quickly, you must keep them most of the year in heat and well watered. If, on the other hand—and this especially applies to the hardier kinds—you want them to flower, you must starve them well through the winter. But I am sure that allowing them to shrivel from want of water is wrong. To prevent this, once the year is turned, I find occasional syringing better than much watering at the roots. Overwatering in winter generally means death, as they then rot at the crown. Sun they must have all through the summer. They are apt to be affected by a fungus blight; this must be cleaned off, of course. Like all the distinct plant families in nature, the more we know about Cactuses the more interesting they are. I have a new sunny window which I am looking forward to filling with Cactuses this summer. I have there now, in a small pot, a red Phyllocactus (see Mr. W. Watson's 'Cactus Culture'), which has upon it two or three flowers in bloom and fifty-two buds. One of my correspondents was exceedingly sceptical about the same bloom of my night-flowering Cereus (see page 121 of my first book) having lasted in a cool, dark hall for two nights; but it certainly did. Last year I was away from home all the precious summer months, so I do not know what happened to the 'bright-blooming Cereus, grand and

s

glorious.' My correspondent adds that some years ago he got into a controversy with experts in 'The Gardener's Chronicle' about these flowers, and one correspondent said that his Cereus remained in bloom six weeks. That must have been a very large plant with many blooms. Some of the most beautiful Cereuses are so large they only seem to flower well if planted in the open ground under glass. I think more than ever that it is worth while to grow Cactuses — for anyone who spends the summer at home. I am obliged to add this, as one says 'Do you take sugar or cream?' at teatime, for hardly anyone now does stay at home. Cactuses have a way of flowering when they choose. They will not wait for you if you are away, and their blooms only last a short time; but when they do condescend to flower, the beauty of them is exquisite — far more rare and lovely than any Orchid that I know. I have lately been able to procure a book for which I have waited a long time, 'Blühende Cacteen,' by Dr. Pfeiffer and F. R. Otto. It was published in Cassel (Germany) in 1843, and is a monograph on Cactuses, in two volumes bound in one. The prints are very well drawn, and the flowers hand-coloured. The text, unfortunately perhaps, is written only in German and French.

For all who wish to increase their Phloxes, Michaelmas Daisies, and hardy Chrysanthemums, it is quite possible in this month or early in May not only to divide them, as I said before, but to take off the shoots and stick them in the ground. This gives you the plants much less tall than if allowed to grow on the original root. Many of the herbaceous things will root in this way in spring. Cuttings of the white Everlasting Pea certainly do.

Cerasus pseudo-cerasus, as sold by Messrs. Veitch & Co., is very like *Cerasus Watereri* in Mr. Robinson's book. The whole family, and especially this one from Mr. Veitch, seems to me as well worth growing as anything I know among spring-flowering shrubs.

April 20th.—We have walked this evening down to the old mill by the river Mole. I have, not unnaturally, a great affection for a watermill, as I passed all my childhood so close to its thumping mysteries, and my bedroom window as a girl was just above the rushing mill-tail, where the brown trout lay under the Laurels. My old mill is all modernised and altered now, while here the miller says with pride : 'I have been here fifty-two years, and I grind the flour with the old stones—no modern china rollers for me !' We buy his flour — his 'seconds' and his 'whole-meal'— and his bran. The latter is what we really went down to fetch, as one of my nieces is fond of bran-water. This wildly stimulating beverage—far too much a tonic for my age—is an American drink. You pour cold water on two handfuls of fresh bran, let it stand for four hours, and then pour it off. It is supposed to contain some of the phosphates in the husks of the wheat, and consequently has much of the nourishing qualities of brown bread.

April 26th.—Last year at this time I was able to go and hear at the Drill Hall, Westminster, Mr. Burbidge's exceedingly interesting address on 'Fragrant Leaves and Sweet-smelling Flowers.' This lecture has since been published in the 'Journal' of the Horticultural Society for October, 1898.

Beyond wishing to remind others how much pleasure and instruction one gets from being a Fellow of the Royal Horticultural Society, I take a sentence from his lecture which seems useful and desirable for all gardeners. He says : 'I want you to rate all fragrant foliage quite as highly as you now profess to value sweet-scented blossoms. I also want to point out some of the essential differences, and advantages even, of foliage leaves as opposed to those floral leaves we call flowers. I am also particularly anxious to try and show that there is a sanitary basis, rather than a merely sensuous reason, for the usage of sweet odours and vegetable perfumes, whether the same be fresh or dried, living, dead, or distilled. Modern researches have amply proved that ozone is developed when the sun shines on most kinds of fragrant plants, such as flowers, Fir and Pine trees, and sweet herbs generally.' It is not much trouble to sow Lemon pips, and yet what is more delicious and reviving than the crushed leaf of a Lemon tree ?

I have found my increased number of Rosemary bushes a great joy. They live everywhere with the slight protection before described—namely, stuffed in all sorts of places under shrubs. But to grow and flower to perfection, as they do in Italy, they want to be under a wall in a warm corner, and fairly well nourished. No doubt their tendency to be killed in hard springs in the open must be the reason that so many gardens, especially small ones, where they are most precious, are content to do without them.

Many books and periodicals praise the old customs of using aromatic herbs, but in old days the smells they had to conceal must indeed have been innumerable. I suppose, unless by reading the accounts of how Russian peasants live even now, we cannot have any idea what England—and indeed all Europe — was, as regards dirt, two centuries ago. Our sweet modern homes are very different. All the same, how many houses are disagreeable from the smell of cooking which pervades them ! Burning dry Lavender, dried Rosemary, dried Cedar-wood, or the essential oils of any of these, entirely does away with this nuisance, from which we have most of us suffered. Burning things of this kind is also most useful in cases of colds, influenzas, etc. Putting a piece of stale bread into the saucepan when Cabbages are being boiled prevents their smelling at all. This is pretty well known, but seldom practised; and the fact is, what causes the nasty smell to pervade a house is not so much boiling the Cabbages, but throwing the water while still hot down the sink. This should never be done till the water has cooled.

Cultivating the art of smelling has certainly been neglected of late, which for every reason is a mistake, as the absence of a sense is a sign of defective health; and if children's smell were tested, it would be noticed when deficient, and the reasons would be diagnosed. In healthy children the power of smell is often very acute. To the blind, sweet-smelling leaves are more valuable than sweet-smelling flowers, which they cannot see; and the leaves last longer, pack easier, and would be much appreciated in hospitals for eye diseases.

Another very interesting letter I received about my last book I will quote: 'I am simply writing with the object of calling your attention to a group of plants which I have in my small way been cultivating for years, and which give me great pleasure every summer. I refer to the night-flowering and night-scented plants. To a business man like myself they are specially welcome, as my time is all occupied with business during the day, and the evening only is left in which we can enjoy our gardens. The most interesting in the group is that exquisite little gem of an annual, *Schizopetalum Walkeri*. It has no English name, unfortunately; you will find it in William Thompson's catalogue. This little flower is pure ivory white, of a Maltese cross form, and after dark throws out a most delicate perfume, not unlike the Almond. I also sow a packet or two of *Mathiola bicornis*, or Sweet-scented Stock. It is powerfully fragrant after dusk, and is of a pleasant character. Then I have a few plants of *Nicotiana affinis* scattered about the garden. These you will know better than myself. There is also the *Hesperis tristis*, which I find somewhat difficult to grow here [Manchester]. Also *Œnothera odorata*, another of the type. So that here you have a small group of plants which kindly reserve their fragrance, store it up during the daytime, and then considerately during the twilight and evening, when the breadwinner of the family comes home after his day's toil, throw out their precious odours and make the garden all the pleasanter and more refreshing for the night stroll after supper.'

April 28th.—Some years ago I was anxious to grow some florist Auriculas, but I must frankly own we were never very successful. They took too much frame-room and wanted too much care ; but for anyone who likes to grow special flowers in a small space I cannot imagine anything more interesting than Auricula-growing. The following directions were written out for me by a most successful Auricula-grower, and they may prove very useful to some few people who are fond of these flowers:

' The fancy or florists' Auricula is divided into green edges, gray edges, white edges, and selfs. These flowers should be grown in pots. One of the most famous growers (and a man of high class, although his station is only that of a Sheffield workman) is Ben Simonite. According to him, a compost of two parts fibrous loam, one part old hotbed manure, one part old leaf-mould, with sufficient charcoal the size of split peas to keep the soil open, is suitable. This should be put together in the autumn, and turned over frequently during the winter. The right time for repotting is after the bloom is

over ; at this moment (early in April) my earliest plants
are in bloom. When potted, the plants require occasional watering, but freedom from drenching rains. If
by chance over-much watered, time should be allowed
for this excess to pass away, and the plants not watered
again until quite dry, although not flagging. Little else
is needed, save to remove decaying foliage and keep
down the aphis or greenfly. All the summer, and until
November, the plants may remain in the open air, save
when they are protected from heavy rains. Early in
November they go into a coldframe, but ventilated by
day whenever the weather is at all fine. Water should
be given seldom, but sufficiently when given at all.
Great dryness will be endured without damage, but there
is a point which must not be overpassed. Towards the
end of January life revives, and water is more needful.
Prior to this, if it be possible, the pots should be so
placed as to receive what light there is, which accelerates
the resumption of growth. About the middle of February, if the growth is evidently progressing, the plant
should be top-dressed with compost, rather stronger than
that used in planting—so fully that side-shoots may be
able to root into the top-dressing. On these offsets depend the reproduction of named kinds. From seed new
varieties may be raised, but the offspring are often very
unlike the parents. In March the flower-stems begin to
rise, and during April the plants flower. In this month
the annual exhibition at the Kensington Horticultural
takes place. It is important to protect the plants in
severe weather by means of matting, also against cutting winds ; but they are hardy, and their great risk is
not cold, but rotting through excessive moisture, which,
affecting the foliage, attacks the neck of the plant if
decaying leaves be not picked off.'

Alpine Auriculas are easily grown from seed, and

require much less care (see 'English Flower Garden').

I am often asked what my vegetable seed bill amounts to. The fact is, I never know. Seeds are so cheap that I get what I want. Where the waste comes in is in sowing them in too large quantities at one time, instead of in succession, not thinning out, etc. It is always worth while to sow all useful vegetables several times over, whether in spring or summer.

The ordinary amateur feels the extreme difficulty of growing flower seeds either in boxes or even out of doors, and says that in the end it is decidedly cheaper to buy plants. This is, of course, true of all the strong-growing herbaceous things. But every gardener soon finds that if you want any quantity of one thing, or if the plant is not particularly suited to the soil, it is infinitely better to grow the plants from seed than to buy one or two specimens, which constantly die. I would always advise beginners to try sowing seeds in little squares in the seed-bed. It is only by this process that they can learn what does well from seed and what does not. Seed-beds in April should be in different aspects —some cool and damp, and some dry and sunny, according to the nature of the plant sown and the country it comes from—and left, only 'weeded, for one or two years. I am quite sure no garden will ever look full and varied all the year round without a great number of plants being grown from seed. It is a later stage of gardening, that is all, just as collecting and saving your own seed is a later stage still.

I saw the other day in a Suffolk newspaper some observations on seed-sowing under glass. They seemed to me so useful just at this time of year that I copied part of the article: 'Sowing seeds may to the superficial observer seem a simple affair; yet it is one of the most important operations in gardening. There is a great difference even amongst gardeners in raising plants from seed. One may succeed with all kinds of seeds, providing the seed is good; whereas another gardener will have the greatest difficulty even in getting ordinary seeds to germinate. Of course, the kind of seeds I mean are choice greenhouse, stove, or Alpine. My experience teaches me that a great many failures are the result of sowing the seed too early in the year. The particular seeds I mean are those sown early in spring, either of plants for conservatory decoration or to bloom in flower beds and borders during the coming summer. Take, for example, those charming greenhouse flowers the Cape Primrose (*Streptocarpus*). Sow this seed in January, and the greatest difficulty is experienced in getting it to germinate; but if sown in April, it will germinate as easily as Lobelia. But perhaps giving choice seeds daily—nay, I might almost say hourly—attention is the most important point of all. The seed may be sown at the proper time and be placed in a suitable place; the soil may be everything to be desired; in fact, everything used—pots, pans, boxes, and drainage —may be all right, yet if they do not receive proper attention for days, weeks, and months before the seed grows, and after, as the case may be, failure will surely follow such neglect. This attention means keeping the compost in that happy condition which is neither wet nor yet too dry.'

Sometimes it is a help to put a little wet *Sphagnum* moss on the top of the pot under the piece of glass, or the pot may be covered with paper. The great thing to aim at with all seeds, whether large or small, is to try to keep the soil sufficiently moist, without having to water them until they begin to grow. This is difficult, well-nigh impossible, with those seeds which are a long time in the soil before they germinate. Still, this is what should be aimed at. Once they are up, it is necessary to water very gently. A good way is to put a small piece of sponge in the hole at the bottom of a flower-pot, and then fill the pot with water of the same temperature as the greenhouse, and move it about so that the water dribbles gently through. With large seeds it is always a good plan to soak them twenty-four hours in tepid water before sowing them. An excellent way of handling very small seedlings is to take a little bit of bamboo, bend it in two like a pair of tweezers, and lay the seedlings on a piece of paper; it is then quite easy to handle the smallest seedlings without injury.

The three or four weeks of severe frosty weather in March has made us very short of vegetables. I never buy when I have not guests, as feeling the pinch makes one alive to one's deficiencies, and causes one to manage better another year. So I thought I would try and see how I liked the root we grow for the cows. We have plenty left, as the winter has been so mild. It is Sutton's Mangold-Wurzel, a yellow kind. We boiled it till tender, whole like a beetroot, and when hot cut it into slices, and ate it with cold butter. It was excellent. In texture it was like a beetroot; in taste, half like a sweet Potato, half like a Chestnut. When Mangolds are young they mash like Turnips.

Early this month Hops begin to show through the ground. When the shoots are about six or eight inches high, before the leaves develop, they can be picked, tied together in a bundle, and cooked exactly like green Asparagus. They have not much taste, but are pleasant in substance, and are supposed on the Continent to be exceedingly wholesome. A vegetable called 'Good King Henry' is worth growing to eat in the same way, and later the leaves cook like Spinach.

It is also worth knowing that at this time of year, when vegetables are scarce in the country, the fresh green leaves of Rhubarb—generally thrown away—make an excellent vegetable dressed like Spinach, either with or without a little butter.

One of the great difficulties in a light soil is a continuous supply of Spinach, and gardeners never will sow a sufficient succession in dry weather, when it must be watered. It has a great tendency to run to seed. In Sutton's book, 'The Culture of Vegetables and Flowers,' he faces the difficulty and gives instruction for its remedy very efficiently. No other Spinach approaches in excellence the real one, *Spinacia oleracea*; but for an extension of the supply two others should be grown in every fair-sized kitchen garden. The New Zealand Spinach (*Tetragonia expansa*) flourishes in the hottest weather, and is best started in a box under glass. The perpetual Spinach or Spinach Beet (*Beta Cicla*) is a most valuable plant for its continuous supply of leaves. Sutton says: 'When the leaves are ready for gathering they must be removed, whether wanted or not, to promote continuous growth.' This is the case with a good many vegetables—Garden Cress, Watercress, Chicory, etc. I shall give special attention this year to sowing Spinach in all sorts of places. Aspect and shade make so much difference in the rapidity with which things grow!

Purslane is a vegetable not often sown in English gardens, but it makes a good summer salad, and is useful in soup or dressed as Spinach.

Last year I tried growing several kinds of Potatoes—five or six varieties recommended by Sutton—but I do not think any turned out better than, if as well as, Sutton's 'Magnum Bonum,' which we have grown for years. 'Ring-leader' is the one we grow for the first early Potatoes; and a red waxy Potato, whose name I do not know, is most useful for cooking in some ways. All must find out for themselves what Potatoes suit their soils best, as it is a subject deserving attention and care.

The small, round button Onions so much used abroad are often omitted in English gardens, though they are merely the result of not thinning out the crop at all. Choose a piece of poor, dry ground; make this fine on the surface; sow in the month of April, thickly but evenly; cover lightly; roll or tread, to give a firm seed-bed. If sown shallow, the bulbs will be round. Besides looking much prettier when braised, this small kind keeps much better through the winter than when made to grow large by thinning.

We grow two kinds of Sorrel now—one with a small, round leaf, and the other the large-leaved ordinary garden kind. It is quite easy, for those who like the vegetable, to lift plants in the spring and grow them on in a frame or greenhouse. It is a thing there is always difficulty about buying, and it is not much liked by English people. It wants to be freshly gathered and well dressed.

There are endless numbers of books on poultry within the reach of everybody; and lately, in Ward, Lock & Co.'s collection of penny handbooks, one has been issued on poultry which is quite useful. But, like all modern books, it is a little above the ordinary keeper of cocks and hens for domestic purposes, making the matter appear unnecessarily difficult. Having a good big field for them to run in here, and the soil being dry and light, I have not had disease amongst my poultry. Among the list of horrible diseases given in this penny book, we come to the following sentence: 'Egg-eating.—This is rather a vice than a disease, and very troublesome to cure.' The author then gives a cruel account of punishment to be used, in the hope of disgusting the offender. This is an excellent instance of the trend of modern thought. Egg-eating is, I am sure, solely the result of giving the poor hens an insufficient quantity of the food required by nature to make their shells hard. Disease among animals is much the same as among people, and is produced often by large quantities of food, but of an improper kind. Diseased poultry means over-crowding, over-feeding — in fact, the fault lies in the way they are managed. Hereditary vice may, we hope, in hens at any rate, be left out of the question. Another thing the author suggests is that when a fowl is killed the entrails should be given to the pigs. This is absolutely wrong, in my opinion, as pigs are essentially vegetarians, and unclean feeding is apt to make them diseased, which is very serious for the eaters of pork.

One is always being asked, Does keeping poultry pay? I never keep strict accounts of what things cost me. Nothing one does at home ever pays, unless one looks into it entirely oneself. I only bring the rules of ordinary common-sense and proportion to bear on the matter.

For early egg-laying it is, I think, desirable to have some of the southern breeds, such as Leghorns, Spanish, etc.

I know very little about my own poultry, as I cannot make pets of things that have to be killed, and they are entirely managed by my gardener and his wife. The following is their account of what they do, and they certainly have been very successful: 'We set the hens as early in January as we can on about nine eggs, as the weather is cold; on thirteen eggs later, being careful that the eggs should not have been frosted. We

make the nests of hay in the henhouse, which is a warm
one. The early-hatched chicks are best for autumn killing, as they begin to lay about July for a short time,
and then stop laying till the next spring. The sitting
hens are fed once a day on barley, about a handful to
each hen; the little chickens on grits the first day, and
then on oatmeal about every three hours. When they
are about a fortnight old they have a little barley in the
middle of the day. The mother hen is kept cooped up,
away from the other fowls, till the chicks are about six
weeks old, when they all run in the field. March- and
April-hatched birds we keep for stock, as they make
the best fowls and layers about October. We shut up
the pullets in a run for laying. We keep no hens older
than two years, and have fresh cockerels every year.
We feed the stock-fowls twice a day—on soft food in
the morning, and barley in the afternoon. The fowl-
houses are white-washed every spring, and kept cleaned
out twice a week, and the floors dusted with slack lime.
The fowls have a good field to run in, so they get
plenty of grass. The shut-up pullets require plenty of
grit and greenstuff, and they are fond of a Mangold to
pick at. Fowls are very fond of bones or scraps, or
anything that amuses them. It is very bad for fowls
to be dull. When we see a fowl not eating or not
looking well, we keep it apart for a day or two, give it
a dose of castor oil, and, if not soon better, we kill and
bury it.' I am sure this is a better plan than trying to
doctor sick birds. I know no more miserable sight than
unhealthy poultry. We rear a few ducks every year,
but kill them in the summer, as they are great consumers of food.

In October I always buy, as I have said before, three
or four young turkeys, and have them fed here for
Christmas-time. It saves three or four shillings on each

bird. Any fowls that are going to be killed ought to be shut up for twelve hours without food. Turkeys and geese require rather longer. Home-grown poultry is much better not plucked or cleaned out till just before cooking. Very young chickens are best eaten quite freshly killed.

For Preserving Eggs.—Put some fresh eggs in a large basin or jar, and pour lime-water over them. Two days after, take out the eggs and look through them carefully. Put away those which are at all cracked. Those which are quite in good condition put into a second jarful of lime-water, and stand this jar in the cellar. See that the eggs are always covered by the lime-water. They will keep for quite six months or more. The first jarful of lime-water can be used to try another lot of eggs.

This is another and even simpler way of preserving eggs, which we find answers perfectly well here : Fill a small shallow box deep enough to cover the eggs— cardboard does quite well—with chaff. Put the fresh eggs, just laid, into this with the points downwards. Tie on the lid ; and when you have more than one box, they can be tied together as they fill. The whole reason of this plan is that the box should be reversed once every twenty-four hours. If this is really done, the eggs keep perfectly fresh for weeks—so fresh that they are not to be distinguished from new-laid eggs, except that they poach beautifully; which, as everyone knows, a new-laid egg does not, any more than a stale one. If the boxes are tied together, it is no trouble turning them over beyond remembering it. The natural history of this is that when the egg is laid the germ is alive, and if the egg lays on its side the germ is not only alive, but grows for many days. When the germ in the egg has consumed its nourishment, it dies from cold, and instantly the egg goes bad. By putting the eggs end downwards, and turning them daily, the germ dies at once and never grows, and the egg remains good. Many will not believe this. I can only say, 'Try it.' If you either turn the box yourself, or have anyone you can depend upon to do it for you, you will not find that it fails.

If you rub perfectly fresh-laid eggs with butter, they keep for a long time. If they have been laid twelve hours before the butter is applied it is no good. Mrs. Roundell says this receipt is of no use : perhaps because she has not tried it with fresh enough eggs.

The word 'egg' reminds me of such an extremely funny anecdote in Mr. Max Müller's 'Auld Lang Syne' that I must crib it. A certain Duke of M——, being very fond of natural history, was much interested in some emus which he possessed. Having occasion to go to town, his agent wired to him : 'The emu has laid an egg. In your Grace's absence we have taken the largest goose we could find to hatch it.'

I am told that the receipts both in my former book and those in 'Dainty Dishes' were considered extravagant. I have now found a cheap little book, called 'Economical Cookery,' by Kate Addison, which meets the want and is true to its name. At the end are two or three most useful hints. If you want your onions to fry a good colour, do not peel them. Another hint is that if you boil corks for five minutes before using them, they fit in the bottles much tighter, and so preserve what is inside much better.

There is a French confectioner named De Bry (45 Southampton Row, and New Oxford street, London), whom I have only lately got to know, and who has the excellent device : 'Vendre bon pour vendre beaucoup.' He sells jams which will be highly appreciated by that increasing class—jam-eaters. I recommend this motto to all those who bottle fruit and make jams, especially in our colonies. I have been lately given a large sample of West Indian jams, but they are not up to the mark. I should imagine there was a great opening for all kinds of preserved fruits, syrups, jams, etc., from abroad, where so many excellent fruits grow almost wild. But they never can be a commercial success if not done carefully. They must look pleasant to the eye, be juicy, and not too sweet. The French alone seem to have the art of knowing how to bottle and preserve fruit. I can buy in London bottled French raspberries, not preserved in sugar at all, and as fresh and good as if newly gathered from a garden ; indeed, better than from my garden, where in dry seasons raspberries always fail.

T

MAY

May 1st.—Gorse thoroughly peeled and wedged (see
first volume) lasts for weeks in water, and the warmth
of the room makes the flower come out so well it is
almost a different-looking plant.

In these light soils all the fruit trees over-flower
themselves so much, like pot-bound plants, that no one
need scruple to pick branches of blossom to put in water
in the house. The trees can never carry even the fruit
that sets.

The evergreens are beginning their spring shoots. I
think it must have been at about this time of year, when
the young leaves on the Holly have no spines, that
Southey wrote :

> All vain asperities, day by day, would wear away,
> Till the smooth temper of my age should be
> Like the high leaves upon the Holly Tree.

A book published in 1857, called 'Curiosities of
Natural History,' by Francis T. Buckland, is very in-
terestingly written, and will be found full of information
on all sorts of subjects—from the anatomy of the water-
rat to Virgil's description of the death of Laocöon.

At this time of year, when the frame double Violets
are over, which do so well for finger-bowl bouquets in

spring, I find a plant or two of *Nicotiana affinis*, sown in the autumn and grown in the greenhouse, very useful. One flower cut off, with a branch of Prince of Orange Geranium or a piece of Sweet Verbena—of which there ought to be plenty now, if they have been properly grown on—make charming little bouquets for this purpose.

The gardener of a friend of mine sowed some self-saved seed of *Nemesia strumosa* in September in a pan, pricking them off twice—the second time a single plant in a small pot. The result was some charming well-grown plants, which flowered beautifully in April, and the flowers were larger and finer than the summer ones out of doors.

The French 'Mange-tout' Peas (Sutton catalogues them as 'French Sugar Peas') are not yet sown generally enough in England. English cooks do not understand (and how should they without explanation?) that they are not shelled, but the pod and the pea are boiled together, and a little butter added before serving.

In the 'Westminster Gazette' of last spring there was an interesting article on the history of Tulips, called forth by the Tulip show at the Royal Botanic Gardens and the general revival of interest in the flower, which has as romantic a history as any plant all the world over. The article being too long to quote here entirely, I give a few extracts: 'In the seraglio of the Shadow of God, when the world was a few centuries younger, there was one festival in early spring which for dazzling splendour outshone the rest of the Eastern fairylike night scenes. Unnumbered artificial suns, moons, and stars lit up the Sultan's beautiful gardens, and in the mystic light which turned night into day tens of thousands of Tulips stood proudly up on their tall, slim stalks, the goblet of each blossom perfect in form and in colour. Among this dazzling dream the Sultan and his harem, and whoever else was great and mighty at the Court of Constantinople, worshipped at the shrine of the Tulip, and the whole of the East echoed the praise of the *thouliban*, or turban flower, the corruption of which term has become our name for the flower.

'The West at that period knew nothing of the Tulip, though it had been great in the East for more years than men remembered. India, Persia, and the Levant had, in the course of ages, woven around it countless legends of love and life and death ; great poets sang its praises ; the heathen laid it at the feet of his gods, and the early Christian of the East pointed to it as the "Lily of the field" which afforded to Christ the subject of a divine sermon to which the world has clung, and still is clinging, as to a never-failing help when the burden of life grows heavy.

'In the sixteenth century an ambassador of the Emperor of Germany to the Sublime Porte, going from Adrianople to Constantinople shortly after midwinter, came upon a wondrous sight. On the roadside, among the weeds and grasses, there rose in glorious beauty clump after clump, bed after bed, of tall, goblet-shaped flowers. As the sun shone upon them they blazed with the colour of fire and sunlight, and the smooth, broad petals formed a deep cup classically simple and perfect, closing over a heart of gold.

'Before long a few Tulip bulbs reached Germany, and thence in 1577 came to England.'

We all know how Tulips were then taken up by Dutchmen. The article says that for the three years from 1634 to 1637 Holland was but a large asylumful of tulipomaniacs. I have just been told how that in one vineyard in Alsace, and in one alone, the pretty wild tulip *Tulipa reflexa* flourishes abundantly. I think more might be done by planting in England the type Tulips, and leaving them to their fate, especially on chalky soils, which they seem to like.

The Crown Imperials are nearly over. They have not been as good as usual this year; the hard frosts in March blackened their poor crowns. A kind correspondent was shocked at my non-botanical language in speaking of the beads of liquid in the hanging flowers as water, not honey. I merely meant that they looked like pure water. He writes: 'I think on examination you will find them honey. As you do not mention it, you may not know of the legend in connection with this flower, which is as follows. Please forgive me if a twice-told tale: When our Lord in His agony was walking in the Garden of Gethsemane, all the flowers save this one alone bowed their heads in sympathetic sorrow. It held its head aloft in supreme disdain; whereupon our Lord gently rebuked it. Smitten with shame at last, it hung its head, and since then has never been able to raise it, and those who care to turn its face upwards always find tears in its eyes.' He closed his letter with the following practical hint: 'For protective purposes—shelters—you may find the bamboo baskets in which moist sugar is sent from South America, about three feet high and nearly six feet round, when split open on one side and flattened out, make good, light shelters.'

I am very fond of reading old 'Edinburghs' and 'Quarterlies,' and one is apt to find in them a helpful contribution to anything that one may have been thinking about. This happened to me the other day when, taking up the 'Quarterly Review' for July, 1863, I came upon a most fascinating article, full of folk-lore and tradition, called 'Sacred Trees and Flowers.' I should delight in quoting several of the stories, but room fails me. Working through all the older traditions of Europe, the writer gives full credit, as is due, to the monks, and says : 'To the Benedictines and Cistercians — the first great agriculturists of Europe and the first great gardeners, the true predecessors of the Hendersons and Veitches of our own day—we are indebted for many of the well-loved flowers that will always keep their places, in spite of their gayer, but less permanent, modern rivals.   The Wallflower, that "scents the dewy air" about the ruined arches of its convent ; the scarlet Anemone, that flowers about Easter-tide, and is called in Palestine the blood-drops of Christ ; the blossoming Almond tree, one of the symbols of the Virgin, and the Marigold that received her name, are but a few of the old friends, brought long ago from Syria by some pilgrim monk, and spread from his garden over the whole of Europe. . . .   In the cloistered garden, too, the monk was wont to meditate on the marvels of the plants that surrounded him, and to find all manner of mysterious emblems in their marks and tracings.   Many displayed the true figure of the Cross.   It might be seen in the centre of the red poppy ; and there was a "Zucca" (fig) at Rome, in the garden of the Cistercian Convent of Santa Potentiana, the fruit of which, when cut through, showed a green cross inlaid on the white pulp, and having at its angles five seeds, representing the five wounds. . . .   The Banana, in the Canaries, is never cut with a knife, because it also exhibits a representation of the Crucifixion, just as the Fern root shows an Oak tree.'   But the fame of the greatest of all such marvels arrived at Rome in the year 1609, when Bosio describes as *maraviglioso fiore* the Passion Flower of the New World.   The first to describe the Passion Flower in England was our own Master Parkinson, who said that it should be assigned to that 'bright Occidental star, Queen Elizabeth, and be named, in memory of her, the Virgin Climber.' The Passion Flower, however, has retained its original name and significance. It is the one great contribution of the western hemisphere to the symbolical flowers of Christendom ; and its starlike blossoms have taken a worthy place beside the mystical Roses and Trefoils of ecclesiastical decoration.

When I replanted the *Ornithogalum pyramidale* in September last year, I planted between them some pieces of *Galega officinalis*, so easily divided in the autumn. The fresh, bright green makes a groundwork for the long spikes of the bulbs, and later it gives a succession of flowers of its own pretty white or pale lilac. In dry seasons it is most useful for picking. In one place I find it is growing quite successfully. In a more shaded corner under a wall—no sun reaching it in winter— every plant of the *Galega* has died. I merely mention this as one more instance of how the hardiest plants do well or not within a few yards of each other. I saw, in a friend's garden to-day, Alstrœmerias growing like weeds all over the place. I remarked on this. 'Yes,' she said, 'it's quite true.' For five years I had never been able to get one seed to grow, and the plants I bought invariably died. Now I have so many that I must dig them out with a spade.'

I do not think I mentioned before that all kinds of Poppies travel beautifully if they are gathered in bud ; and if, on arrival, the hard husk is peeled off from the buds, they revive and flower and last longer. Forcing open the buds exhausts the flowers, and then they open, but to fade and die. The Shirley and Iceland Poppies are prepared in this way for the London market. Some of the Campanula tribe do best dry and starved ; they flower well instead of going to leaf. This is especially the case with the little *C. cæspitosa* and with *C. grandis*, which is so useful for covering the ground under shrubs and in bare, dry places. *C. pyramidalis*, though it likes half shade, enjoys a rich, rather moist place. *C. persicifolia* is never quite so beautiful here as I have seen ·it on stiff soils.

It is well in spring and early summer to make constant cuttings of the white Swainsonia. It does well out of doors and in, and is a very refined, pretty little plant.

RECEIPTS

To Cook Spaghetti (small Italian macaroni).—Put some bacon-fat, or any pieces of fat, in a saucepan with onions, carrots, herbs, etc., all chopped up, and a little sugar. Fry them slightly. Pour off the fat. Cut up some tomatoes, add a little stock, and simmer it all together till the tomatoes are cooked. Pass the whole through a sieve, so that the sauce may be quite smooth. Boil the spaghetti separately till quite tender, then drain off the water, and mix with the tomato sauce. If cheese is liked, mix in some grated Parmesan the last thing before serving; also a little fresh butter, which can be added without the cheese, if preferred.

Italian Way of Dressing a Cabbage with a Hard Heart.—Plunge the cabbage into boiling water. Take out the heart, cut it into ribbons. Mix with it bacon, chopped meat or game, onion, garlic, parsley, ¦herbs, and, above all, some Gruyère and Parmesan cheese — in fact, almost anything. Bind this mixture with egg. Replace it in the cabbage, and tie it up well to prevent the stuffing from escaping. Boil fast till done. Serve with brown or white sauce, or butter only.

Another Risotto à la Milanaise.—Italian rice is the best of all, though rather difficult to get. It is different from either Carolina or Pata. Failing it, boil half a pound of best Carolina rice. When it is about half cooked, drain it off and replace it in the stew-pan. Add a good quarter of a pound of butter, stand it on the side of the stove, allow it to fry gently till the rice is quite done, stirring very frequently to prevent burning, which it will do unless constant attention is given. Then mix about half a pint of good *demie glazè de volaille*, or, if that should not be convenient, a little ordinary half-glaze. Add about a quarter of a pound of grated Parmesan, some tongue cut to size of a shilling, and about four or five truffles cut in slices, also bits of chicken the size of a shilling. Season to taste, and serve *very* hot in a silver souffle-dish, with a very little Parmesan grated over the top. It is an improvement, as a change with risotto, to press it into a round basin and turn it out before serving.

A very good way of cooking young potatoes is to put them into a black frying-pan, whole, in hot butter. Cover them up, and let them cook for an hour. This does very well for small old potatoes also.

A very creamy *purée* of potatoes (see 'Dainty Dishes'), put into scallop-shells and browned in the oven, handed round with roast mutton, is rather a pretty change.

Fresh summer spinach, plain boiled and chopped (not too fine), and rolled in the middle of a large pancake, is excellent.

A good *purée* of sorrel (see 'Dainty Dishes'), with small asparagus cut up into little pieces, is an excellent May or June dish.

Asparagus Salad.—Thin boiled asparagus, cut up into short lengths (*pointes d'asperges*) and mixed with oil and lemon-juice, makes a nice salad. It is much improved by the addition of an apple ('New Zealand') peeled and cut up into thin Julienne shreds.

When apples get scarce and tasteless in the spring, a very good 'charlotte' can be made in exactly the same way as 'apple charlotte' (see Dainty Dishes') by making a smooth *purée* from stewed sun-dried apricots, to be had of all London grocers and stores.

A good cookery book is called 'A Younger Son's Cookery Book, by a Younger Son's daughter' (Richard Bentley & Son).

May 22nd.—When I made up my mind last year to go to Florence, I thought I would try and collect a few appropriate books to enlighten my ignorance and refresh my memory. I asked my friends what I should take, merely reminding them that Mr. Hare's volumes on Italy and George Eliot's 'Romola' had naturally occurred to myself. I got very little help before I went; but by degrees, during the month I was in Florence and since my return, I have collected and read several books which I should have been glad to have had last year, and which may help those who go straight from a busy home life and take a short trip to Florence. Of course, the literature on Florence is so enormous, and people's taste in books differs so greatly, that to write a mere list of names would enlighten no one. I shall only mention those books which I either possess or have had lent to me to read; and if I describe them a little in detail, I think it may help the inexperienced to make a selection of those which they themselves would enjoy. At Florence there is a most excellent lending library; in fact, probably more than one.

As an example of 'art' teaching at the end of the last century, there is now a cheap edition of Sir Joshua Reynolds' 'Discourses,' which are full of wisdom and general instruction. He shares with the greatest— Michael Angelo especially—the misfortune that those who came after him degenerated, which seemed at one time to justify the condemnation of his teaching. Here is a sentence from one of his 'Discourses' which comes

home to me as a reason why, instead of giving my own
superficial opinions, I try to help others by recommending books which· I think will greatly add to their enjoyment of a visit to Florence :

'The great business of study is to form a mind
adapted and adequate to all times and all occasions; to
which all nature is then laid open, and which may be
said to possess the key of her inexhaustible riches.

'A detail of instruction might be extended with a
great deal of pleasure and ostentatious amplification ;
but it would at best be useless. Our studies will be for
ever in a very great degree under the direction of chance.
Like travellers, we must take what we can get and when
we can get it, whether it is or is not administered in the
most commodious manner, in the most proper place, or
at the exact minute when we would wish to have it.

'The habit of contemplating and brooding over the
ideas of great geniuses, till you find yourself warmed by
the contact, is the true method of forming an artist-like
mind.   It is impossible to think or invent in a mean
manner ; a state of mind is acquired that receives those
ideas only which relish of grandeur and simplicity.

'I do not desire that you should get other people to
do your business, or to think for you.   I only wish you
to consult with, to call in as councillors, men the most
distinguished for their knowledge and experience, the
result of which counsel must ultimately depend upon
yourself.   Such conduct in the commerce of life has
never been considered as disgraceful, or in any respect
imply intellectual imbecility ; it is a sign rather of that
true wisdom which feels individual imperfection, and is
conscious to itself how much collective observation is
necessary to fill the immense extent and to comprehend
the infinite variety of nature.   I recommend neither self-
dependence nor plagiarism.   I advise you only to take

that assistance which every human being wants, and which it appears, from the examples that have been given, the greatest painters have not disdained to accept.

'Let me add, the diligence required in the search, and the exertion subsequent in accommodating those ideas to your own purpose, is a business which idleness will not, and ignorance cannot, perform. Men of superior talents alone are capable of thus using and adapting other men's minds to their own purposes, or are able to make out and finish what was only in the original a hint or imperfect conception. A readiness in taking such hints, which escape the dull and ignorant, makes in my opinion no inconsiderable part of that faculty of the mind which is called genius.'

Before I begin my list of books, I think I will say that there are few more useful things for young people to take with them to Italy than a biographical dictionary of the painters. I have two ; but they are old ones. I have had them all my life. Doubtless there are better and more modern ones now, which I have not taken the trouble to look up. One is Pilkington's 'Dictionary of Painters' by Allan Cunningham, and the other a 'Dictionary of Italian Painters' by Maria Farquhar, edited by R. M. Wornham. This is a dear little book published in 1855, and light and portable, but probably long out of print. In studying art, nothing is more necessary than to know — not only the chronology of the pictures themselves, but also to a certain degree the evolution of the minds of the men who painted them. This we can partly arrive at by the dates of their births and deaths. The galleries, as a rule, are not arranged to help one much, though many pictures now have dates on their frames. Still, it requires a peculiar head — certainly, I think, one not possessed by most women — to arrange these dates of the painters' lives, overlapping each other as they do, on the spur of the moment, in a way that is of the smallest use for judging the merits of the pictures, and, above all, the mind of the man that shines through his work.

One should know the date of a picture, as in biography everything depends upon the age at which incidents occur. Men of genius often do at twenty what is usually not done at forty; so every now and then a painter anticipates by centuries the thought or the execution of future ages.

In accordance with the taste of her day, Maria Farquhar gives five double-columned pages of her little book to Raphael, and half a single column to Botticelli. In this she did not differ from her contemporaries, for, as Mr. Hewlett says in 'Earthwork out of Tuscany': 'Seriously, where in criticism do you learn of an earlier painter than Perugino until you come to our day? And where now do you get the raptures over the Carracci and Domenichino, and Guercino, and the rest of them, which the last century expended upon their unthrifty soil? Ruskin found Botticelli; yes, and Giotto. Roscoe never so much as mentions either.'

I have four little daintily printed volumes published in 1834 — an early work of the well-known authoress, Mrs. Jameson, who has written so much on Italian art. These books are not without interest to the student of life, art, or art criticisms. The last two volumes are a reprint of a still earlier work, which had a success in its day, called 'The Diary of an Ennuyée.' The book is still interesting to me, not only for its *démodée* style, but also as being a kind of '*Pot-Pourri*' of the day. This 'Diary of an Ennuyée' contains an account of the author's stay at Florence, which is my reason for

mentioning the book here. Her reflections are young
and genuine, and the courage with which she lays them
down gives them a human interest. I feel considerable
sympathy with what she says about Michael Angelo.
She thus speaks of the Medici statues: 'In a little
chapel in San Lorenzo are Michael Angelo's famous
statues—the Morning, the Noon, the Evening, and the
Night. I looked at them with admiration rather than
with pleasure; for there is something in the severe and
overpowering style of this master which affects me dis-
agreeably, as beyond my feeling and above my
comprehension. These statues are very ill-disposed
for effect; the confined cell (such it seems) in which
they are placed is so strangely disproportioned to the
awful and massive grandeur of their forms.

'There is a picture by Michael Angelo, considered a
chef-d'œuvre, which hangs in the Tribune to the right
of the Venus. Now, if all the connoisseurs, with Vasari
at their head, were to harangue for an hour together on
the merits of this picture, I might submit in silence, for
I am no connoisseur; but that it is a disagreeable, a
hateful picture, is an opinion which fire could not melt
out of me. In spite of Messieurs les Connoisseurs and
Michael Angelo's fame, I would die in it at the stake.
For instance, here is the Blessed Virgin—not the
"Vergine Santa d'ogni grazia piena," but a Virgin
whose brickdust-coloured face, harsh, unfeminine
features, and muscular, masculine arms give me the idea
of a washerwoman (*con rispetto parlando!*)—an infant
Saviour with the proportions of a giant! And what
shall we say of the nudity of the figures in the background?—profaning the subject and shocking at once
good taste and good sense. A little further on the eye
rests on the divine Madre di Dio of Correggio. What
beauty, what sweetness, what maternal love and humble

adoration are blended in the look and attitude with which she bends over her Infant !'

Just as a contrast to this bald dislike of Michael Angelo, which I more or less share, I will copy, as an example of modern subtle scholarly criticism, a sentence on the same picture from Pater's 'Renaissance'—a book to be read indeed :

'When the shipload of sacred earth from the soil of Jerusalem was mingled with the common clay in the Campo Santo at Pisa, a new flower grew up from it, unlike any flower men had seen before—the Anemone, with its concentric rings of strangely blended colour, still to be found by those who search long enough for it in the long grass of the Maremma. Just such a strange flower was that mythology of the Italian Renaissance which grew up from the mixture of two traditions, two sentiments — the sacred and the profane. Classical story was regarded as so much imaginative material to be received and assimilated. It did not come into men's minds to ask curiously of science concerning the origin of such story, its primary form and import, its meaning for those who projected it. The thing sank into their minds, to issue forth again with all the tangle about it of mediæval sentiment and ideas.

'In the *Doni* Madonna in the *Tribune* of the *Uffizi*, Michael Angelo actually brings the pagan religion, and with it the unveiled human form, the sleepy-looking fauns of a Dionysiac revel, into the presence of the Madonna, as simpler painters had introduced there other products of the earth, birds or flowers; while he has given to that Madonna herself much of the uncouth energy of the older and more primitive "Mighty Mother."'

Is it possible to see side by side more different criticisms of the same picture? And it is not only the difference of a young woman and a scholarly man; it means the immense march the world has made altogether in the understanding of its own evolution.

To return to Mrs. Jameson. She runs on with her criticisms through the sights of Florence. Most of the pictures she admires are certainly not those that excite the greatest admiration in these days. The name Botticelli is never once mentioned by her, any more than it is thirty years later by George Eliot in her notes on Florentine art in the diary published in her Life. Pater, on the contrary, tells us that Sandro Botticelli is the only contemporary mentioned, whether by accident or intention, by Leonardo in his treatise on painting.

I only possess the translation of this treatise published in 1835. Just lately a new 'Life and Works' of Leonardo, by Eugene Muntz, has been published by Heinemann, but it is 42s. net.

To leave high things for low, Mrs. Jameson touches on the society of the day at Florence and parties at the Countess of Albany's, etc. She gives an amusing story of a travelling young lord who, when presented with the Countess of Albany's card, exclaimed:

'The Countess of Albany! Ah!—true—I remember! Wasn't she the widow of Charles the Second who married Ariosto?' There is in this celebrated *bévue* a glorious confusion of times and persons.

For those interested in the byways of history, a well-known modern author, Vernon Lee, has written a 'Life' of this Countess of Albany. I think it the most interesting of Vernon Lee's books that I have read. It was published in the 'Eminent Women' series—why, I cannot imagine; for it seems to me as incongruous as Hawthorne's 'Life' being in the 'English Men of Letters,' or Lady Hamilton's picture having a place in the National Portrait Gallery.

Vernon Lee's 'Studies of the Eighteenth Century in Italy' I have not read ; but if they are half as interesting as this 'Life,' I have something to look forward to. The pictures of even a portion of society in Florence drawn in this 'Life' of the Countess of Albany set one wondering how a hundred years can have brought about such changes. Vernon Lee's later works, mostly about Italy, 'Limbo and Other Essays' and 'Genius Loci,' there seems no need for me to praise ; they have been so recently in the reading public's mind, and so much appreciated.

It seems to me very clearing to the mind to read French or German criticisms at the same time as English, especially with regard to Italy, as at all times the French, of whom I know most, take such an absolutely different point of view. 'L'Italie d'Hier,' by the brothers De Goncourt, written in the winter of 1855-56, is entirely devoid of what we should call 'the feeling for Italy.' To read this description of Italy is very like taking up a book illustrating the contents of the first Exhibition of 1851, when all sense of the beautiful seemed absolutely lost. Georges Sand, in her youthful bitterness, exclaimed, in the 'thirties, that Italy was ' Peintures aux plafonds, ordure sous les pieds'; but that criticism is again of a totally different kind. Edmond de Goncourt looks at a picture and says : 'La Vierge chez ce peintre, c'est la Vierge du Vinci, mais avec une expression courtisanesque.' The drawings by one of the brothers in this book are rather clever, and in describing a ball at the Pitti, in the Grand Duke's time, he gives an absurd caricature of our English Minister of the day, Lord Normanby, which no one who remembers him can read now without a smile. The book is well worth looking at as typical of French criticism of that day, and anybody who cares to enjoy a

U

strong literary contrast has only to take up afterwards Paul Bourget's 'Sensations d'Italie' (published in 1891, and dedicated to Robert Lord Lytton by his affectionate friend and admirer) and his most daintily illustrated little gem called 'Un Saint,' published in 1894. Here the forty years have indeed altered sentiment, feeling, aspiration, and description. Both are French ; I prefer the Bourget.

The famous 'Voyage en Italie' by H. Taine (1866) is literature of a much more serious kind. It is descriptive rather than critical in the modern sense, and the chapter 'La Peinture Florentine' should be read by anyone seriously interested in the Florence galleries. It contains an enlightened sentence on the famous Venus de' Medici, forcing one to remember—what so many forget—that the arms were a restoration by Bernini, and are very likely the cause of much that fails to please in this statue. What he says of the galleries are only slight sketches, but these are by the hand of a master. The end of the second volume is Venice ; the first volume is Rome.

'The Makers of Florence,' by Mrs. Oliphant, is a most helpful book and one of her best. It should be read, I think, before the more detailed 'Life and Times of Savonarola,' by Professor Pasquale Villari, as the mind then will be in a more receptive condition for absorbing the greater detail of the larger book. It is almost inconceivable that Savonarola's skull formation should have been as low as it is represented in the portrait reproduced in this book of Mrs. Oliphant's, with the head covered with his Dominican cowl.

'The Life and Times of Savonarola' by Villari, translated as it is into English by his wife, has been lately republished in a cheap edition by Fisher Unwin.

Signora Villari has also written a pretty little book

of her own, called 'On Tuscan Hills and Venetian Waters.'

I have long had that amusing classic, the 'Memoirs of Benvenuto Cellini' by himself, translated by Thomas Roscoe (1823), on the title-page of which is a saying of Horace Walpole's: 'Cellini was one of the most extraordinary men of an extraordinary age. His Life, written by himself, is more amusing than any novel I know.' This book was again translated into English by John Addington Symonds, and published in 1888. It is pleasanter reading than Roscoe's, but the engraved portrait in the old book is infinitely better than in the new.

I found Symonds' 'Life of Michael Angelo' a book of rare interest. Symonds is often criticised for inaccuracy of detail. The same accusation is always brought against Froude; but both writers have a power of popularising information which, joined to their gift for vivid description, make one *live* in the past, in spite of the atmosphere of modern thought through which they present it.

Symonds' 'Italian Sketches,' which are so conveniently published in the Tauchnitz edition, speak of many things in a charming way, but do not actually touch on Florence itself.

Amongst the books I have been reading none seem to me more remarkable or stamped with a stronger or more interesting individuality than Walter Pater's. His 'Renaissance,' which he calls 'Studies in Art and Poetry,' and 'Marius the Epicurean,' with its vivid word-painting and its pictures of old Italy, so unchanged even to-day, are books which must be immensely admired by those who read them, or not liked at all. They are certainly not light reading, and more fitted for the study than the railway carriage; but they are books which I believe will live in English literature when many of the productions of this period will have passed into the unknown. They are full of study, thought, and knowledge, and it is not only a knack of beautiful writing which is their chief attraction and merit.

Many years ago two old ladies, Susan and Joanna Homer, lived in Florence, and wrote one of the first and the most satisfactory of the detailed guide-books I have ever seen, called 'Walks in Florence.' An interesting new French book by A. Geffroy, called 'Études Italiennes,' published in 1898, I thought worth reading, as it gives another historical view of the Renaissance ; Art being only indirectly alluded to. The chapters are on 'Les Grands Médicis,' 'Savonarola,' 'Guichardin.' He quotes of 'Laurent,' 'Ce refrain resté populaire qui résonne encore comme un écho lointain et gracieux de la Renaissance !

> Quanto è bella giovinezza
> Che si fugge tuttavia !
> Chi vuol esser lieto, sia,
> Di doman non c' è certezza.'

The second part of the book is called 'Rome Monumentale.' In this there is a chapter on 'La légende de la Cenci,' in which he also sweeps away the whole story.

Only last summer a book appeared called 'Tuscan Artists, their Thought and Work,' by Hope Rea. Sir W. B. Richmond writes the preface, and says : 'I desire success to this little volume, so interesting, so full of sympathy with those various emotions whose expression in all forms of art has made Italy their foster mother.'

A book has just been sent me, called 'Stray Studies from England and Italy,' by John Richard Green, the author of the famous 'Short History.' The title is not quite correct, as there is an excellent chapter or two on the south of France, and an exceedingly interesting historical paper on the home of our Angevin kings, which

was also the home of the Renaissance in France ; and it
has a still earlier interest for the modern English tourist
who rides through Touraine by the Loire to Saumur, for
as Mr. Green says, 'Nothing clears one's ideas about the
character of the Angevin rule, the rule of Henry II., or
Richard or John, so thoroughly as a stroll through
Anjou.' Another charming chapter is 'The Florence of
Dante.' In fact, I have most thoroughly enjoyed this
little gem of desultory information.

For serious modern criticism of Italian painters and
their work, I have found nothing that has interested me
so much and which seems to me so new as Mr. Bernhard
Berenson's three little volumes—'The Venetian Painters
of the Renaissance,' 'The Florentine Painters of the
Renaissance,' and 'The Central Italian Painters of the
Renaissance.' The author evidently aims at representing the modern scientific school of art criticism, started,
as far as I know, by Giovanni Morelli. The indexes at
the end of each volume will be found valuable, though
many of Mr. Berenson's conclusions will be cavilled at ;
and his attributions of pictures, differing, as they do,
from the official catalogues, raise much antagonism.

Where doctors differ, the public may be amused, and
art critics of the future must worry out their various
opinions.

'Italian Literature,' by Richard Garnett, is one of
those books for which the public ought to feel grateful,
as it condenses an incredible amount of labour and
study into a very small, convenient volume. It brings
us down to the present day, D'Annunzio's novels, etc.

In 1897 Mr. John Morley published one of his brilliant lectures, delivered in the Sheldonian Theatre, on
Machiavelli. He begins by a reference to Dante's liken-
ing of worldly fame to the breath of the wind, that
blows now one way, now another, and changes name as

it changes quarter. He says of Machiavelli : 'In our age, when we think of the chequered course of human time, of the shocks of irreconcilable civilisations, of war, trade, faction, revolution, empire, laws, creeds, sects, we seek a clue to the vast maze of historic and prehistoric fact. Machiavelli seeks no clue to his distribution of good and evil. He never tries to find a moral interpretation for the mysterious scroll. We obey laws that we do not know, but cannot resist. We can only make an effort to seize events as they whirl by, and to extort from them a maxim, a precept, or a principle, to serve our immediate turn. Fortune, he says—that is, Providence, or else circumstances, or the stars—is mistress of more than half we do. What is her deep secret, he shows no curiosity to fathom. He contents himself with a maxim for the practical man ("Prince," xxv.), that it is better to be adventurous than cautious, for Fortune is a woman and, to be mastered, must be boldly handled.'

Mr. Morley's defence of Machiavelli is on the lines of his concluding words : 'It is true to say that Machiavelli represents certain living forces in our actual world; that science, with its survival of the fittest, unconsciously lends him illegitimate aid ; that "he is not a vanishing type, but a constant and contemporary influence." This is because energy, force, will, violence, still keep alive in the world their resistance to the control of justice and conscience, humanity and right. In so far as he represents one side in that eternal struggle, and suggests one set of considerations about it, he retains a place in the literature of modern political systems and European morals.'

I wind up by taking from my list of books that were recommended to me a few I have not yet had time to read : 'Christ's Folk in the Apennine,' by Miss Alexander; 'Roadside Songs of Tuscany,' by the same; 'A Nook in the Apennines,' by Leader Scott; 'Italian Sketches,' by Mrs. Ross; 'Histoire des Médicis,' by Dumas; 'Une Année à Florence: Impressions de Voyage,' by Dumas; 'Italian Commonwealth, or Commonwealth of Florence,' by Trollope.

Last year, on May 26th, I left my Surrey garden for three months. The account of this time I had abroad and the return in August will bring my year to its conclusion.

My spring gardening was spoilt by the feeling that the buds I had watched so carefully would be seen in flower by others and not by myself; and there is no denying I left home with a considerable wrench. The garden looked very full, but green and flowerless; only one or two large Oriental Poppies were out. I do not know why, but I travelled by night to Paris, resting some hours in an hotel in order to go through by the Cenis train, arriving at Florence early in the evening instead of in the middle of the night. I might just as well have slept in Paris; it would have cost no more than the six hours' rest. I started from there to travel alone, for the first time in my life.

I did not want to feel sad or lonely, which would have been foolish, as I was deliberately going to please myself; and I could not help smiling as I thought over a sentence in the journal of Marie Bashkirtseff, and what she says about travelling with one's family: 'Je comprend qu'on soit heureux de vivre en famille, et je serais malheureuse seule. On peut aller faire des achats en famille, aller au Bois en famille, quelquefois au Théâtre. On peut être malade en famille, faire des cures en famille, enfin tout ce qui est de la vie intime et des choses nécessaires; mais voyager en famille ! ! ! C'est comme si on prenait plaisir à valser avec sa tante.

C'est ennuyeux mortellement, et même quelque peu ridicule.'

Railway travelling is always such a joy to me. I never know which I like best — looking out of the window, or feeling that I can read in peace without the disturbances which are perpetually occurring elsewhere. Going through France, I am always struck afresh by the thinly populated look of the country, except just near the towns.

I had in my travelling bag a cutting from the 'Daily Telegraph' of January 5th, 1898: Mr. Gladstone's account of Hallam,— a remarkably interesting paper, one of those rare gifts sometimes bestowed upon us by the daily press. It must have been almost the last, if not quite the last, thing of any importance the old man ever wrote.

Has it ever been explained why the recollections of youth are so engraven on the brain and flash out in old age with such vivid clearness? Educated and uneducated, clever and stupid, all seem to share the same experience. The dullest of old people are interesting if allowed to talk of their youth and themselves. The only drawback is that they enjoy repeating over and over again what they remember. Gladstone's half-jealous criticism of Hallam spending eight months in Italy between Eton and Cambridge includes so excellent a description of travelling in the days that are gone that it haunted me as I flew and rushed in my express in one bound from Paris to Florence:

'The agencies of locomotion have, within the last seventy years, been not only multiplied, but transformed. We then crept into and about countries; we now fly through them. When Arthur Hallam went with his family to Italy, there was not so much as a guidebook. It was shortly afterwards Mrs. Starke, under the auspices of Murray, founded that branch of literature, and within the compass of one very moderate volume expounded in every particular the whole continent of Europe. But this is only the outside of the case. A visit to Italy was then the summit of a young man's aspirations ; it now supplies some half-dozen rapid stages in larger tours, where we run much risk of losing in discipline and mental stimulus what we gain in mile-age. When it took sixteen or eighteen days to post to Rome, each change of horses was an event. The young traveller could not but try to make the most of what he had bought so dear. Scene, history, and language now flash before the eye ; then they soaked into the soul. Men were then steeped in the experiences of Italy ; they are now sprinkled with the spray. Its scenery, its art, its language, which was a delight and luxury to learn ; its splendid literature ; its roll of great men, among whom Dante himself might serve to build up the entire fame of a nation ; and its place in history, which alone connects together the great stages of human civilisation —all these constituted a many-sided power which was brought to bear almost in a moment on the mind of Arthur Hallam. I knew it, for I suffered by it. The interval between his progress and my own, always long, became such that there was no joining hands across it. I was plodding on the beaten and dusty path, while he was

> Where the lost lark wildly sings,
> Hard by the sun.'

Everyone takes with him to Florence Mr. Hare's 'Cities of Central Italy.' In his introduction to the 'Cities of Northern Italy,' he puts it well as regards the changes that have in my life-time come over travelling. I can remember things as he describes them :

' The old days of Italian travel are beginning to pass out of recollection — the happy old days, when, with slow-trotting horses and jangling bells, we lived for weeks in our *vetturino* carriage as in a house, and made ourselves thoroughly comfortable there ; halting at mid-day for luncheon, with pleasant hours for wandering over unknown towns and gathering flowers and making discoveries in the churches and convents near our resting-place. All that we then saw remains impressed on our recollection as a series of beautiful pictures set in a framework of the homelike associations of a quiet life, which was gilded by all that Italian loveliness alone can bestow of its own tender beauty. The slow approach to each long-heard-of but unseen city — gradually leading up, as the surroundings of all cities do, to its own peculiar characteristics — gave a very different feeling towards it from that which is produced by rushing into a railway station.'

This is all perfectly true ; but when we think that hundreds can now see and enjoy the great cities of Italy, which in old days was only the privilege of the idle, the rich, and the few, we can without regret give up the more romantic methods of travelling of bygone days.

The only book I had with me, given me before I left for Florence, was called ' Earthwork out of Tuscany,' being ' impressions and translations ' of Maurice Hew-lett (J. M. Dent & Co., 1895). It describes Florence, not as I saw it, but in autumn and early winter, the usual tourist time. It is very modern in tone, and although slightly affected, yet the enthusiasm and delight in Italy are as great as, or even greater than, those of writers of a past generation. His preface, which he calls ' Proem,' is an apologia for writing at all on such well-known ground, for he feels his book must risk the charge of being ' a *réchauffé* of Paul Bourget and Walter Pater with *ana* lightly culled from Symonds, and perchance the questionable support of ponderous references out of Burckhardt.' My journey was shortened for me by the pleasure I got from reading this book, and it made me feel glad, as I sat in the train, that I was on my way to this Italy of undying interest.

I had, of course, the usual luggage scare at the Custom House at Modane in the middle of the night. I was idiotic from sleep, and the officials declared my boxes were not in the train. I felt like the French cabman with a heavy load when a passing friend asked him how he was. 'Pour moi, je suis plongé dans la misère jusqu'au cou.' Just as the train was starting, to my intense relief I spied my boxes, and could once more complacently smile and remember a nice little story I had just been told. An American lady, having lost all her luggage, said : 'Any great trial sent by the Almighty I can bear, but these collateral smacks are too much for anyone to endure.' How true it is !

One of the drawbacks of the facility of modern travel is that it enables people who have a short holiday — say, of three weeks — to rush through Italy from place to place. Disappointed with the climate, they imagine sunshine is to be found further on. I heard a young man, who spent his three weeks at Rome, Florence and Venice, say that he had 'done *that* tour, and that Florence was the vilest climate on the face of God's earth.' Whereas a great deal more pleasure is to be had, and one gains a much more lasting impression, by going straight from home and spending the whole time in one place.

Everyone warned me so much against the heat I should find in Italy in June. But I began my disappointment by finding the Alps all cloud and rain, and, in spite of its being the last days of May, the weather was quite cold.   At Turin the sky was as inky black as in London.   The torrents were bursting, and the roads floating with water over black mud.   As we got near Genoa, of which absolutely nothing can be seen from the railway, it was like a gray July day at home, the hay cut and the Acacias in flower.

The journey along the seashore is a most irritating series of tunnels.   When I arrived at Florence, all loneliness was at an end.   Kind friends met me, and we drove through the town, which I had not visited, except for one night, since I was twenty.   In the gray, damp drizzle it did not look its best, but no weather can spoil the majestic appearance of the Ilex and Cypress avenue outside the Roman gate — the approach to what was once a Medicean villa.   Through this we had to drive to reach the village of Arcetri, where my journey ended.

The joy of being once more in Italy was, indeed, great ; my *pension* close — to the Torre del Gallo — was a large, fine house, quite empty.   All the upper floor was my own, and I could roam from room to room and enjoy the most beautiful views conceivable.   The whole country is like a gigantic rockwork — hill and vale and sloping sides and varied aspects, and all that can be imagined as perfect for the growth of vegetation.   I was rather disappointed at the excessive greenness of everything on my arrival.   Even the Olives, in spite of the green corn underneath them, looked green — not gray — from the masses of small yellow flowers that covered them.   One cannot look at all this redundant vegetation without realising that Florence must be blessed with an abundant rainfall.

They talk here of the probability of a wet ' San Giovanni ' as we talk of ' St. Swithin ' — meaning, of course, there is generally much wet about that time.

The Italian papers were naturally full of Mr. Gladstone's recent death, and one of them published his translation of Cowper's hymn, 'Hark, my soul,' which seems already, at the end of a year, almost a literary curiosity :

> Senti, senti, anima mia
> (Fu il Signor che sentia)
> Gesù parla e parla a te:
> 'Di, figliuolo, ami Me ? '
>
> 'Te legato svincolai,
> Le tue piaghe risanai,
> Fuorviato rimenai,
> Notte e dì per te mutai.'
>
> 'Vien la madre a quando a quando
> Il suo parto obliando ?
> Donna il può, non posso Io,
> Mai non viene in Me l' obblio.'
>
> 'L' amor Mio sempre dura,
> Alto più d' ogni altra altura,
> Tocca già le nere porte,
> Franco e fido, in fino a morte.
>
> 'Tu la gloria Mia vedrai,
> Se le piene grazie avrai,
> Te del trono meno al piè;
> Di, figliuolo, ami Me ? '
>
> 'Ah, Signor, mi duole il core
> Pel mio stanco e fiacco amore,
> T' amo pure, e vo' pregare
> Che ti possa meglio amare.

My food in my out-of-town *pension*, as I had it all to myself, consisted of vegetables, macaroni, rice, Alpine strawberries, etc. I learnt the secret of the delicious little vegetable they call 'Zucche,' which I had often heard of. It is called in the English Vilmorin vegetable book Italian Vegetable Marrow, 'an extremely distinct

variety, stems not running very thick, and short.   The
luxuriant foliage forms a regular bush.   All through
Italy, where this gourd is very commonly grown, the
fruit is eaten quite young, just before the faded flower
drops off.   The plants, deprived of their undeveloped
fruits, continue to flower for several months most profusely, each producing a great number of young gourds,
which, gathered in that state, are exceedingly tender
and delicately flavoured.'   'This should be tried in England,' adds Mr. Robinson.   The same excellent way of
gathering them quite young might, I think, be adopted
for other gourds and Vegetable Marrows.

What I saw from my window at Arcetri — Fireflies — Cypresses —
Youthful memories in the 'Cascine' — Deodar in cloister of
San Marco — Fête at Santa Margharita — Villas — Gardens —
Want of colour in Tuscany at midsummer — Slight allusion
to picture galleries — The Cabinet of Cardinal Leopoldo de'
Medici — June 24th in Florence — Botanical Garden — Silence
of birds and summer sounds.

June 1st.—I alluded in May to a book called 'Earthwork out of Tuscany.' The introductory chapter contains the following passage, which comes home to me most
strongly, as I begin to write a few notes about my visit
to Florence : 'Has any city, save perhaps Cairo, been
so written out as Florence ? . . . . Florence has often
been sketched before — putting Browning aside, with his
astounding fresco music — by Ruskin and George Eliot
and Mr. Henry James, to name only masters. But that
is no reason why I should not try my 'prentice hand.
Florence alters not at all ; men do. My picture, poor as
you like, shall be my own.' I, too, can only, in great
humility, beg you to accept this little account of my
June near Florence, 'not as what I would fain offer, but
what I am able to present.'

June 2nd.— The weather is getting finer and warmer,
and I am more and more delighted with my large, empty
house and with the views all round. A more perfect
spot could not be found even here. The actual town I
cannot see ; it is hidden by the undulating ground that
rises behind San Miniato, ending in the Torre del Gallo,
close to the villa where Galileo was exiled, when blind

and old, to die. Tradition says that he worked from the top of this tower. I wonder whether he did, or whether Milton was right in saying that he studied the moon from the top of Fiesole. Milton only saw Galileo on his second visit to Florence, as during his first visit the astronomer was kept a close prisoner by the Inquisition.

What was really at the bottom of Galileo's persecution ? Religious people thought it militated against the dignity and importance of man that this planet of his should go spinning round the sun — with men's hopes and feelings hanging on by their eyelids — instead of remaining quiet, in a dignified manner, while the sun did its duty in going round, warming and lighting, the earth.

Galileo's blindness seems to have had a 'prophetic fascination' for Milton, and the deep impression left by the sight of the Tuscan astronomer is shown by the way in which Milton once or twice alludes to him in 'Paradise Lost,' not published till nearly thirty years later.

Mr. Stephen Phillips' fine poem to Milton blind, might almost apply to Galileo :

> The hand was taken by Angels who patrol
> The evening, or are sentries to the dawn,
> Or pace the wide air everlastingly.
> Thou wast admitted to the presence, and deep
> Argument heardest and the large design
> That brings this world out of woe to bliss.

Ouida says of Galileo's tower in 'Pascarel,' perhaps the most imaginative and delightful of her Italian books (so true to nature, and so false to human nature !): 'The world has spoilt most of its places of pilgrimage, but the old star-tower is not harmed as yet where it stands amongst its quiet garden ways and grass-grown slopes, up high amongst the hills, with sounds of dripping water on its court, and wild wood flowers thrusting their bright heads through its stones. It is as peaceful, as simple, as homely, as closely girt with blossoming boughs and with tulip-crimsoned grapes now as then, when, from its roof in the still midnight of far-off time, its master read the secret of the stars.'

But to Galileo at seventy and blind, I wonder what was the use of the old fighting tower? The sight of it was a ceaseless joy to me, flanked by splendid Cypresses, standing ochre colour against the blue, or dark against some 'billowy bosomed cloud'; and at evening it was 'one red tower that drinks its fill out of the sunset sky.'

This was as I looked to the east. Moving round to the south, the view widened and spread right up the valley of the Arno, where the little puff of gray smoke curled along the base of the hill, and showed where the train sped on its way to Rome, through the mountains, as they folded one over the other in tints of pearly gray. Still more south came the hill where Vallombrosa stands, and then a long stretch of villa-dotted low hills. At the end of the ridge was a little grove of pointed Cypresses, and the well-known favourite peasant church of all the country round stood out on its own little hill in the middle distance. Towards the west came a hillock crowned with a flat, white villa, cut by the Cypresses that surround nearly all the houses, sinking and swelling with Olive and Vine towards the distant view of the Certosa of the Val d'Arno. And so round to the whole beautiful broad valley running towards Pisa, ending in the blue shadows of the Carrara Mountains, with the top of Bellosguardo in the middle distance sharp and black against the gray mist of the plain. Evening after evening I used to try and get home to see the sunsets from my windows, as nowhere

else were they so beautiful, and nowhere else did the
air blow so fresh, and yet so warm, as in my home of
the winds, the 'Pension d'Arcetri.'

The only sadness that I know of in these southern
summers is that the twilights are so short. I missed
much the long, pale primrose evening skies of June,
which at home throw up their faint northern brightness
right into the indigo of the star skies of night, and
almost meet Aurora at her waking.

But the dark evenings are wanted to show the beauty
of those wonderful fairy-like things that flit about in
millions under the Olive trees and in the corn. I had
never seen the fireflies since the summer I passed under
Fiesole, when I was a little child of ten, but I had not
forgotten them. The poetry that hangs around them is
endless ; their natural history is prosaic. They are
beetles. Both sexes are luminous, though that is not
the general belief in Italy. They are nearly related to
our glowworm. The colour of the fireflies is warmer
and more golden than the blue light of the glowworm,
and their beauty is enhanced and made more mysterious
because the light comes and goes, and shows much more
brightly at intervals. These fireflies are usually only to
be met with in quite the south of Europe, but in fine
hot summers they can be seen in rarer numbers as far
north as Switzerland, and even the middle of Germany.
The Italians call them *lucciole*, and associate them with
all sorts of pretty poetical stories. Ouida says : 'One
cannot wonder that the poets love them, and that the
children believe them to be fairies carrying their little
lanterns on their road to dance in the magic circle under
the leaves in the wood. Some say they die in a day ;
some say they live on for ages. Who shall tell ? They
look always the same.'

On one side of my house was a much-neglected, but

lovely little square, walled garden with beautiful tall iron gates. The beds and paths, edged with stone, were of a simple, formal pattern, which gave great dignity to the weedy little wilderness; and there were the usual large terracotta pots with strong, well-grown Lemon trees in them, the pride of the Tuscan peasant's heart. The flowers on them scented the air; the peasants sell the pale fruit at a special price all the summer through in the town, as we sell glass-grown Peaches. I think that if we tried to grow plants of this sort of Lemon at home in pots or tubs, it would be far better than trying to grow the more delicate Oranges usually seen on terraces in England. I was told I should find it too hot, but I never did once. Indeed, at first I was disappointed; it was not warm enough. But in England they had snow early in June. The Irises, the Tulips, all the wild spring flowers were over. I found the fields in places filled with a curious orchidaceous-looking plant which, terrible weed as it was, I thought would look beautiful as a spring pot-plant. It turned out to be a cruel parasitical growth, called *Orobanche pruinosa*, which grows on the roots of the Broad Beans, destroying whole crops—to the ruin of bad farmers. It also grows on the roots of Geraniums, I am told; which will be convenient in making it a pot-plant at home.

My villa *pension* was surrounded with fine Cypresses of all sizes and ages. I wonder when and how they came to be planted round the houses? Some say the peasants from all time have planted one as a kind of dower when a daughter was born in the house. In justification of this, Mr. Loudon says that Pliny tells several extraordinary stories about the durability of the wood, and that the plantations of Cypresses were cut down every thirteen years for poles, rafters, joists, etc., which made the wood so profitable that a plantation of Cypresses was thought a sufficient marriage portion for a daughter. Theophrastus states that it grew naturally in the isle of Crete, and that those who wish to have the Cypress flourish must procure a little of the earth from the isle of Cyprus for it to grow in. The early botanists supposed that the upright and spreading Cypresses were male and female of the same plant — *C. horizontalis* the male, *C. stricta* the female. This is not the case. The horizontal Cypress is quite a distinct species, which comes from the Levant. The evergreen Cypress is a flame-shaped, tapering, and cone-like tree. The male catkins are yellowish, about three inches long, and very numerous. The female catkins are much fewer and of a roundish oblong form; but both grow on the same tree. I have a sentiment for Cypresses that amounts to a passion. All my life they have remained in my mind as emblems of the fairest land I have ever known.

June 5th.—To-day being warm, I went down to Florence; and dropping my companion — who had to call on a sick friend — I went on alone to the 'Cascine,' the well-known public park, which I had not seen for over forty years. The ghost of my youth sat beside me in the little shabby carriage; and as I drove along the well-remembered alley, with the racecourse on the right, and the shaded roads where I used to ride, the past all came back to my mind. To the outward eye all seemed very much the same — a little smartened up and modernised perhaps. As I drew up on the Piazzone, there was another carriage with a mother and three young daughters, as we used to be. It was a strange, lonely, sepulchral sort of feeling — that in all that gay crowd very few were even born when we lived in Florence and I used to go daily to the 'Cascine' and dance half the night through at balls. That winter at Florence seemed to me at the time to be the last of my youth, and it altered all my life.

How strange are the depressions of youth! Life seems over when really it has scarce begun! It was in such a mood I left Florence at twenty. De Musset has expressed this sadness of youth with concentrated pathos:

> J'ai perdu ma force et ma vie
> Et mes amis et ma gaieté;
> J'ai perdu jusqu'à la fierté
> Qui faisait croire à mon génie.

> Quand j'ai connu la vérité
> J'ai cru que c'était une amie;
> Quand je l'ai comprise et sentie
> J'en étais déjà dégoûté.

> Et pourtant elle est éternelle,
> Et ceux qui se sont passé d'elle
> Ici bas ont tout ignoré.

> Dieu parle, il faut qu'on lui réponde,
> Le seul bien qui me reste au monde
> Est d'avoir quelquefois pleuré.

As I drove back into Florence the air was heavy with the perfume of the Lime trees — such Lime trees as I have never seen before. The leaves are few and small, and were absolutely hid by the size and number of the yellow flowers, with their big sheaths on each side like wings. The evening sky was reflected in the Arno in the old, familiar way, and the air was warm and still. I called for my friend, and once more shut up the memory of the past in that far-away corner of the brain where such things remain. We drove through the town, and I first saw the Duomo with its façade completed. In my day, of course, it was rough bricks, with the holes for the scaffolding left in it. Beautifully as it is done, and I do

think it is a noble piece of restoration, the new façade
at first gave me a shock.   It seemed to cheapen Giotto's
lovely tower, and made one feel that what had seemed
inimitable could be copied.

My first fortnight at Florence was spent in driving
about seeing old gardens, and dropping into dim
churches on summer evenings before returning home.
My critical feelings were all absolutely dead. I could do
nothing but gasp and admire, and with it always the
dim memory of somehow having seen it all before, as in
a dream.   The churches in the fading evening light
looked very solemn and very beautiful — portals to death,
perhaps, rather than windows into heaven.   But I do
not know that I liked them less for that.   I found
Florence very little changed in its general aspect, in
spite of the many alterations which have been such pain
and grief to the English inhabitants.   It is almost, if
not quite, unspoilable.   There are trams and omnibuses
and incongruous things, no doubt; but, oh! it is wonderfully unchanged — from the time-worn stones of its
pavements to the black eaves of its roofs against the
brilliant sky.

One need not be in Florence to give one's entire
sympathy to the good people there who are trying their
utmost to save the beautiful old city from destruction.
To destroy old streets to build hotels may defeat its own
object, for if Florence becomes less beautiful the demand
for hotel rooms may diminish; though, honestly, I
think that, to keep up the influx of strangers, sanitary
precautions and a certain content among the people
are more necessary still.   Five thousand English and
other tourists left Florence the week before I arrived, in
consequence of a very slight riot which followed on the
two days' Socialist outbreak at Milan.   The departure of
strangers means ruin to the hotel-keepers and poverty

to all those they employ; so my sympathy to a certain extent goes with the difficulties of the Italian Government, who have to consider the material benefit to the city and its people that may come from wider streets and bridges. When I see protests such as have appeared lately in the columns of our newspapers, a feeling of shame always comes over me at the wholesale destruction that has gone on within my memory in our own poor old London, and which few people think about,—for instance, the destruction of Temple Bar, because it was thought too expensive to make a road each side of it. Also the clearing away of sixteen or eighteen of Wren's beautiful churches. I would far rather see them used in some way for the people's good than destroyed. I cannot see why they should not be put to some useful service, as the monasteries and convents have been in France and Italy. If this is sacrilege, surely it is much more so wantonly to destroy ! At least, we might still have the beautiful spires of the kind which Mr. Watson describes :

> It soars like hearts of hapless men who dare
>   To sue for gifts the gods refuse to allot;
> Who climb forever toward they know not where,
>   Baffled forever by they know not what.

Not to speak of the hideous spoiling of the Thames by the railway and other bridges, narrow streets and old houses are constantly pulled down. Only the other day the picturesque almshouses of Westminster ceased to exist. Last, but not least, Wren's work is being disfigured, as most people feel, by the modern decorations in St. Paul's. I often wish a deputation of influential Italians, with a petition signed by hundreds of non-influential names, would come here and protest against this destruction of old buildings and our many other

municipal shortcomings. May the Italians respect their
lovely buildings !— and I believe they will—better than
we do. They certainly restore — with apparently only
the wish to copy and maintain — a great deal better than
any other European nation I know. I cannot make up
my mind that in this they are wrong, in spite of the constant protests of the Anti-Restoration Society, with
whose work I have been in much sympathy all my life.
It seems hard to say that the beautiful buildings of the
Middle Ages ought to be allowed to fall into ruins, and
the effort to preserve what we admire will, I think, earn
the gratitude of the ages to come. In the eighteenth
century, ruins, *as* such, were admired even to the extent
of making artificial ones, and the landscape painters not
only steeped all nature's bright colours in black and
brown, but painted the ruined columns under thunder-
clouds, with Roman soldiers in togas walking about. And
our grandfathers bought and admired their pictures !

June 6th.— When I was young, in Florence, a great
mystery hung over the convent of San Marco, as women
were not allowed to visit it, and we young ones thought
of it principally in connection with its perfumery shop,
where the Iris-root powder and pale pink lip-salve were
better than anywhere else. It was with a real feeling of
curiosity that I saw the interior and the famous frescoes
that have survived so many centuries. I found them
very sweet and child-like—these decorations of the little
cells by the humble Christian monk ; but I suppose I
had expected too much, for, as works of art, they disappointed me. In the little square surrounded by the
cloister of San Marco, where Fra Girolamo sat *sotto un
rosajo di rose Damaschine* preaching to his contemporaries, the monks — or rather, I suppose, some unimagi-
native official who has charge of the public buildings in
Florence, has planted, instead of the gentle damask Rose

and the Lavender and Rosemary, a huge flourishing Deodar. No doubt this tree is beautiful enough on the high,
steep sides of the Lower Himalayas, but with its symmet-
rical growth, and the size to which it has already attained,
it is a most unsightly and inappropriate object in the
restricted cortile of Savonarola's monastery. It puts
everything out of all proportion, and is such an anachronism ! Deodars are quite modern trees in Europe, and
are not pretty, even in villa gardens. I do wish it could
be cut down ; plain, daisy-spangled turf would be much
better. Nothing is so striking or so general as the want
of imagination in planting. Sometimes plants are put
in entirely out of character with the rest of a garden ;
another time trees are planted which, when they grow
well, entirely obscure the view or shut out the summer
sunset. One curious anachronism I have noticed is that
an artist, in painting a scene for the background of a
Greek or Roman play, introduces American plants in his
foreground! So many places are merely spoilt in an
effort to improve them, and this is especially the case all
around Florence.

Of all that I have read about Florence since my
return, I think nothing is more attractively clever or
more full of character, both of the place and of the
writer, than a chapter called 'A Florentine Mosaic' in
'Tuscan Cities,' a little volume by W. D. Howells, the
American. It is published in the 'English Library'
series at Leipzig. Half the book is about Florence. It
is a perfectly charming mixture of humour and history,
bewildered tourist and most cultivated man of letters.
It takes one so instantly into the very heart and core of
the Middle Ages that one purrs with a delightful feeling of 'Oh, certainly ! Yes, I always did know all about
it.' Popes and parties, blacks and whites, the ins
and outs, etc. Art, which generally forms such a large

portion of a book about Florence, is left out altogether, or at any rate is only like a brilliant tapestry background to his living, moving figures. It is so clear and so comprehensive that it satisfies the idle and whets the appetite of those who wish to know more. Mr. Howells has a masterly way of sketching, and his appreciation of the cloisters is so real that, to my mind, he makes one feel it would be worth while to go all the way to Florence to see them and nothing else. Cloisters are, perhaps, the most characteristic things in Italy. He thus writes :

' The thing that was novel to me, who found the churches of 1883 in Florence so like the churches of 1863 in Venice, was the loveliness of the deserted cloisters belonging to so many of the former. These enclose nearly always a grass-grown space, where daisies and dandelions began to abound with the earliest consent of spring. Most public places and edifices in Italy have been so much photographed that few have any surprise left in them ; one is sure that one has seen them before. But the cloisters are not yet the prey of this sort of pre-acquaintance. Whether the vaults and walls of the colonnades are beautifully frescoed, like those of Santa Maria Novella or Santa Annunziata or San Marco, or the place has no attraction but its grass and sculptured stone, it is charming ; and these cloisters linger in my mind as something not less Florentine in character than the Ponte Vecchio or the Palazzo Publico. I remember particularly an evening effect in the cloister of Santa Annunziata, when the belfry in the corner, lifted aloft in its tower, showed with its pendulous bells like a great graceful flower against the dome of the church behind it. The quiet in the place was almost sensible ; the pale light, suffused with rose, had a delicate clearness ; there was a little agreeable thrill of cold in the air ; there could not have been a more refined moment's pleasure offered to a sympathetic tourist loitering homeward to his hotel.'

As I write, I feel 'Of course everyone knows this book,' but it is often not so, and no one told me of it till long after I got back. I experienced one of those 'refined moments of pleasure' when one beautiful . June afternoon — warm, but not one bit too hot — we drove to the Certosa, and, sending the carriage round, walked up its steep Olive slopes to the monastery. A few of the white-robed monks still remained in possession. I did not make out if they are renewed or not, but their presence preserves the character of the place. I had never seen it before ; for of course years ago, like San Marco, it was not shown to women. The garden was peaceful to a degree, shimmering in the golden-veiled summer sunshine. Never did I see such lovely lavender ; it was as different from our northern plant as could be. The flowering part was just double as long, and one mass of grey-blue flowers, which gave a general effect in the garden as of blue haze. One side of the cloister had been thrown down by the earthquake of three years ago. They were beginning to repair it — with the usual Italian patient fidelity in restoration.

No one who goes to the Certosa should fail to take special notice of the remarkable *pietra tombale* — so different from our dull interpretation of the 'tombstone' — of Cardinal Lionardo Buonafede. I am told it is often missed. This recumbent statue is as fresh and well preserved as the day it was made, which is very rare with any of these peculiar effigies. The figure of the old Cardinal lies on the tessellated marble floor. His head is propped by costly pillows, and he wears his jeweled mitre. His stockinged feet and simply crossed hands, with the long, straight draperies of his robe, are a most perfect example of the realistic sculpture of the

Middle Ages — as true as waxwork, with none of its vulgarity — so different from the degeneracy of modern Italian art. I wish I knew why it has been a Christian custom to clothe the feet of the dead; they are especially beautiful. If all else is changed, they remain the same.

June 9th. — This being the Festival of Corpus Christi, we went in the afternoon to the little church close by of Santa Margharita. Ouida describes, much better than I can do, 'the little, brown, square church, with its bell clanging in the open tower high above in the sweet air on the hills; there is level grass all about it; and it has a cool, green garden, shut within walls on every side except where a long parapet of red, dusky tiles leaves open the view of the Valdarno; underneath the parapet there are other terraces of deep grass and old, old Olive trees, in whose shade the orchids love to grow and the blue Iris springs up in great sheaves of sword-like leaves.

'There are trees of every sort in the cloistered garden, the turf is rich and long, the flowers are tended with the greatest care, the little sacristy grows red in the sun, an Acanthus climbs against it; the sacristan's wife comes out to you plaiting her straw, and brings you a cluster of her Roses; you sit on the stone seat, and lean over the parapet and look downward; birds flit about you; contadini go along the grass paths underneath and nod to you, smiling; a delicious mingled loveliness of Olive wood and Ilex foliage and blossoming vineyards shelve beneath you; you see all Florence gleaming far below there in the sun, and your eyes sweep from the snow that still lies on Vallombrosa to the blue shadows of the Carrara range.

'It is calm and golden and happy here at Santa Margharita's, high in the fragrant hill air, with the Guelder Roses nodding above head, and the voices of the vine-dressers echoing from the leaf-veiled depths below.'

That is an exact description of the spot ; we went there often, and we, too, hung over the parapet and thought of the *tempo passato*. I could see the little church tower always from my bedroom window.

On this beautiful June afternoon we saw the most picturesque and characteristic procession — the Host carried from the church to the chapel of a villa about half a mile off. The houses round, year by year, take it in turns to be so honoured. The priests in general were very ugly and common-looking, but the young man who on this occasion carried the Host was superb, like the Giorgione in the Pitti. The lighted candles in the outdoor evening light, the white-robed priests, the long procession of peasants, were most striking. Arriving at the villa, they passed to the chapel under a loggia, the tessellated pavement of which was drawn out in a beautiful coloured pattern made of the petals of flowers — Poppies, Roses, Larkspurs, the brilliant yellow Broom — and all between the pattern filled in with little leaves of bright green Box. The effect was to me quite new and very decorative. The procession passed on each side, and the priest alone, carrying the Host, was esteemed worthy to walk straight down the middle of this nature-coloured carpet. Nothing could have been more rurally peaceful and lovely than the whole scene. In the earlier days of the century we were taught to believe the troubles of Italy, like the troubles of Ireland, were owing to Catholicism. Now the theory is that the Latin races are dying out ; but if this is true, is it certain they are dying of Catholicism ? Is it not quite wonderfully clear the Italians have never lost their Paganism ? I confess, as I watched the whole scene, I could only think of Pater's opening to 'Marius the

Epicurean,' in which he describes how the purer forms
of Paganism had lingered in the villages after the
triumph of Christianity—'a religion of usages rather
than the facts of belief, and attached to very definite
things and places.'   Then comes the description of the
'little' or private Ambarvalia in the home of the youth
Marius, and it almost exactly describes what I saw this
June day quite at the end of the nineteenth century.
'At the appointed time all work ceases; the instru-
ments of labour lie untouched, hung with wreaths of
flowers; while masters and servants together go in solemn procession along the dry paths of vineyard and
cornfield. . . . The old Latin words of the Liturgy,
to be said as the procession moved on its way, though
their precise meaning has long since become unin-
telligible.

'Early on that day the girls of the farm had been
busy in the great portico, filling large baskets with
flowers cut short from branches of Apple and Cherry,
then in spacious bloom, to strew before the quaint
images of the gods — Ceres and Bacchus, and the yet
more mysterious Dea Dia—as they passed through the
fields, carried in their little houses on the shoulders of
white-clad youths, who were understood to proceed to
this office in perfect temperance, as pure in soul and
body as the air they breathed in the firm weather of
that early summer-time. The clean lustral water and
the full incense-box were carried after them.'

So far the description is exact. The butchery which
disgusted Marius, Christianity has swept away; but
everything else remains almost entirely the same.

All trace of costume amongst the peasants has disappeared even in this Arcetri neighbourhood, the most
simple and countrified side of Florence. The people,
from the outside, look well-to-do and comfortable, and

on festal days the young of both sexes walk about the roads in cheerful, happy bands. They never go in couples, as we everlastingly see them on the same occasions in England; but the boys were together, and the girls together. The figures of the women in the long, plain skirts and coloured shirts struck me as very graceful and dignified. George Eliot says of Romola: 'Let her muffle herself as she will, everyone wants to see what there is under her veil, for she has that way of walking like a procession.' That is just what one may say of many of these young Tuscan women. She also says: 'There has been no great people without processions, and the man who thinks himself too wise to be moved by them to anything but contempt is like the puddle that was proud of standing alone while the river rushed by.'

All my early time at Florence was spent in driving about, seeing villas, wandering through the poderes, resting and drawing. For the amateur sketcher, what a mental struggle it is!—whether to give the time to drawing, or to see all one can. One day we started at eight, and drove up to Monte Sennaria, fifteen miles or so, on the Bologna Road. This took us past the villa we lived in as children. I found that all had been much changed and grown up. Even the road—which in my day passed between walls out of which grew the large, handsome house—was now turned to the left, and the space between it and the villa thickly planted with evergreens, thus entirely depriving it of its original Italian character.

I can remember now the mysterious tremble with which I used sometimes to lie awake at night and hear the tinkle of the bell of the dead-cart, as it passed under the windows up to the cemetery on the hill. I had been told no coffins were used, and I always thought some one might wake during the long drive. The morning we went to Monte Sennaria the weather was lovely, and, though rather hot on starting, it soon got delicious; and as we reached the higher ground many spring flowers remained. I particularly noticed quantities of the blue Italian Borage, growing small and low on dried banks, and a sheet of gentian-blue bloom. Grown in good soil in English flower borders, it is coarse and leafy, and flowers but little; at least, that is my experience. I shall find it a most valuable plant in Surrey if it will grow in poor, dry places. Last autumn, after I got home, I immediately moved some of my plants of Italian Borage to the driest, sunniest spot in the garden. I shall see if it will flower as abundantly as it did in Italy. The Rush or Italian Broom ought to be sown every year in light soils, as it is such a useful July-flowering plant, and rarely seen — not being quite hardy — in Surrey.

The villas of the rich that I saw round Florence — and, of course, there are a great many which I did not see — are to be recognised by the fact that the Vine and Olive, Lemon and Pomegranate, Fig and Mulberry, are turned out for the planting of Laurels, Deodars and other conifers, Rhododendrons, and coarse-growing, un-pruned shrubs. The beautiful old walls are often levelled to the ground, to make a slope of coarse-growing grass; or the wall formerly used for the trained and well-pruned Vine is smothered with a mass of untended creepers. The newly planted Crimson Rambler is doing very well and making excessive growth, though it will never be a general favourite, as it flowers too late and is not a marketable Rose; so the gardeners despise it, which is lucky, as its colour is not good. The greatest crime of all, as regards the spoiling of Italian gardens, is destroying the effect of space and coolness, and at the same time entirely shutting out the view by planting trees—say, even a row of Poplars. The old gardens, as perhaps Dante and Boccaccio saw them, are now smothered in Virginia Creeper, and made to look as much like a villa at Hampstead or Putney as possible. Magnolias are crowded out, and Camellias seem no longer cultivated (I suppose, because they are out of fashion in English conservatories); and instead of the cool, gray gravel, so easily kept raked and weeded in the old days, unsatisfactory grass paths are attempted. In the garden that I especially remember, having spent months there twice in my life, the view towards the city and the Val d'Arno right away to the Carraras — which on favoured evenings are rubies or sapphires or beaten gold against the sky — all this, so ineffaceably impressed on my memory, is now hidden from sight by a dark, gloomy, tangled mass of evergreens. As regards the modern treatment of newly made gardens in Florence, it is only fair to say that I saw them much too late, all attention being given to make them beautiful up to the end of May, as at about that time most of the English visitors fly northward.

The gardens which gave me most pleasure were those which had remained in the hands of Italians and retained their old character. All over the world the English have an insane, inartistic, though perhaps natural desire, not to develop the capabilities of the soil and climate in which they are forced to live, which would give a real interest to every plot of cultivated ground inhabited by the white man, but to have a garden as like 'home' as possible—to make a lawn, which fails and is ugly, and to plant a shrubbery, which grows apace and chokes everything really worth growing.

I got last year from Seville a letter describing what a southern garden should be: 'The Alkasar garden is the most beautiful I ever saw: very neglected as regards

W

individual plants, but so lovely as a whole. The beds
are all *sunk*. You walk between dwarf Myrtle hedges
on tiled, paved, or brick paths, and every now and then
you come to a round point with coloured tile seats.
Some of the outside Myrtle hedges are waist-high and
very fine. The beds are eighteen inches below the path,
and again divided by little Myrtle hedges six inches
high (no doubt the origin of our Box edgings). They
are mostly filled with Violets and sweet-scented shrubs,
and above tower great Magnolias, Lemons, Oranges,
Verbenas, Heliotrope, Jasmines in clumps, and a host of
other things I do not know the names of. Here and
there the path leads to a great raised marble tank or
Moorish bath. There are innumerable small fountains
sunk and tiled; round one of these is a great tiled walk
with Orange trees sunk in round holes about two feet
deep, making a fine double avenue. I fancy the garden
is pretty much as it was originally laid out by the
Moors. I wish you could see it. The Spaniards have
added their favourite Carnations grown in pots, but little
else. It seemed to me that the style might well be
copied in England, making the beds much less; certainly the little shallow fountains would look lovely
anywhere. We have seen one or two other gardens,
always the sunk beds and tiled or paved paths, and
always Violets used as grass round the roots of anything. Where we are has been an eye-opener to me
about the English abroad and their narrowness in
household management. Our garden was made by an
Englishman, so all our beds are raised, and are washed
away in every storm, and the would-be gravel path is
most of it in the high road below. Your book has been
of the greatest use in our tiny garden. Even though
the conditions are so different, the spirit is the same.'
My dear young friend a little misses the spirit of

what I mean when she thinks the system of the garden she describes can be brought to England. Where there is frost and damp, such things get soon spoilt and injured, and look mournful and decayed. Broken-up paving-stones are pretty in a formal garden, and — planted with Lavender, Pinks, Carnations, Rosemary, Saxifrages, and Roses — can be made to look lovely at all seasons. But sunk beds as she describes them, which are perfect for irrigation in the South, would never do here. The plants would damp off. Raised beds, however, are undesirable even in England in light soils. We can no more imitate what is best in the South than they can imitate our velvet lawns and our sweeping Beech trees. Planting the *Viola odorata* (the Old English garden Violet) under every shrub or tiny Gooseberry and Currant bush, in both flower and kitchen garden, has been a great success with me in Surrey. If tried with even Czar Violets, which require more care and cultivation, it would be a failure. The cultivation of Carnations in pots might be more carried out in England—with advantage, I think. And it would be better if the pots were painted or glazed half-way down, as done on the Continent, to prevent evaporation. The single-branching Larkspurs of all colours were grown in pots at Florence, and looked so well. I am trying some. They are far prettier than the double annual Larkspur generally grown in England.

The two most beautiful villas I saw truly carried out, with their lovely grounds, the half-monkish ideal expressed by Newman: 'By a garden is meant mystically a place of spiritual repose, stillness, peace, refreshment, and delight.' Our gay, modern, brilliant, flowery English parterres and Scotch and Irish gardens express, to my mind, none of this. Apart from everything else, their limited size renders this impossible. They tell us

a garden is the reward of toil; the earth's cry of delight
that winter is over and gone; the full enjoyment of
plenty and rich colour, requiring constant care; not a
place of 'spiritual repose, stillness, and delight.'

The more splendid of these two villas was, tradition
says, designed by Michael Angelo, and it is worthy of
his brain and hand. In its large simplicity it reminds
one of his will: 'Lascio l' anima a Dio e la mia roba ai
più prossimi parenti.' This villa stands many miles
high on the hillside southwest of Florence, and is
approached by the usual stately Cypress avenue. Its
massive plain front and its open arcade are most impressive. On the right was the solemn shade of the
Ilex grove, and beneath was the boundless view of sunlit Florence.

The other villa, most wonderful of all as regards its
surroundings and views, was Villa Gamberaia (which
means, 'Pool of the Crayfish'), four or five miles from
Florence, beyond Settingiano. I suppose everyone who
goes to Florence sees it, or used to do so; now it is
more difficult. Napoleon IH. lived in it at one time. I
wonder if in after-life his thoughts sometimes turned
with sorrowful regrets to the peaceful days passed
there! Here were Cypresses taller and straighter than
any I had ever seen; long, green alleys, ending in small
temples; high walls over which Oleanders tossed themselves, their branches heavy with the bloom of their
exquisite pink flowers; and all the long afternoon of
the late June day the nightingales sang. Why, in colder
climes, do they stop singing so much earlier in the year,
and here they sing well into midsummer! With the
exception of these nightingales in favoured woods, the
birds are very silent in Italy in June. But the sounds
are many—frogs, insects, the constant singing of the
grasshoppers. Keats says: 'The poetry of Earth is

never dead. When all the birds are faint with the hot . sun and hide in cooling trees, a voice will run from hedge to hedge about the new-mown mead. That is the grasshopper's.'

For associations with the South, there is nothing in the way of sounds to equal the sad call of the little night-owl—or *aziola*, as the Italians call it. The following colloquial poem of Shelley's, if not a gem amongst his lyrics, expresses the tender affection we must all feel for this little bird :

> 'Do you not hear the aziola cry?
> Methinks she must be nigh,'
>   Said Mary, as we sate
> In dusk, ere stars were lit or candles brought;
> And I, who thought
> This aziola was some tedious woman,
>   Ask'd, 'Who is Aziola?' How elate
> I felt to know that it was nothing human,
>   No mockery of myself to fear or hate!
> And Mary saw my soul,
> And laughed and said, 'Disquiet yourself not;
> 'Tis nothing but a little, downy owl.'
>
> Sad aziola! many an eventide
>   Thy music I had heard
> By wood and stream, meadow and mountainside,
> And fields and marshes wide,—
> Such as nor voice, nor lute, nor wind, nor bird,
>   The soul ever stirr'd;
> Unlike, and far sweeter than them all.
> Sad aziola! from that moment I
> Loved thee and thy sad cry.

One of my first inquiries on my arrival in Florence was about an old villa that in my time belonged to a rich Russian. They said it was all swept away and the treasures gone to St. Petersburg. The reason this villa made so deep an impression on me was that there I saw for the first time a picture of ' Paolo and Francesca '; it was by Ary Scheffer. I was so young that it set me wondering how Dante could call it Hell and yet leave them together. The same thought has been rendered finely, I think, by a young friend who signs himself ' M. B.' His sonnet was written on seeing the much stronger and more beautiful representation of the same subject by Mr. Watts :

> Though borne like withered leaves upon a stream,
>   Perished and dead, they would not live again,
>   Nor in the hard world face the wiles of men;
> Their past is but the haunting of a dream.
> And yet they would not sleep in Asphodel,
>   Nor — for without remorse is their regret —
>   Drink deep of bliss and utterly forget;
> Not for all Heaven would they exchange their Hell.
> And they give thanks because their punishment
> Is sealed and sure, because their doom shall be
> To go in anguish through eternity
>   Together on the never-resting air.
> Beyond all happiness is their content
>   Who know there is no end to their despair.

At the end of June the whole colour of the country had changed and become much richer from the corn ripening. This restored to the Olive trees once more their gray colour in the sunlight, and in evening light they again looked cool and almost blue against the warm madder and ochre of the corn. How endless in nature is the making of colour by contrast !

Custom often has in it more reason than at first appears. I never could understand why so few people go to Italy in summer. But the fact is, they hunger for bright, strong colour — blue skies and yellow sunsets, purple mountains and brilliant flowers. These they find in spring and autumn, to their hearts' content ; but summer in Florence is mellow and veiled, and very tender in colour, truly represented in Mason's pictures, and so totally unlike the typical water-colour drawings of Italy from the brush of Richardson or Aaron Penley, much the fashion fifty years ago.

At one villa I saw a pond of lovely Burmese goldfish, quite different from any I had ever before seen alive, and exactly resembling the fish in Japanese drawings and Chinese bowls — little, fat bodies, and large, swimming bladders, and long, waving tails which made their movements very swift and graceful. They were fed with little bits of wafer, the same as that used in Catholic churches, and also used all over the Continent for wrapping up powders so that you should not taste the medicine. The fish pounced on these delicate morsels with extraordinary rapacity and greed. I have never dared feed the goldfish in my fountain, as they remain so much healthier with only the natural food they are able to procure. Where the fountains are kept very clean, the best food for them, if these wafers cannot be procured, is crumbled vermicelli.

June 17th.—My time was half over in Florence before I went to the picture galleries at all — not because I did not wish to go, but there was so much else to see and enjoy and admire. It is almost useless to speak of the pictures themselves. Those who have seen them know what they are; and to those who have not, no words would convey any idea. It was very interesting to me to realise how my own taste had altered. The outside of the Pitti, grand and massive as the building is, gives me no pleasure. Under the archway, and beyond the public entrance into the building, there is a little yard where a wonderful sight can be obtained of the Arabesque patterns which adorn the outside of the old Medici passage to the Uffizi. It is worth while to go through to look at them. Inside the galleries, pictures that used to be pointed out to me as the great gems in my youth seemed now comparatively uninteresting. Botticelli, whom I at that time never heard of, stands indeed a head and shoulders above his contemporaries. Two quite little cabinet pictures in one of the small rooms at the Uffizi gave me much to think of. One was the exquisite little 'Judith.' His rendering of the subject first gave me a kind of understanding why the old masters were so fond of the ghastly story which must have appealed to them from their own wars and dissensions. I have always hated the usual treatment of this subject — the bleeding corpse on the bed and the uplifted head in Judith's hand. But here the beautiful heroine widow, her deed accomplished, her country saved, trips home again with stately pride across the open country. Warriors are in the distance, fields and flowers in front, and her child-like, innocent face is turned full towards one. In one hand she holds the emblem of peace, an Olive branch; in the other the sword of power. Behind her comes the maid, with the handsome head of Holofernes in the meat-bag on her head. The maid's expression of mingled awe and admiration is quite as much beyond the time in variety of expression and powerful story-telling as is Judith's own, which shows one how she will shortly say, with a loud voice: 'Praise, praise God, praise God, I say; for He hath not taken away His mercy from the House of Israel, but hath destroyed our enemies by mine hands this night.'

The other picture, 'Calumny,' is hung quite near. It is a little larger, and is unique and remarkable in every way: an allegorical picture full of thought. The idea was suggested to Botticelli by Lucian's description of a painting by Apelles. For the benefit of those as ignorant as I was, I may as well say that Apelles was a famous painter at the Court of the first Alexander, and then of Ptolemy, about 330 B.C.: and that Lucian was a Greek writer of the time of Marcus Aurelius, and that his manuscripts were brought from Constantinople to Italy about 1425, and printed for the first time at Florence in 1496, Botticelli's own date being 1437–1515.

The whole picture is painted with the greatest finish and delicacy, and with an immense wealth of detail. In the background are three highly decorated arches, with a pure, blue sky, tenderly graduated, showing through. In the middle of the picture is Calumny, hurrying towards the Judge, and attended by two women, representing Hypocrisy and Treachery. Calumny drags a rather feeble young man, without clothes, by the hair of his head along the ground. He holds his hands up in an attitude of supplication, and is supposed to represent Innocence. Envy, a male figure clothed in shabby garments, stands between this group and the Judge's throne. Ignorance and Distrust are whispering into the long donkey's ears of the Judge. On the left of the picture is the black, draped figure of Remorse, who turns and looks at a beautiful naked young woman representing Truth. Calumny has seized and is carrying before the Judge Truth's lighted torch. It is impossible to look at this picture and not have brought to one's mind the wretched fate of the modern prisoner on the Devil's Island.

Had nothing been preserved to us of Botticelli's but these two pictures, I think we should have known that he was one of the men who were most in advance of their time, and one of the greatest painters the world has ever known. To my mind, the Botticellis in our own National Gallery give no sort of idea of his gifts and powers as seen at Florence.

An old friend, to whom I had written of my love of the early Tuscan painters when I was at Florence as a girl of twenty, answered me as follows, and I suppose many would agree with him:

'The modern taste for the very early Florentine masters must, I think, be an acquired one, and, though in your own case it may have seemed spontaneous, I doubt whether any intellectual taste or tendency is wholly self-formed in the case of a girl of nineteen. At that impressionable age living in a mental atmosphere congenial to it, you with your quick receptive temperament probably imbibed from those around you, whose opinions on art were entitled to your respect, and without any conscious effort or critical process of your own, that sentiment about the early Florentine masters to which the writings of Ruskin had already given so strong an impulse, and which was then the pervading sentiment of connoisseurs and persons interested in pictorial art. Perugino is the earliest master in whose works I can find beauty—a quality essential to my enjoyment of art as such. The earlier masters, Giotto, Cimabue, Taddeo Gaddi, Masaccio, Lippo Lippi, etc., seem to me only interesting.'

With regard to Botticelli, I feel that he alone perhaps among the Tuscans strikes the note which Berenson alludes to in the following passage from his 'Venetian Painters,' and I like to feel that Berenson's optimism about modern art and life is true:

'Indeed, not the least attraction of the Venetian masters is their note of modernity, by which I mean the feeling they give us that they were on the high road to the art of to-day. We have seen how, on two separate occasions, Venetian painters gave an impulse to Spaniards, who in turn have had an extraordinary influence on modern painting. It would be easy, too, although it is not my purpose, to show how much other schools of the seventeenth and eighteenth centuries—such as the Flemish, led by Rubens, and the English, led by Reynolds—owed to the Venetians. My endeavour has been to explain some of the attractions of the school, and particularly to show its close dependence upon the thought and feeling of the Renaissance. This is perhaps its greatest interest, for, being such a complete expression of the riper spirit of the Renaissance, it helps us to a larger understanding of a period which has in itself the fascination of youth, and which is particularly attractive to us because the spirit that animates us is singularly like the better spirit of that epoch. We, too, are possessed of boundless curiosity. We, too, have an almost intoxicating sense of human capacity. We, too, believe in a great future for humanity, and nothing ·has yet happened to check our delight in discovery or our faith in life.'

The head of Rembrandt in his youth, painted by himself, in the Pitti (not either of those in the Uffizi) is perhaps the most beautiful of his many self-painted portraits. None, certainly, in the Rembrandt Exhibition at Burlington House this winter came near to it for beauty, in my humble opinion.

There is also an unusual portrait of Charles I. and Henrietta Maria, painted together in one frame, divided only by the twisted column of an Italian window. I have never before seen a double portrait treated in quite the same way. It is Van Dyke at his best—so finished, so refined! Perhaps he took extra pains, knowing it was going to the young Queen's Medicean relations, in the then far-away beautiful Florence.

I find I am doing exactly what I meant not to do, and must stop noticing pictures, as any guidebook describes all the best pictures quite enough.

I found a treasure in one of the smaller rooms at the Pitti which Mr. Hare, at any rate, does not mention. It was the most remarkable piece of furniture, from some points of view, I think I ever saw in my life, though perhaps many would call it unartistic. Historically, it is interesting from the religious attitude it represents. It was a large cabinet on a raised stand. It belonged to Cardinal Leopoldo dei Medici, and was placed in his dressing-room. One side of it, when the doors were opened, acted as an altar, with a delicately-carved crucifix in a recess, before which the Cardinal could say mass. On the other side the doors opened on to an elaborate toilet table of a most luxurious kind, with looking-glasses and every other appliance. The whole piece of furniture contained a number of small drawers, many of them secret. The black wood of which it was made was highly polished and a beautiful specimen of cabinet work. The whole was richly inlaid, outside and in, with various marbles, stones, and alabasters of different colours and sizes. The veinings and colourings of these were used and adapted as the landscape backgrounds of wonderfully delicate little oil paintings, representing almost the whole of the Bible stories, both Old and New Testament. It requires hours to see this cabinet properly, and among all the treasures in this wonder palace it is, perhaps, the object that gives one the greatest idea of the wealth and luxury of that God-and-mammon period that can possibly be seen. It is supposed to have been made in Germany and painted by Breughel. Some paintings on wood, using the graining of the wood as suggestive of the landscapes, are the only attempts I have seen in modern art to carry out this idea of Breughel's paintings on stones. The natural markings of the wood give great variety to the composition of the landscape. This is very much increased by the varied materials used for the decoration of this marvellous cabinet.

Of course I re-read 'Romola'; everyone does and ought, as being in the atmosphere of Florence extraordinarily increases the enjoyment of what is in many ways a very wonderful book, full of fine things and passionately sympathetic with women's trials.

In a very old notebook of mine, I find the following sentence. I have no idea by whom it was written; but it so exactly describes why certain books, and indeed certain people, appeal to me when others that are in many respects better leave me cold and indifferent, that I repeat it now in my old age, agreeing with it as I did at twenty:

'We readily overlook all that is tasteless and ignorant for the sake of that power which, in reminding us of the misery of the world, translates it into something softening, elevating, uniting. We should fully allow that some immortal work, and a great deal of the most popular work, is almost entirely without the feeling. There is scarcely a touch of it in Homer; there is not a touch of it in many a novel much sought for at the libraries. But to us it appears one of the greatest gifts of the writer of fiction. It is not that we desire to be always contemplating the misery of the world; when we take up a novel we often desire to forget it. But an author who does not know it cannot make us forget it; and a writer who is to deliver us from its oppressive forms must be able to translate the manifold troubles of life, with all their bewildering entanglement, their distracting pettiness, into something that releases such tears as the foreign slaves shed on Hector's bier. "Their woes their own, a hero's death the plea." '

No modern novelist that I know does this better than George Eliot.

In Florence, with the sky and the sunshine and the whole mind in a receptive condition, no effort was necessary fully to appreciate 'Romola.' What a difference that does make ! Reading some books at unfavourable times is as great an injustice towards the author as looking at pictures, no matter how beautiful, in the dark.

June 19th.—Sad news has come from England to-day of the death of Sir Edward Burne-Jones. What a loss!

The following very simple little poem by Byron—not much known, I think—is not modern in feeling, but fits singularly, for those who believe in spirit-land, the death of a man like Burne-Jones :

> Bright be the place of thy soul!
>   No lovelier spirit than thine
> E'er burst from its mortal control
>   In the orbs of the blessed to shine.
>
> On earth thou wert all but divine,
>   As thy soul shall immortally be;
> And our sorrow shall cease to repine
>   When we know that thy God is with thee.
>
> Light be the turf of thy tomb!
>   May its verdure like emeralds be!
> There should not be the shadow of gloom
>   In aught that reminds us of thee.
>
> Young flowers and an evergreen tree
>   May spring from the spot of thy rest;
> But no Cypress nor Yew let us see,
>   For why should we mourn for the blest?

Those who do not believe in spirit-land in any thinkable form—and I fancy they are many more than is generally supposed—when brought face to face with death, mourn not for the peace and rest of those that are gone, but for themselves—their own personal grief and loss and misery—and feel a kind of humiliation that what they themselves prized most, or the person who loved them most, is gone from them. Such grief, like all our other selfishness, should be fought and controlled as much as we have strength for. The old notion of those who prayed against sudden death was of a death unprepared, unsanctified by the Church, that did not give the same chance of eternal happiness to some one they loved which was freely granted to the majority. This indeed was a thought only to find relief in wailing and gnashing of teeth. Now we say: 'What was best for them was worst for us, but what does that matter?'

In speaking of Burne-Jones' work many years ago, Mr. Ruskin said: 'His work is simply the only art-work at present produced in England which will be received by the future as classic. I know that these will be immortal, as the best things the mid-nineteenth century in England can produce, in such true relations as it had through all confusion retained with the paternal and everlasting art of the world.' And do we not all feel this is true?

June 24th.—This is the great Florentine 'Festa,' of which I had often heard and never seen. We were too idle to go down to the ceremonies at the cathedral in the morning, but in the afternoon there were vespers at the baptistery, and the sight was most characteristic and curious. Every child that is born in Florence is still baptised there, and the water is still salted as of old. There were men, women, and children crowding through —both of the large doors being opened wide to the sunny piazza. These openings were veiled during the service by a long, black, thin curtain. In the middle, raised on an altar and again raised on steps, was the beautiful jewelled Benvenuto Cellini John the Baptist shrine. The people went up and touched it, and mothers, after touching the shrine, then touched the babies in their arms, who held up their tiny hands to receive the touch, and afterwards reverently kissed their own fingers.

Strong peasant men were there, young and old. It cannot be one of the least of the mysterious Florentine bonds, this baptistery which brings back to the inhabitants the recollection of every child that is born to them, more especially as the infant mortality must be prodigious. A handsome mother and daughter knelt just before me on the marble floor, types of to-day. The mother, old and tired and hot, mumbled prayers, but not with devotion. The cold hand of Time had laid hold on her. If the old are religious it is mentally, not passionately, and it takes the form of 'calm repose and peace divine.' The daughter, handsome though not very young, with coal-black hair, said her prayers with closed eyelids and a passionate pathos in her face, softening for a time her somewhat masculine features — a perfect example of life's disappointments, not yet utterly without hope.

Passing out into the glorious evening sunshine, we went inside the large, bare Duomo, beautiful to me from its size, its majesty, its cool shades, illuminated by the pouring in of the bright summer western sun, which formed rays of light across the darkness. A full choral vesper was not yet quite ended, and the boys threw back their heads and flung out their high notes, echoing into the dome. It was not very reverent or beautiful, but it sounded well, as it mounted, in wave upon wave of sound, into the echoing cavities of the great vault. Many people think the inside of the Duomo ugly, and of course one can see how it was the origin of much ugliness that came afterwards; but it has a grand beauty of its own, and the jewelled glass is the exact sort of old glass I admire—most vague in design, but strong in colour, and glowing with a richness beyond the finest enamel.

Later in the evening we went on to a balcony on the Lung' Arno, to see the fireworks let off from the opposite hill of San Miniato. I had not seen good fireworks for many years. They may be as good at the Crystal Palace, and no doubt are, but never can the whole scene be anything like as lovely as those fireworks on this night of San Giovanni, with the background of the San Miniato hill, and the river in front a mirror of reflections. Every street poured its crowd in all directions on to the Lung' Arno. We had excellent places, and my companion, in a burst of enthusiasm, seized my arm and said : 'I don't care, it is simply the most beautiful thing in art or nature I have ever seen.' High over all hung the young moon, in the clear lapis lazuli sky. The crowd poured along in a ceaseless stream, but it was impossible to imagine anything more quiet and orderly. From the absence of strangers, the streets were so empty in the daytime one wondered where the people could possibly all come from now.

June 26th.—I was faithful to my tastes, and though I had little time I went to the Botanical Garden in the town. It had nothing in it very remarkable ; all the greenhouse plants were out in the open, and many of our northern plants were growing somewhat shabbily in pots as botanical curiosities, in the way we grow southern things at home. The beautiful *Catalpa syringæfolia* was in full flower here, and in all other good Florentine gardens. The same with *Trachelospermum jasminoides*, which hung over all the walls in the greatest profusion, scenting the air for yards round. I am sure this plant is generally too much coddled at home, and would do better if sunk out during the summer and well watered; it is a greenhouse plant well worth growing. *Asclepias incarnata* and *Asclepias tuberosa* were very sweet ; both these and *Solanum glaucum* are quite worthy of a place in a fair-sized greenhouse. *Rupelia juncea*, from Mexico, struck me as a pretty greenhouse plant, with red flowers and weedy growth. *Iris pseudacorus* was growing in a huge sunk pot, half earth, half water.

There was a large collection of Hydrangeas — plants so easy to increase that I think our greenhouses ought to contain greater varieties. These four struck me as good : *Hydrangea quercifolia*, *H. macrocephala*, *H. hortensis*, and *H. chinensis*.

Variegated Maple is grown a good deal at Florence, and, when skilfully used and much pruned, it can be made a considerable feature in any large garden—mixed with dark evergreens, such as Hollies, Privets, Irish Yews, etc., as it has almost the whiteness of flowers at a distance. *Cassia australis* struck me as being a handsome greenhouse evergreen.

The garden was full of sunk tubs for watering, with pieces of stone and small plants round the edge. *Convolvulus mauritanicus* is a plant to grow at home in considerable abundance ; it comes easily from seed, and was lovely in this garden in half shade under shrubs. Mine has lived out now three winters, its roots protected by a small shrub. It is also very pretty grown in baskets in the greenhouse.

I was disappointed at seeing no Lilies growing in gardens in Florence, though plenty of the *Lilium candidum* were sold in the market. How excellent is Mr. Stephen Phillips' line on a Lily garden : 'A tragic odour like emotion rose.' That is a complete description in words of the scent of some flowers, such as I had long sought for, but, I think, never found before.

Apparently nothing in my first book really offended the reviewers, and perhaps even the public, so much as my non-appreciation of Virginia Creeper and *Ampelopsis Veitchii*. The remarks of one critic are typical of many others: 'Very gently and respectfully we would say "Avoid the dictatorial attitude," and we would point our meaning by an ancient horticultural saying of the Midlands: "Different people have different opinions—some like apples, and some like inions." Mrs. Earle, it seems to us, might well consider that occasionally others may, without being guilty of sin against art, admire that which revolts her sense of the beautiful. Frankly, her denunciation of *Ampelopsis Veitchii* hurt our feelings. But the dictatorial tone, the inability to recognise two sides to a question, is characteristic of even the greatest gardeners.'

What I did not sufficiently explain is that it is not a plant that I condemn in itself, but what I do condemn is the placing of it in wrong situations, or allowing it to destroy architectural beauty. I have, under my own bedroom window, an ugly piece of slate roofing which this autumn was covered with a mixture of Virginia Creeper and Ampelopsis—the latter still green, the former one mass of ruby and gold. Nothing could be more beautiful. But then it is growing where hardly anything else would grow, which is different to sacrificing a good south or west wall for this one week of beauty in the year.

My objection to *Ampelopsis Veitchii* was certainly increased while in Florence, as it grew with the greatest profusion in every direction, and as a picturesque object (say, for sketching) the beautiful old Porta Romana was entirely destroyed and put out of tone, both with sky and earth, by being almost entirely covered with this terrible brilliantly green Japanese Ivy.

June 27th.—Just before I left I went to see the Riccardi Palace, in the Via Cavour. The chapel I thought, as I suppose everyone does, one of the most interesting gems in Florence; it is so wonderfully fresh in colour. The frescoes are by Benozzo Gozzoli. We are told his mind was less exalted than Fra Angelico's. That may easily be. His pictures are quite mundane, but the costumes and the landscape backgrounds are thoroughly interesting, and the luxurious grandeur in these wonderfully preserved frescoes give one a thrilling idea of the times. I was especially interested in the garden backgrounds. The Roses were quite cultivated Roses and very large. The Cypresses were faithfully painted as I have seen nowhere else; some were quite natural, others again were cut in rounds and shapes, probably the earliest representation of topiary work in the world. The flower beds were cut out in the grass, with hedges such as one sees to-day round any modern hotel. The extraordinary preservation of the frescoes is owing to their having been in the dark. Now the owners have made a large window, and a Philistine proprietor years ago cut a door through the principal fresco. The portraits of the Medicis on horseback, and the splendid clothes, figure, and horse of the eastern Emperor, impressed me with the feeling it was quite the finest thing of the kind I had seen.

I suppose everyone climbs up to the top of the old Palazzo Vecchio and sees that old Medicean room, once the library, where the huge white doors of the book-cases are panelled with the most beautiful old maps. If I remember rightly, America is represented by the island of Cuba! The colour of them is splendid. Even modern maps would make a beautiful decoration for a white room, I think. German modern maps are exceedingly well coloured, and some representing seas and currents have a mystery and poetry quite their own.

The comparatively new public road on the San Miniato hill, which Mr. Hare calls 'an enchanting drive,' struck me as extremely well done, very well planted, and all the plants well blocked together. In a few more years, when it has lost its 'new' look, it will be very beautiful, even from a gardener's point of view. The variety of Oleanders—from snow-white to darkest red— were the best I have ever seen.

The interior of San Miniato is one of the most curious, old, and impressive churches in all Florence; but the strange burial-ground, dug apparently into the rock, is to my mind pathetically ugly. The utter bad taste of it is not on so large a scale as the famous cemetery at Genoa, which, to the very utmost, carries out Mr. Ruskin's words on modern Italian sculpture : ' Trying to be grand by bigness and pathetic by expense.'

Who that has ever been there does not share that pining for the beauty and sunshine of the South ? It is common to so many natures, and almost universally expressed by the poets. The return need of the South for the strengthening influence of the North I have rarely read in prose or poetry. Mrs. Browning seems to have realised that there is such a need :

> 'Now give us lands where the Olives grow,'
>   Cried the North to the South,
> 'Where the sun with a golden mouth can blow
>   Blue bubbles of grapes down a vineyard-row!'
>   Cried the North to the South.

> 'Now give us men from the sunless plain,'
>   Cried the South to the North,
> 'By need of work in the snow and the rain
>   Made strong, and brave by familiar pain!'
>   Cried the South to the North.

> 'Give lucider hills and intenser seas,'
>   Cried the North to the South,
> 'Since ever by symbols and bright degrees
>   Art, child-like, climbs to the dear Lord's knees,'
>   Said the North to the South.

'Give strenuous souls for belief and prayer,'
  Said the South to the North,
'That stand in the dark on the lowest stair,
 While affirming of God, "He is certainly there,"'
  Said the South to the North.

'Yet oh! for the skies that are softer and higher,'
  Sighed the North to the South;
'For the flowers that blaze, and the trees that aspire,
 And the insects made of a song or a fire,'
  Sighed the North to the South.

'And oh! for a seer to discover the same,'
  Sighed the South to the North;
'For a Poet's tongue of baptismal flame,
 To call the tree or flower by its name,'
  Sighed the South to the North.

JULY

July 1st.—I left Florence on one of the last days of June, with oh ! such a sad heart and a feeling I should never see it again.   I am so conscious, as I said before, of the wisdom of spending the rest of my life at home and foregoing the pleasures of travel, as with my nature long absences unfortunately diminish the pleasure and interest I take in my own concerns, and regret at what I leave behind comes between me and my happiness when I am away.   The weather had been wet, and directly the sun was obscured the temperature was, if anything, rather too cool.   I do love a night railway journey, because of the chance it gives one of seeing that most wondrously lovely effect of nature which we so seldom do see—this growth of the famous 'more light,' Goethe's last words—the triumphal march of the coming on of day.   I determined to enjoy it in spite of the presence of seven Italians, one more than the carriage was intended to hold, who got in at Genoa at four o'clock in the morning and never ceased talking amongst themselves.

It is not only the beauty of the growing light, but the mysterious human awakening, the early smoke that coils from some cottage chimney, the opening window,

the man who goes out to his work along the road—every
little incident seems to be full both of the poetry and
pathos of life. In a tiny volume lately published, of
remarkable verse by A. E., 'Earth Breath and other
Poems,' the poem called 'Morning' expresses in part
my feeling :

> We had the sense of twilight round us;
>   The orange dawn lights fluttered by;
> And thrilling through the spell that bound us
>   We heard the world's awakening cry.
>
> We felt the dim appeal of sorrow
>   Rolled outward from its quiet breath,
> To waken to the burdened morrow,
>   The toil for life, the tears for death.
>
> And out of all old pain and longing
>   The truer love woke with the light.
> We saw the evil shadows thronging,
>   And went as warriors to the fight.

The last line is to me an especially true note. Indifference, blindness, despondency, all these I hate ; but
to meet life with courage, both for oneself and others,
that must be the real aim. But courage is rather
strength than happiness.

Professor Blackie said somewhere, ' There is nothing
fills me with more sorrow occasionally than to see how
foolishly some people throw away their lives. It is a
noble thing to live ; at least, a splendid chance of playing a significant game—a game which we may never
have the chance to play again, and which is surely
worth while to try to play skilfully ; to bestow at least
as much pains upon it as many a one does on billiards
or lawn tennis. But these pains are certainly not
always given, and so the game of life is lost, and the
grand chance of forming a manly character is gone, for
no man can play a game well who leaves his moves to

chance, and so, instead of fruitful victories, brilliant blunders are all the upshot of what many a record of distinguished lives has to present.' All this from a night journey. It was broad daylight as we came down the beautiful flowery slopes of the Cenis in a luxurious French corridor carriage, so superior in every way to the Italian one we had just left.

The English used to be accused of being the great eaters of Europe when I was young. I do not think that is the case now. In our carriage was a middle-aged couple—I should imagine, brother and sister—and evidently, as is so often the case with other couples, the gray mare was the better horse. She travelled with curious deliberation; first she wrapped up both the hats in beautiful bright Italian silk handkerchiefs, to preserve them from dust. Her black hair, I suppose she thought, could be cleaned without expense. She frizzled up her curls and wiped her dark, fat, ugly face. She then produced a huge powder-puff, and powdered her face well all o er. The man bore all this patiently; he was thin and bald, and much more refined-looking than she was. He placed a black silk cap on his head. Then she opened a large dog-basket filled with a most dainty luncheon. Sandwiches, folded up in a beautifully clean, damp napkin, began the meal. Then were eaten large slices of meat and bread, mugs full of rich milk, cheese (of which she must have eaten eight or ten ounces), and all this with a resigned calm, as if she were performing a sacred duty which she owed, not to herself, but to society. The meal wound up with beautiful ripe Apricots—grown, I am sure, on their own Lombardy estate—and a home-made plum cake, like an English one. The remains, which were carefully packed up, would have fed a carriageful, and, I confess, made me feel quite greedy, my humble bread and cherries having nearly come to an end. When they had eaten their fill, superior peppermint lozenges were produced by the lady and shared by her companion; not one, but six or seven were slowly consumed in the same resigned, sad way. This was to assist digestion, I presume. Calm sleep then supervened to both, and their labours were over. In the seat opposite me was a man in the dress of an ecclesiastic, with a face that might have belonged to Rousseau's famous Savoyard vicar—a calm, intellectual face, that would have looked well carved in the mellow, amber-coloured marble of a Florentine tomb. My travelling companions—externally, at any rate—were strong contrasts!

I never can pass through this valley of Chambéri, with its beautiful mountains all around, without a strange thrill at the thought that here Rousseau lived and botanised for so many happy years in his youth, or calmly worked in the garden of his early love, Mme. de Warens. Her house is still shown. Some years ago I spent a day in Chambéri, but only saw this house from the top of the castle tower, my companions preferring other sights to the romantic pilgrimage I wished to make to the abode where lived those two, who little dreamt they were weaving one of the strangest romances that was ever publicly confessed.

I saw at that time in the museum a curious example of how, in certain stages of civilisation, the same customs prevail. They have there a large collection of curiosities taken from the remains of Lake villages; amongst other things, beautiful pins and brooches, like those found in Scotland and Ireland. My attention was attracted to a halfmoon-shaped piece of wood scooped out and delicately carved and ornamented. I asked the custodian what it was. He pointed to a small photograph placed beside it, which represented a Japanese woman lying on the floor with a piece of similar wood under her little head. Perhaps without this photograph from the far east the use of this primitive pillow from the Lake villages might have remained an unexplained curiosity.

I spent a few days in the neighbourhood of Geneva, to see some friends in one of the water-cure establishments so common now on the Continent — part hotel, part cure — very different from those primitive water-cures started in the early half of this century by Preissnitz, at Graafenberg. I picked up on an old bookstall, some years ago, a curious little pamphlet by Bulwer Lytton, called 'Confessions of a Water Patient.' He described how he had found his faith in the system strengthen, but he shrank from the terrors of a long journey to Silesia, 'the rugged region in which the probable lodging was a labourer's cottage, where the sulky hypochondriac would murmur and growl over a public table spread with no tempting condiments.' It is the modern luxury of hotel life which, I think, now militates so much against all these cures. The patients have two large hotel dinners of doubtfully wholesome food, and lie about all day on luxurious chairs. This is very different from the return to primitive life, an essential part of the cure in the old system, and which in modern days has been better practised by l'Abbé Kneipp than by any other that I have heard of. Now luxury and self-indulgence hold the poor modern, civilised patients in their grip wherever they go, and often they return no better than they went, in spite of douches and baths innumerable.

I must confess I found it rather trying coming from Florence to a hydropathic establishment in Switzerland. Illnesses, and especially what, for want of a better name, are called nerve-illnesses, are from their very obscurity quite extraordinarily depressing, and bring prominently forward the eternal injustice of nature. Looking out of my window at the gravelled yard and the heavy grove of trees gave me the feeling that I might be in a private lunatic asylum, or even in a prison, though I have never lived in either. The thought may have been specially presented to my mind from the remarkable poem which appeared last year, 'The Ballad of Reading Gaol,' for, looking up out of my window, I too could see over the opposite roof that little square of blue which suggested these two verses :

> I never saw a man who looked
>   With such a wistful eye
> Upon that little tent of blue
>   Which prisoners call the sky,
> And at every wandering cloud that trailed
>   Its ravelled fleeces by.
>
> He did not wring his hands, as do
>   Those witless men who dare
> To try to rear the changeling Hope
>   In the cave of Black Despair :
> He only looked upon the sun,
>   And drank the morning air.

Looking down in the early morning, I saw the patients, in various quaint costumes, hurrying to the morning douches. One, a middle-aged man, could not walk unless he pushed a large brown basket-work per-ambulator before him. He did not lean on it, and was very cheerful, but apparently it steadied his nerves, and with it his legs obeyed his wishes and he walked perfectly. Many people were, of course, quite well — merely accompanying the invalids. All these bathing-places strike me as being deadly dull and tiresome for those who are well, but foreigners seem to be much more patient about spending their holidays in health resorts than we are, for they look upon absolute idleness as the correct thing, and are content to spend their waking hours in talking. This can be noticed any day at seaside places in France. To my mind, the perfect holiday for people in health is change of scene and occupation and interest; certainly not what is called 'rest,' which means sitting out all day long, doing absolutely nothing but chattering to people you have never seen before and will never see again. Without the object of being a companion to those we love, I can imagine no greater trial.

When I could stand the feeling of being surrounded by invalids no longer, I used to get outside the place and walk by the deep-cut cliffs, rather than banks, of the roaring, rushing river. The land was losing all its wildness, and was being built over; but nothing can ever alter those steep-cut sides, which in old days might have been the scene of the following poem:

By the hoof of the wild goat uptossed
From the cliff where she lay in the sun
    Fell the stone
To the tarn where the daylight is lost—
So she fell from the light of the sun,
    And alone.

Now the fall was ordained from the first
With the goat and the cliff and the tarn,
    But the stone
Knows only her life is accursed
As she sinks in the depths of the tarn,
    And alone.

Oh! Thou who hast builded the world,
Oh! Thou who hast lighted the sun,
Oh! Thou who hast darkened the tarn,
    Judge Thou
The sin of the stone that was hurled
By the goat from the light of the sun
As she sinks in the mire of the tarn
    Even now—even now—even now!

Beautiful, bright Geneva struck me as hard and ugly, after the mellow softness of Florence. I had hoped to have seen many interesting places in the neighbourhood, the homes of those who are familiar to us as our own relatives. Ferney I have never seen, nor Coppet, nor the house on the south side of the lake where Byron lived, close to the one taken by the Shelleys and Clair that memorable summer after Byron's separation from his wife and before the birth of Allegra. Is it not all told in one of the best, most complete, and most interesting biographies of our day, Dowden's 'Life of Shelley'? George Eliot spent a happy time at Geneva as a girl, and I would gladly have seen 18 Rue des Chamoines, where she lived and rested and enjoyed herself with kind friends. And last of all, there is the quiet corner where Amiel worked and lived and wrote. Some time after his death a very interesting review (by Lucas Malet) of Mrs. Humphry Ward's translation of Amiel's 'Journal Intime' appeared in the 'Fortnightly Review' for May or June, 1896. She alludes several times to the short biography of Professor Amiel by Mlle. Berthe Vadier, which was published in Paris, and thus describes the place where he lived: 'His windows overlooked a well-filled flower garden; the walls of it were draped with Ivy and Virginia Creeper, above which rises the ancient college of Calvin, while through a side opening he could see the trees on the Promenade Saint-Antoine, and the Russian church, its gilded cupolas backed by the purple hillside of the Grand Salève.' Amiel's biographer says: 'Il était toujours beau.' Lucas Malet adds: 'The dome of his head is very fine, reminding one in height and purity of curve of the head of Shakespeare, or of the modern writer who in looks so curiously resembles him—Dante Rossetti. But with the brow all likeness to the great or lesser poet ceases: the eyes and lower part of the face lacking the glorious audacity and robustness of the first—we accept the witness of the Stratford bust and picture, rather than that of the fancy portrait in Westminster Abbey—equally with the sensuous heaviness that so mars the beauty of the second. For Amiel's face and head belong to a type not infrequent in French Switzerland, combining a certain largeness of ground plan with an almost pinched delicacy of detail. Refinement rather than strength is its characteristic : a head in porcelain rather than a head in granite.' I copy this excellent description, as it exactly fits a large number of student men of our own day. Lucas Malet goes on to say : 'And truly—though perhaps at the risk of seeming a little fantastic—we may say that in Amiel's face there is more than a hint of that singular temper, the predominance of which in his printed utterances, whether in prose or verse, prevents their rising into the first rank of excellence. Both are a trifle artificial ; marked by something of over-civilisation and over-intellectuality. He wants body, so to speak. He is utterly deficient in what Mr. Henry James has so delightfully called "the saving grace of coarseness." In his case there is too complete a severing of those cords which bind us to the lower creation. Not only ape and tiger, but song-bird and sea-wind, have died in him, as they must always run the chance of dying in highly educated persons—of dying so effectually indeed that such persons forget the very alphabet of that mysterious, primitive language to speak in which is not only the instinct of external nature, but the highest achievement of art.' Do we not all know people whom this description fits as admirably and completely as it doubtless did the Geneva professor, though they may but partly share the intellectual gifts which made his journals so interesting a portrait, not only of himself, but of the type of human being whom he represents — always aspiring and never satisfied, always working and producing comparatively little result !

During my stay I was not able to see any of these houses, as I had wished, and only once did I stand in the town on the ever wonderful ˌbridge where the Rhone, as blue as melted sapphires, tears through the arches. In spite of endless scientific investigations, no explanation has ever been arrived at to account for the wonderful colour of the Rhone water. A few miles below the town, as we all know, the Arve rushes down from the valley of Chamounix, muddy in tone and charged with solid matter, and it colours for miles the blue waters of the Rhone. At length the Arve gains the mastery, and the Rhone, once polluted, does not recover its purity before reaching the sea. So remarkable a freak of nature, however often one has heard of it, strikes one afresh with its obvious allegory.

Instead of all the things I wished to see in Geneva, the one and only thing I did see was the new museum with its newly planted grounds, a short drive from the town, and called (goodness knows why) Ariana. The building is commodious and light, and well suited for its object. It is a pleasure to visit a museum with all the windows wide open ; they are generally such airless, stuffy places. But one cannot help being severe on modern buildings on one's return from Italy. Local museums always have an interest, and one generally finds something one could have seen nowhere else. In this case it was a most instructive and comprehensive collection of old china, very well arranged, named, and dated. Several specimens and manufactories were quite new to me — which is not astonishing, as I know so little about china. A tea service with butterflies and beetles on a white ground, catalogued 'Nyon, 1780 to 1800,' struck me as exceedingly pretty. Also some

Charlottenburg of 1790 was rough in shape, but beautifully painted, clear and clean. The only really ugly china was that of about the middle of this century.

There were some curious old pictures, interesting rather chronologically and historically than from any artistic reason. A picture of the 'Roi de Rome' at about twelve years old, stated to be by Gerard, was curious, and if authentic would be a joy to a Napoleonic collector. Otto Marcellis and Auger Meyer, two insect and leaf painters of the end of the last century, interested me, as their oil-paintings resembled a curious water-colour I have, on a black ground, done by the well-known flower painter, Mme. Mariani.

I spent two charming afternoons with the famous Alpine gardener, Monsieur H. Correvon. Though at this time of year his garden near Geneva was almost a dry desert, yet it was full of interest to the true gardener. M. Correvon said that gardening, as we understand it, had made but small way on the continent of Europe, and that almost all of his clients were English. Such observations as I have been able to make quite confirm this assertion. A talk with him is alone well worth any trouble, and no garden-lover should fail to visit a man who has done so much to keep together and cultivate the mountain flora of Europe. I still hope I may go some spring on purpose to see his Alpine garden, which is high up on the edge of the snows of the great St. Bernard, a huge rockery cultivated under natural conditions. I cannot imagine anything more interesting to plant-lovers. M. Correvon is the author of many charming little books on Alpine and herbaceous flowers — 'Fleurs Coloriées de Poche dans les Montagnes de la Suisse,' 'Les Orchidées Rustiques' (very enlightening to the ignorant on the numbers of these plants), and 'Le Jardin de l'Her-

boriste,' carrying on to our day the theory of the health-
giving virtues of medicinal plants, and often quoting
l'Abbé Kneipp.   M. Correvon is a poet, too, and can
express as well as feel, which is not given to all of us.
This is what he says on Linnæus' humble flower:

> Sur les flancs de nos monts il est une fleurette
>   Au suave parfum
> Qui fuit l'éclat du jour, dérobant sa clochette
>   Aux yeux de l'importun.
>
> Sa patrie est au loin, sous un ciel plus sévère,
>   Près des glaces du Nord,
> Et nos torrents ont vu la charmante étrangère
>   Croître aussi sur leur bord.
>
> Ses jolis rameaux verts s'étalent sur la mousse
>   De nos vallons alpins,
> Formant, près des vieux troncs sous lesquels elle pousse,
>   Le plus beau des jardins.
>
> Il semble qu'un reflet d'aurore boréale,
>   A survivre obstiné,
> S'attarde et se mélange à la teinte d'opale
>   De la fleur de Linné.

I have tried in many places for years to grow this
plant; it does not die exactly, but it pines and looks
sad, and has never once flowered with me.

In some gardens round Geneva I saw several fine
specimens of *Hemerocallis fulva*.   The kind sold by
nurserymen generally is the one figured in the 'English
Flower Garden,' and slightly double.   This probably
makes them rather shy flowerers, and in England they
are usually seen in mixed flower borders.   The flowers
of those I saw in Switzerland were quite single, probably a strong-growing type.   They were planted in
small, rather sunk beds in gravel or grass, in quite full
sun, and copiously watered.   They were one mass of

flower in July, and really most effective, handsome plants — quite as effective as the Cape Agapanthus, so much commoner with us. They would look showy on lawns, and would, I think, do well in tubs, if they got sun and water enough.

The lovely yellow Day Lily, which flowers earlier, has done well with me in full sun, never moved at all, but mulched and watered in dry weather at the flowering time.

There are several so-called new varieties of *Hemerocallis*, and all seem worth growing when they can be made really to succeed; but, though apparently coarse-growing plants, they must be fed, and in a shrubbery in this soil they would hardly make healthy leaves.

The shrubberies round about the villas in the neighbourhood of Geneva were quite as badly pruned — often all on one side, and as much choked up — as ours in England, or more so. All that the inhabitants seem to care for is what makes dense shade, which, of course, they need more than we do. A large Privet, called *Ligustrum sinense*, was flowering very well, and is effective and worth growing in villa gardens, in spite of its rather disagreeable smell. It is a good flowerer in July, a rare quality among shrubs.

July 8th.—I carried out my wish and remained a night at Bâle, resisting the greater convenience of the station hotel for the old, famous, and handsomely rebuilt post-house of 'The Three Kings,' with its balconies over the rushing, splendid Rhine. To the ignorant this river looks as if its water-power were stupendous; as a fact, it cannot even be used to make the electric light for the town, the level of the river varies so immensely.

Time was short and the weather wet, so I only saw the museum or picture gallery, which was what I had come to see. Bâle to me meant two things — Erasmus and Boecklin. It was at Bâle that Erasmus lived and died. Froude's lectures on 'The Life and Letters of Erasmus' had so recently brought that memorable time vividly before me; and they enable us to look 'through the eyes of Erasmus at all events as they rose, with the future course of things concealed from him. This is the way to understand history. We know what happened, and we judge the actors on the stage by the light of it. They did not know.' Holbein's portrait of Erasmus is intensely interesting, and much more beautiful than the one at Hampton Court, by the same painter, of this thin-lipped, intellectual, sensitive 'Trimmer' of the Middle Ages. Froude says: 'In early life death had seemed an ugly object to Erasmus. When his time came, he received it with tranquility. He died quietly at Bâle on July 12, 1536, and was buried in state in the cathedral.' The last words of Froude's last lecture are: 'I have endeavoured to put before you the character and thoughts of an extraordinary man at the most exciting period of modern history. It is a period of which the story is still disfigured by passion and prejudice. I believe you will best see what it really was if you will look at it through the eyes of Erasmus.' It is not always so easy to see through the eyes of wisdom, especially for those who are passionate and prejudiced.

With regard to the typical pictures of Boecklin bought by his native town, I must confess my first impression was one of disappointment, in spite of their great power. His large figure-pictures of mermaids and mermen, fighting centaurs, etc., though in a way striking and remarkable, are to me positively ugly, both in colour and form, their only redeeming point being the beautiful cloud effects. In skies he seems never to fail. But there is one small picture of exquisite beauty, which reaches the height of the *Todten-Insel*, called

'The Sacred Grove'—a deep, dark Ilex wood, just like those I had lately been seeing near Florence. On the right a sunlit plain or valley was only indicated, and the light seemed to beat upwards, as in nature. Along the dark wood came a white-robed procession of worshippers. On the left was a tiny stone altar, on which burnt the sacred fire, the smoke rising straight up into the absolutely still evening air. It was a beautiful picture —a thorough example of Mr. Ruskin's description, in one of his Oxford lectures, of landscape painting. He says: 'Landscape painting is the thoughtful and passionate representation of the physical conditions appointed for human existence. It imitates the aspects and records the phenomena of the visible things which are dangerous or beneficial to men; and displays the human methods of dealing with these, and of enjoying them or suffering from them, which are either exemplary or deserving of sympathetic contemplation.'

On my return home, I found a criticism of M. Arnold Boecklin's work in the 'Revue des Deux Mondes' for November, 1897, by a fellow-countryman of his, M. Edouard Rod. He describes how admiring crowds came from all parts of Switzerland and the adjoining countries, as if for a pilgrimage, to see the loan collection of Arnold Boecklin's paintings, brought together that year and exhibited on the occasion of his having attained the age of threescore and ten. Many strangers came, somewhat doubtful as to the admiration to be bestowed on a painter almost entirely unknown out of Germany and German Switzerland. But the display seems to have convinced all that the work showed wonderful power and originality, executed in a novel manner. He was born rich and became poor, and for years his art seems to have had a hard and uphill fight with the world that did not appreciate him, and poverty that dogged his steps from Rome back to Bâle. At last he went to Munich, where the distinguished novelist, Paul Heyse, seems to have held out to him a friendly and helping hand. Must one believe that success is necessary to an artist? The fact is that Boecklin never really became himself till his individuality was recognised. His best works all belong to this latest period, and his admirers hope for him an illustrious old age. M. Edouard Rod adds: 'In looking at his later works I thought, what a beautiful thing is old age when it remains healthy, brave, and laborious. I thought of those luminous evenings that sometimes are the end of glorious summer days.' Boecklin's work will be all the more interesting in the days that are to come, because it is singularly devoid of French influence. In a closing sentence of an admirable article on the Millais Exhibition, Mr. Claude Phillips says: 'A vast wave, starting from France as a centre, is now more or less rapidly spreading itself over the whole expanse of the civilised globe, enveloping even us, who, with a wise obstinacy, most strenuously interposed our barriers of race and position as a defence. If it continues to advance, steady and resistless as heretofore, will there not, before the next century has spent half its course, be practically but one art?' But, as time goes on, will not individuality always assert itself, and may we not hope for Boecklins in the future who will struggle and be free of all schools, even the French?

July 12th.—After Bâle I came back once more to Cronberg. Nothing is so interesting, next to one's own garden, as the gardens one knows well, belonging to one's friends, especially when they have very different situations and soil. At Cronberg the soil is very strong and tenacious, and bakes into a hard crust, about as different to my Bagshot sand as can be imagined. In all I say or recommend, it is most important to remember that in stiff, heavy soils, everything that grows well with me would do badly and require a perfectly different cultivation. The amateur should always recognise that when things do badly it is probably because of some mistake in cultivation, and that it is always worth while to try some other method.

I went for the first time to the famous 'Palmengarten,' at Frankfort, which, in its way, is really beautiful, and a very well-kept, interesting public garden — half pleasure garden, half botanical. The greenhouses are clean and orderly, and arranged in much better taste than they would have been at home. There is much more attempt at grouping foliage plants, Mosses, Ferns, etc., than one generally sees. The same with the outdoor planting; though artificial and formal, it was done with considerable thought and originality, the beds being thoroughly carpeted to keep away weeds, which in that style of gardening is the only possible plan. The colour contrasts were good; a brighter, hotter sun than ours, together with much watering, perfects this kind of garden. I found planting of effective groups in the grass was a distinct feature in gardens about Cronberg, and better done than I have ever seen in England, save in very exceptional cases. It is an art that can rarely be understood by gardeners, as I think it requires a certain amount of real art-training to be able to imagine effects, both of form and colour. A well-planted White Variegated Maple ought to be in every garden, but it should not be allowed to get large and coarse. A contrast should be planted near it in the shape of broad-spreading leaves of some strong-growing, dark-foliaged plant.

A much more delicate mixture, is a small red-leaved Japanese Maple and the *Spiræa Ulmaria*, the common

British Meadow-sweet. In strong soils this is a lovely combination on grass. In this kind of planting, it is most important to remember that if two spiral or two bushy things are planted together they interfere with the grace of form which is aimed at. In the just mentioned plants the small red Maple would stand out strong from the grass, and would represent massiveness of form and colour. The well-grown specimens of the Spiræa—sure to do well, as they are wild plants—represent the grace of spiral growth and light, soft, white or cream colour. I find *Eucalyptus Gunnii* the hardiest of all the gum trees, and most especially pretty in colour and form for this kind of gardening; and it is also good for picking, as it lives well in water. These contrasts may be carried out in endless variety, even in small gardens.

When in Germany I was much struck by a green-house full of the healthiest tree and winter-flowering Carnations I have ever seen. The gardener told me that the secret of the entire absence of injured leaves and spots from rust was, that from July onwards, whether they are in pots or planted out, he syringed them once a week with the following mixture, which is also good for many other plants that are often blighted, especially Hollyhocks and Madonna Lilies :

Mixture for Killing Carnation Disease.— (1) Two pounds of vitriol (copper); (2) four pounds of lime, fresh slaked; (3) twenty-seven gallons of water; (4) two pounds of sugar. (1), (2) and (3) should be mixed together till no longer blue, but clear. Then mix the sugar with the rest. Syringe with an insecticide every week in the early afternoon. The syringing should be done quickly and finely. The ordinary garden syringe with a fine rose does quite well.

Here is the real Bordeaux mixture, slightly different

from the last receipt, used throughout the whole of
France against the phylloxera on the Vines ; it is also a
cure for the Potato disease :

Bordeaux Mixture.— Dissolve three-quarters of a
pound of carbonate of copper in a little warm water ;
place it in a vessel that will hold six gallons of water.
Slake half a pound of freshly burnt lime and mix it
with the water so that it is about the thickness of
cream.   Strain it through coarse canvas into the solution of copper.   Then fill up the vessel with water.

With these two receipts, it seems to me possible to try
endless experiments on plants in any way affected by
disease or rust.   I shall certainly try it on *Humea elegans*
when the plants begin to go off.   For a few years I gave
up growing this charming annual, the disease always
making its appearance.   I cannot bear being beaten
by a blight.

Everywhere on the Continent I find abundant
supplies of what used to be called Wild Strawberries,
the cultivation of which is receiving the greatest attention.   The soil at Cronberg, being strong, is very good
for growing Strawberries.   When I arrived last year the
main crop was just over, but the cultivated Alpines
appeared in large quantities at every meal.   These
improved Alpine Strawberries last all through the summer and late on into the autumn.   I never can understand why this class of Strawberries is so much neglected
in all English gardens.   They are rather troublesome to
pick, and have to be done with clean hands, as they
come to table without their stalks.

In the 'Horticultural Journal' for January, 1899, there
is a most interesting article by the great improver of the
whole family of Alpine Strawberries — M. Vilmorin —
which will do away with any excuse of not understanding their cultivation.   But I will not quote from it, as

anyone can get the number of the 'Journal' who is sufficiently interested in the subject to wish for the last
word.   Up to the present, I have never been successful
in producing fruit in any sufficient quantity to make the
growing of these Strawberries seem worth while, but I
mean to try, with improved knowledge, to see if it cannot
be done even on this sandy soil.   A neighbour of mine
has been most successful; but a vein of clay runs
through his garden, which is a helpful point, not to
mention his greater knowledge and experience on the
subject, having previously grown them in France.   He
kindly wrote out for me the system which he practises
in the growing of this most useful and healthful little
fruit, called the 'Improved Alpine Strawberry': 'To
obtain these large and abundant, it is necessary to grow
them on young plants (certainly not more than three
years old) and plants originally grown from seed.   The
fruit degenerates rapidly if grown on runners from an
old plant.   Select the best seed.   I grew mine from Vilmorin's No. 17,239—*fraisier des quatres saisons* "Berger"
—0.60 centimes per packet.   This is cheaper than yourself selecting, maturing, and preparing the seeds, which
probably would mature less thoroughly here than under
the hot summer sun in France.   Sow in March, in a
shallow box or pan under glass, well watered, in soil as
follows : One half of thoroughly well-rotted leaf-mould,
one quarter of sand, one quarter of light loam.   Cover
with a glass, as usual, until they begin to grow.   Very
moderate heat.   Prepare, in a well-sheltered border exposed to the sun, a strip of soil two and a half feet wide.
Mix in plenty of well-rotted manure from an old hotbed with the light loam of the open border.   Plant the
young seedlings in a row down the middle of this strip
about five inches apart.   Water them well, and shade
them for a few days till their roots have taken good hold

of the ground. Then they will grow rapidly and produce large leaves and strong runners, which must be laid out across the piece of ground on either side of the plants. Any runners beyond this first break should be cut off. The runners and the plant are left to grow together till about September, when the offsets will have rooted and grown, and the strip of soil will be covered with rich leaves and strong, healthy young plants. In winter, or early next March, prepare the bed in which they are intended to fruit: light loam with fair quantity of old leaf-mould or rotted old hotbed manure. There should not be more than four rows in one bed without a small path, in order to facilitate the cropping and the cutting-off of runners later on. The rows should be fifteen to eighteen inches apart, and in these rows plant, in March, the rooted runners of the seedlings, with as good balls as you can get. They will begin to bear about July, and will go on bearing until the frost comes in October or November, if they have been kept well watered in hot weather, and the runners trimmed off. In November cut off any remaining runners, mulch them well, and they will stand all through the winter. The second year they will bear, from May to November, good, large fruit about an inch long and half an inch across. They should be gathered with clean hands and allowed to drop off their stalks into the basket. If they do not drop to-day, they will next day or the day after, as they should be quite ripe. They will stand plenty of sunshine if they are watered in proportion to the heat of the weather. The fruit-bearing stems, in the best kinds, are strong and stand up above the leaves, so that the bloom coming on may be in full light and warmth. The leaves should never flag. Treat the bed the same way in the next winter, mulching, etc. This is the result: First year, sowing and producing the plants ; second year, a good half-crop, July to November ; third year, a spring crop and autumn crop. The fourth year the autumn crop will not be so large ; but if they are sown every year, as they should be, a subsequent sowing will be bearing its first autumn crop. It is possible to try a late summer sowing to crop the following autumn ; the runners must be taken off in the same way. Although the plants bear any amount of frost, a short, light frost during blooming time will turn the yellow centres of the flowers black, which means no fruit there. It is well, therefore, to be able to protect the beds by tiffany or bracken fixed between two laths. It is well, also, to have some natural shelter against the north and northeast winds.' This last sentence is a most useful hint for any Strawberries, and I shall certainly adopt it, as my first crop is constantly destroyed by these spring frosts.

While in Germany I saw beautiful beds of these Alpine Strawberries bearing profusely. The gardener told me that the way he managed them was to strike the runners off the young plants early in August and plant them for the winter under a wall, water well till rooted, mulch for the winter, and leave in the same place till April. Prepare a bed then in full sunshine with plenty of good cow-manure. Take up the young plants from under the wall ; plant them in the bed a foot apart, alternating the next row ; mulch again, and water copiously while the plants are flowering. Pick off all runners except those required for propagation.

The only real difference between this and the former receipt is that the first one prescribes the constant sowing and taking runners from the young plants, whereas the German gardener, apparently, took his runners from older plants. This difference would be quite accounted for by the difference between a soil naturally suited to Strawberries and one that is not.

Last year I heard of an American way of growing Strawberries, a man in New York having made a large fortune by inventing the following method: A petroleum barrel is made clean by burning it out. Holes, about two inches wide, are drilled into it in alternate rows from base to top, at intervals of about six inches in all directions. The barrel is then raised on bricks or stones, ample holes having been bored in the bottom of the cask for drainage. The bottom is filled with crocks and broken pots, and then a layer up to the height of the first holes is filled in with good mould. The Strawberry runners, well rooted, are planted by drawing the crown of the plant through the hole and spreading out the roots. Then fill up with soil till you reach the next layer, and so on up to the top. The top is not filled to the very rim, so as to admit of rain soaking down, and to hold the watering and liquid-manure soaking which it requires in the spring. A small drain-pipe should be let in, down the middle of the barrel, to ensure the water and liquid-manure reaching the lower plants in sufficient quantity. I am bound to own that my gardener says the cask did not ripen well last year; but I was not here, so I cannot say what was the reason. I suspect it was that the moisture did not penetrate sufficiently into the barrel. I have planted two more tubs this autumn in the same way with 'Viscountess' and 'Royal Sovereign,' and shall await results. It is just possible there is not sun enough in this country to ripen them grown in this way, though I do not believe it. The advantages, if successful, would be great economy of ground, the fact that you can water without fear of drawing up the roots, that no straw or cocoanut fibre is required to keep the fruit clean; and I imagine, grown in that way, the birds would not touch the fruit.

I saw two pretty decorations for a luncheon-table in

Germany. One was : four baskets painted white, with
high handles and sprays of any small mixed flowers
that do not fade quickly tied to the handles, the baskets
well piled up with common summer fruit—Strawberries,
Currants, Raspberries, Cherries, Gooseberries—each in a
separate basket, and a small vase with the same mixed
flowers in the centre.

The other—a pretty, daylight table decoration—was a
vase in the middle, filled with blue Cornflowers (which
of course grow wild in Germany), standing out on a
ground-work of Maidenhair. There were small vases
round with wild yellow three-fingered Trefoil, or any
other yellow wild flower, such as Buttercups. Between
the dishes of fruit were laid on the table sprays of
Maidenhair, Cornflower, and yellow flowers together.

RECEIPTS

Timbale Napolitaine.—To be served either in a
silver *casserole* or in an open French high pie-crust,
shaped like a flower-pot, and filled while baking with
dry peas to keep it in shape. Boil a small quantity
of medium-sized macaroni ; drain it well. Take two
sweetbreads, scald and trim well, parboil, and cut into
regular pieces about half an inch square. Make a good
brown sauce (not too dark), to which add two or three
spoonfuls of concentrated tomato *purée*, some good fresh
mushrooms cut in dice or strips, some truffles or morels,
and tiny little *quenelles* of chicken breast (if you have
any cold chicken to use up). Put the sweetbreads into
this thick sauce. Mix all well together, let it stew
gently for a few minutes, then finish your macaroni in
the usual way with cheese, only using far less butter
than for plain macaroni. Now fill the silver *casserole* or
the pie-crust by putting alternate layers of macaroni

and of the stew. Finish at the top with a little layer of sauce and truffles, and serve very hot.

The remains of this Timbale, if the sauce has been kept thick and concentrated enough from the first, can be made into excellent croquettes or rissoles by being cut up quite small, with hardly any of the sauce mixed with it. Shape as croquettes, roll in egg and bread-crumbs, and fry.

Poulet à l'Indienne.—Boil a large fowl in thin chicken or veal stock, with two or three onions. When done, take these out, strain the stock (which ought to look quite pale and clear), cut the fowl in pieces, cover with leaves of tarragon, add one or two to the stock, pour over the fowl hot, and serve. Boil a large cupful of Patna or Italian rice, strain, and dry. Make apart, while the fowl is cooking, a curry sauce with onion, butter, apple, stock, and curry powder (as described in my former book), no flour. When the rice is ready to serve, stir enough of this sauce into it to colour it thoroughly without making it sloppy or greasy. I saw this once at a French luncheon party, and it was called *Poulet à l'Indienne*, though of course it is not Indian in our sense at all. I have often done it successfully, but never had a receipt for it.

Croûtes of Ham and Beans.—Take four ounces of lean ham and grate or chop very fine. Put it into a stewpan with a little cayenne pepper and a spoonful of sherry; then dish it upon small fried *croûtes* of bread. Dish round these a *purée* of broad beans or white haricot beans. Serve hot.

Lentils.—Put a breakfastcup of Egyptian lentils into a saucepan, cover with about an inch and a half of water, boil very slowly for an hour. Heat half a tumbler of the best olive oil in a small saucepan. Cut up very small half an onion, and fry it till yellow in the oil.

Pour the whole on to the lentils, and let them boil another half-hour. Wash and pick a good handful of Italian rice. Dry on a cloth, and mix with the lentils when the rice is cooked. Add a little salt and pepper, and serve.

French beans or scarlet runners well boiled in salt and water, slightly drained, and then mixed at once (all hot) with olive oil and very little vinegar, and eaten as a salad, are much better than when allowed to get quite cold. I think this is the same with all cold vegetables —beetroot, asparagus, beans, etc. Our weather so seldom admits of quite cold things being palatable. These receipts, however, are useless unless the olive oil is of the best. I always buy my oil and vinegar from Mrs. Ross, Poggio Gherardo, Via Settignanese, Florence.

A Chocolate Pudding.—Take five ounces of fresh butter; four ounces of chocolate, grated; four ounces of pounded sugar; one ounce of flour. Mix these in a small pan with a cup and a half of milk. Boil till quite thick, and then pour into a dish with five yolks of eggs and some scraped peel of a lemon. Stir for half an hour. Beat up well the whites of the five eggs, and add them slowly to the rest. Smear with butter a conical tin mould, sprinkle with cinnamon; pour in the mixture. Boil it for two hours in water. A cream sauce flavoured with vanilla should be served with it or poured round it.

Norwegian Fruit Jelly.—Take two pounds of red currants and two pounds of raspberries (raw) rubbed through a cloth to extract the juice. Measure the juice in a good, clean wine-bottle, and pour it out. Put in the rest of the juice, and fill up the bottle with cold water so as to make two wine-bottles of liquid in all. Put this liquid in a large brass saucepan, and add half a stick of vanilla and three-quarters of a pound of lump sugar. Put the saucepan on the fire. Mix five ounces of the best corn flour and two ounces of Groult's French starch flour (*farine d'amidon*) with half a bottle of cold water. When quite smooth, pour it gradually, stirring all the time, into the boiling fruit juice. Let the whole boil until it thickens. Rinse out a china mould or basin with cold water, pour in the mixture, and put it for some hours in a cool place or on the ice. Turn it out, and serve with cream.

Cherries and Semolina.—Boil four pounds of good cherries in a quart of water till quite soft, then pass through a hair sieve. Put the juice back on the fire, with a piece of vanilla and half a pound of lump sugar. Let it boil for twenty minutes. Take a packet of French semolina ; drop in a sufficient quantity to thicken the juice, stirring all the time ; when this has boiled up, proceed as in the former receipt. Rhubarb might be tried in this way.

Much the same sweet can be made in winter in the following way: A pint and a half of red wine, and a pint and a half of bottled fruit syrup. These must be mixed together and brought to the boil. Mix four spoonfuls of cornflour with a little cold syrup kept back for the purpose, and stir this into the boiling liquid. It is most important to keep stirring all the time. It must be boiled for fifteen or twenty minutes.

Currants—red, white, and black—are excellent left on their stalks, well washed, and then dipped into the white of a very fresh raw egg, rolled in finely pounded sugar, and put for one minute into the oven to dry.

AUGUST

August 9th.—For the first time in my life, I went to a Horticultural Society Show at the Drill Hall, Westminster, in August. The interest centered chiefly in the new hardy Water Lilies which everyone with small ponds or lakes ought to try and cultivate, I think. There were a few new Lilies that I had never seen before; but what particularly attracted my attention was an exceedingly good strain of my favorite *Campanula pyramidalis*, exhibited by the Syon House gardener, and flowered under glass. He afterwards gave me an interesting account of how he cultivates them, which I quote:

'I am glad you liked the Campanulas, but I am sorry they were not quite as good as some I have shown in previous years, as we forced some of the plants, and they do not like much heat. There is no special way of cultivating the plants. Those you saw were sown early in April, '97, in pans in a coldframe, and pricked off end of May into boxes, potted up six weeks later into forty-eight pots, singly. Up to this they had been grown in a coldframe, but from July till October they were stood outside on ashes, but well watered. In winter we place rough boards round these, or stand in coldframes. Too much moisture is worse than frost, and very little water is given in midwinter. Early in March we place them in seven- or eight-inch pots, and stand in the open or on ashes to keep out the worms, potting in a good soil with a little manure, but as firm as possible, and they then flower the end of July or early in August.

'The flowers are purer in colour if they are placed under glass when opening. We do not grow any plants over sixteen or seventeen months. I would advise sowing in March for flowering in following August twelvemonth. Ours is a very fine strain — the Syon House variety — and a compact grower. I do not plant out at all for conservatory decoration. By planting out and lifting in spring, you would get larger plants.'

I am quite sure these flowers can never be seen in anything like perfection except grown under glass when the flower is appearing.

Not the least interesting sight was the variety in shades of blue — some very soft and delicate-looking, almost gray; some a good china-blue. There were many more of the white ones, and I find them rather easier to grow.

Another way of growing the *C. pyramidalis*, especially any good colour you want to preserve, is to cut up the roots and repot small pieces. I do not think the plants will be as strong as those grown from seed, but it is less trouble.

I was pleased the other day to read in the papers that the old Chelsea Physic Garden has been saved from being built over by the London Parochial Charities. The garden was presented by Sir Hans Sloane to the Society of Apothecaries, on condition that fifty new varieties of plants should be grown in it and annually furnished to the Royal Society till the number amounted to two thousand. These gardens and the

Botanic Gardens at Oxford are the oldest of the kind in England. The land at Chelsea was acquired by the Apothecaries as far back as 1674. Evelyn visited the Chelsea Gardens in 1685, and mentions that he saw there a Tulip tree and a Tea shrub. Here, too, it has been said, one of the first attempts was made to supply plants with artificial heat, the greenhouse having been heated by means of embers placed in a hole in the ground. Poor plants! they must have been rather smoke-dried, I fear. It was here, too, that Philip Miller, the 'prince of gardeners'—so styled by Linnæus—spent nearly fifty years. He managed the gardens from 1722 to 1771, during which period they attained a great reputation throughout Europe. Miller was the author of the much-admired 'Gardener's Chronicle.'

August 14th.—Towns are never so pleasant as when out of season. Florence in June, and London in August, how immensely emptiness increases their charm!

Flat-hunting in London is more bewildering and difficult even than house-hunting, so I was indeed lucky to find one with perfect views, very high up, with a lift, and just what I wanted in every way. I always have thought the garret was the nicest part of a London house. It has the best air and generally some sort of view. A high flat has all these advantages, and the lift does away with the fatigue of the stairs. A French landlady once said, when we had panted up her five stories to her airy apartment and complained a little of the pull up: 'Le cinquième n'est au cinquième que pour les monstres de la rue. C'est au premier pour les Anges!' One does feel nearer the sky, and the gulls fly by the windows in stormy weather. The cloud effects can be endlessly studied, and often smoke rather adds to than detracts from the beauty of sunsets, as Mr.

Ruskin puts it in that beautiful chapter on the truth of colour in the first volume of 'Modern Painters': 'When Nature herself takes a colouring fit, and does something extraordinary—something really to exhibit her power— she has a thousand ways and means of rising above herself, but incomparably the noblest manifestations of her capability of colour are in these sunsets among the high clouds. I speak especially of the moments before the sun sinks, when his light turns pure rose-colour, and when this light falls upon a zenith covered with countless cloud-forms of inconceivable delicacy, threads and flakes of vapour which would in common daylight be pure snow-white, and which give, therefore, fair field to the tone of light. There is then no limit to the multitude, and no check to the intensity of the hues assumed. The whole sky from the zenith to the horizon becomes one molten, mantling sea of colour and fire; every black bar turns into massy gold, every ripple and wave into unsullied, shadowless crimson and purple and scarlet, and colours for which there are no words in language and no ideas in the mind—things which can only be conceived while they are visible—the intense hollow blue of upper sky melting through it all, showing here deep and pure and lightless; there modulated by the filmy, formless body of the transparent vapour, till it is lost imperceptibly in its crimson and gold.' All this, and indeed much more, can be seen now and again from the top of a high London house by those who have eyes to see and a heart to appreciate. There are other effects—white clouds sailing on pure blue, storm-clouds rising and dispersing, and (in autumn) the sun lying like a little gold ball on the mist, the lights glimmering through the fog in the streets below, which are in darkness, whilst we dress and breakfast without ever having to touch the switch which produces the magic light. One more evening pic-

ture is the new moon shining in at the windows, high
up and above a long, graduated space of evening sky
and a far, mysterious purple vista, half town-lights,
coming through the darkness as in one of Whistler's
harmonies, painted as he alone can paint such effects.
The distance is cut off by the black roofs and gables of
the houses opposite.

Hitherto I have always moved from smaller houses to
larger, which is comparatively easy. Changing from a
large house to a small flat is the most difficult thing I
have yet had to do. All the flats I have ever seen are,
to my mind, spoilt by being so much overcrowded, and
yet, in many cases it is for the preservation of property
that the flat or smaller house is taken at all. To help
the non-crowding of these small rooms, I got rid of as
many superfluities as possible. I reduced the bulkiness
and heaviness of curtains, and, where I could, made a
broad hearth with no fenders at all. I think tiles and
painted wood for fireplaces have been overdone of late.
I hope we shall return to more marble and stone. A
green Irish Connemara marble makes a beautiful hearth,
and this and other marbles could be adapted in many
ways where tiles have been used.

I find that many people have been puzzled by my advice to have inner curtains and no blinds. When they
are there, of course it is cheaper to keep the blinds.
One friend wrote that she could not make up her mind
to have no blinds, as she thought the little curtains attached to the sash looked so untidy when pulled aside,
like a petticoat hung up. I do not think this at all, and
have lately found two stuffs which are most useful for
curtains in the place of blinds. One is green bunting,
which does not fade, and is very cheap, but narrow. It
can be got in several colours from Cayler & Pope, 113
High street, Marylebone, and I dare say at many other

places. It is very pretty in white. The green looks well from the outside of the house, as does the red twill I recommended before. White cotton-twill sheeting also makes very pretty inner curtains. They are specially pretty with outer curtains of white muslin. This in a small room makes a very pretty effect, and there is nothing to fade or to detract from the beauty of plants, etc., inside the room. My friend who was afraid to use the small curtains said the only use of blinds is in case of death. It is for that very reason I should like blinds done away with. Drawing down blinds in cases of death seems such a foolish fashion, when in time of sorrow one wants the help of all the sunshine that can be had. I must own sash windows are difficult to manage with curtains. I myself do not like them cut in two; but even then they are not so ugly as smart blinds edged with embroidery or lace.

Many ask if white paint, especially on staircases, does not prove unserviceable. I think white paint knocks off less than any other, and there is no wear and tear on a staircase except on the carpet in the middle. It is very desirable to have a piece over at both ends of the stair-carpet, so that when it gets worn it can be shifted either up or down. This is a touch of economy beginning with expense, as it requires a little more carpet. I have never heard it suggested by the shopman who sells or lays the carpet. To return to paint, it is essential that white paint should be good, which depends entirely on using the very best white lead. This is perfectly well known in the trade, but it naturally costs more than the inferior qualities, and so is seldom used. I never use varnish except in London, as even the best varnish always turns the paint yellow after a little time. I am obliged to own that, though very cheap in the first instance, my favourite whitewashed walls do seem extravagant, as they are not pretty unless constantly renewed and kept spotlessly white, and that is what the holder of the purse-strings will rarely agree to. White-washed walls soiled by smoke look very unsatisfactory. A paper will look cleaner after sixteen or seventeen years of wear than whitewash does after two or three.

August 29th.—Several of my young friends complained that the chapter headed ' Daughters' in my first book, though it sympathised with the woes of childhood, was addressed rather to mothers than to daughters. They say : ' We want a chapter about ourselves, on our own difficulties and trials, on love and marriage, and the proper conduct of life between seventeen and twenty-five.' So now, partly from memory of my own experience (for I was a girl once), and partly from observing others, I am going to talk on these subjects as well as I can, only referring as before to the well-to-do classes, the only ones about which I know anything. Where I find that my own thoughts have been expressed by others, I shall deliberately quote ; and as these quotations will be from the writings of both men and women, some mothers may not think them suitable for the reading of very young people.

So far as I have been able to judge, the first difficulty which most commonly presents itself to a grown-up girl is her position with regard to her mother, no matter how excellent that mother may be, and even when the girl remembers the devotion she bore to her up to the age of (say) fifteen or sixteen. When a girl is about this age a barrier seems often to arise between them, usually caused by some want of confidence on the girl's part. The difficulty, however, is only aggravated if the mother resents or is hurt by this reticence. George Eliot refers to this subject with Titanesque touches. She says : ' We are bound to reticence most of all by that reverence for the highest efforts of our common nature which commands us to bury its lowest fatalities, its invincible remnant of the brute, its most agonising struggles with temptation, in unbroken silence.' But, on the other hand, the same author thus describes the downward career of one of her best-drawn characters : 'Tito had an innate love of reticence—let us say, a talent for it—which acted as other impulses do, without any conscious motive, and, like all people to whom concealment is easy, he would now and then conceal something which had as little the nature of a secret as the fact that he had seen a flight of crows.' Some natures are born so secretive and shy that it is a real difficulty to them to speak out or ask advice, so that they cannot learn in any way except from that exceedingly bitter source—personal experience. I would advise the young to fight as much as they can against concealment. There is of course one subject which by its very nature can only live in privacy. We all go through the stage sooner or later of understanding what love means, and we all think at the time there is only one thing in the world of importance—that our hearts should not be unveiled. But with genuine and open natures this passes, and they end very often by open confession later on of that which torture would not have drawn from them at the time. Why reticence, to my mind, is so bad is that it so quickly grows into deception, and the smallest events develop into something quite different from what they really were.

Yet no one can recognise more than I do the necessity of some kinds of hypocrisy; it is 'the respect that Vice pays to Virtue,' and a form both of truth and strength. 'The Englishman kisses and does not tell, the Frenchman kisses and tells, and the Italian tells and does not kiss !'—so went the old saying. Admitting the facts, the concealment of the Englishman is the best.

When one is young, one thinks just the contrary, and people are very apt to say: 'If I have a passion, why should I hide it under a bushel? So long as there is no concealment there is no harm.' This kind of argument may take people into very deep water. A parent of reserved nature rather encourages concealment in the children, and indeed thinks it 'beautiful,' forgetting that the children may inherit from the other side of the family a need for sympathy and the expression of affection, and that these are as absolutely necessary to some natures as food for the body. In my experience, I can most honestly say that the people who have done best in life are those whose temperament has enabled them to talk out their difficulties with friends or relatives, and who have learned to ask advice. Advice should be taken to develop one's own judgment — and, as I said before, need never be followed. It is useful to understand how matters strike other people who are not personally concerned. The non-understanding of this is often the cause of a bad influence being exercised by one sex over the other. It is more easy to pardon faults than to forgive those who assume virtues they do not possess.

The mere forming of one's trouble into words makes it seem lighter to bear. We have all sometimes, if not often, known the extreme worry experienced on waking because of some trivial thing we have done or left undone, which disappears entirely or assumes its proper proportions after our morning bath. Talking out to a friend often plays the part of the bath.

I can trace a change in my whole life from the kindness of a Jewish old maid to me when I was a precocious little monster of ten years old. We were at Leghorn during a fearful earthquake, and the hotel where we were staying, though not actually thrown down, was so shaken and injured as to be considered unsafe to live in.

This good lady took us all in, and was kindness itself
to us. My heart went out to her with a genuine out-
pouring of love and gratitude, and when we left, having
observed my many little childish selfishnesses, she wrote
me the following letter :

'MY DEAREST THERESA :—As I feel quite certain you
really love me, you will listen with attention to the few
remarks I have to make, and at the same time convince
me of your affection by reading occasionally these lines
in remembrance of me. Now, dearest, I must tell you
that patience is one of the greatest requisites, not only
for our own happiness, but for everyone about us. Be
careful to keep *that* in mind. At meals (be you ever so
hungry) do not show impatience; look round and observe whether those dearer than yourself have all they
require, before you think of yourself. This will prevent
your being selfish, which is of all things the most odious.
Think first of your dearest mother, for rarely in health
and never in suffering does she give one thought on herself. Therefore you, my darling, have but to follow her
bright example, and you will be an ornament to society,
a pattern of good breeding, and an example to your
infant sisters, who will look up to and listen to your
affectionate advice. Remember that love towards all
who instruct you is absolutely necessary, and patience
and good feeling for the servants will make them both
love and respect you. This is my affectionate advice to
you, my dearest Theresa; and whenever you feel inclined to be impatient or selfish you will read this and
remember me.'

To my mind, this letter is an absolute gem as regards
the understanding of child-nature. There is no mention
of anything that could possibly make the little being

of ten feel her youth or the writer's age. There is no word of religion. Love terrestrial is the moving power throughout. The motive for life suggested in it is not exactly happiness, which none can command, but the regulating of one's life, with ambition as an object. The incorporation of eastern ideas into the West is responsible for much of that spirit which attributes all evils to the will of God, as trials to be accepted with resignation rather than difficulties to be fought against and overcome, and, if possible, provided against beforehand. 'Sufficient unto the day is the evil thereof' is a saying that has, *I* think, been twisted into many senses never intended.

Advice, however, may be offered too young, and bear no fruit. I once heard a kind grandmother preaching unselfishness to a little boy of four or five: 'No one loves selfish people;· you won't be happy if you are selfish.' And he, the rosy-faced little rascal, looked up and said, earnestly: 'Oh! but, gran, that is not quite true; for I am so selfish and *so* happy!'

Many mothers prefer to remain in ignorance rather than find out that the tastes and views of their daughters are different from their own. If, as is sometimes thought, this difference is greater now than it used to be, I cling to my opinion that it is largely due to sending girls away from home for educational purposes. Freedom and a good education have many advantages, but the corresponding disadvantages should be faced when the plan is originally decided upon.

Some years ago there came out a book, 'Le Journal de Marie Bashkirtseff,' which made a considerable sensation at the time, and raised — so far as I could judge — a good deal of anger and irritation amongst English mothers of the day. It was accused of being strained, exaggerated, and morbid; and so perhaps it is. One accusation, I believe, was true—that the heroine made herself two years younger than she really was, *i.e.*, she begins the journal nominally at the age of twelve, whereas she was really fourteen. In spite of its faults, I believe this book will remain for all time a most useful introduction to the knowledge of that strange being—a young girl, say, from sixteen to twenty-one. Its exaggeration is that of a microscope, which reveals nature without distorting it. This constitutes its utility for all mothers who have girls growing up around them.

A girl should bear in mind that it is quite possible she is a cause of considerable disappointment to her mother, and this possibility should be thought of humbly and affectionately rather than with resentment. For though, perhaps, it is due to no fault of her own, the disappointment is none the less real to her mother. She should do her utmost to make herself as pleasant in her home as she can. What elders expect from the young is a fair amount of willingly given assistance and unselfish cheerfulness. Few things, I think, contribute more to happiness in the home than a certain power of conversation; and, if it does not come naturally to them, girls would do well to try and acquire it. Any moderately intelligent woman can learn 'to talk'; and to be absolutely silent in society is not modesty, but a form of selfishness, for it casts a gloom over everyone present. The true greatness of individuals lies in their own hearts, and conversation is as much a question of kindness as of cleverness. Mr. George Meredith, in 'Beauchamp's Career,' describes delightfully the charm of conversation in a girl. Of course all cannot have this, but all can try for it: 'Renée's gift of speech counted unnumbered strings, which she played on with a grace that clothed the skill and was her natural endowment—an art perfected by the education of the world. Who cannot talk! But who can? Discover the writers in a day when all are writing. It is as rare an art as poetry, and in the mouths of women as enrapturing—richer than their voices in music.' With young girls silence often becomes a habit from not being trained to join in the conversation of their elders—a fault in many English homes. But if a girl realises this is a mistake, she can get over it after she is grown up if she chooses. If, on the contrary, she is silent merely from being socially bored, she had better learn that a very simple remedy for boredom in society is to try and amuse others. There is sure to be some-one uglier or duller or older than she is, to whom she can devote herself. One of the chief uses of society is the constant self-discipline it imposes. Depend upon it, as George Eliot says, we should all gain unspeakably if we could learn to see some of the poetry and pathos, the tragedy and the comedy, lying in the experience of a human soul that looks out through dull gray eyes and that speaks in a voice of quite ordinary tones. Such a thing is almost impossible to some girls, whose great amusement in life is to chatter. This has its charm to many; but girls of this temperament should, on the contrary, try to cultivate the art of listening, to draw forth information from others, and to understand their attitude without forming too hasty judgments. 'To communicate our feelings and sentiments is natural. To take up what is communicated just as it is communicated is culture.' A power to sympathise with others is one to be much cultivated, ever remembering it has to be paid for.

> For he who lives more lives than one,
> More deaths than one must die.

Happiness and cheerfulness were not at all cultivated by serious-minded good people in my youth, who were much affected by the teaching, even if not under the influence, of the Quakers and Wesley. To be sad was almost considered a virtue. The High Church movement began the change, as I remember it, against the gloom of the Low Church teaching. The practical sense of the present day is now fighting the morbid tendencies, which have taken a hold on so many, reflected from the writings of Ibsen and Maeterlinck. Those not naturally of a happy temperament should cultivate happiness from within, not artificially assume it.

A lecture on 'Happiness,' given by Miss Lucy Soulsby in 1898 (published by Longmans, Green & Co.), is an excellent example of the teaching to which I refer, and would, I think, be helpful to many a girl.

A very common grievance to-day between mothers and daughters is that the girls while still young refuse to go out into society at all, feeling how tiresome and unprofitable it is. This is all very well if the girl has mapped out her fate, and knows exactly what sort of a life she is going to lead; but if she is merely drifting, it is only a form of selfishness, and rather a foolish one. Until life is really settled, the more varied and open to change it can be kept the better. After marriage, I am sure the more people stay at home the better for ten or fifteen years.

The state I have referred to of more or less antagonism between mother and daughter ought not to cause the amount of distress that it often does. Time, the great healer, constantly rights things again, and, as a rule, a girl never turns with more true love to her mother than just after her marriage. But my advice to girls under these circumstances is to be conciliatory and hide from others the irritation which often they cannot help feeling. This I should recommend, even if from no higher motive than that the casual observer should not judge them too harshly. It is a rooted idea in the minds of many men that a bad daughter makes a bad wife. Was not Iago's strongest argument in the poisoning of Othello's mind against poor Desdemona, 'She did deceive her father marrying you'? Not long ago I heard a young man say: 'I mean to marry for a mother-in-law—that is to say, I will never marry a girl who does not love her mother, nor would I marry a girl with a mother whom I thought unworthy of her love.'

The French, of course, exact an outward expression of devotion from both sons and daughters unknown in this country, and I doubt whether our literature could produce a parallel passage to these opening lines of Florian's poem of 'Ruth':

> Le plus saint des devoirs, celui qu'en trait de flamme
> La nature a gravé dans le fond de notre âme,
> C'est de chérir l'objet qui nous donna le jour.
> Qu'il est doux à remplir ce précepte d'amour !
> Voyez ce faible enfant que le trépas menace ;
> Il ne sent plus ses maux quand sa mère l'embrasse.
> Dans l'âge des erreurs ce jeune homme fougueux
> N'a qu'elle pour ami dès qu'il est malheureux ;
> Ce vieillard qui va perdre un reste de lumière
> Retrouve encore des pleurs en parlant de sa mère.

Last summer, while waiting at a hot railway station and pondering in my mind how I could bring together a few notes that might help to solve some of the difficulties in girls' lives, I caught sight of a little yellow publication on the bookstall, called 'The Modern Marriage Market.' It will be remembered that this consisted of four articles, by ladies, reprinted from magazines. I bought it at once, thinking that these ladies would probably say what I wanted to say better than I could do it.

It was interesting to find that they severally took what, roughly speaking, might be called the four sides of the question, though the last article held the philosophic view that, as with most affairs of life, there is much to be said on all sides. Miss Marie Corelli holds up the little blind god Love as the only one worthy to regulate our lives and destinies. Lady Jeune is surprisingly satisfied with things as they are. Mrs. Steel prefers even eastern to western customs rather than ignore the importance of the future generation. Lady Malmesbury takes, as I have already said, a broader and more moderate view as regards the *pros* and *cons* of the various points at issue. Most people would agree that the matter is one on which it is almost impossible to generalise, as so much depends on the enlightened bringing up of the girl herself. The whole question has been treated with stronger and more philosophic consideration in an essay called 'Marriage,' which I mentioned before, in Sir Henry Taylor's 'Notes from Life.' His essay has the additional advantage of being addressed to both men and women, which is certainly to be desired. He begins with a quotation from Webster's play, in which the Duchess of Malfy asks: 'What do you think of marriage?' and Antonio answers:

'I take it as those that deny purgatory;
It locally contains or heaven or hell;
There is no third place in it.'

Sir Henry Taylor goes on to say that when he was young he did not agree with this, but that increase of years made him think Antonio's view the correct one. It seems to me that the last fifty years have wrought a considerable change in these matters. Nowadays members of society, so far as I am acquainted with them, consider it very inconsistent with their own dignity to

AA

admit that marriage has turned out 'hell' for them, and see that a more philosophical attitude of mind enables them to expect less and really find a great deal of happiness on the lines of the quotation at the conclusion of Lady Malmesbury's article : 'Two are better than one ; because they have a good reward for their labour. For if they fall, the one will lift up his fellow; but woe to him that is alone when he falleth, for he hath not another to help him up.' In my youth I used to think that the gain in marriage was almost entirely on the woman's side; but as I grow older I am inclined to think the advantages and the disadvantages to men and women are nearly equal.

The crux of the whole position as regards the girl seems to me to be hinted by Lady Jeune when she implies that the mother should take the matter into her own hands—if not of making, at any rate of unmaking, marriages. And from this point of view, I think I have something to suggest.

The questions that are constantly put to me on this subject by girls more or less young, prove to me that a great part of the difficulty arises from the injudicious ignorance in which they are allowed to grow up. Let us begin at the beginning. A young girl of eighteen or nineteen once said to me : 'What is the harm of kissing ?' And it is not altogether an easy question to answer if the girl herself has no feeling about it. When I was twelve years old my mother deliberately explained to me that for girls to kiss boys and men was childish and *infra dig.;* that grown-up women thought most gravely of kissing, and reserved it for those they loved very much, and who had asked them to marry them. This gradually puts the matter on a sounder basis. We have to be much older to understand that 'kisses are like grains of gold and silver found upon the ground, of

no value in themselves, but showing that a mine is near.'
On the other hand, some girls may think, in perfect
innocence, that a kiss means a great deal more than it
really does, especially as it is generally taken, not given;
and I have even heard of a girl of seventeen who
thought she was so lowered by having been kissed by a
man that she was bound to marry him to save herself
from disgrace. So one girl takes it; another may think,
having once begun, there is no going back, and the
onward course is the only possible one. To another,
one accidental kiss may be only a great help and protection, teaching her by fear to understand and distrust
herself. This state of ignorance ought never to be in
a girl who has reached a marriageable age. If the stop-
ping of kissing is desirable at twelve, it is equally
important that at fifteen or sixteen the mother or an
elder sister, or some kind friend, should explain the
facts of nature sufficiently to prevent forever the possibility of such distorted notions as to the facts of life.
There are hundreds of ways of expanding and enlarging
a girl's mind so as to increase, rather than diminish, the
modesty which is her greatest safeguard, and certainly
not the least of her attractions. Indeed, it is a favourite
theory of mine that the instincts of life are apt to grow
before their protector—modesty—which is more the
result of cultivation and civilisation than particularly
pertaining to what is natural. All prohibitions wound
liberty and increase desire. We, none of us, can defend
ourselves from a danger as to the very existence of
which we are ignorant. If a girl is trained to understand that we are part of that great whole which is
called nature, and that, in fact, our common development
is shared by every flower that blooms, she is neither
surprised nor shocked when further knowledge gathers
round her as life expands. This, I believe, will serve as

a very wholesome check against an overpreponderance being given to the romantic attitude so much advocated by Miss Marie Corelli. She describes marriage as the 'exalted passion which fills the souls' of a man and woman, 'and moves them to become one in flesh as well as one in spirit.' Mrs. Steel says, and I must say I agree with her, that this so-called 'exalted passion' is quite as often likely to lead to evil as to good.

Whether girls realise it or not, certainly an immense number of them associate marriage with the very healthy desire of having children of their own. With a little further cultivation they will come to think of the man they wish to marry as the father of these unborn children ; and most women — even girls — can early discriminate between the man they enjoy dancing with, and the man they would like to be some day head of their house and father of their children. This develops what I hold to be of such great importance : that the girl herself should feel respect, or at any rate approval, of the man she thinks of marrying. There should be many solid reasons for entering into so important a partnership beyond the fact of love, even if that be ever so real. At the same time, I do not mean to imply that the man's moral standard in the past should necessarily have been the same as the woman's. The man who understands women extracts far more love from them — and so, in the end, makes them happier — than the man who knows little about them. I hold it to be a great mistake for a man to have that kind of fear of the girl he is engaged to, or of his wife, which leads him to think it is desirable to deceive her. That seems the great danger of the tone of the present day, a woman expecting too much of men.

One of the chief difficulties in talking or writing of love is that the word may be interpreted in so many ways. To generalise on love is almost as difficult as to define it; it means such different things to different people. Girls who read novels and poetry are apt to think that the fancy they feel for the first man they meet is the great passion which they will never get over; whereas, broadly speaking, strong feeling most often belongs to inconstant natures. As I think of it, real love never exists until it is tried by adversity; but I am the last to deny that the *real* thing—however you define it—gives dignity and nobility to life, and makes it worth living. 'C'est bien à l'amour qu'il en faut venir à toute époque, en toutes circonstances, en tout pays, tant qu'on veut chercher à comprendre pourquoi l'on vit sans vouloir le demander à Dieu.'

Thomas Moore puts it:

> When first the Fount of life was flowing,
>   Heavy and dark and cold it ran,
> Every gloomy instant growing
>   Bitterer to the lips of Man;
> Till Love came by one lucky minute,
>   Light of heart and fair of brow,
> And flung his sweetening cordial in it,
>   Proudly saying, 'Taste it now.'

Mr. Austin has a pretty definition of love:

> 'Tis a fifth season, a sixth sense, a light,
> A warmth beyond the cunning of the sun.
>   Another element; fire, water, air,
> Nor burn, nor quench, nor feed it, for it lives
>   Steeped in its self-provided atmosphere.

Doubt and fear were linked with it in very early days, for Plotinus says of love: 'It is worth the labour to consider well of Love, whether it be a god, or a devil, or a passion of the mind, or partly god, partly devil, partly passion.' Dr. South puts it: 'Love is the great instrument and engine of nature, the bond and cement of society, the spring and spirit of the universe. It is of that active, restless nature that it must of necessity exert itself; and like the fire, to which it is often compared, it is not a free agent to choose whether it will heat or no, but it streams forth by natural results and unavoidable emanations, so that it will fasten upon an inferior, unsuitable object rather than none at all. The soul may sooner leave off to subsist than to love; and, like the vine, it withers and dies if it has nothing to embrace.' Here are some lines by a French woman who feels the sadness of love:

Car la douleur, hélas ! est l'ombre de l'amour
Et le suit, pas à pas, et la nuit et le jour ;
Elle est même à tel point sa compagne fidèle,
Que l'amour à la fin ne peut vivre sans elle.
Or s'il en est ainsi, qui pourrait me blâmer
Qu'ayant peur de souffrir je n'ose pas aimer !

This kind of cowardice, however, lasts a very short time, and the father's advice to his child, in George Eliot's poem, comes much nearer to what we, most of us, practise :

' Where blooms, O my father, a thornless Rose ?'
　' That can I not tell thee, my child;
Not one on the bosom of earth e'er grows
　But wounds whom its charms have beguiled.'

' Would I'd a Rose on my bosom to lie !
　But I shrink from the piercing thorn.
I long, but I dare not, its point defy;
　I long, and I gaze forlorn.'

' Not so, my child — round the stem again
　Thy resolute fingers entwine;
Forego not the joy for its sister — pain.
　Let the Rose, the sweet Rose, be thine.'

Here is one more example of the many forms love takes—perhaps the noblest and the best: renunciation, no matter why or wherefor, but for duty's sake. It is one of Mrs. Browning's 'Sonnets from the Portuguese':

Go from me. Yet I feel that I shall stand
    Henceforward in thy shadow. Nevermore,
    Alone upon the threshold of my door
Of individual life, I shall command
The uses of my soul, nor lift my hand
    Serenely in the sunshine as before,
    Without the sense of that which I forbore—
Thy touch upon the palm. The widest land
Doom takes to part us, leaves thy heart in mine
    With pulses that beat double. What I do
And what I dream include thee, as the wine
    Must taste of its own grapes. And when I sue
God for myself, He hears that name of thine
    And sees within my eyes the tears of two.

Tennyson's two lines everlastingly contain the true test :

Love took up the harp of Life, and smote on all the chords with
    might—
Smote the chord of Self, that—trembling—pass'd in music out
    of sight.

And now, to wind up the definitions of love, I will quote from two clever modern novels. Lucas Malet, in 'The Wages of Sin,' attempts to describe the little god, who, we are told, still has something of the sea from which his mother, Venus, rose :

'Love is quiet and subtle and fearless ; yet he comes softly and silently, stealing up without observation ; and at first we laugh at his pretty face, which is the face of a merry earthly child—but his hands, when we take them, grasp like hands of iron, and his strength is the strength of a giant, and his heart is as the heart of a tyrant. And he gives us to drink of a cup in which sweet is mingled with bitter; and the sweet too often is soon forgotten, while the taste of the bitter remains. And we hardly know whether to bless him or curse him, for he has changed all things; and we cannot tell whether to weep for the old world we have lost, or shout for joy at the new world we have found. Such is love for the great majority; a matter terrestrial rather than celestial, and of doubtful happiness after all.'

Mr. Mallock, in one of his clever novels, takes the matter further in a way that may console those who suffer from what appears such a wasted experience : 'A serious passion is a great educator. But its work only begins when the pain it causes has left us. Strong present feeling narrows our sympathies; strong past feeling enlarges them. Thus, a woman of the world always should have been, but should not be, in love. She should always have had a grief; she should never have a grievance.'

How true it is, even with the commonplace, glorified at the moment by their suffering : 'On a tant d'âme pour souffrir et si peu d'esprit pour le dire' !

While on this subject, for the sake of those who have not the pleasure of knowing Mr. Wilfred Blunt's poems, I quote three of his sonnets. First, because I think them beautiful; and secondly, because they strike a note, very well recognised by those who have a knowledge of human nature, of the danger of too great suppression in youth. And I hold the sonnets up as a looking-glass to some, and those by no means the worst, that they may recognise what perhaps will be the trials and temptations of their own future. These poems describe very truthfully the phases many women go through, in a more or less degree, according to their kind — women, who, to all appearances, are just like everyone else, who lead their quiet, dutiful lives, in all sincerity and honour. During my lifetime the fact has been much more recognised that the temptations and trials of women are not really so very different from those of men, though in our civilised life they come to them in a different way and often at a different age. This fact was, I believe, well understood in the old world, though covered over and distorted during the Middle Ages. Here are the sonnets, so rightly called the 'Three Ages of Woman':

I.

Love, in thy youth, a stranger knelt to thee,
　With cheeks all red and golden locks all curled,
And cried, ' Sweet child, if thou wilt worship me,
　Thou shalt possess the kingdoms of the world.'
But you looked down and said, ' I know you not,
　Nor want I other kingdom than my soul.'
Till Love in shame, convicted of his plot,
　Left you and turned him to some other goal.
And this discomfiture which you had seen
　Long served you for your homily and boast,
While, of your beauty and yourself the queen,
　You lived a monument of vain love crossed,
With scarce a thought of that which might have been
　To scare you with the ghost of pleasures lost.

II.

Your youth flowed on, a river chaste and fair,
　Till thirty years were written to your name.
A wife, a mother, these the titles were
　Which conquered for you the world's fairest fame.
In all things you were wise but in this one,
　That of your wisdom you yourself did doubt.
Youth spent like age, no joy beneath the sun,
　Your glass of beauty vainly running out.
Then suddenly again, ere well you knew,
　Love looked upon you tenderly, yet sad.
'Are these wise follies, then, enough for you ?'
　He said ; ' love's wisdom were itself less mad.'
And you : ' What wouldst thou of me?' ' My bare due,
　In token of what joys may yet be had.'

III.

Again Love left you. With appealing eyes
    You watched him go, and lips apart to speak.
He left you, and once more the sun did rise
    And the sun set, and week trod close on week,
And month on month, till you had reached the goal
    Of forty years, and life's full waters grew
To bitterness and flooded all your soul,
    Making you loathe old things and pine for new.
And you into the wilderness had fled,
    And in your desolation loud did cry,
'Oh for a hand to turn these stones to bread !'
    Then in your ear Love whispered scornfully,
'Thou too, poor fool — thou, even thou,' he said,
    'Shalt taste thy little honey ere thou die.'

As grown-ups have such difficulty in understanding
children, so do men and women find it hard to understand each other. Many a young husband, often 'one
of the best,' deeply wounds and pains his wife quite
unintentionally. It is a mistake to be too sensitive ; we
must take people as they are. To most men it will
always be as Coventry Patmore so prettily says :

A woman is a foreign land,
    Of which, though there he settled young,
A man will ne'er quite understand
    The customs, politics, and tongue.

Owen Meredith translates the same thought in the
reverse way, and with a more personal note, thus :

Dearest, our love is perfect, as love goes !
    Your kisses fill my frame and fire my blood ;
And nothing fails the sweetness each bestows
    Except the joy of being understood.

If for one single moment, once alone,
    And in no more than one thing only, this
Moreover only the most trivial one,
    You could but understand me — Ah, the bliss !

One of the ideas I find most common in women, and not only young ones, is that in starting a Platonic affection with a man, sometimes at a certain sacrifice to themselves, they believe they do it for his sake, and that they are raising his moral nature. I am very doubtful whether the influence that comes through that kind of love between men and women, which in these days is called 'friendship,' ever works very much for good, as the influence savours of that old-fashioned education I have already condemned, which tries to make persons what we wish them to be, in contradistinction to making them understand that their only possible growth or improvement must come through their own self-development. Self-deception comes in when the woman persuades herself that she is helping the man to do that which he could not do alone. This means that at best she is only a temporary prop, which never yet strengthened anybody. The man who sees the position, and wishes to continue the 'friendship,' always uses the argument that the matter rests with the woman, but that if she gives him up things will be worse with him than they ever were before. In a publication I have already mentioned, called 'The London Year-Book,' there is a long poem on social life with the title 'Flagellum Stultorum' (The Flogging of Fools). In it I find a passage which once more lays bare the absurdity and false sentiment of such a position :

> . . . Woman's saddest mental dower
> Is not to know the limits of her power.
> And thus 'tis chief of woman's wild intents
> To know men's motives and their sentiments.
> Believe me, gentle sex, there's not a man,
> However mean his intellectual scan,
> But comprehends us better far than do
> The wisest, keenest, cleverest of you.
> The street-boy understands, upon my life,
> The Lord High Chanc'llor, better than his wife.

So, when a woman turns her wits again,
And hopes to modify the ways of men,
I look to see, when faith and practice meet,
Her tears bedew the pathway to defeat.

Samuel Johnson, who married a widow twenty years older than himself, and quarrelled with her on his way to church, as he said he was not to be made the slave of caprice, and was resolved to begin as he meant to end, also said in after-life: 'Praise from a wife comes home to a man's heart.' I am sure this is equally the case with the wife. I have known many happy couples, but never one that did not beam with joy at real praise and appreciation from husband to wife, or wife to husband. Of course, however, all flattery must be given with discretion.

Every girl, after marriage, should expect to be not understood, and to remember this is part of the mysterious scheme of life which probably, on the whole, tends to good; at any rate, it sharpens the interest of life. How far do we not go to find 'an undiscovered country'? Besides, if it is a trial it is lightened by remembering it is the same for all. Lucas Malet seems to think it is universal:

'Do two human beings, especially of the opposite sex, ever fully understand one another? Have any two ever done so, since the world began? History and personal observation alike answer in the negative, I fear; for, alas! the finest and liveliest imagination stops short of complete comprehension of the thoughts, aims, predilections of even the nearest and best loved. In truth, is not each one of us, after all, under sentence of something very like perpetual solitary confinement in the prison-house of our own individuality?'

One of the many pranks love plays us is that, when women love, one of their chief joys is to pour out their whole souls — past, present and to come — thinking that, because the man enjoys it and shows sympathy, he understands ; but he does not a bit, and quickly forgets all she has told him. One reason why the early months of marriage are so often the least happy is that the two individuals expect each to understand the other. Mr. Lecky somewhere puts it that the art of a politician in a great measure is that of skilful compromise, and that someone whose name I forget 'was ever ready with the offer of a golden bridge or *via media* in order to reconcile effectually differences of opinion.' Does not this wisdom equally extend to married, and indeed to all family life ? If one of the two is always offering this golden bridge, I do not see how things can go very far wrong. I have known many married people of all ages — some older, some contemporary, and some younger — and my astonishment is that, on the whole, so few marriages have been real failures. What gives the impression of failure to the young is that they often judge of the happiness or unhappiness of married life from the generation of their parents. When people have been married for eighteen or twenty years, the conditions of their lives are entirely different from what they were in earlier years. Even if mutual devotion is still there, the display of it is subdued, and children instinctively assume that neither their parents nor their parents' friends were ever in love with each other. Also it is true that this middle life is frequently the most trying time in the marriage tie. Early love is over, time has developed the differences of the two individuals, and they have not yet attained to the more reasonable calm that often supervenes in later years. And yet this half-way time is just what is presented to the critical eyes of the young as they are growing up.

There is a love which never tries to call itself by any

other name, and which in time may grow into a very
real and noble friendship. This is perhaps the most
perfect developement of happiness in marriage that can
occur, but no doubt it is rare.

Mr. Michael Field, in a little poem of great delicacy,
shows how Cupid may sometimes heal the wound he has
himself inflicted:

> Ah, Eros does not always smite
>   With cruel, shining dart,
> Whose bitter point, with sudden might
>   Rends the unhappy heart—
> Not thus forever purple stained
>   And sore with steely touch,
> Else were its living fountain drained
>   Too oft and over much.
> O'er it sometimes the boy will deign
>   Sweep the shaft's feathered end:
> And friendship rises, without pain,
>   Where the white plumes descend.

Mrs. Holland, in her charming letters, remarks on a
saying of Mr. George Meredith's in 'The Egoist': 'The
scene in which, while his mother's death is imminent, he
pictures his own, and wants to make Clara swear, is
extraordinarily good, and that word of hers—"I can
only be of value to you, Willoughby, by being myself"
—contains, to my mind, the very gospel of marriage.
So many marriages are more or less spoilt by the man
wanting the woman to be his echo—not his friend.'
Perfect friendship between men and women can only
come, I think, after love—not before it.

Jowett felt the extreme difficulty of friendship between
men and women, and said: 'Hegel was right in con-
demning the union of souls without bodies. Such
schemes of imaginary pleasure are wholly unsatisfactory.
The characters of human beings are not elevated enough
for them. The religious ideal, the philosophical ideal, is

far better than the ideal of female friendship. If any pleasure is to be gained from this, it must be strictly regulated — never allowed to pass into love or excitement — of a noble, manly sort, with something of protecting care in it.'

Jowett also speaks of the sadder side of friendships, which we have all experienced. Though friendship is often represented as love eternal, it is not so at all, and needs as much, if not more, maintaining than love of another kind.

He says: 'I do not know whether friendships wear out, like clothes — not if they are kept in repair, and are not too violent. Then they last, and are a great comfort in this weary world.'

As I am known to be a strong advocate of marriage, girls often say to me: 'Do you mean that we are to marry somebody who wants to marry us, whether we really like them or not?' To this there seems to me only one answer: 'If you are perfectly certain that you like one man better than anybody else, you must get over that before you can marry another. While this strong feeling lasts, and to my belief it will last only so long as, at the back of everything, there is some hope, I would advise you not to marry anyone else—in fact, under the circumstances, to think of it would be revolting.' Of course this is the same for men and women. When this feeling has died down to a memory, almost the most real, and yet the most unreal fact in one's whole life, then I think a girl should try and make her future by keeping herself for the best type of man who may wish to marry her, not expecting to be ever again —at any rate, in her youth — blindly in love.

A common saying, and one upon which I have seen many people hang their lives, is *Tout vient à qui sait attendre*. This is the version current in England. The correct French proverb is *Tout vient à point à qui sait attendre*, which, however, does not alter the sense. I have always considered it one of the most untrue sayings with an appearance of wisdom that there is. The only thing that surely comes to those who wait in this manner is death. Stating this opinion of mine the other day, someone else maintained that they took it in another sense, and that the crux of its meaning lay not in the word *attendre*, but in the word *sait* ('Everything comes to those who know *how* to wait'). Skill in waiting, how to utilise to a given end all events that occur —such waiting brings about the coming of desired things. This was perhaps the original meaning of the saying; it is certainly not the accepted popular interpretation of to-day.

One of the virtues that I think is over-praised at all ages, in women especially, is constancy. Constancy is splendid, and much to be admired where two people are constant; but where it is one-sided, and neither wanted nor appreciated by the other sex, I think it is rather of the same order as the non-changing of opinions in Blake's comparison in 'Heaven and Hell': 'The man who never changes his opinion is like standing water, and breeds reptiles of the mind.'

Mr. Henry James says, with a strength that is almost crushing to us women, who cling with such persistency to our delusions: 'Illusions are sweet to the dreamer, but not so to the observer, who has a horror of a fool's paradise.'

Shelley gives us strength by saying: 'The past is death's, the future is thine own. Take it while it is still yours, and fix your mind, not on what you may have done long ago to hurt, but on what you can now do to help.'

Jowett, like most teachers of the young, placed a

great, it may be an excessive, value on success. It distressed him to see his pupils making a mess of life. He wished them to take their part in the work of their generation with energy and effect. And yet one of his pupils writes, 'that it was Jowett, as much as anyone, who taught me that work, not success, made life worth living.' I quote this here in my chapter to young women, though it is intended for men, because it applies equally to women, and has a cheerful ring. Women's work is seldom crowned with success, but it is always there in some shape or another, ready for them to take up ; and if they do so the result, if there is none other, will at least be the strengthening and improving of their own lives, not by escaping their trials, but by learning to bear them better.

Goethe says : 'Everything that happens to us leaves some trace behind; everything contributes imperceptibly to make us what we are. Yet it is often dangerous to take a strict account of it. For either we grow proud and negligent, or downcast and dispirited ; and both are equally injurious in their consequences. The surest plan is just to do the nearest task that lies before us.'

I do not believe the state of mind which improves a woman's character ever comes without some intellectual effort. Most women of a certain type generally fly to music and desultory reading. Both these may be turned to serious use. Both may be only another form of the excitement which brings on reaction. Drawing and art were the saving of me. The creative work and the endless intellectual ramifications independent of — in fact, active against — a society life made drawing most useful to me. It does not much matter what the occupation is, so long as it is a mental gymnastic — something which stretches and strengthens the mind, and consequently, I think, the character—something which takes us away from the accusation which George Eliot puts as follows : 'We women are always in danger of living too exclusively in the affections. And though our affections are perhaps the best gifts we have, we ought also to have our share of the more independent life—some joy in things for their own sake. It is piteous to see the helplessness of some sweet women when their affections are disappointed—because all their teaching has been, that they can only delight in study of any kind for the sake of a personal love. They have never contemplated an independent delight in ideas as an experience which they could confess without being laughed at.' Many will smile at my thinking it necessary in these days to make this quotation; but women's natures remain the same—yesterday, to-day, and for ever—and in certain phases of family life, and surrounded by the difficulties they entail, George Eliot's caution may be as much wanted by some young women as it was, more universally, forty years ago. Of course this is an entirely different thing from cramming children in early youth.

There was nothing Jowett spoke of with so much bitterness as useless learning. 'How I hate learning !' he exclaimed. 'How sad it is to see a man who is learned and nothing else, incapable of making any use of his knowledge !' If this is true of men, is it not doubly true of women ? 'Is learning of any use ?' he asks himself in one of his notebooks; and the answer is : 'Men are often or always unable to use it. It keeps men quiet, it clogs their efforts, it is creditable, it gratifies curiosity ; but, for progress to mental improvement, learning without thought or imagination is worse than useless.'

Goethe says : 'To the man of superficial cleverness,

almost everything takes a ridiculous aspect ; to the man of thought, almost nothing is really ridiculous.'

I quote Jowett's strong condemnation of useless learning, as it should put us on our mettle to learn in such a way as is most likely to be useful to fill the vacuum in our individual lives. But we must remember that Jowett lived in an atmosphere where learning for learning's sake surrounded him, and the choice for him lay between well-directed and misdirected learning. I cling, however, to the idea that even somewhat useless learning is better than none, as the mere effort to learn does good.

Mothers who like keeping their girls at home, and who see them content in a round of empty gaiety and excitement, often say : 'I am in no hurry for my girls to marry ; they are happy and merry at home.' As men's bachelor lives often unfit them for marriage, so girls' lives are just as apt to do the same. They have to fit themselves for either marriage or old-maidism, and this is not done by prolonging unduly the life described in one line by La Fontaine : *La cigale ayant chanté tout l'été*, etc. I remember my mother telling me that she had rather pitied a sad-looking, elderly girl at a Newcastle ball. Her partner remarked : 'Yes, no wonder, poor girl ! she is just recovering from her seven-and-twentieth disappointment.' This, of course, is an exaggeration, but it is characteristic of what may happen. After a certain amount of rushing about, a girl should herself realise that she can no more live on social excitements without deterioration than her body can thrive on sal-volatile. These remarks must always apply only to the large average. Women who are very attractive to men, as I said in my first book, have the ball at their feet, and, as regards the other sex, can do as they like.

One of the best, noblest, and most useful old maids I have ever known once said to me : 'Why was I not warned ; why did no one remind me that to most women the chances do not come often, and that if we do not take them while we are young and have something to give, they do not come again, or not, at any rate, in the way, that, being older, we can accept?'

When women turn to practical work, their high hopes are even more frequently disappointed than those of men —so many things weight their career, and the sense of failure is so frequently all that they reap.

> Have you thought, in your moments of triumph,
>   Oh, you that are high in the tree,
> Of the days and the nights that are bitter—
>   So bitter to others and me ?
> When the efforts to do what is clever
>   Result in a failure so sad,
> And the clouds of despondency gather
>   And dim all the hopes that we had !
>
> Have you thought when the world was applauding
>   Your greatness, whatever it be,
> Of the tears that in silence were falling—
>   Yes, falling from others and me ?
> When the hardest and latest endeavours
>   Appeared to be only in vain,
> And we've curtained our eyes in the night-time
>   Indiff'rent to waking again !

Those who just miss their lives are those I pity. It seems to me that, of all bad teaching, the worst is to live only in the present, and try in no way to look to the future.

Great sorrow or trouble, or loss of money or sickness, seem mercifully to preserve in some women certain qualities of youth which always remain attractive to men, even far on into middle life. Such misfortunes embalm

the qualities which the more ordinary experiences and
pleasures of life destroy. Hence the unexpected and
deep love episodes at an age when young people imagine
such a thing is impossible. I remember quite well
thinking at eighteen: 'What does it matter what
women of thirty do?' Has not the world been lately
given an example of this kind of love, for which it will
eternally be the richer, in the Browning love-letters?

That clever old French wit Chamfort, when he was
reproached by a lady for not caring about women, answered: 'Je puis dire sur elles ce que disait Madame de
C. sur les enfants: "J'ai dans ma tête un fils dont je
n'ai jamais pu accoucher"; j'ai dans l'esprit une femme
comme il y en a peu, qui me préserve des femmes comme
il y en a beaucoup; j'ai bien des obligations à cette fem-
melà.' I believe this kind of feeling keeps many, especially cautious men, bachelors. This is a mistake,
even from their own point of view, as these are the very
men who are apt to fall victims to strong fancies when
it is least wise for them to do so; and when they are on
the borders of old age nature often has her revenge.

I quote the Chamfort story to remind girls that good
and sensible men require certain qualities in a woman
whom they are thinking of marrying, and the reason
why ordinary women are wise to consider twice about
refusing to marry young is that perhaps that gift of
youth is the only real thing they will ever have to give a
man. When a dead level of mediocrity is reached, think
how large is a man's choice, in England especially!
What is there in a woman of from thirty to thirty-five,
who has knocked about the world, flirted and amused
herself, given and taken all she could get, that should
particularly make a man desire to marry her? Her
freshness is gone, and her want of wisdom is often
sadly apparent.

We all know 'Punch's' advice to a man about to marry: 'Don't.' My advice is exactly the contrary. I say: Do, and don't wait till love of your bachelorhood becomes too strong a custom. But except when very young, in which case the wild oats will probably be sown in an undignified way at the end of life, don't marry exclusively for what is called love. Let the heart and the head go together. For a woman, I think it is wise and often right to marry a man out of a sort of gratitude; it rarely answers for a man to marry for this reason a woman who has loved him not wisely but too well.

I do not, for one, entirely condemn the French customs as regards marriage, though I believe they themselves are modifying them. When marriages are a question of reason and arrangement, I think it is better that such things should be managed by the elders than by the young people; and if Englishmen of sense, when they make up their minds to marry, would take the help and advice of older women in seeking a wife, instead of going about with the hope that they may be fancy-stricken through the eye, I think more suitable marriages would be brought about, both as regards character and the very natural wish that the woman should have a certain proportion of money to help the joint *ménage*.

If a man who has married with his best judgment really cares to win the love of a girl after marriage, and takes pains to do so, he is sure to succeed—it is so natural for a good, affectionate woman to love her husband and the father of her children.

Of course if a girl, with no sense of duty, merely sells herself to shine in the world, or for admiration and notoriety, which she thinks she will get better married than single, there is nothing to be said. Such things will always be; but a girl of that type is rare, and almost as mischievous single as married. The type of women that men often know most about was thus described to me by a man. He gave it as his deliberate opinion of women as he had found them: 'They are curious creatures; in religion they can believe fifty times as much as any man. In love they only believe when they see and hear you; as soon as your back is turned they scream and cry out you have abandoned them. Before you come they want you, when you have gone you have betrayed them, and they wonder that a man cannot bear that sort of thing for ever. Do you call me practical for speaking in this way? Very well, I am practical—and tell you what I know.'

To go back to our original text, 'The Marriage Market.' The writers of all four articles seem to me too much under the impression that marriages are decided by the parents. So far as my experience goes, in England this is not the case. The girls take their lives in their own hands, though often with very insufficient knowledge. I have known girls who distrust to such a degree the feelings they may have for a man who is rich that they have actually refused him for fear they should be influenced by worldly reasons, everyone about them taking it for granted that they could never be so foolish as not to marry him. Many girls think of marriage solely as a means of escaping home duties, and assume that the duties will be lighter after marriage than before.

I hear many people condemn the girl who 'marries for money'; and Marie Corelli vituperates against the women who 'sell themselves,' as she calls it. This seems to me unfair. Marriage and even love do not alter a nature; and if a girl knows herself, and is quite well aware that she cares most for the things that money alone can give her, I think there is more of wickedness if she makes the misery of the man she may like best by marrying him if he is poor, than in accepting the rich man if she can get him. I speak only of those whose standard of life is a low one. What is supremely idiotic, and distinctly the fault of the mother, showing a general want of training, is to imagine that when you marry a man for his money, whom you neither love nor admire, you are to have as well all the joys of life which no money can buy. The thing is ridiculous. There are few who, like Danaë, can have god and gold together. Marrying for money or position may be a high or a low line; it is often the only vent for a woman's ambition. But if she does it of her own free will, thoroughly understanding and facing what she undertakes, in nine cases out of ten she will carry it through and make the best of it. The person who 'has gained the world' is perhaps the one least likely to throw it away. It is the sentimental, warm-hearted, impressionable girl, who marries some man of the world not knowing what she is doing, who turns to someone else for consolation in bitterness of spirit when she finds out her mistake.

The tone of the day, as it is often represented in ephemeral literature, is that, so far as the moral life goes, the sexes should be equal. This has given rise to a very natural feeling amongst girls : that it is a matter of no importance which loves most or even first, the man or the woman. The stronger feeling on the woman's side is a phase of the relations between men and women which always has been and always will be; but the open acknowledgment of it is certainly much more common now than forty years ago. Nothing changes nature, and especially in youth it is natural for the man to take the initiative. The cultivation of pride in a woman is much to be desired, and would never deter a man who was really in earnest in his pursuit. In fact,

we all value what is difficult of attainment. I found
this well expressed in an American periodical which I
took up by chance last year; it was called 'The Way of
Man':

> There was many a Rose in the glen to-day
>   As I wandered through,
> And every bud that looked my way
>   Was rich of hue.
> But the one in my hand,
>   Do you understand ?
> Not a whit more sweet, not quite so fair,
>   But it grew in the breach of the cliff up there.

A question I have frequently heard discussed by
people who perhaps would be the very last to be themselves in such a situation, is whether a woman with a
'past' is bound to tell it to a man who has proposed to
her, and whom she wishes to accept. A large proportion
of these people who now go in for 'equalising' the sexes
say, 'No; she is not bound to tell,' and they argue that
a man does not lay *his* past before a woman when he is
engaged to marry her. It may be very unjust, but I
cannot see that the cases are parallel. The woman fears
that if she tells her story to the man, he will not marry
her. If this is really the case, her acceptance of his
offer is a species of fraud. To begin a life of partnership under such circumstances means that the woman
puts herself on the level of a man who cheats his friend
at cards or sells him a bad horse. The reason why the
position of the woman differs from that of the man is
due to that unwritten law accepted amongst civilised nations. The man who does not recognise this law will be
unaffected by the confession of her past; the man who
does recognise it ought not to be deceived.

I think most girls of to-day understand that there is
a veiled side to many men's lives, and that a man's past

has to be accepted, not cavilled at, by a girl who understands life when she marries a man who is not very
young, and who has knocked about the world. She
would scarcely wish him to tell her details of passing
love affairs; but I would go so far, without any insult
to him, as to recommend that a girl who knows what she
is doing should solemnly, and in all tenderness and love,
just before marriage, put the question to the man she
is engaged to whether his particular past entails any
serious ties upon him. By this I mean that she should
know whether he has children whom he ought to edu-
cate and look after, in order that she may not only
face the fact, but also help him to do his duty by them.
No secret should come between them, especially not one
which, if ignored, might perhaps bring forth future
trouble. If he has no such ties, so much the better for
everybody. If he has, she who is about to marry him
should share the troubles and privations that they entail.
So many problems in this life are solved by courage.
Facing such a position does not make it, whereas ignor-
ing it may weave difficulties and misery.

Optimism I have always believed to be the right rule
of conduct both for men and nations. Yet there is truth
in what I have somewhere read that it must not be an
optimism without intelligence. It should not be that
kind of optimism which, to keep cheerful, must blot out
menace by looking another way, and obliterate coming
peril by turning the back. Neither in private nor in
public life should it be the spurious optimism which is
part dullness of perception, part moral weakness, part
intellectual timidity, part something worse—I mean,
refusal to recognise approaching danger because open
recognition would have to be followed by the worry or
expense of prevention.

As I said before, it is so difficult to generalise—not

only because every individual case has a different aspect, but also because every ten years makes an entirely different platform for our conduct of life. This seems to me to be not sufficiently acknowledged. Once more I return to a bundle of letters, to find one written by a very old friend of our family, which talks of the decline of life, from a man's point of view, in a way that is individual and yet applicable to many:

'I quite agree with you that it is very disagreeable to grow old, and I have always thought that if *I* had been Providence I would have made life *begin* with dotage and decrepitude, and go on freshening and improving to a primal death. But as I am a humble individual, and not Providence, I make up my mind to things as they are. Neither old women nor old men can hope to be loved amorously or sentimentally, whatever other love they may obtain. I confess that for long years the ruling feeling of my life was a love of women, and a desire to be loved by them, not exactly with a passionate love, but with a love having in it some touch of amorous sentiment. It was for this that I chiefly valued my youth, my intellect, my celebrity, and whatever else I possessed that might help me to it. And it was through loving women, "not wisely but too well," that I made myself unpopular both with men *and* women; for I cared nothing about men, and they saw it and resented it, and yet women are in the hands of men, and he who would be popular with women should take care first to get men's good word. Even if I had taken count of this in time, perhaps, I should not have taken heed to it, for I was rather reckless and heedless in my youth, and more disposed to trust to fortune than to take means, and perhaps I had also a sort of latent consciousness that what I desired was not good for me, and thus was I, in the absence of better safeguards,

'From social snares with ease
Saved by that gracious gift, inaptitude to please.

'Youth is dead and gone at eight-and-twenty, and one may mourn it for a year or two then ; but at thirty it is time to rise and eat bread, and after fifty one no more desires to be young than one desires to be the Archangel Michael or Henry VIII. One does not desire it, because one cannot conceive it. The past is so long past that it is past being a subject for regret ; and as to the future, one has to look forward to losing one's eyes and ears and brains, and some of the powers of one's stomach, but one has not the loss of youth to look forward to, and that is one source of sadness removed — and to me it used to be, thirty or forty years ago, a source of sadness ; for I was very fond of my youth, and cared more for it than for eyes, ears, brains, stomach, and all the rest. Now they have a fair share of my regard, and I shall be sorry for their decay. I think you make too much of my imagination as a resource. It is true that from time to time I join a party of phantoms, and find them pleasant to live with on the whole, though they sometimes give me a good deal of trouble, and at other times wear my nerves a little. But my main resource is in my business. Acting to a purpose with steadiness and regularity is the best support to the spirits and the surest protection against sad thoughts. Realities can contend with realities better than phantoms can . . . For the rest, Sydney Smith's precept is "Take short views of life." Henry Taylor expressed the same thing :

'Foresight is a melancholy gift
Which bares the bald and speeds the all-too-swift.

'To invest one's personal interests in the day that is passing, and to project one's future interests into the children that are growing up, is the true policy of self-love in the decline of life, and as commendable a policy as it is in the nature of self-love to adopt.'

I have recommended no books for girls. The question is much too big a one. But I cannot refrain from saying that within the compass of one small book I know nothing that comes up in wisdom and sagacity to Emerson's essays called 'The Conduct of Life,' and 'Society and Solitude.' He says: 'Youth has an access of sensibility before which every object glitters and attracts. We leave one pursuit for another, and the young man's year is a heap of beginnings. At the end of a twelvemonth he has nothing to show for it, not one completed work. But the time is not lost.' If this is true of young men, it is doubly true of young women. Every experience is a growth, and every growth tends towards completion of life rightly understood. There should never be hopelessness and despair, whatever happens. The future is always ours, to conquer and make noble. No one can really crush us. Trodden under foot, if we choose we *may* rise again better, even nobler, than all the fortunate ones around us. It all depends on ourselves. That is why I admire Mr. George Moore's 'Esther Waters' almost above all modern novels, although Messrs. Smith & Son, whose stalls are covered with translations of French novels, refused to sell it.

In spite of age and experience, I feel that on all these difficult subjects I have said very little that can be of use to anybody. There is no receipt by which we can regulate our lives. 'As our day is, so shall our strength be' is a fact to those who train their natures to meet with courage the difficulties as they arise.

One of our old divines states that 'Our infancy is full of folly; youth, of disorder and toil; age, of infirmity. Each time hath his burden, and that which may justly work our weariness; yet infancy longeth after youth; and youth after more age; and he that is very old, as he is a child for simplicity, so he would be for years. I account old age the best of the three, partly for that it has passed through the folly and disorder of the others; partly, for that the inconveniences of this are but bodily, with a bettered estate of the mind; and partly, for that it is nearest to dissolution.' I wish I could agree with Bishop Hall, but I do not. I very often feel that quite the worst part of old age is that it brings us near to dissolution. My sympathies all remain with the young, and I only feel at times inclined to cry out, with Thomas Moore:

> Give me back, give me back the wild freshness of Morning;
> Her clouds and her tears are worth Evening's best light.

I fear everyone will think this is not at all as it should be; and I only feel it sometimes, and perhaps even that won't last.

This is good-bye, dear reader. Collecting these notes has given me pleasure and also cost me trouble. I cannot do better than close them by quoting what were almost the last lines ever written by my kind friend and brother-in-law, Owen Meredith. I owe him as large a debt of gratitude as one human being can owe another. It was due to his friendly advice and his kind encouragement that my mind was saved from that sense of failure and disappointment so common—to women, at any rate —in middle life. He taught me how all ages have their advantages, and gave me courage to go on learning, even to the end. He always seemed able to see the line of the other shore with a brightness not granted to me:

> My songs flit away on the wing:
> They are fledged with a smile or a sigh:
> And away with the songs that I sing
> Flit my joys, and my sorrows, and I.

For time, as it is, cannot stay :
  Nor again, as it was, can it be :
Disappearing and passing away
  Are the world, and the ages, and we.

Gone, even before we can go,
  Is our past, with its passions forgot,
The dry tears of its wept-away woe,
  And its laughters that gladden us not.

The builder of heaven and of earth
  Is our own fickle fugitive breath :
As it comes in the moment of birth,
  So it goes in the moment of death.

As the years were before we began,
  Shall the years be when we are no more :
And between them the years of a man
  Are as waves the wind drives to the shore.

Back into the Infinite tend
  The creations that out of it start :
Unto every beginning an end,
  And whatever arrives shall depart.

But I and my songs, for a while,
  As together away on the wing
We are borne with a sigh or a smile,
  Have been given this message to sing —

The Now is an atom of sand,
  And the Near is a perishing clod :
But Afar is as Faëry Land,
  And Beyond is the bosom of God.

INDEX

cc

(449)

INDEX

ELIZABETH AND HER GERMAN GARDEN

BY

The Author of "A Solitary Summer"

12mo. Cloth. $1.75

"The moment such a volume is taken up the pleasant spell acts upon eyes and finger-tips, and one likes the book before it is read."

—KATE SANBORN.

"Reading on, we find ourselves in the presence of a whimsical, humorous, cultured, and very womanly woman, with a pleasant, old-fashioned liking for homeliness and simplicity; with a wise husband, three merry babies, a few friends, a gardener, an old German house to repose in, an agreeable literary gift, and a slight touch of cynicism. Such is Elizabeth. It is a charming book."

—*The Academy* (London).

THE MACMILLAN COMPANY

66 Fifth Avenue, NEW YORK

THE SOLITARY SUMMER

BY

The Author of " Elizabeth and Her German Garden "

$12mo.   Cloth. $1.50.

"A continuation of that delightful chronicle of days spent in and about one of the most delightful gardens known to modern literature.   The author's exquisite humor is ever present, and her descriptions . . . have a wonderful freshness and charm."

—*Washington Post.*

"Perhaps even more charming than the fascinating original, which is saying a great deal. . . . . It is the kind of book in which one likes to dip into much the same spirit of enjoyment that makes one linger on the quiet, shady banks of some secluded stream.   There are few authors who have thrown so companionable a personality into their books as this charming woman has succeeded in doing."

—*The Glasgow Herald.*

THE MACMILLAN COMPANY

66 Fifth Avenue NEW YORK

JESS

BITS OF WAYSIDE GOSPEL

BY

JENKIN LLOYD JONES

12mo. Cloth. $1.50

There is narrative enough in it to justify the characteriza-tion of it as a book of summer stories, roadside experiences gathered by one who traveled now on foot, now on horseback, sometimes alone, sometimes in genial wagon company, in search of rest, strength, mental quickening, spiritual poise and peace. Were it not for the unconventional handling, it might be char-acterized as a volume of sermons, dealing with the universalities of religion. The lessons and inspirations of nature here found carry the reader far afield from the realms of doctrine, ceremony, or denominational issues. Jess, who gives the title roll to the book, was a loving and lovable horse that companioned the author through many hundred miles of travel, much of it through the beautiful scenery of southwestern Wisconsin, the Berkshire Hill country of the Mississippy valley.

The book, therefore, represents religion in its humane and humanitarian expression. The author of the book shows his sym-pathy with all forms of life, and his openness to truth, whether revealed in nature, through science, human history, or the peren-nial inspirations of literature. "The Religion of the Bird's Nest," "Earth's Fullness," "My River," "A Dinner of Herbs," "The Uplands of the Spirit," "Near to the Heart of Nature," are some of the titles of these sermon stories, which may hint at the fresh-ness, hopefulness and tenderness of the spirit expressed in this book.

THE MACMILLAN COMPANY

66 Fifth Avenue, NEW YORK

Lightning Source UK Ltd.
Milton Keynes UK
UKHW011844201118
332627UK00013B/956/P